21世纪经济管理类精品教材

商务统计双语案例精析

（第2版）

杨楠◎编著

清华大学出版社
北京

内 容 简 介

本书以商务统计的原理、案例、操作为主线，围绕统计中常用的概念，从描述统计到推断统计，进行系统而图文并茂的阐述。本书精选的案例，契合大数据时代读者对商务与经济统计领域数据可视化、辨识与推断层次提升的强烈需求，涉及金融、制造、医疗、大宗商品等众多行业，有助于培养读者运用商务统计理论和方法分析与解决实际问题的能力。

本书是一本视野开阔、资料丰富、通俗易懂的双语统计学案例教材，具有专业性、前沿性和实用性的特点，不仅可以作为普通高等院校经济管理专业的本科生和研究生学习商务统计的教材，也可以作为相关从业人员的自学辅导用书。

图书在版编目（CIP）数据

商务统计双语案例精析 / 杨楠编著. —2 版. —北京：清华大学出版社，2021.1（2023.1重印）
21 世纪经济管理类精品教材
ISBN 978-7-302-57175-9

Ⅰ. ①商…　Ⅱ. ①杨…　Ⅲ. ①商业统计—案例—双语教学—高等学校—教材　Ⅳ. ①F712.3

中国版本图书馆 CIP 数据核字（2020）第 260268 号

责任编辑： 杜春杰
封面设计： 刘　超
版式设计： 文森时代
责任校对： 马军令
责任印制： 宋　林

出版发行： 清华大学出版社
网　　址：http://www.tup.com.cn，http://www.wqbook.com
地　　址：北京清华大学学研大厦 A 座　　邮　　编：100084
社 总 机：010-83470000　　邮　　购：010-62786544
投稿与读者服务：010-62776969，c-service@tup.tsinghua.edu.cn
质量反馈：010-62772015，zhiliang@tup.tsinghua.edu.cn
印 装 者： 三河市龙大印装有限公司
经　　销： 全国新华书店
开　　本： 185mm×260mm　　**印　　张：** 16.5　　**字　　数：** 377 千字
版　　次： 2012 年 2 月第 1 版　　2021 年 3 月第 2 版　　**印　　次：** 2023 年 1 月第 2 次印刷
定　　价： 59.80 元

产品编号：084967-01

作者简介

杨楠，上海财经大学统计与管理学院教授、博士生导师，教师教学发展中心副主任，计算科学与金融数据研究中心特聘教授，上海市人工智能学会副秘书长。主要从事经济与金融统计研究和统计学教学工作。清华大学理学学士和硕士，上海财经大学经济学博士，美国哥伦比亚大学和英国伦敦政治经济学院访问学者。

曾主持完成国家自然科学基金项目 1 项，教育部人文社会科学研究项目、全国统计科学研究项目、上海市哲学社会科学规划项目、上海市教委科研创新项目、上海市决咨委招标项目等省部级课题 8 项，三次获得省部级科研奖。出版《房价指数的编制、管理与应用》《家庭资产统计研究》等专著和《商务统计双语案例精析》《应用回归分析》《应用时间序列分析》等多部教材，在《金融研究》《国际金融研究》《财经研究》《数理统计与管理》等国内外刊物发表学术论文 30 余篇。

为本科、硕士和博士开设多门专业课程，作为负责人建设的“Statistics”课程获评上海高校全英语教学示范课程，主讲的“数据时代的推断陷阱”在线课程在中国大学慕课、超星尔雅等多个平台播出。曾获上海市级教学成果二等奖 1 项，被评为上海市“三八红旗手”，上海财经大学“我心目中的好老师”“教书育人标兵”，三次获评上海财经大学商学院“明星教师”。

第 2 版推荐序

有则故事让我印象特别深刻。十九世纪中期，英国国内爆发霍乱疫情，最初人们并不清楚这个疾病到底如何传播，政府的几次尝试最终都无法根除霍乱的流行。直到一位内科医生约翰·斯诺（John Snow）针对性地收集了大量的数据并进行统计分析，得出了疾病的传播与水源有关的结论，于是政府限制并迁移了许多公用抽水机，疫情才得到有效控制，而他本人也因此获得现代流行病学之父的美誉。

数据分析带来价值，而统计学则是数据分析的理论基础。自从人类发展出统计学，这门学科已被应用于无数领域，而我粗浅地认为，其在商业领域的应用就称为商务统计或商务分析。在互联网高度普及的背景下，数据收集的深度与广度都显著增加，因而又衍生出大数据、数据科学、人工智能等新兴领域。在可见的未来，统计分析之于商务发展的重要性可以说是有增无减。

不过，是否脑中放入所有的统计知识，就能成为商务分析的高手呢？可能还必须加一样东西，那就是与实际的商业问题和应用场景的紧密连结。数据本身并没有价值，而通过分析萃取出的知识，才会对决策产生指导意义，进而落实潜在价值。如同上述故事，数据收集与统计分析皆紧扣着阻断霍乱传播的目的，因此可做到有的放矢。

本书更加难能可贵的地方是列举了各个商业案例，不仅详述如何寻找模式从数据建立统计模型，以及所用的分析方法及其背后思路，而且分析过程皆指向特定、具体的目标。理论分析的价值在于应用，而应用是否成功则取决于分析方法与场景是否匹配。本书对于个别案例的深入剖析，相当成功地连结理论与实务应用，值得读者反复咀嚼其中奥妙。

值得一提的是，本书所提供的中英文对照让读者在学习统计知识的同时，还能知道相应的英文表达方式，特别是对于有英语沟通需求的统计分析从业人员来说，这是一个特别且帮助很大的设计。

在互联网快速渗透人们生活的时空背景下，将来的商务环境对数据的依赖极有可能日益增加，数据分析虽不是万能的，但没有数据分析却可能万万不能。我认为无论是对企业经营者、统计分析从业人员、在校学生，还是对普罗大众，这本著作都是学习商务统计和商务分析的难得佳作，极具理论基础和实践价值。

eBay 全球副总裁、中国研发中心总经理

田　卫

2020 年 9 月

第 1 版推荐序

发现统计的商务价值

在市场咨询与民意研究行业工作了十多年，这使得我有机会与成百上千的外企、民企、国企、政府机关、民间机构等各种类型的客户进行广泛的接触。在这个过程中，我深深感到统计数字之美，只有在实践中得到应用，其价值之美才能得到充分的展现，否则就是一堆枯燥的数据。我也曾在一些高校中多次进行过“市场研究在商业中的应用”之类的讲座，其中我也能感受到：讲概念时同学们的眼神多有游离，而一旦进入案例，尤其说到一些关键数据如何对客户的商业决策产生支撑作用，并获得商业的巨大成功时，同学们的眼神就会变得炽热而有互动。我也曾应杨楠博士之邀在上海财经大学进行过相关讲座，她曾代表学生就讲题提出要求：多讲案例。所有这些让我对统计有了一个基本的认识，那就是，统计的价值之美在于应用，而应用的范例最为直观而有趣。

作为一个研究咨询行业中天天与统计数字打交道的从业者，即使在我自己的眼中，统计也曾经是一门枯燥艰涩的学科。看见统计数字头晕想来是很多人都有过的体验。因此，如何让统计更加有趣而易懂、易懂而有用，是很多与统计分析有关的从业人士一直想解决的问题。

当看到这本《商务统计双语案例精析》时，我意识到杨楠博士在多年的教学与研究工作中，已然成为“有趣而易懂、易懂而有用”这一逻辑的践行者。我仔细拜读了这本书，全书以商务统计的概念、案例、操作为主线，围绕统计中常用的概念，从描述性分析到整合性分析，从参数统计到非参数统计，从数值统计到假设检验，进行系统而图文并茂的阐述。尤其是书中的案例，涉及金融、制造、医疗、大宗商品等众多行业，从商务的角度展现了统计在各行各业的商业价值。并且，其双语编排使得读者在阅读时能够英汉对照，更有助于读者有效地汲取西方商务统计方面的知识与体系。

这本书对于读者而言，个人觉得至少有三方面的作用：第一，读完此书，读者能够快速掌握商务统计中的基本概念，因为书中即使是枯燥的概念，也分析得图文并茂；第二，读完此书，读者能够将统计概念应用到实践中去，因为书中的案例是商业世界中活生生的案例；第三，读者还可以把这本书作为工具书，因为书中每一章都有一个如何应用 Excel 和 SAS 等软件进行统计实现的操作小技巧，这一点在以往的统计类书籍中不多见。

实现了这三方面的作用，其实就是发现了统计的价值。通常情况下，统计类的书很难体现商务价值，商务类的书着眼于统计的并不多，而这本《商务统计双语案例精析》则将两者进行了有机的结合。让我们一起开启商务统计价值的发现之旅吧!

零点研究咨询集团副总裁
周林古
2012年1月

第 2 版前言

《商务统计双语案例精析》出版的 8 年，恰逢大数据的话题被广为传播之时，数据分析的应用日益增加。正如《大数据时代》中所描绘的："只要一点想象，万千事物就能转化为数据形式，并一直带给我们惊喜。"在商业与管理领域，产生了更多的数据和更多基于数据进行的分析，研究者和决策者更加倾向于以事实为依据进行决策，这其中，对商务统计学理论与技能的需求尤为强烈。

此次第 2 版的编写体现了过去 8 年间统计学的发展变化和学科应用特点，契合大数据时代读者对商务与经济统计领域数据可视化、辨识与推断层次提升的强烈需求，增加了更为鲜活的案例，以便教师教学实践及读者自学时提高运用商务统计理论和方法分析与解决实际问题的能力。

在编写过程中，编者充分考虑了历年教授本科生、MBA 学生和 iMBA 学生过程中收集的教学反馈、国内同行和读者们的反馈，同时吸取了 AMBA、AACSB 两个国际商学教育认证专家组对于"商务统计学"课程的反馈建议。此外，编者还收集研究了国内外名校在同名课程内容上的最新资料，并于 2017 年 7 月赴美国参加哈佛大学商学院关于案例教学教法的 GloColl 培训项目，学习教法上的最新理念。基于以上多种途径的学习和分析，最终对本书的修订方向有了明确的把握，也有信心在未来使用第 2 版教材中不断进行案例授课内容与教法上的持续改进。

编者相信，未来，在商务分析领域，统计分析仍将处于重要位置，最好的决策将来自那些对商业时代潮流进行精准地感知和把握、能够将量化分析的科学与来自经验和对问题的领悟良好结合的决策者。如果运用得当，统计分析可以既简单又有价值。因而第 2 版教材仍然传承第 1 版的结构设计，带领读者从具体的案例问题和现实数据出发来考虑如何分析，力争做到生动、具体、真实。第 2 版教材对第 1 版教材的相关内容进行的具体完善和改进如下：对第 1 章、第 2 章、第 7 章、第 8 章的案例数据进行了更新；新增了第 1 章"我国健身人群画像"案例、第 4 章"下降的信用卡利率"案例；原书的第 4 章和第 5 章合并为第 2 版的第 4 章，并新增了第 5 章"培训是否有效"案例。各章节的最后，在 Excel 软件分析之外，还新增了 R 语言分析，便于不同读者参考。

本案例集的编著是多位成员协同努力的结果，其中莫雅杰、亓旻昊参与了策划与设计、内容整合与修改，以及方差分析、非参数方法部分的工作，王栋慧、亓旻昊、刘子萱参与了探索性数据分析之图示法部分的工作，桂希凯、鲜东良、蒋超宇参与了探索性数据分析之数值法、区间估计、假设检验部分的工作，方茜、黄锦晖、李碧琳参与了一元线性回归、多元回归部分的工作，金敏参与了时间序列预测部分的工作，梁正溜教授对部分章节的英文表达给予了有效的修改建议。在此，对团队成员的辛勤工作表示深深的谢意！期盼同行专家和广大读者提出宝贵的批评和建议，使本书日臻完善。

杨　楠

2020 年 9 月

于上海

第 1 版前言

全英语及双语教学是高等教育适应经济全球化挑战、培养高级经济管理类人才的重要途径。近年来，师资的国际化、生源的国际化和教材的国际化，已经使统计学这门经济管理专业人才培养中的核心数量方法课程面临前所未有的挑战与发展机遇。如何更为有效地汲取西方经济管理统计的积淀成果，服务于国内经济建设与对外经济交往，已经成为我们迫切需要解决的问题。

培养学生准确观察数据、进行科学分析和正确决策的能力往往很难完全通过统计学课程教学来实现。理解统计思想、掌握统计方法的关键在于结合现实问题进行思考和分析。对此，案例教学不失为一种事半功倍的学习途径。具有生动性、启发性和可操作性的案例能够作为统计理论课程教学内容的有益补充，而小组合作讨论、运用软件实施、撰写结果分析报告的过程可以使学生留下深刻的印象，促进其快速掌握通过统计分析进行判断与决策的思路与方法，以更好地解决实际问题。

本书撰写的初衷来自于笔者过去多年为经济、金融、会计、工商管理等本科中外合作专业学生，以及本科统计学双学位学生、MBA 学员讲授双语统计学课程的案例教学环节。作为国外原版教材的有益补充及案例教学环节的重要参考，笔者深刻感受到了编撰一本视野开阔、资料丰富、通俗易懂的双语统计学案例集的必要性。对于采用中英文对照的双语形式编著，笔者经过了较长时间的考虑，这种方式既可以准确呈现英文原有含义和表达句式、国际标准统计软件输出结果，也可以方便各个层面的读者同时通过对照中英文来精确理解各部分内容。

本书所呈现的案例，有的是笔者从国外畅销的经济管理统计学、商务统计学经典教材中精选出来的典型案例，也有的是笔者基于美国劳工部、世界黄金协会、《福布斯》杂志等网站上的热点问题与数据自行编撰的与现实生活密切相连的案例，基本涵盖了基础统计学的各部分内容，并具有实用性、权威性和前沿性的显著特点。这些案例多为开放式，即使在原版教材中也未给出完整的解答分析。笔者在教学过程中，经过案例教学的探索实践，总结出科学合理的解答过程，经过精心编排，呈现在这本案例集中。

本书每一章内容的展现形式如下：首先是该章所对应统计方法的概括性描述，接着是一个具体案例问题的背景描述和数据呈现，之后是对该案例的分析框架、计算过程与结果以及对结果的延伸讨论和软件应用实施过程解释，最后是关键公式与注解。通过这样一种结构设计，希望读者能从具体的案例问题和现实数据出发来考虑如何分析，而不是从理论推导出发，因而更加生动、具体、真实，也更加符合从事商务工作的人员在现实工作中使用统计学方法解决现实问题的逻辑。

本书可以作为经济管理类非统计学专业的本科生学习统计学课程的辅助教材，也可以作为 MBA、MPA 学生学习统计学课程的辅助教材，还可以作为商务领域的广大工作者学习统计方法应用的参考书。

本书的编著是多位成员协同努力的结果，其中张希参与了最初的策划与设计，以及探索性数据分析之数值法、区间估计、方差分析、多元回归部分的工作；胡瑶参与了假设检验、一元线性回归部分的工作；龚逸君参与了非参数统计、时间序列分析部分的工作；蔡志文参与了探索性数据分析之图示法部分的软件输出及图表设计的工作，在此，对团体成员的辛勤工作表示深深的谢意！由于笔者水平有限，本书难免存在不妥之处，恳请同行专家和广大读者给予我们宝贵的批评和建议。

杨　楠

2012 年 1 月

于上海财经大学

目 录

Contents

Chapter 1

Displaying and Exploring Data: Graphical Presentations

第 1 章　探索性数据分析之图示法

There are many ways to present data in pictures. Sometimes a unique picture is used to fit a particular situation. The purpose of a plot, graph, or picture of data is to give you a visual summary that is more informative than simply looking at a collection of numbers. Done well, a picture can quickly convey a message that would take you longer to find. Done poorly, however, a picture can mislead all but the most observant of readers.

用图形来展现数据的方法有多种，特定情况下要使用特定的方法。借助图形，可以了解数据集的大致特征，形成清晰的视觉化的总结。如果使用得当，图形可以快速准确地传递信息；相反，若使用不当，图形也可以具有相当的欺骗性，误导除行家以外的所有读者。本章将介绍常用的图示法，并通过案例让读者体会如何用图示来展现概括数据集的基本特征。

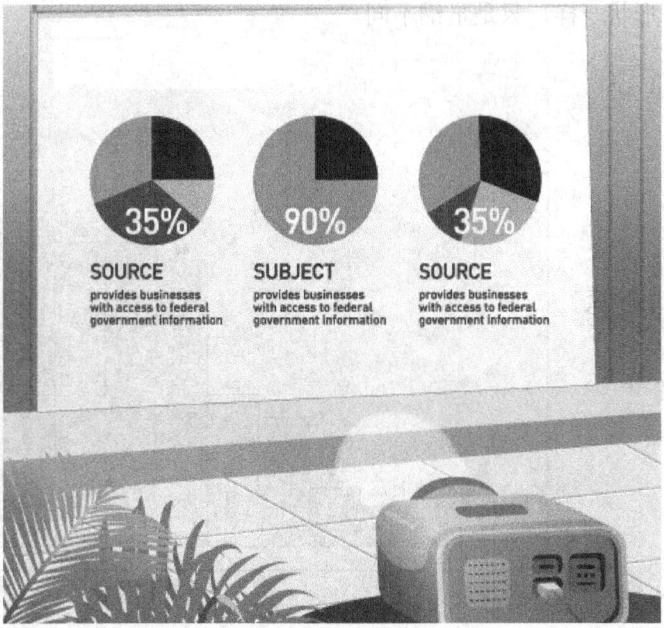

1.1 Graphs to Describe Quantitative Data

1.1 定量数据的图示分析

1. 直方图

直方图是在每个分组区间上绘制一个长条形而产生的图形，它可以用来描述已表示成频数或频率的数据。从直方图可以看出数据分布的疏密。

1. Histogram

A histogram is a graph that consists of vertical bars constructed on a horizontal line that is marked off with intervals for the variable being displayed. The intervals correspond to those in a frequency distribution table. The height of each bar is proportional to the number of observations in that interval. The number of observations can be displayed above the bars.

2. 绘制直方图

在绘制直方图时，一般用横轴（X 轴）表示所研究的变量，用纵轴（Y 轴）表示每组观测数据的频数或频率。纵坐标也可用百分比（见图 1.1），即把频数除以样本量，这样与用频数得到的形状一样，只是量纲不同。

2. Creating a Histogram

To create a histogram, simply divide the range of the data into intervals, and then count how many data fall into each part of the range. Draw a bar whose height is equal to the count for each part of the range—or, equivalently, make the height equal to the proportion of the total count that falls in that interval.

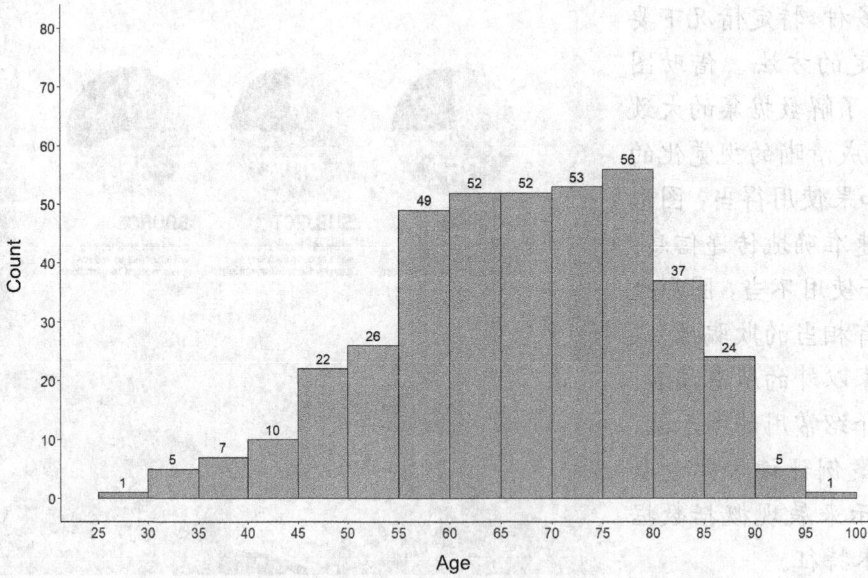

Figure 1.1　Histogram

图 1.1　直方图示例

3．茎叶图

探索性数据分析主要使用简单的算术或易画的图形来快速总结数据集的特征，很多方法最初是使用笔和纸就能完成的。时至今日，茎叶图这种古老的方法仍然被广为使用，它可以既展示数据的分布形状又同时带有原始数据信息。

3．Stem-and-leaf Display

The techniques of *exploratory data analysis* consist of simple arithmetic and easy-to-draw graphs that can be used to summarize data quickly. Many of these techniques were initially developed to provide a simple overview of a data set using pencil and paper. However, one technique, referred to as the stem-and-leaf display, is still widely used. A stem-and-leaf display can be used to show both the rank order and the shape of a data set simultaneously.

4．绘制茎叶图

茎叶图（见图 1.2）像一片带有茎的叶子。茎为较大位数的数字，叶为较小位数的数字。

步骤 1：把每个观测数据分解成茎和叶两部分，一般取前几位数为茎、最后一位数为叶。在一个垂直竖线的左侧将观测值的茎依次列出，在该竖线的右侧将对应叶依次列出。

步骤 2：把所有的数据由小到大排序，每个都按 1 中步骤分成茎和叶，然后按茎和叶的大小排列成图。

4．Creating a Stem-and-leaf Display

Only two steps are needed to create a stem-and-leaf display.

Step 1: First, arrange the leading digits of each data value to the left of a vertical line. To the right of the vertical line, record the last digit for each data value as we pass through the observations in the order they were recorded.

Step 2: Sort the digits on each line into rank order.

1 | 8
2 | 02344578
3 | 023445689
4 | 0

Figure 1.2　Stem-and-Leaf Display

图 1.2　茎叶图示例

5．盒形图

盒形图又称箱形图、箱线图、盒子图。它使用一个矩形盒

5．Box-Plot

A visually appealing and useful way to present a **five-number summary**[①] is through a box-plot,

① 五点法（Five-number Summary）中的统计量指的是一组数据的最小值、第一四分位数、中位数、第三四分位数和最大值，它们可以提供该组数据的重要位置及分散程度信息。

子形状来展示数据分布中五个最关键的点的位置。使用盒形图可以便于比较多个数据集的分布情况。

sometimes called a box-and-whisker plot. This simple picture also allows easy comparison of the center and spread of data collected for two or more groups.

6. 绘制盒形图

步骤 1：画一个封闭矩形，左右两边分别对应于数据集的上、下四分位数（点）。

步骤 2：在盒子的中间、数据集的中位数处，画一竖线。

步骤 3：盒子的宽度即是数据集的四分位距。

步骤 4：在盒子左右两边，分别向外画出延伸线，长度为 1.5 倍的四分位距。如果最小或最大值在此范围内，则线就画到最小、最大值为止。

步骤 5：用星号标出在延伸线范围外的数值。

6. Creating a Box-plot[①]

Step 1: Draw a box with ends at the lower and upper quartiles.

Step 2: Draw a line in the box at the median.

Step 3: Compute the width of the box; this is defined as the interquartile range.

Step 4: Draw whiskers at each end with length equal to 1.5 times the interquartile range. If the minimum or maximum occurs before the full length is reached, stop there.

Step 5: Use an asterisk to indicate any additional data points beyond the range covered by the box and whiskers.

7. 盒形图释义

盒形图（见图 1.3）将一个数据集分为四部分，最小的四分之一位于盒子左边以左，接下来的四分之一位于盒子内部左半边，第二大的四分之一位于盒子内部右半边，最大的四分之一位于盒子右边以右。异常值也很容易识别。

7. Interpreting Box-plots

Notice that box-plots essentially divide the data into fourths. The lowest fourth of the data values is contained in the range of values below the start of the box, the next fourth is contained in the first part of the box (between the lower quartile and the median), the next fourth is in the upper part of the box, and the final fourth is between the box and the upper end of the picture. Outliers are also easily identified.

8. 散点图

散点图（见图 1.4）是展示两个数值型变量间关系的直观图形，其中一个变量在横轴方

8. Scatter Diagram

A **scatter diagram** is a graphical means of showing the relationship between two quantitative variables. One variable is shown on the horizontal axis

① 不同的软件及不同选项所生成的盒形图两头线长的定义不尽相同，但封闭盒子长度的定义基本一样。

向，另一个变量在纵轴方向。散点图比单纯的线性图复杂，它提供了更多关于两变量间关系的信息。

and the other variable is shown on the vertical axis. Although a scatter diagram can be more difficult to read than a line graph, it displays more information.

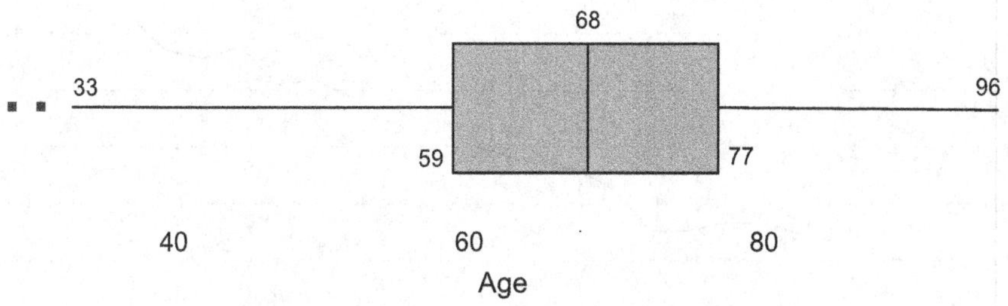

Figure 1.3　Box-Plot

图 1.3　盒形图示例

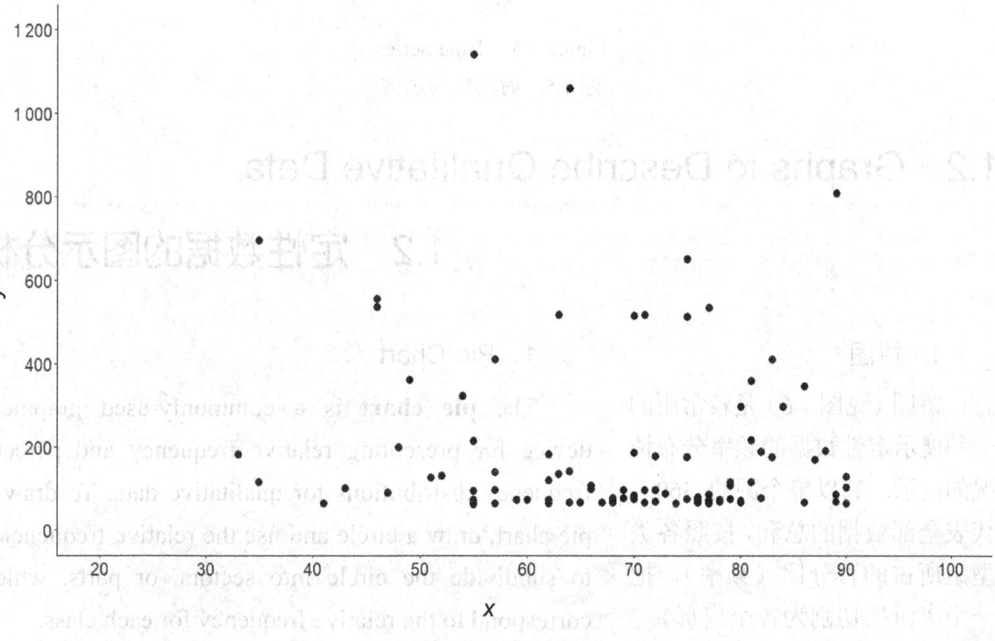

Figure 1.4　Scatter Diagram

图 1.4　散点图示例

9. 时间序列

时间序列（见图 1.5）是一组依据时间排列的数据点。在时间序列中，时间为自变量，构建时间序列的目的往往是预测有关因变量的未来发展趋势。

9. Time Series

A time series is simply a series of data points ordered in time. In a time series, time is often the independent variable and the goal is usually to make a forecast for the future.

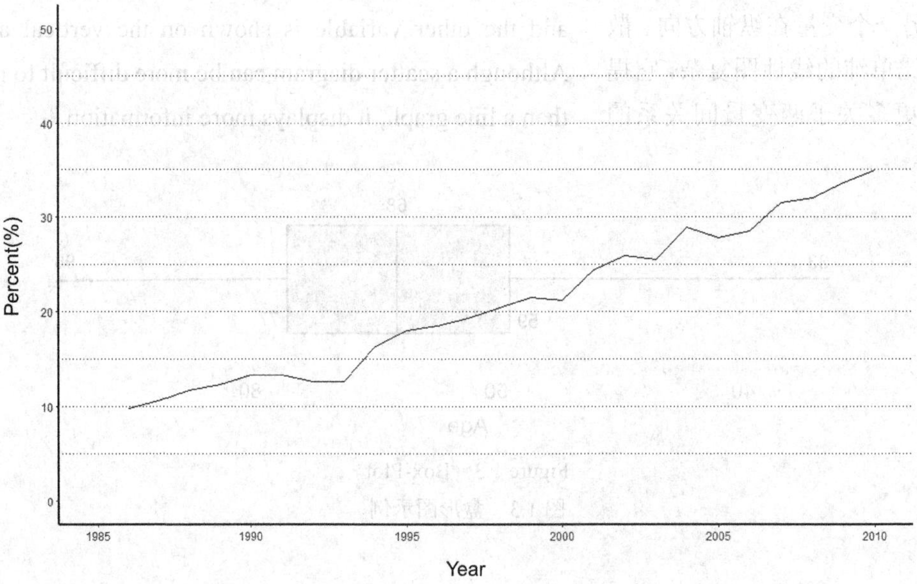

Figure 1.5　Time Series

图 1.5　时间序列示例

1.2　Graphs to Describe Qualitative Data

1.2　定性数据的图示分析

1. 饼图

饼图（见图 1.6）是较常用的一种展示定性数据的频率分布情况的图示。它以整个圆的 360° 代表全部数据的总和，按照各类型组所占的百分比（频率），把一个“饼”切割为各个扇形。

2. 条形图

条形图（见图 1.7）也是一种展示定性数据频率分布的图形。在条形图中，每一分类组被表示成一个条形，条的长度代表了这个组中所含数据的频数或频率。

1. Pie Chart

The **pie chart** is a commonly-used graphical device for presenting relative frequency and percent frequency distributions for qualitative data. To draw a pie chart, draw a circle and use the relative frequencies to subdivide the circle into sectors, or parts, which correspond to the relative frequency for each class.

2. Bar Graph

A **bar graph** also shows percentages or frequencies in various categories, and it can represent two or three categorical variables simultaneously. One categorical variable is used to label the horizontal axis. Within each of the categories along that axis, a bar is drawn to represent each category of the second variable. Frequencies or percentages are shown on the vertical axis.

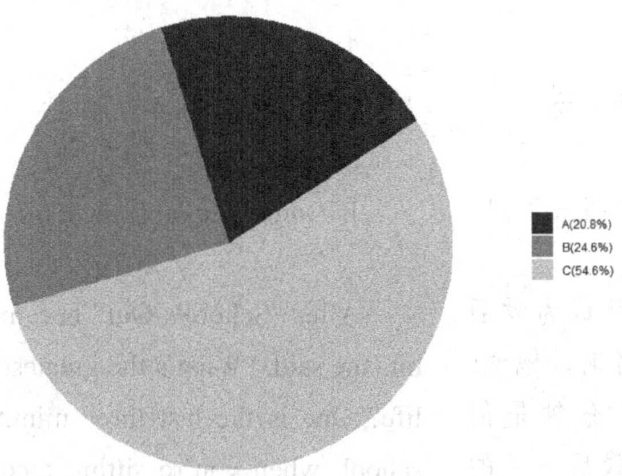

Figure 1.6　Pie Chart

图 1.6　饼图示例

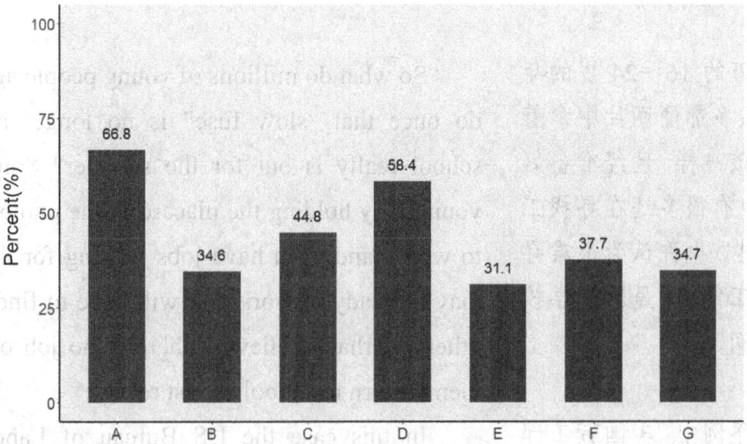

Figure 1.7　Bar Chart

图 1.7　条形图示例

Case 1.1　School's Out

案例 1.1　年轻人暑期工作情况分析

1. 案例介绍

“暑假里，离开学校，
直到秋天，
我们也许就不再回来了。”

当“离开学校”成为爱丽斯·库珀的第一要务时，她说：“一生中最棒的三分钟是何时？也许在学校的最后一天的最后三分钟。就是这样的时间，你坐在那里就像保险丝快要慢慢熔断。”

对上百万的16～24岁的年轻人来说，很多都像图片中拿着标语牌的女孩一样，已经准备好去工作了，也有很多还在寻找工作。还有一些，也许认为很难寻找到合适的工作，于是回到学校休息一段时间。

在这个案例中，美国劳工部希望分析近年年轻人暑期工作的相关情况，如：他们参加暑期学校的比例，他们工作的行业，失业情况等。相关数据被收集整理在表1.1、表1.2、表1.3中。其中包括从1986—2010年的每年暑期学校参加率、2007—2010年每年7月的失业率、2010年7月调查得到的16～24岁青年人的就业数据。美国劳工部希望对已有数据进行一些初步分析。

1. Introduction[①]

“Out for summer
Out till fall
We might not be back at all.”

After “School’s Out” became Alice Cooper’s first hit, she said, “What’s the greatest three minutes of your life? One is the last three minutes of the last day of school, when you’re sitting there and it’s like a slow fuse burning.”

So what do millions of young people aged 16 to 24 do once that “slow fuse” is no longer burning and school really is out for the summer? Some, like the young lady holding the placard in the photo, are “ready to work” and even have jobs waiting for them. Others may be ready to work, but will have to find a job. Still others, perhaps believing there is no job out there for them, return to school or just relax.

In this case the US Bureau of Labor Statistics takes a look at the numbers of young people over the past years, the proportion of young people who are working, the industries in which they work, the unemployment rate among young people, and the proportion who are in school in the summer. Four data sets obtained are shown in Tables 1.1, 1.2, 1.3. They report the yearly percentages of summer school attendance from 1986 to 2010, the unemployment rates in July from 2007 to 2010, the number of employed persons aged 16 to 24 in July 2010. The US Bureau of Labor Statistics decided to do some preliminary analysis of the data already collected.

① www.bls.gov/spotlight.

Table 1.1　Percentage of Summer School Attendance

表 1.1　暑期学校的参加率

July, of year	16 to 24 years	20 to 24 years	July, of year	16 to 24 years	20 to 24 years
1986	9.8	8.4	1999	21.5	16.8
1987	10.6	8.6	2000	21.2	16.2
1988	11.7	10.7	2001	24.4	18.7
1989	12.3	10.5	2002	25.9	19.7
1990	13.3	11.4	2003	25.5	19.3
1991	13.3	12.0	2004	28.9	21.7
1992	12.6	11.9	2005	27.8	20.7
1993	12.6	11.6	2006	28.5	21.1
1994	16.3	13.8	2007	31.5	23.2
1995	18.0	14.8	2008	32.0	23.9
1996	18.5	15.5	2009	33.6	24.4
1997	19.3	15.3	2010	34.9	26.3
1998	20.4	16.4			

Source: Current Population Survey

Table 1.2　Unemployment Rate, Persons aged 16 to 24, by Age, Sex, Race, and Hispanic or Latino Ethnicity, not Seasonally Adjusted, July, 2007—2010

表 1.2　2007—2010 年每年 7 月 16～24 岁青年人的失业率

（按年龄、性别、种族划分，未经季节性调整）

Age, Sex, and ethnicity 年龄、性别、种族	2007（%）	2008（%）	2009（%）	2010（%）
16 to 24 years of age, total（合计）	10.8	14.0	18.5	19.1
Women（女性）	10.4	12.8	17.3	17.5
Men（男性）	11.1	15.0	19.7	20.5
White（白人）	9.3	12.3	16.4	16.2
Hispanic or Latino ethnicity（西班牙及拉丁裔）	11.8	16.0	21.7	22.1
Black or African American（黑人及非洲裔）	20.5	24.8	31.2	33.4

Note: Persons whose ethnicity is identified as Hispanic or Latino may be of any race.

Source: Current Population Survey

Table 1.3 Data for Employed Persons, Aged 16～24, by Industry and Sex, July 2010

表1.3 2010年7月调查得到的16～24岁青年人的就业数据（按行业、性别划分）

Industry（行业）	Men（男性）		Women（女性）	
	16～19岁	20～24岁	16～19岁	20～24岁
Total（合计）	2 680 000	6 857 000	2 609 000	6 418 000
Accommodation and food services（住宿和餐饮服务）	726 000	1 032 000	859 000	1 229 000
Retail trade（零售业）	540 000	1 312 000	622 000	1 244 000
Education and health services（教育和医疗服务）	149 000	537 000	338 000	1 802 000
Professional and business services（专业及商业服务）	212 000	718 000	105 000	540 000
Manufacturing（制造业）	148 000	634 000	77 000	192 000
Arts, entertainment, and recreation（艺术、娱乐及休闲）	260 000	326 000	267 000	196 000
Construction（建筑业）	192 000	690 000	2 000	33 000
Other services（其他服务业）	90 000	318 000	145 000	285 000
Financial activities（金融业）	57 000	319 000	53 000	380 000
Transportation and utilities（交通运输和公共事业）	55 000	257 000	17 000	80 000
Public administration（公共管理）	42 000	137 000	22 000	197 000
Information（信息）	55 000	163 000	62 000	107 000
Agriculture and related（农业及相关行业）	117 000	164 000	24 000	67 000
Wholesale trade（批发业）	35 000	200 000	13 000	53 000
Mining, quarrying, and oil and gas extraction（挖掘、采矿、石油和天然气开采）	2 000	50 000	3 000	12 000

Source: Current Population Survey

这个案例涉及描述统计中的一些图示方法，我们将基于直方图、盒形图及散点图，对青年人的暑期工作情况进行分析。

In this case, appropriate descriptive graphic methods are mainly used to analyze the data related to young people's work in summer. Based on the graphs, we can discuss the information further.

2. 暑期学校的参加率

2. Summer School Attendance

在就业率逐渐下降的同时，参加暑期学校的年轻人的数量逐渐上升。图1.8绘制了1985—2010年16～24岁的年轻人参加暑期学校比例。近年来，参加暑期学校的学生比例已经达到历史新高：16～19岁的群体中达

The declining employment-population ratio has been accompanied by a growing number of young people attending summer school. Figure 1.8 displays the time series of proportions of 16-24-year-olds enrolled in school in July, from 1985 to 2010. In fact, the percentage of young people attending summer school recently set record highs: 45.6 percent for

到 45.6%，20～24 岁的群体中达到 26.3%。尽管工作与学校学习不是绝对冲突的，但在学校注册的年轻人并不倾向于出去工作。这种从工作场所回到教室的趋势无疑是与衰退的经济、高学历带来高工资的可能密切相关的。

16-to-19-year-olds, and 26.3 percent for 20-to-24-year-olds. Although work and school are not exclusive, young people enrolled in school are less likely to be working than their non-enrolled peers. This movement of young people from the workplace to the classroom is no doubt related to some combination of the weakening economy, realization of the tremendous potential earning power of higher levels of education, and other factors unique to individual young persons.

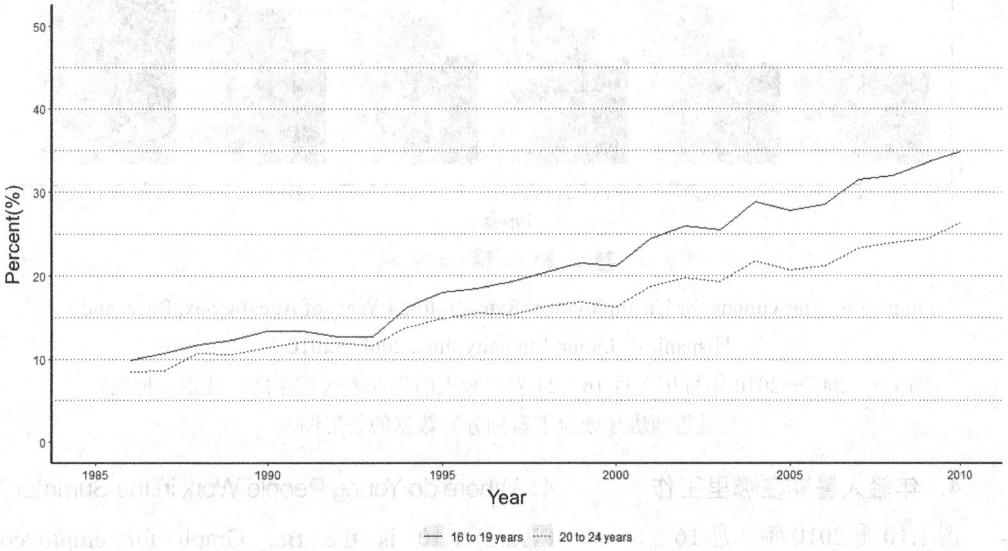

Figure 1.8　Time Series Plot for Proportion of 16-to-24-Year-Olds Enrolled in School in July, 1985—2010

图 1.8　1985—2010 年 16～24 岁青年人注册暑期学校比例的时间序列图

3．年轻人的失业率

图 1.9 是 2007—2010 年 7 月 16～24 岁的年轻人的失业率的条形图，按照性别、种族、西班牙及拉美裔等进行分类。在这段时间，男青年的失业率持续高于女青年。此外，那些传统意义上更倾向于雇用男性的行业，如建筑和制造业，雇用率持续低于其他那些倾向于雇用女性的行业，如教育和健康护理。与以往相同的是，年轻白人的失业率仍低于年轻黑人和西班牙裔。

3．Youth Unemployment

Figure 1.9 shows a bar graph for unemployment rate, 16～24 years of age, by sex, race and Hispanic or Latino ethnicity for the month of July, from 2007 to 2010. The unemployment rate for young men was consistently higher than that for young women between July 2007 and July 2010. During this period, employment in industries that generally hire more men than women (such as construction and manufacturing) declined more than employment in industries that tend to employ more women than men (such as education and health care). Unemployment among white young people tended to be lower than that among black and Hispanic young

2007—2010 年，无论哪个青年群体的失业率都有显著增加。

people, as is also typical of their older counterparts. Unemployment among all groups of young people increased markedly between 2007 and 2010.

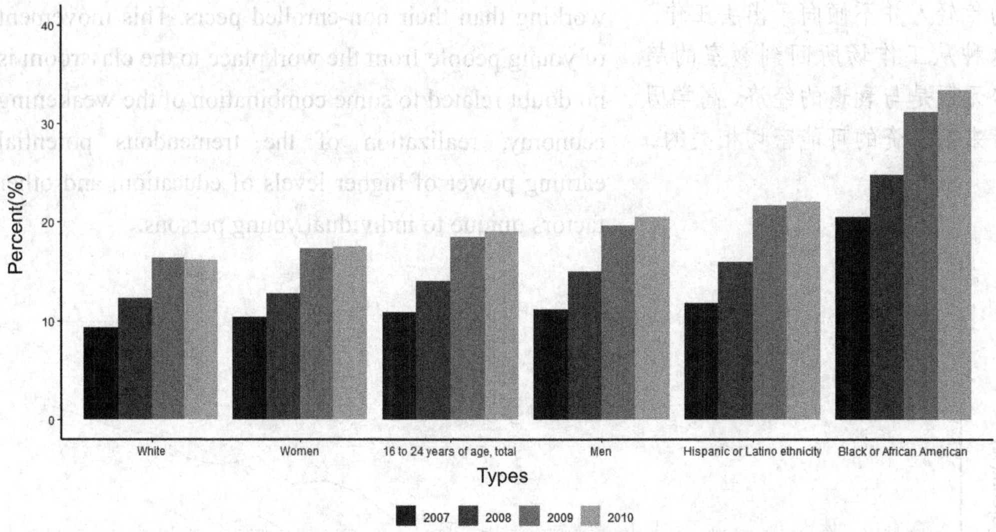

Figure 1.9 Bar Graphs for Unemployment Rate, 16-to-24 Years of Age, by Sex, Race, and Hispanic or Latino Ethnicity, July, 2007—2010

图 1.9 2007—2010 年每年 7 月 16～24 岁年轻人的失业率（按年龄、性别、种族、是否西班牙或拉丁裔划分）数据的条形图

4. 年轻人暑期在哪里工作

图 1.10 是 2010 年 7 月 16～24 岁被雇用的年轻人人数的条形图，按照行业和性别进行分类。每年 4 月到 7 月间，劳动力市场上年轻人的数量激增，因为很多高中生、大学生都在找暑期工作，毕业生们也进入工作大军。对那些准备秋天回到学校的年轻人来说，在酒店、食品、零售等行业找一个暂时的工作是一个不错的选择。整体来说，暑期大约有相同数目的男青年和女青年被雇用。在教育和健康护理行业，女性人数更多些；在制造业和建筑业，男性人数更多些。

4. Where do Young People Work in the Summer?

Figure 1.10 is the Bar Graph for employed persons, 16–24 years of age, in July 2010, categorized by industry and sex. The figure implies that the youth labor force grows sharply between April and July each year, when large numbers of high school and college students take or search for summer jobs and graduates enter the labor market in search of permanent employment. For those young people who intend to return to school in the fall, temporary summer jobs—often found in the accommodation and food services industries and the retail sector—are a good fit. Overall, roughly equal numbers of young men and young women are employed during the summer. Young women outnumber young men in the education and health services industries; in the manufacturing and construction industries, there are more young men than young women.

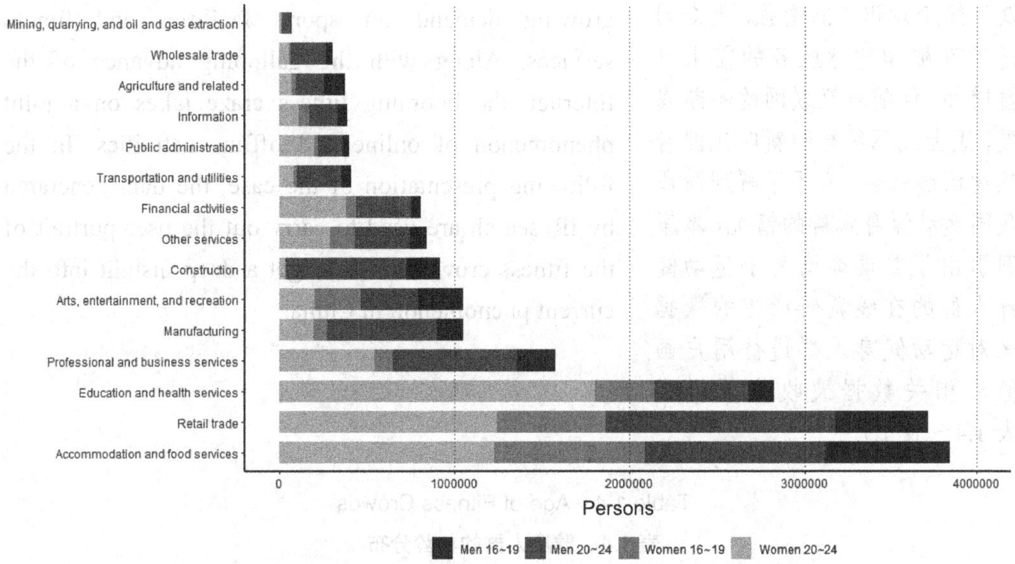

Figure 1.10　Bar Graphs for Employed Persons, Age 16～24, by Industry and Sex

图 1.10　2010 年 7 月 16～24 岁就业数据的条形图（按行业、性别划分）

Case 1.2　The User Portrait of the Fitness Crowds

案例 1.2　我国健身人群画像

1. 案例介绍

随着我国大众生活水平的提高，消费力和消费意愿逐年上升，生活方式快速转变升级，大

1. Introduction①

In China, the improved living standards have come to exert a positive impact on the nationals' lifestyles and promote their health awareness, as indicated by the

① http://report.iresearch.cn/report/201903/3345.shtml.

众的健康意识不断增强。大众对运动设施和健身服务的需求日益增加，伴随着互联网的不断发展，线上线下结合的新时代健身热潮已然来袭。为了了解现阶段我国运动健身人群的情况，本案例引用了艾瑞咨询关于运动健身人群的在线调研产生的数据来对运动健身人群进行用户画像。相关数据被收集整理在表 1.4～表 1.7 中。

growing demand for sports facilities and fitness services. Along with the galloping advance of the Internet, the booming fitness craze takes on a joint phenomenon of online and offline activities. In the following presentation of the case, the data generated by iResearch are used to carry out the user portrait of the fitness crowds so as to get a deep insight into the current phenomenon in China.

Table 1.4 Age of Fitness Crowds

表 1.4 健康人群的年龄分布

Age（年龄）	Percentage (%)［百分比（%）］	Age（年龄）	Percentage (%)［百分比（%）］
<20	5.7	41～50	14.7
20～30	31.5	>51	6.4
31～40	41.7		

Table 1.5 Reasons Behind Workout

表 1.5 锻炼的原因

Reasons（原因）	Percentage (%)［百分比（%）］
Stay Healthy（保持健康）	66.8
Strengthen Body（提升身体素质）	58.4
Relieve Stress（缓解压力）	44.8
Enjoy Exercise（享受锻炼过程）	37.7
Improve Confidence（增加自信心）	34.7
Enhance Willpower（锻炼意志）	34.6
Gain Pleasure（提升愉悦感）	31.1

Table 1.6 Fitness Period

表 1.6 锻炼时间

Period (Mins)［锻炼时间（分钟）］	Percentage (%)［百分比（%）］	Period (Mins)［锻炼时间（分钟）］	Percentage (%)［百分比（%）］
<10	0.00	41～50	29.0
11～20	2.1	60～90	16.2
21～30	16.8	>90	3.4
31～40	32.5		

Table1.7　The Consuming Structure of Fitness Crowds

表 1.7　健身人群的消费结构

Consumption（消费）	Program（课程服务）	Sports（运动场景）	Shoes & Clothes（鞋服设备）
Percentage[百分比（%）]	20.8	24.6	54.6

Source:http://report.iresearch.cn/report/201903/3345.shtml

2. 健身人群年龄分布饼图

如图 1.11 所示，在健身人群的年龄分布方面，20 岁以下占比 5.7%，20～30 岁占比 31.5%，31～40 岁占比 41.7%，41～50 岁占比 14.7%，51 岁以上占比 6.4%。从数据分布中不难发现，健身人群主要集中在中青年群体，40 岁以下为主体人群，共占比 78.9%。

2. Characteristics of Fitness Crowds

As shown in Figure 1.11 regarding the age distribution of the fitness crowds, those aged under 20 accounted for 5.7%; those aged 20～30, 31.5%; those aged 31～40, 41.7%; those aged 41～50, 14.7%; and those aged over 51, 6.4%. The results suggest that the majority (78.9%) belonged to the middle-aged group under the age of 40.

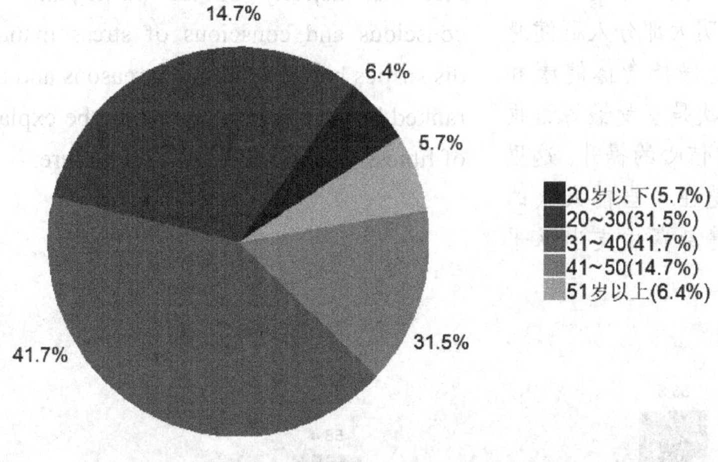

Figure 1.11　Pie Chart of the Fitness Crowds' Age

图 1.11　健身人群的年龄分布饼图

31～40 岁用户占比最高，主要原因是这部分用户生活已经趋于稳定，精力较为充沛，且收入稳定，有一定的闲暇时间。其次是 20～30 岁的比例也较高，主要原因是这个群体中大部分未结婚成家，休闲时间较多，经济压力较小，有时间也有经济

It was found that those who were aged 31～40 constituted the highest proportion of the users, which could mainly be explained by the fact that they have stable income and were physically energetic. Below the highest proportion was those were aged 20～30, the main reason of which was that most of them were unmarried having more leisure time and less financial pressure. With the advent of the Internet and artificial

实力参与健身活动。随着移动互联网、人工智能的发展，代表未来新趋势的 20～30 岁年轻用户群体健身习惯和健身意识逐渐养成、经济能力逐步提高，预计在未来的 3～5 年，该用户群体有可能成为健身行业的消费主力军。

intelligence, the young users aged 20 ～ 30 may represent a new trend in the near future; they are expected to contribute to the major consumption in the sports and fitness industries in the next three to five years.

3. 健身原因分布条形图

图 1.12 显示出在健身原因中，“保持健康”占比 66.8%，“提升身体素质”占比 58.4%，“缓解压力”占比 44.8%，“享受锻炼过程”占比 37.7%，“增加自信心”占比 34.7%，“锻炼意志”占比 34.6%，“提升愉悦感”占比 31.1%，说明大部分人群健身的主要原因是保持身体健康和缓解压力，其次是享受锻炼过程中意志力和自信心的提升。这里的差别主要是在于当前大众的健身需求和健身费用支出水平处于不同层次。

3. Reasons behind Workout

As indicated in Figure 1.12, the seven reasons accounted for 66.8%, 58.4%, 44.8%, 37.7%, 34.7%, 34.6%, and 31.1%, respectively, presenting a gliding decrease in percentage. The first three of staying healthy, strengthening body and relieving stress, ranked high in percentage, the main explanation of which was that the majority of the participants were health-conscious and conscious of stress management. The disparities between the three reasons and the rest which ranked lower in percentage could be explained in terms of fitness demand and cost expenditure.

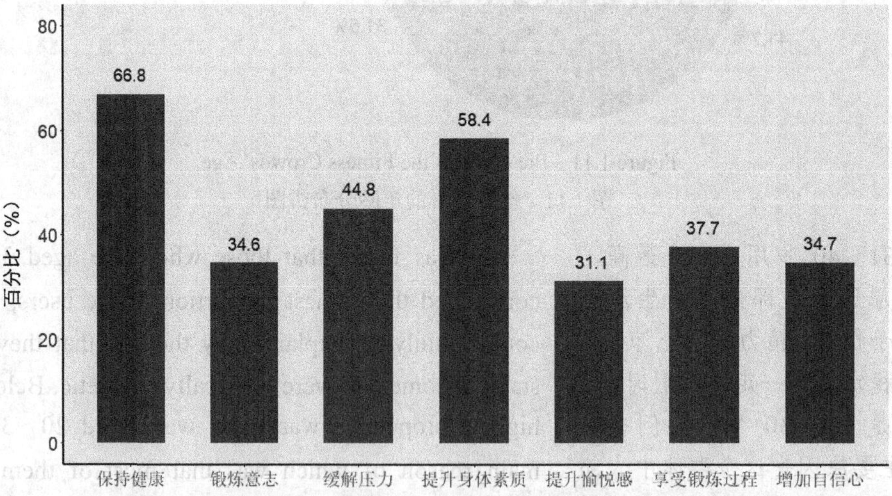

Figure1.12 Bar Chart of the Purpose of Fitness

图 1.12 健身的原因分布条形图

当前大众的健身主体需求是在适当的支出下保证身体健康，而同时可以看到追求时尚美丽的“减肥+塑形”和“纯粹喜欢运动”的健身理念也慢慢被大众接受，由此带来了健身需求的细分，课程形式和内容将趋于多样化。

Additionally, the different proportions reflect diversity in the growing demands such as vogue beauty and pure enjoyment. Such diversity facilitates the development of new fitness programs for the public.

4. 平均健身时长分布条形图

如图 1.13 所示，在单次运动时长上，“10 分钟以下”占比 0%，“11～20 分钟”占比 2.1%，“21～30 分钟”占比 16.8%，“31～40 分钟”占比 32.5%，“41～50 分钟”占比 29.0%，“60～90 分钟”占比 16.2%，“90 分钟以上”占比 3.4%。由此可见，没有用户单次运动时长在 10 分钟以下，用户运动健身时长多集中在 30 分钟到 1 个小时，六成用户运动健身时长为 20～40 分钟。

4. Fitness Period

As shown in Figure 1.13 pertaining to the duration of single exercise, those who lasted less than 10 minutes accounted for 0%; those who did 11～20 minutes, 2.1%; those who did 21～30 minutes, 16.8%; those who did 31～40 minutes, 32.5%; those who did 41～50 minutes, 29.0%; those who did 60-90 minutes, 16.2%; and those who did more than 90 minutes, 3.4%. From the range of different periods, we can see that no user exercised less than 10 minutes; that most of them would have a workout that lasted 30～60 minutes; and that 60% of them exercised for 20～40 minutes.

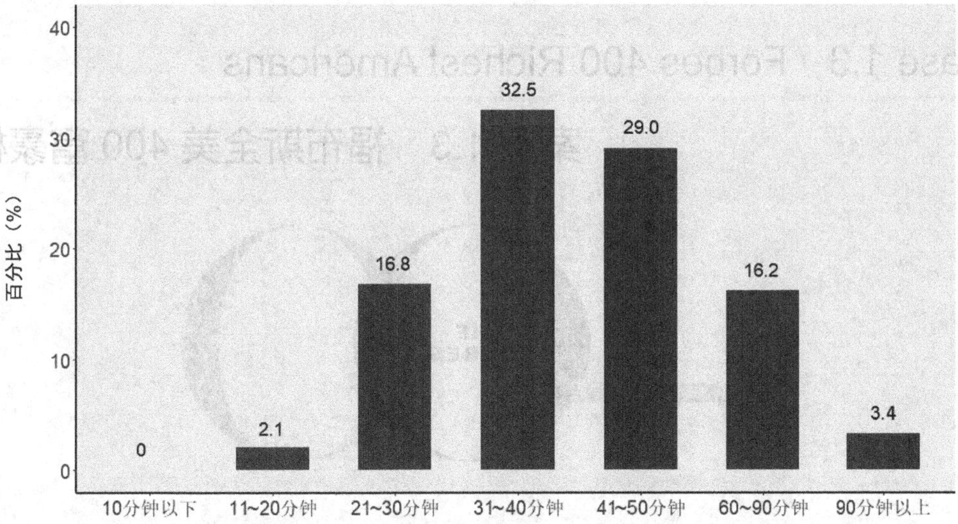

Figure 1.13 Bar Chart of the Fitness Time

图 1.13 健身时间分布条形图

5. 健身人群消费结构分布饼图

从图 1.14 来看，购买鞋服装备仍然是健身人群消费的主要部分，占到了消费总体的 54.6%，而随着用户运动生活方式和消费观念的升级，投入运动场景和课程服务的消费也上升至 45.4%的份额。随着未来运动健身企业对用户需求的进一步挖掘，用户在运动健身方面的消费投入仍然有很大上升空间。

5. The Consuming Structure of Fitness Crowds

As shown in Figure 1.14, the purchase of sports shoes and clothes still constituted the main part of the total consumption, accounting for 54.6%. With the upgrading of the sports and consumption concept, the consumption of sports services and programs increased up to 45.4%. Furthermore, the sports and fitness enterprises never stopped exploring and accommodating the needs of users; as expected, the consumers' spending on sports and fitness would be bound to grow significantly in the future.

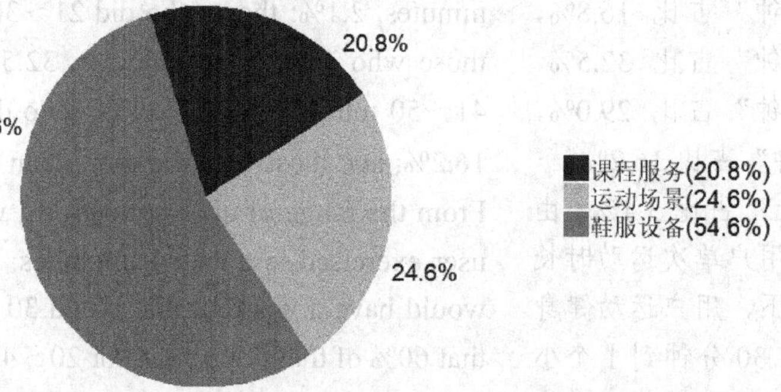

Figure 1.14 Pie Chart of the Consumption Structure of Fitness People

图 1.14 健身人群消费结构分布饼图

Case 1.3 Forbes 400 Richest Americans

案例 1.3 福布斯全美 400 富豪榜

The Forbes 400: The Definitive Ranking Of The Wealthiest Americans

1. 案例介绍

福布斯全美 400 富豪榜是《福布斯》(*Forbes*)杂志每年公布的按净资产排名的美国最富有的400人名单。它由Malcolm Forbes 于 1982 年创建,截至2019年已有38期,其影响遍及全球,能够反映杰出人士与经济潮流的最新动向。

在最新一期的榜单中,《福布斯》400名最富有的美国人的总净资产创历史新高,达 2.96 万亿美元,比 2018 年增长了 2.2%。其平均净资产增加了 2 亿美元,达到 74 亿美元。

在榜单中,亚马逊创始人杰夫·贝佐斯(Jeff Bezos)以净收入1 140亿美元第二次位居榜首。比尔·盖茨位列第二,与2018 年相同,但他和贝佐斯的差距比 2018 年大幅缩小,仅为 80 亿美元。杰夫·贝佐斯的前妻麦肯齐·贝佐斯和其他 18 位新人也首次登上了福布斯全美400 富豪榜的榜单,其中包括视频游戏公司 Epic Games 的首席执行官蒂姆·斯威尼(Tim Sweeney),私人股本公司 Thoma Bravo 的联合创始人、首位波多黎各亿万富豪奥兰多·布拉沃(Orlando Bravo),以及流媒体公司 Roku 的创始人 Anthony Wood。

榜单展示了最富有的 400 名美国人的姓名、净资产、年龄、所在地和所属行业等信息。由于篇幅所限,表 1.8 列举了部分原

1. Introduction[①]

The Forbes 400 or 400 Richest Americans (first published in 1982) is a list published by Forbes Magazine showing the 400 wealthiest Americans, ranked by net worth. The list is published annually, and 2019 marks the 38th issue. The 400 was started by Malcolm Forbes in 1982 and treats those in the list like celebrities. It was intended to capture each year's extraordinary individual and entrepreneurial energy.

In the latest release, the Forbes 400 richest Americans are worth a record-breaking $2.96 trillion, up 2.2% from 2018. The average net worth of a Forbes 400 member has risen to $7.4 billion, up $200 million.

Amazon founder and CEO Jeff Bezos keeps his spot as the richest person in the US for the second year. He clocks in at $114 billion. Bill Gates came in at number 2, also the same rank as last year, but the gap between him and Bezos has narrowed dramatically to just $8 billion. Besides MacKenzie Bezos, Jeff Bezos' ex-wife, 18 other newcomers join the ranks, including Tim Sweeney, CEO of the video game company Epic Games, private equity dealmaker Orlando Bravo, who is the first Puerto Rican-born billionaire, and Anthony Wood, founder of streaming technology firm Roku.

The Forbes 400 list displays information about name, net worth, age, residence, and source. Table 1.8 shows selected items from the list, and the whole list is in an appendix. Here we want to achieve a more

① www.forbes.com/lists/.

始数据，全部数据表参见书后附录。在这里，我们希望借助图示方法得到更为直观的理解。

intuitive understanding by using graphical methods.

Table 1.8 Selected Data from the Forbes 400 Richest Americans

表1.8 福布斯全美400富豪榜的节选数据

Rank （排名）	English name （姓名）	net worth($) [净资产（美元）]	Age （年龄）	Residence （所在地）	Source （所属行业）
1	Jeff Bezos 杰夫·贝佐斯	114B	55	Washington	Amazon 亚马逊
2	Bill Gates 比尔·盖茨	106B	64	Washington	Microsoft 微软
3	Warren Buffett 沃伦·巴菲特	80.8B	89	Nebraska	Berkshire Hathaway 伯克希尔·哈撒韦
4	Mark Zuckerberg 马克·扎克伯格	69.6B	35	California	Facebook 脸书
5	Larry Ellison 拉里·埃里森	65B	75	California	Oracle 甲骨文
6	Larry Page 拉里·佩奇	55.5B	46	California	Google 谷歌
7	Sergey Brin 谢尔盖·布林	53.5B	46	California	Google 谷歌
8	Michael Bloomberg 迈克尔·布隆伯格	53.4B	77	New York	Bloomberg 彭博
9	Steve Ballmer 史蒂夫·鲍尔默	51.7B	63	Washington	Microsoft 微软
10	Jim Walton 吉姆·沃尔顿	51.6B	71	Arkansas	Walmart 沃尔玛
11	Alice Walton 艾丽斯·沃尔顿	51.4B	70	Texas	Walmart 沃尔玛
12	Rob Walton 罗伯·沃尔顿	51.3B	75	Arkansas	Walmart 沃尔玛
13	Charles Koch 查尔斯·科赫	41B	83	Kansas	Diversified 多元化经营
14	Julia Koch & family 茱莉亚·科赫及家族	41B	57	New York	Diversified 多元化经营
15	MacKenzie Bezos 麦肯齐·贝索斯	36.1B	49	Washington	Amazon 亚马逊
16	Phil Knight & family 菲尔·耐特及家族	35.9B	81	Oregon	Nike 耐克
17	Sheldon Adelson 谢尔登·阿德尔森	34.5B	86	Nevada	Casinos 赌场

续表

Rank （排名）	English name （姓名）	net worth($) [净资产（美元）]	Age （年龄）	Residence （所在地）	Source （所属行业）
18	Michael Dell 迈克尔·戴尔	32.3B	54	Texas	Dell 戴尔
19	Jacqueline Mars 杰奎琳·马尔斯	29.7B	80	Virginia	Confectionery 糖果
20	John Mars 约翰·马尔斯	29.7B	84	Wyoming	Confectionery 糖果

Source: www.forbes.com/lists

这个案例仍然涉及描述统计中的一些图示方法，我们将基于直方图、茎叶图、盒形图及散点图，对富豪们的净资产与年龄这两个定量变量进行分析。

In this case, appropriate descriptive graphical methods can be used to analyze the two quantitative variables, net worth and age, of the 400 richest Americans. Based on a histogram, stem-and-leaf display, box plot and scatter diagram, we can discuss the information further.

2. 福布斯全美 400 富豪的年龄分布直方图和茎叶图

2. Histogram and stem-and-leaf display of Age Data for Forbes 400 Richest American

图 1.15 是福布斯全美 400 富豪的年龄数据直方图。从图中可以看出他们的年龄分布大致成钟形，略微左偏。大多数人的年龄为 50～85 岁，中心位置为 65～75 岁。最年轻的四位为 20～30 岁，最年长的十余位为 90～100 岁。

Figure 1.15 is a histogram of the Forbes 400 richest Americans' age data. From the figure we can see that the age variable takes on an approximate bell shape and has a tiny skewness to the left. Most of the ages are within the interval of 50 to 85, and the central location seems to be within the interval of 65 to 75. The youngest four people are aged between 20 and 30, and the ten or so oldest people are aged between 90 and 100.

图 1.16 是福布斯全美 400 富豪们的年龄数据茎叶图。它与直方图最大的不同在于它还可以展示出原始数据。在这个案例中，我们将每行的茎和一个叶组合就得到一个原始年龄数据。例如，可以看出，30～40 岁的富豪有 12 位，年龄分别是 31 岁、33 岁、34 岁和 35 岁。

Figure 1.16 presents the data in another way: a stem-and-leaf display. Although it may appear to offer the same information as the histogram, it differs in showing the original data. In Figure 1.16, we can find the original age of each person in the Forbes 400 by combining each stem with a leaf. For example, for those aged between 30 and 40, we know that there are 12 people, and their actual ages are 31, 33, 34, and 35.

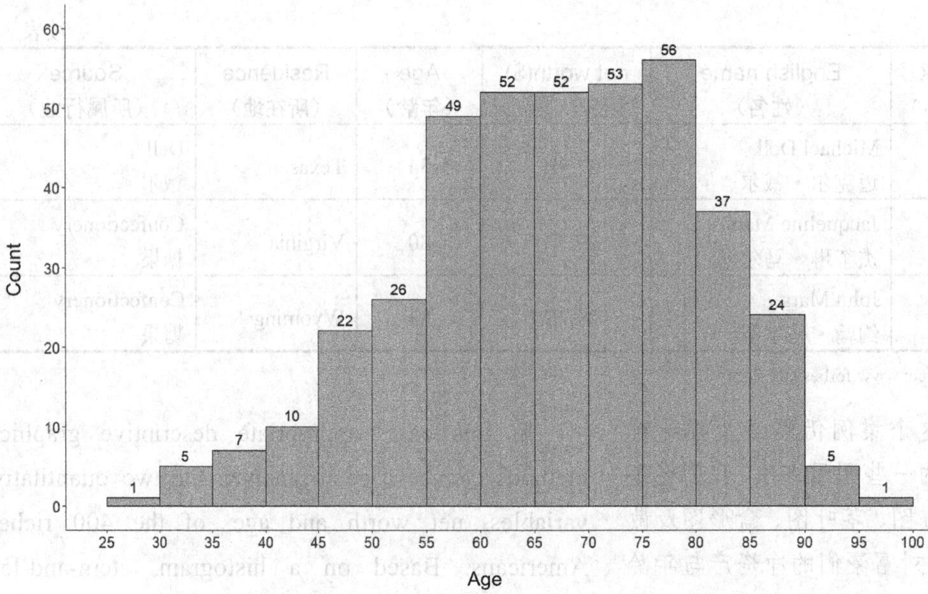

Figure 1.15 Histogram of the Forbes 400 Richest Americans' Age

图 1.15 福布斯全美 400 富豪的年龄分布直方图

```
The decimal point is 1 digit(s) to the right of the |
2 | 9
3 | 134
3 | 556677889
4 | 11223334
4 | 5566677777889999999
5 | 000011223333344444444
5 | 55555555666677777777777778888888899999999999
6 | 000000000000011111222222222222233333333333333344444444444
6 | 5555555555566666666666677777888888888888888899999
7 | 000000000000001111111112222222223333333333333344444444
7 | 55555555555555556666666666666777777777777777777888888888889999999
8 | 000000001111111222222222223333344444
8 | 55555555666666777777888999
9 | 00000013344
9 | 6
```

Figure 1.16 Stem-and-Leaf Display of the Forbes 400 Richest Americans' Age

图 1.16 福布斯全美 400 富豪的年龄分布茎叶图

3．福布斯全美 400 富豪的年龄分布盒形图

图 1.17 是福布斯 400 富豪

3．Box-Plot of Age Data for Forbes 400 Richest American

Figure 1.17 is the box-plot of the age date for

的年龄数据盒形图。图中显示了五个关键位置，从左到右分别是 $Q_1-1.5IQR$、Q_1、中位数、Q_3 和 $Q_3+1.5IQR$。中间三个数值 59、68 和 77 对应于 Q_1、中位数和 Q_3。由于数据集最大值超出了此上限，右侧虚线就画到最大值 96 为止，左侧有两个数小于此下限，被识别为异常值，左侧虚线就画到下限 33 为止。

the Forbes 400 richest American. In the box, the key positions[①] labeled are, from left to right, $Q_1-1.5IQR$, Q_1, median, Q_3, and $Q_3+1.5IQR$. The three middle values of 59, 68, and 77 correspond to Q_1, the median, and Q_3 respectively. Since the maximum value is smaller than the upper limit, the right whisker stops at the maximum of 96. Because two small values exceed the lower limit, the left whisker still stops at the lower limit of 33 and the two points outside are identified as outliers.

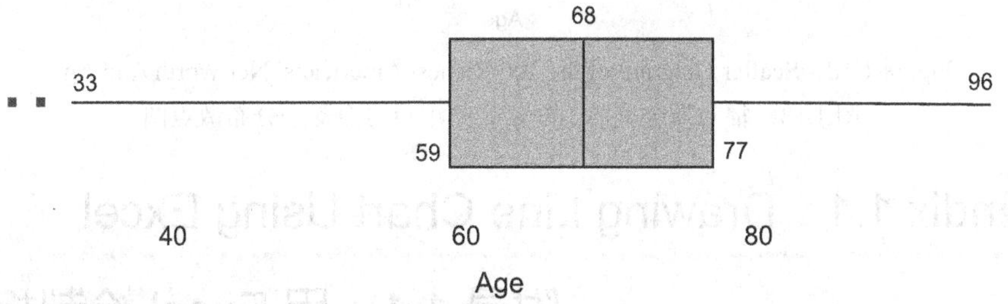

Figure 1.17 Box-Plot of The Forbes 400 Richest Americans' Age
图 1.17 福布斯全美 400 富豪的年龄分布盒形图

图 1.17 中盒子明显呈现非对称形态，两边的胡须长度也不对称，说明数据为左偏，右侧分布较紧密，左侧分布较分散。

The box is not symmetrical, and neither are the whiskers. This means the data set is skewed to the left. The right part is more compact and the left part is more dispersed.

4. 福布斯全美前 100 富豪的年龄-财富散点图

4. Scatter Diagram of Net Worth and Age of 100 Richest American

这里想探究最富有的 100 人的年龄与财富之间是否存在线性相关关系。图 1.18 是对应的散点图。可以看到，随着年龄增加，财富并不必然增加。若用直线拟合散点，则斜率接近零。这说明年龄与财富不存在线性相关关系。

Here we want to investigate whether a linear relationship can be found between the richest 100 Americans' net worth and age data. A scatter diagram is drawn, as shown in Figure 1.18. We can see that as age increases, net worth doesn't increase accordingly. If a straight line is drawn to represent the trend of all these points, its slope will approximate zero. This means that almost no linear correlation exists between net worth and age for the 100 richest Americans.

① 第一四分位点减 1.5 倍四分位距，第一四分位点，中位数，第三四分位点，第三四分位点加 1.5 倍四分位距。

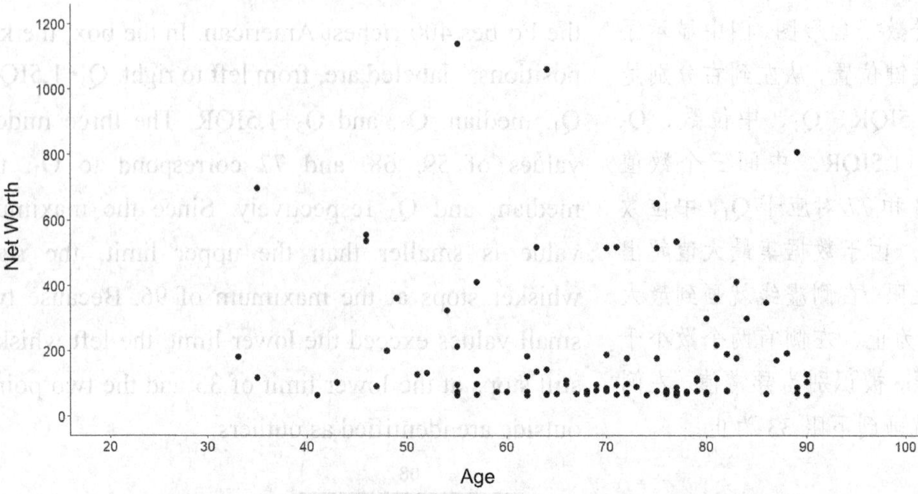

Figure 1.18 Scatter Diagram of the 100 Richest Americans' Net Worth And Age

图 1.18 福布斯全美前 100 富豪的年龄与净资产分布散点图

Appendix 1.1 Drawing Line Chart Using Excel

附录 1.1 用 Excel 绘制折线图

步骤 1：选定数据（见图 1.19）。

Step 1. Select the data as below.

	A	B	C	D
1	July, of year	Percentage of Summer School Attendance		
2		16 to 19 years	20 to 24 years	
3	1986	9.8	8.4	
4	1987	10.6	8.6	
5	1988	11.7	10.7	
6	1989	12.3	10.5	
7	1990	13.3	11.4	
8	1991	13.3	12	
9	1992	12.6	11.9	
10	1993	12.6	11.6	
11	1994	16.3	13.8	
12	1995	18	14.8	
13	1996	18.5	15.5	
14	1997	19.3	15.3	
15	1998	20.4	16.4	
16	1999	21.5	16.8	
17	2000	21.2	16.2	
18	2001	24.4	18.7	
19	2002	25.9	19.7	
20	2003	25.5	19.3	
21	2004	28.9	21.7	
22	2005	27.8	20.7	
23	2006	28.5	21.1	
24	2007	31.5	23.2	
25	2008	32	23.9	
26	2009	33.6	24.4	
27	2010	34.9	26.3	
28				

Figure 1.19 Selecting Data

图 1.19 选取数据

步骤 2：单击“**插入**”按钮，单击图表中“**所有图表**”，选择你喜欢的折线图，如图 1.20 所示。

Step 2. Select **Insert**, choose the **Line Chart**, then choose the style of bar you like.

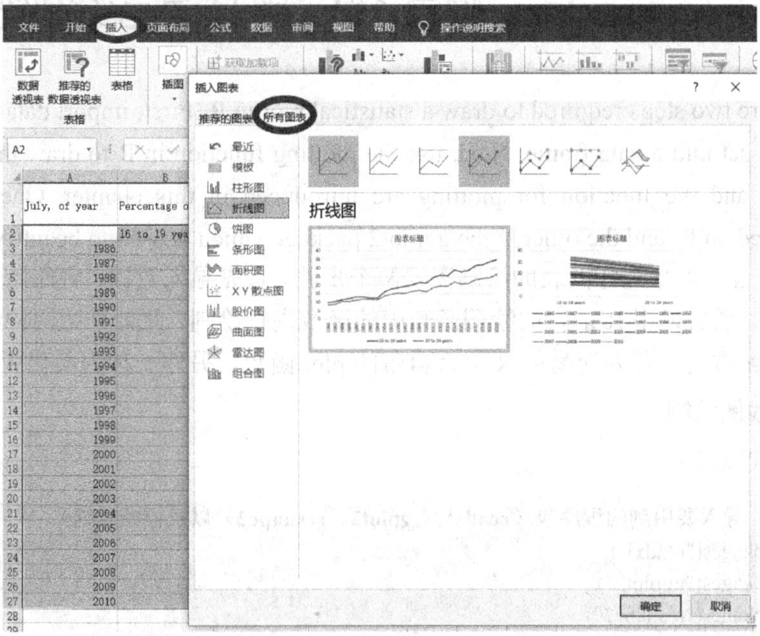

Figure 1.20　Plotting Process

图 1.20　绘图过程

步骤 3：单击“**确定**”按钮即可画出折线图（见图 1.21）。

绘制条形图、饼图方法类似。

Step 3. Select **OK**, then the line chart appears. Bar graph and pie chart could also be drawn in this way.

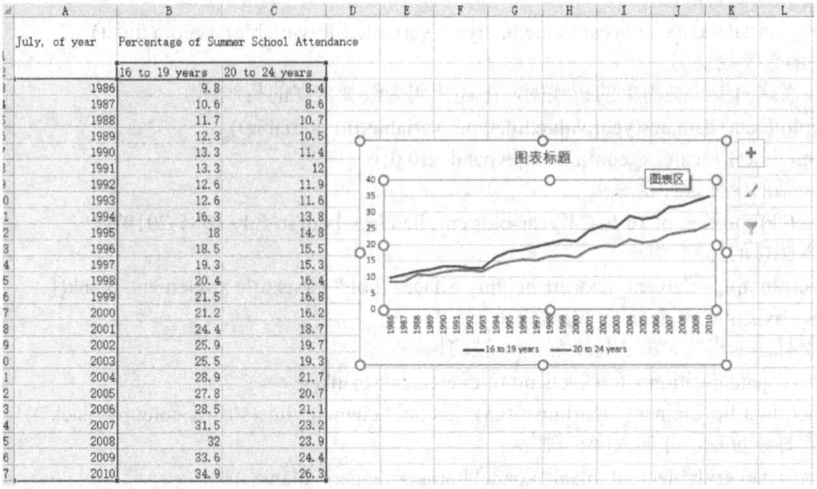

July, of year	Percentage of Summer School Attendance	
	16 to 19 years	20 to 24 years
1986	9.8	8.4
1987	10.6	8.6
1988	11.7	10.7
1989	12.3	10.5
1990	13.3	11.4
1991	13.3	12
1992	12.6	11.9
1993	12.6	11.6
1994	16.3	13.8
1995	18	14.8
1996	18.5	15.5
1997	19.3	15.3
1998	20.4	16.4
1999	21.5	16.8
2000	21.2	16.2
2001	24.4	18.7
2002	25.9	19.7
2003	25.5	19.3
2004	28.9	21.7
2005	27.8	20.7
2006	28.5	21.1
2007	31.5	23.2
2008	32	23.9
2009	33.6	24.4
2010	34.9	26.3

Figure 1.21　Outcomes of Plotting

图 1.21　绘图结果

Appendix 1.2 Graphical Presentations Using R

附录 1.2 用 R 语言绘制统计图表

There are two steps required to draw a statistical plot in R. First, import data and turn the original data set into a data frame. Next, use the plotting function in R to draw the plot. Both the package and the function for plotting are introduced in this chapter. One is the plot function based on R, and the other is the ggplot2 package which is used to beautify the plot.

在 R 语言中进行统计图表的绘制需要两个步骤。首先导入数据，将原始数据集转为数据框模式。然后调用 R 语言的绘图函数中的函数进行绘制，此处介绍两种绘制图表的 packages 和函数，一种为简易的 R 语言自带的 plot 函数，另外一种为美化版的 ggplot2。

1．折线图绘制

（1）代码

```
#步骤一：导入要用到的程序包（readxl、ggplot2、reshape2）以及原始数据
install.packages("readxl")
install.packages("ggplot2")
install.packages("reshape2")
library(readxl)
library(ggplot2)
library(reshape2)
data <- read_excel("D:/data/Chapter 1-Case 1-School's Out.xls",
                   sheet=1,range = "A2:C27")
data <-melt(data,id.vars='year')

#步骤二：绘制折线图
#gp<-ggplot(data=data,aes(year,value,linetype=variable,fill=variable))+geom_line()
#详见*函数参数说明
#gp #只需这两步绘制简单的折线图，下述代码为绘制美观的折线图
gp<-ggplot(data=data,aes(year,value,linetype=variable,fill=variable))
  +geom_line() +scale_x_continuous(expand=c(0,0))+
  #将 x 轴的坐标延伸至原点
  ggtitle("Proportion of 16-to-24-year-olds enrolled in school in July,1985-2010")+
  #加入图像的标题
  theme(plot.title=element_text(lineheight=.8,face="bold"),axis.title.x=element_blank(),
        axis.title.y=element_blank()) +
  #调整标题的格式，并去除 x 轴和 y 轴的标题
  theme(legend.position="top", legend.title=element_blank()) +
  theme(plot.title=element_text(hjust=0.5),axis.line=element_line(size=1,colour="black"))+
  #设置标题位置，并加入坐标轴
  theme(panel.grid=element_blank(),panel.border=element_blank())+
  theme(panel.background=element_blank())+
  #删去背景中的网格线与边界线，并将背景色调更改为白色
```

```
    geom_hline(yintercept = c(5,10,15,20,25,30),linetype="dotted")+
    ylim(0,50)+ xlim(1985,2010) +
    ylab("%")+theme(axis.title.y=element_text(angle=0,vjust=1.0,hjust=0.1))
gp
#调用函数绘制图像
```

（2）具体过程分析

步骤 1：安装并调用 readxl、ggplot2 和 reshape2 程序包。

步骤 2：导入原始数据，并利用 melt 函数将原数据转换为 ggplot2 程序包可识别的数据结构。

步骤 3：利用 ggplot2 函数绘制折线图，并设置坐标轴格式、调整字体大小。

（3）*函数参数说明

```
gp<-ggplot(data=data,aes(year,value,linetype=variable,fill=variable)) + geom_line()
```

☑ aes(year,value)：将 year 视作折线图的横坐标，value 作为折线图的纵坐标。

☑ linetype=variable：表示线的类型取决于变量。

☑ geom_line()：确定要画图像的种类为折线图。

（4）绘制结果（见图 1.22）

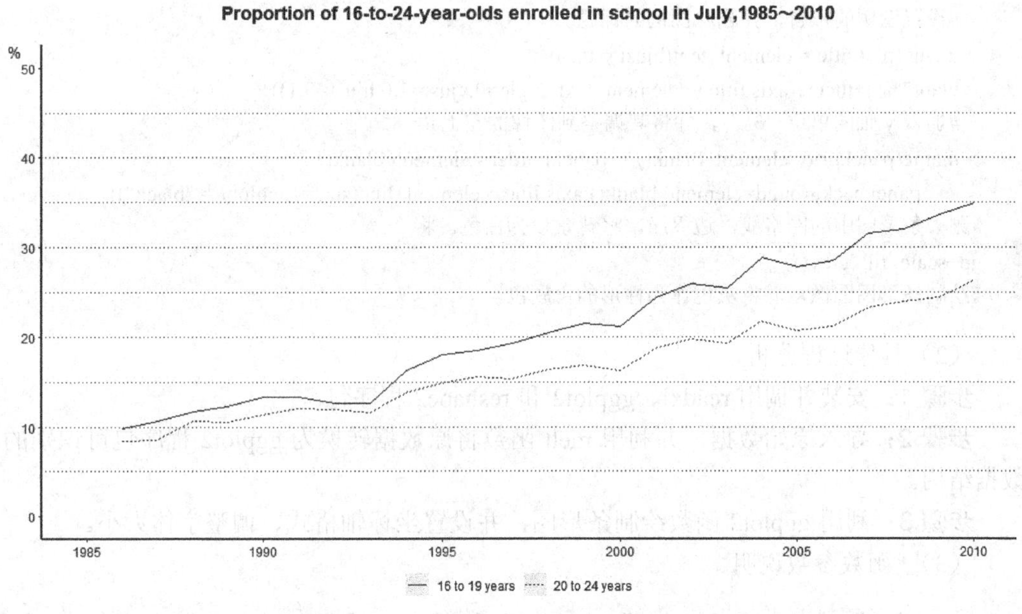

Figure1.22　Line Chart

图 1.22　折线图

2. 条形图绘制

（1）代码

```
#步骤一：导入要用到的程序包（readxl、ggplot2、reshape2）以及原始数据
library(readxl)
```

```
library(ggplot2)
library(reshape2)
data <- read_excel("D:/data/Chapter 1-Case 1-School's Out.xls",
                    sheet="Table 1.2")
data <- melt(data, id.vars = "Sex, race, and ethnicity")

#步骤二：绘制条形图
#gp<-ggplot(data=data,aes(x=reorder(`Sex, race, and ethnicity`,value),
     y=value,fill=factor(variable))) +
#geom_bar(stat='identity',position=position_dodge())                详见*函数参数说明
#gp#只需这两步绘制简单的条形图，下述代码为绘制美观的条形图
gp<-ggplot(data=data,aes(x=reorder(`Sex, race, and ethnicity`,value),
     y=value,fill=factor(variable))) +
  geom_bar(stat='identity',position=position_dodge()) +
  ggtitle("Unemployment rate, person 16 to 24 years age, by sex, race, and
     hispanic or latino ethnicity, July, 2007-2010") +
  #加入条形图的标题
  theme(plot.title = element_text(lineheight=.8, face="bold"),axis.title.x=element_blank()) +
  #设置条形图标题的格式，并删去 x 轴的标签
  theme(legend.position="top") +guides(fill=guide_legend(title=NULL))+
  #设置图例的位置，并删除图例的标题
  theme(plot.title = element_text(hjust = 0.5))+
  ylab("%")+theme(axis.title.y=element_text(angle=0,vjust=1.0,hjust=0.1))+
  #加入 y 轴的单位“%”，并将其调整到图像的左上角
  theme(panel.grid=element_blank(),  panel.border =element_blank(),
     panel.background=element_blank(),axis.line = element_line(size=1, colour = "black"))
#删去条形图中的网格线，边界线，将背景设为白色。将
gp+scale_fill_grey()
#绘制条形图图像，并将灰色作为柱形的主题色。
```

（2）具体过程分析

步骤 1：安装并调用 readxl、ggplot2 和 reshape2 程序包。

步骤 2：导入原始数据，并利用 melt 函数将原数据转换为 ggplot2 程序包可识别的数据结构。

步骤 3：利用 ggplot2 函数绘制条形图，并设置坐标轴格式、调整字体大小。

（3）*函数参数说明

```
gp<-ggplot(data=data,aes(x=reorder('Sex, race, and ethnicity',value),
     y=value,fill=factor(variable))) + geom_bar(stat='identity',position=position_dodge())
```

☑ x=reorder('Sex, race, and ethnicity',value)：将'Sex, race, and ethnicity'列按照值的大小排序，再将排序后的数据作为 x 轴。

☑ geom_bar()：ggplot2 中绘制条形图的函数。

☑ position=position_dodge()：避免相邻的两个条形重叠。

☑ stat='identity'：表示依据 x 与 y 一一对应的方式绘制图像。

（4）绘制结果（见图 1.23）

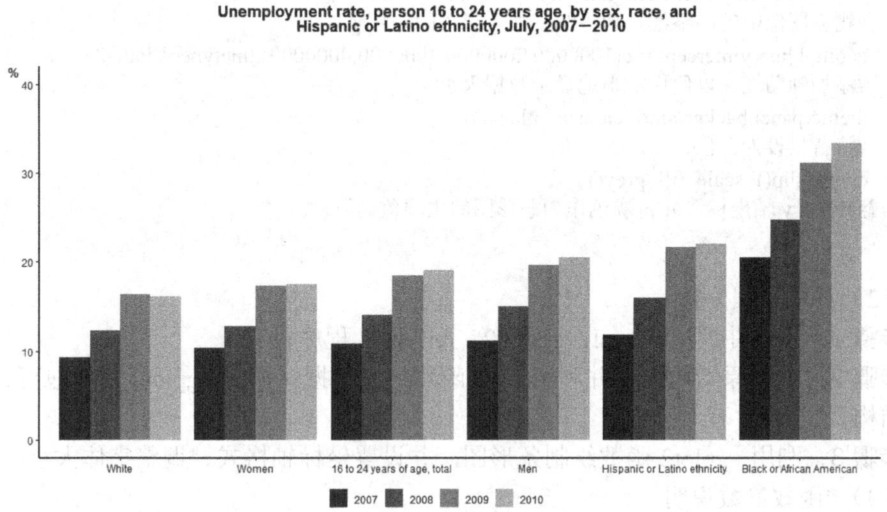

Figure 1.23　Bar Graph

图 1.23　条形图

3．堆积条形图绘制

（1）代码

```
#步骤一：导入要用到的程序包（readxl、ggplot2、reshape2）以及原始数据
library(readxl)
library(ggplot2)
library(reshape2)
data <- read_excel("D:/data/Chapter 1-Case 1-School's Out.xls",
                   sheet="Table 1.3",range=("A1:E16"))
data <- melt(data,id.vars ='Industry')

#步骤二：绘制堆积条形图
#gp<-ggplot(data=data,aes(x=reorder(Industry,-value),y=value,fill=variable)) +
#geom_bar(stat="identity",position="stack",width=0.7)+
#coord_flip()                                  详见*函数参数说明
#gp#只需这两步绘制简单的堆积条形图，下述代码为绘制美观的堆积条形图
options(scipen=200)   #取消科学计数法表示
gp<-ggplot(data=data,aes(x=reorder(Industry,-value),y=value,fill=variable)) +
    geom_bar(stat="identity",position="stack",width=0.7) +
    ggtitle("Employed persons,age 16-24,by industry and sex,July 2010")+
    #加入堆积条形图的标题
    theme(plot.title=element_text(lineheight=.8,face="bold"),axis.title.x=
    element_blank() ,axis.title.y=element_blank()) +
    #设置标题的样式，并删去 x 轴和 y 轴的标签
    theme(legend.position="top") +
    guides(fill=guide_legend(title=NULL))+
    #设置图例的位置，并删去图例标题
    theme(plot.title = element_text(hjust = 0.5))+
    #设置标题的位置
```

```
    theme(panel.grid=element_blank(),panel.border=element_blank(),
          axis.line= element_line(size=1, colour = "black"))+
    #删去图像中的网格线，边界线。加入黑色的坐标轴
    geom_hline(yintercept = c(1000000,2000000,3000000,4000000),linetype="dotted")+
    #添加辅助线，以便更清晰地显示数据大小
    theme(panel.background=element_blank())+
    #将背景设为白色
    coord_flip()+scale_fill_grey()
  #翻转 x、y 轴坐标，并将灰色作为条形图的主题色
gp
```

（2）具体过程分析

步骤 1：安装并调用 readxl、ggplot2、reshape2 程序包。

步骤 2：导入原始数据，并利用 melt 函数将原数据转换为 ggplot2 程序包可识别的数据结构。

步骤 3：利用 ggplot2 函数绘制条形图，并设置坐标轴格式、调整字体大小。

（3）*函数参数说明

```
gp<-ggplot(data=data,aes(x=reorder(industry,-value),y=value,fill=variable)) +
  geom_bar(stat="identity",position="stack",width=0.7)+
  coord_flip()
```

☑ x=reorder(industry,-value)：将 industry 列从大到小排列后得到的向量作为 x 轴。

☑ position="stack"：指定画出的条形图为堆积条形图。

☑ coord_flip()：将绘制出的图像横纵坐标轴转换。

（4）绘制结果（见图 1.24）

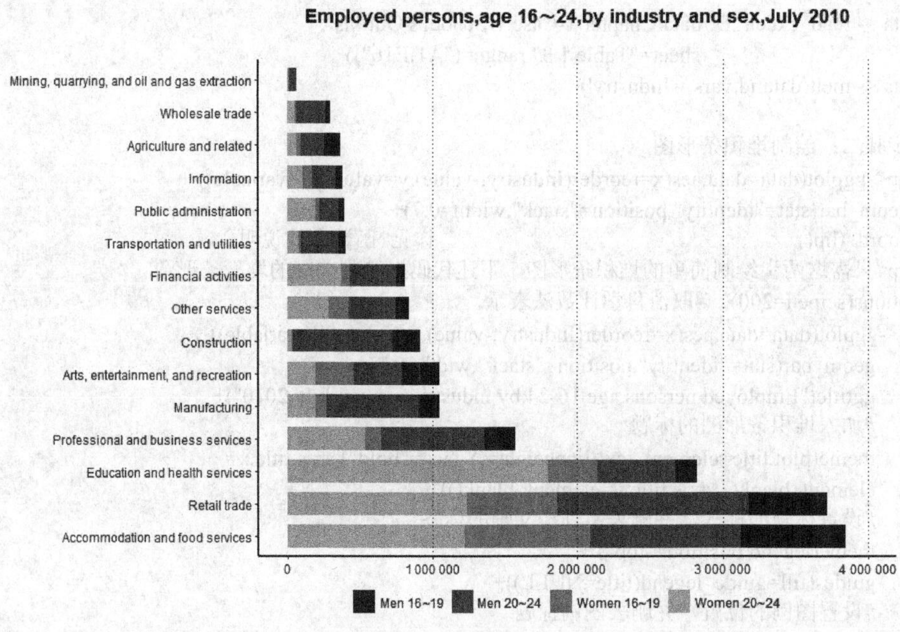

Figure 1.24 Stacked Bar Graph

图 1.24 堆积条形图

4．饼图绘制

（1）代码

```
#步骤 1：导入数据和数据分析需要用到三个程序包（xlsx、ggplot2、scales），我们安装并调用这三个程序包。注：计算百分比用到的 percent 函数属于 scales 程序包。
install.packages('xlsx')
install.packages('ggplot2')
install.packages('scales')
library(xlsx)
library(ggplot2)
library(scales)

#步骤 2：统计图表的绘制
age <- c(5.7,31.5,41.7,14.7,6.4)
label <- c("20 岁以下","21-30","31-40","41-50","51 岁以上")
dt = data.frame(value = age, group = label)
label_value <- paste('(', round(dt$value/sum(dt$value) * 100, 1), '%)', sep = '')
label <- paste(dt$group, label_value, sep = '')
ggplot(dt, aes(x = "", y = value, fill = group)) +
  geom_bar(stat="identity")+
  coord_polar("y",start=1) +                                  #利用条形图转换为饼图
  geom_text(aes(y=value/3+
                c(0,cumsum(value)[-length(value)]),x = sum(value)/62,
              label=percent(value/100)),size=5)+              #生成数据标签
  theme_minimal()+
  theme(panel.grid = element_blank(),panel.border = element_blank(),axis.title=element_blank(),
        axis.ticks=element_blank(),
        axis.text = element_blank(),
        legend.title = element_blank())+                      #设置图例
  labs(title="Pie chart of Age distribution")+                #设置图表标题
  theme(plot.title = element_text(hjust = 0.5,size = 18))   +
  scale_fill_grey(labels=label)                               #用灰色填充
```

（2）绘制结果（见图 1.25）

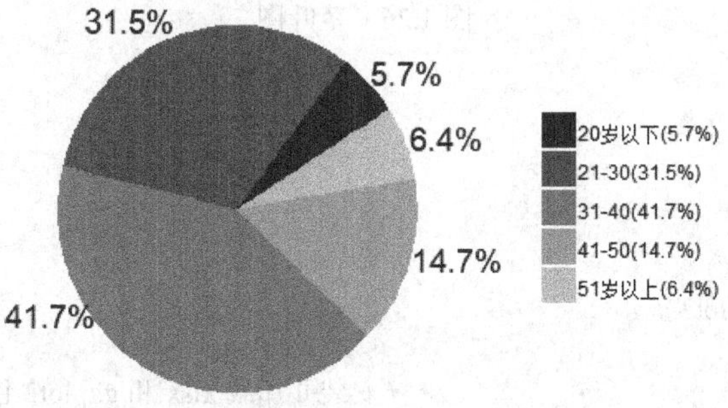

Figure 1.25　Pie Chart

图 1.25　饼图

5. 茎叶图绘制

（1）代码

```
#步骤一：读取数据
install.packages('xlsx')
install.packages('ggplot2')
library(xlsx)
library(ggplot2)                              #安装并加载 xlsx 和 ggplot2 包以读取数据和绘图
data=read_excel("Chapter 1-Forbes.xls")       #单引号内为文件存放位置
data=data.frame(data)                         #转换为数据框格式

#步骤二：直接用 R 语言中的 stem 函数来进行绘制
stem(data$age)
```

（2）绘制结果（见图 1.26）

```
The decimal point is 1 digit(s) to the right of the |
 2 | 9
 3 | 134
 3 | 556677889
 4 | 11223334
 4 | 55666777777889999999
 5 | 00001122333334444444
 5 | 5555555556666777777777777888888899999999999
 6 | 000000000000011112222222222222333333333333344444444444
 6 | 555555555556666666666667777888888888888888999999
 7 | 000000000000011111111222222222333333333333344444444
 7 | 555555555555555566666666666667777777777777777888888888889999999
 8 | 0000000011111111222222222222333333344444
 8 | 5555555566666677777788899 9
 9 | 00000013344
 9 | 6
```

Figure 1.26　Stem-and-Leaf Display

图 1.26　茎叶图

6. 盒形图绘制

（1）代码

```
#步骤一：读取数据
install.packages('xlsx')
install.packages('ggplot2')
library(xlsx)
library(ggplot2)                              #安装并加载 xlsx 和 ggplot2 包以读取数据和绘图
data=read_excel("Chapter 1-Forbes.xls")       #单引号内为文件存放位置
data=data.frame(data)                         #转换为数据框格式
```

```
#步骤二：绘制盒形图
#方法一：直接用 R 语言自带的 boxplot 函数绘制
boxplot(data$age,main="BOX-PLOT OF THE FORBES 400 RICHEST AMERICAN'S AGE")
#方法二：利用 ggplot 进行绘制
ggplot(data, aes(y=age)) +
  geom_boxplot(fill = "grey",
  outlier.colour="red",
  outlier.shape=15,
  outlier.size=3,size = 2.5)+
  xlim(-0.6,0.6)+                        #标注异常点，用"x"来表示，颜色设置为红色
  theme(panel.background = element_blank(),
        axis.text.x = element_text(size=20),        #y 轴刻度大小
        axis.title.x = element_text(size = 20))+
  coord_flip()                                      #将盒形图（箱线图）平行放置
```

（2）绘制结果（见图 1.27）

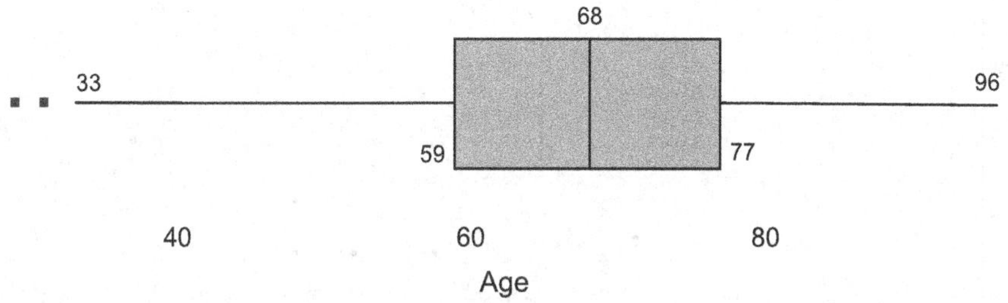

Figure 1.27 Box-Plot

图 1.27 盒形图

7．散点图绘制

（1）代码

```
#步骤一：读取数据
install.packages('xlsx')
install.packages('ggplot2')
library(xlsx)
library(ggplot2)                         #安装并加载 xlsx 和 ggplot2 包以读取数据和绘图
data=read_excel("Chapter 1-Forbes.xls")              #单引号内为文件存放位置
data=data.frame(data)                                #转换为数据框格式
age100 = data$age[1:100]
worth100 = data$worth[1:100]
forbes100 <- data.frame(age_new=age100,worth_new=worth100)
#将前 100 富豪的年龄和净资产重新组成一个新的 dataframe，命名为 forbes100
#步骤二：绘制图像
#方法一：直接用 R 语言自带的 plot 函数绘制
plot(x=forbes100$age_new,y=forbes100$worth_new,      #x 轴为年龄，y 轴为财富
main="age_worth 散点图",xlab="age",ylab="worth")      #设置图表与坐标值标题
#方法二：利用 ggplot 进行绘制
ggplot(data=forbes100, aes(x=age_new, y=worth_new)) +
  geom_point(shape = 19,size = 3,color = "blue")+
```

```
scale_x_continuous(limits   = c(20,100),breaks = seq(20,100,10)) +
scale_y_continuous(limits   = c(0,1200),breaks = seq(0,1200,200)) +
labs(title="Histogram of the Forbes 400 richest American Age *
     Netwotrh",x="Age",y="Net Worth")+
theme(plot.title = element_text(hjust = 0.5,size = 16),
      axis.text.x = element_text(size=15),
      axis.text.y = element_text(size=15),
      axis.title.x = element_text(size = 15),
      axis.title.y = element_text(size = 15),
      panel.grid.major =element_blank(),
      panel.grid.minor = element_blank(),
      panel.background = element_blank(),
      axis.line = element_line(colour = "black"))
```

（2）绘制结果（见图 1.28）

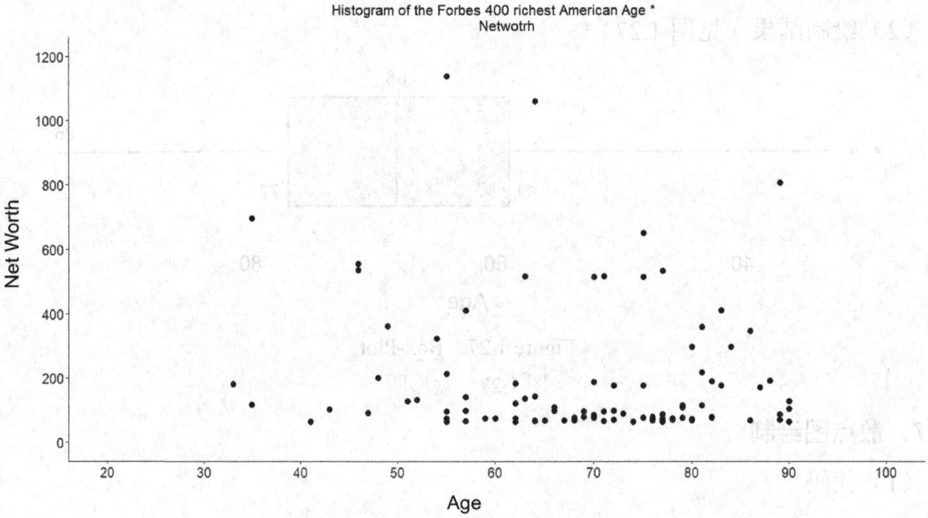

Figure 1.28　Scatter Diagram

图 1.28　散点图

8．直方图绘制

（1）代码

```
#步骤一：读取数据
install.packages('xlsx')
install.packages('ggplot2')
library(xlsx)
library(ggplot2)                            #安装并加载 xlsx 和 ggplot2 包以读取数据和绘图
data=read_excel("Chapter 1-Forbes.xls")     #单引号内为文件存放位置
data=data.frame(data)                       #转换为数据框格式
age100 = data$age[1:100]
worth100 = data$worth[1:100]
forbes100 <- data.frame(age_new=age100,worth_new=worth100)
#将前 100 富豪的年龄和净资产重新组成一个新的 dataframe，命名为 forbes100
```

```
#步骤二：绘制图像
方法一：直接用 R 语言自带的 hist 函数绘制
hist(x=data$age,breaks = seq(25,100,5),                        #数据为 age，自定义区间
main="Histogram of the Forbes400 richest American",            #设置图表标题
xlab="age",ylab="count")                                       #设置 x 轴和 y 轴标题
方法二：利用 ggplot 进行绘制
Picture1<-ggplot(data, aes(x = age))+
  geom_histogram(breaks = seq(25,100,5),fill = "grey", colour = "black")+
  #区间定义为（25,30），（30,35）……
  scale_x_continuous(limits= c(25,100),breaks = seq(25,100,5))+
  scale_y_continuous(limits=c(0,60),breaks=seq(0,60,10))+      #设置横纵坐标刻度以及范围
  geom_text(aes(label=as.character(..count..)),stat="bin",breaks=seq(25,100,5), vjust=-0.5,size = 5)+
                                                               #显示数据标签
  labs(title="Histogram of the Forbes 400 richest American")+  #添加题目
  theme(plot.title = element_text(hjust = 0.5,size = 16),      #标题的位置及大小
        axis.text.x = element_text(size=15),                   #x 轴刻度大小
        axis.text.y = element_text(size=15),                   #y 轴刻度大小
        axis.title.x = element_text(size = 15),                #x 轴标题大小
        axis.title.y = element_text(size = 15),                #y 轴标题大小
        panel.grid.major =element_blank(),
        panel.grid.minor = element_blank(),                    #去除网格线
        panel.background = element_blank(),
        axis.line = element_line(colour = "black"))            #显示坐标轴
Picture1
```

（2）绘制结果（见图 1.29）

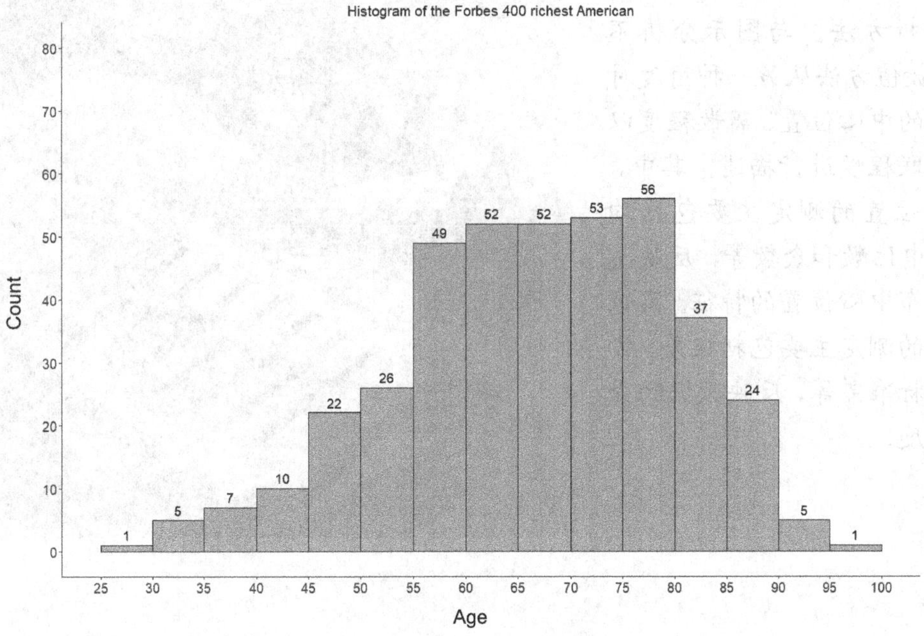

Figure 1.29　Histogram

图 1.29　直方图

Chapter 2

Displaying and Exploring Data: Numerical Measures

第2章　探索性数据分析之数值法

In this chapter, we continue the study of descriptive statistics. Unlike tabular and graphical methods, numerical measures of location, dispersion, shape, and association provide additional alternatives for summarizing data. Measures of central location include the mean, median, and mode, which describe the center of a set of data. Measures of dispersion include the range, variance, and standard deviation, which show the variation or spread in a set of data.

本章继续探讨描述性统计分析方法。与图示分析不同，数值方法从另一种角度对数据的中心位置、离散程度以及关联程度进行描述。其中，中心位置的测定主要包括均值、中位数和众数等，反映总体分布中心位置的特征。离散程度的测定主要包括极差、方差和标准差等，反映数据的分散程度。

2.1 Numerical Measures of Central Location

2.1 中心位置的测定

1. 均值

均值是一组数据的算术平均数。均值容易受异常值的影响。因此在没有极端值的情况下，均值的运用更有效。

$$\bar{x} = \frac{\sum_{i=1}^{n} x_i}{n} \quad (2.1)$$

式中：$\bar{x}$ 表示样本均值，n 表示样本个数，x_i 表示样本中某一观察值，$\sum_{i=1}^{n} x_i$ 表示将样本中所有观察值加总。

1. Mean①

The mean is the numerical average of a set of numbers. We add up the values and divide by the number of values. The mean can be distorted by one or more outliers, and is thus most useful when there are no extreme values in the data.

$$\bar{x} = \frac{\sum_{i=1}^{n} x_i}{n} \quad (2.1)$$

Where:

$\bar{x}$ represents the sample mean.

n is the number of values in the sample.

x_i represents any particular value.

$\sum_{i=1}^{n} x_i$ is the sum of the values in the sample.

2. 中位数

中位数是对数据按大小顺序排列之后，处于中间位置的数值。

2. Median

The median is the midpoint of the values after they have been ordered from the smallest to the largest, or the largest to the smallest.

3. 众数

众数是一组数据中出现次数最多的数。

3. Mode

The mode is the value of the observation that appears most frequently.

2.2 Numerical Measures of Dispersion

2.2 离散程度的测定

1. 极差

极差是一组数据中最大观测值与最小观测值之差。

1. Range

The range is the difference between the largest and the smallest values in a data set.

$$\text{Range} = \text{Largest value} - \text{Smallest value}$$

① 此处介绍样本均值与样本方差。总体均值与总体方差的介绍详见本章“关键公式与注解”部分。

2. 方差

方差是所有观测值与样本均值的离差的平方和的算术平均数。

$$s^2 = \frac{\sum_{i=1}^{n}(x_i - \overline{x})^2}{n} \qquad (2.2)$$

式中：

s^2表示样本方差，x_i表示样本中某一观察值，$\overline{x}$表示样本均值，n表示样本个数。

3. 标准差

标准差是方差的平方根。方差与标准差是最主要的测定离散程度的指标。

$$s = \sqrt{\frac{\sum_{i=1}^{n}(x_i - \overline{x})^2}{n}} \qquad (2.3)$$

式中字母代表的含义与方差中字母代表的含义是完全一致的。

2. Variance①

The variance is the arithmetic mean of the squared deviations from the mean.

$$s^2 = \frac{\sum_{i=1}^{n}(x_i - \overline{x})^2}{n} \qquad (2.2)$$

Where:

s^2 is the sample variance.

x_i is the value of an observation.

$\overline{x}$ represents the sample mean.

n is the number of values in the sample.

3. Standard Deviation

The standard deviation is the square root of the variance. It is a measure of how spread out the numbers are.

$$s = \sqrt{\frac{\sum_{i=1}^{n}(x_i - \overline{x})^2}{n}} \qquad (2.3)$$

The meanings of the letters are the same as for the calculation of variance above.

Case　National Health Care Association

案例　全美护士工作满意度调查研究

1. 案例介绍

美国全国医疗保健协会正关注将来医疗保健行业中护士短缺的问题。为了了解护士们对目前工作的满意程度，协会对全国的护士进行了一次调查。作为这项研究的一部分，样本中的50名护士从工作、薪水和晋升机会三个方面做出评判。每个方

1. Introduction②

The National Health Care Association is concerned about the shortage of nurses the health care profession is projecting for the future. To learn about the current degree of job satisfaction among nurses, the association sponsored a study of hospital nurses throughout the country. As a part of this study, 50 nurses in a sample indicated their degree of satisfaction with their work, their pay, and their opportunities for

① 此处仅介绍样本方差，总体方差的介绍见于本章“关键公式与注解”部分。

② David R. Anderson, Dennis J. Sweeney, Thomas A. Williams, et al. Statistics for business and economics[M]. Boston: Cengage Learning, 2005.

面都由 0～100 分来衡量，数值越大表示越满意。数据也显示了那些护士所在医院的种类，分别为私立医院、退伍军人管理医院和大学医院。数据如表 2.1 所示。

promotion. Each of the three aspects of satisfaction was measured on a scale from 0 to 100, with larger values indicating higher degrees of satisfaction. The data collected also showed the type of hospital employing the nurses. The types of hospitals were Private, Veterans Administration (VA), and University. The data is shown in Table 2.1.

Table 2.1　Data For National Health Care Association

表 2.1　全美医疗保健协会调查数据

Nurse（护士编号）	Hospital（医院类型）	Work（工作情况）	Pay（薪水）	Promotion（晋升机会）	Nurse（护士编号）	Hospital（医院类型）	Work（工作情况）	Pay（薪水）	Promotion（晋升机会）
1	Private	74	47	63	26	Private	84	28	62
2	VA	72	76	37	27	Private	71	45	68
3	University	75	53	92	28	VA	72	37	86
4	Private	89	66	62	29	VA	84	60	29
5	University	69	47	16	30	Private	82	49	91
6	Private	85	56	64	31	VA	90	76	70
7	University	89	80	64	32	Private	88	49	42
8	Private	88	36	47	33	University	74	70	51
9	University	88	55	52	34	VA	78	52	72
10	Private	84	42	66	35	University	85	89	46
11	Private	90	62	66	36	Private	74	59	82
12	University	72	59	79	37	University	76	51	54
13	VA	82	37	54	38	VA	82	60	56
14	University	90	56	23	39	Private	77	60	75
15	Private	64	43	61	40	VA	63	48	78
16	Private	85	57	67	41	VA	86	72	72
17	Private	71	25	74	42	University	77	90	51
18	University	71	36	55	43	VA	86	37	59
19	Private	70	38	54	44	Private	87	51	57
20	VA	71	49	58	45	University	79	59	41
21	VA	90	27	67	46	University	84	53	63
22	VA	73	56	55	47	University	87	66	49
23	Private	72	60	45	48	VA	84	74	37
24	VA	65	42	68	49	VA	95	66	52
25	VA	94	60	52	50	Private	72	57	40

在这个案例中，我们主要运用了描述性统计方法，尤其是数

In this case, methods of descriptive statistics, especially numerical measures, are mainly used to

值方法，通过分析关于工作情况、薪水和晋升机会的数据来了解护士对工作的满意程度。

与图示方法不同，对中心位置、离散程度、总体分布的形状以及总体间的关联度进行描述的数值方法给数据的分析带来了另外一种视角。均值、中位数和众数等对数据的中心位置进行了描述。极差、方差和标准差等则展示了数据的离散程度。此外，当涉及两个变量时，协方差和相关系数可以描述两者的关联程度。

analyze the data on work, pay, and promotion in order to study the degree of job satisfaction among nurses.

Unlike tabular and graphical methods, numerical measures of location, dispersion, shape, and association provide additional alternatives for summarizing data. Measures of location such as the mean, median, and mode are values used to describe the center of a set of data. Measures of dispersion such as range, mean deviation, and standard deviation show the variation or spread in a set of data. Furthermore, when it comes to two variables, covariance and correlation can be used to describe the relationship between them.

2. 分析步骤

步骤1：根据对数值方法中中心位置的衡量，判断护士对于工作最满意以及最不满意的方面。讨论医院在哪些方面需要改进。

步骤2：根据离散程度的度量，指出护士们看法差异最大的方面，并解释原因。

步骤3：根据医院的种类，在某些类型的医院，护士似乎对工作满意程度更高。研究医院类型并且对了解和改进工作满意程度提供建议。

步骤4：讨论可以了解和改进工作满意程度的其他描述性统计方法。

以上四个步骤的具体分析如下。

步骤1：根据对数值方法中中心位置的衡量，判断护士对于工作最满意以及最不满意的方面。讨论医院在哪些方面需要

2. Analytical Procedures

Step1: On the basis of the entire data set and measures of central location, decide which are the most satisfying and the least satisfying aspects of the job for the nurses. Discuss in what areas improvements should be made.

Step2: On the basis of descriptive measures of variability, indicate the measure which generates the greatest difference of opinion among the nurses and explain why.

Step3: According to the types of hospitals, a particular type of hospital seems to have better levels of job satisfaction than the others. Study the types and provide recommendations for learning about and improving job satisfaction.

Step4: Discuss additional descriptive statistics and insights which can be used to learn about and possibly improve job satisfaction.

Analytical Procedures are described in follows.

Step1: On the basis of the entire data set and measures of central location, decide which are the most satisfying and the least satisfying aspects of the job for the nurses. Discuss in what areas improvements should

改进。

如表 2.2 所示，工作情况均值为 79.8，是三个方面得分中最高的。中位数是 82，表示工作情况最中间的得分。众数是 72，表示频数出现最多的得分。不难看出，就中心位置而言，在三个方面中工作情况指标的满意度最高。相对地，薪酬得分均值为 54.46，满意度最低。因此，医院在薪酬和晋升机会这两个方面需要做出改进。

be made.

As the following data shows, the mean of work is 79.8, which is the largest among the three aspects. The median value, which shows the center of work, is 82. The mode, which is the value that appears most frequently, is 72. It is not difficult to see that on the basis of measures of location, work is the most satisfying aspect of the job. Relatively, the of pay is 54.46, which indicates it is the least satisfying aspect of the job. The pay and promotion aspects should be improved.

Table 2.2 Outcomes of Descriptive Statistics

表 2.2 描述统计输出结果（a）

	Work	Pay	Promotion
Mean（均值）	79.8	54.46	58.48
Median（中位数）	82	55.5	58.5
Mode（众数）	72	60	52

步骤 2：根据离散程度的度量，指出护士们看法差异最大的方面，并解释原因。

如表 2.3 所示，晋升机会极差为 76，标准差为 16.00，两值皆为三方面指标中的最大值，说明这个指标波动性较大。工作情况标准差最小，说明这组数据离散程度小。因此，可以看出护士们针对晋升机会的满意度分歧最大。

Step2: On the basis of descriptive measures of variability, indicate the measure which generates the greatest difference of opinion among the nurses and explain why.

As the following table shows, the range of promotion is 76 and the standard deviation is 16. Both of these are the largest values among the three aspects, which presents a quality of high variability. The standard deviation value of work is the smallest, which means lower variability. As a result, promotion appears to generate the greatest difference of opinion among the nurses.

Table 2.3 Outcomes of Descriptive Statistics

表 2.3 描述统计输出结果（b）

	Work	Pay	Promotion
Std. Deviation（标准差）	8.29	14.75	16.00
Range（极差）	32	65	76
Minimum（最小值）	63	25	16
Maximum（最大值）	95	90	92

步骤3：根据医院的种类，在某些类型的医院，护士似乎对工作满意程度更高。研究医院类型并且对了解和改进工作满意程度提供建议。

根据医院类型，将表2.1所示的50个观察值分为3组，分别以私立医院、退伍军人管理医院和大学医院命名，重组后的数据如表2.4所示。

Step3: According to the types of hospitals, a particular type of hospital seems to have better levels of job satisfaction than the others. Study the types and provide recommendations for learning about and improving job satisfaction.

The 50 observations in Table 2.1 are separated into 3 groups, which are named Private Hospitals, VA Hospitals, and University Hospitals, and then restructured as shown in Table 2.4.

Table 2.4 Rearranged Data For National Health Care Association

表2.4 重组数据

Private（私立）				VA（退伍军人管理）				University（大学）			
N	Work	Pay	Promotion	N	Work	Pay	Promotion	N	Work	Pay	Promotion
1	74	47	63	2	72	76	37	3	75	53	92
4	89	66	62	13	82	37	54	5	69	47	16
6	85	56	64	20	71	49	58	7	89	80	64
8	88	36	47	21	90	27	67	9	88	55	52
10	84	42	66	22	73	56	55	12	72	59	79
11	90	62	66	24	65	42	68	14	90	56	23
15	64	43	61	25	94	60	52	18	71	36	55
16	85	57	67	28	72	37	86	33	74	70	51
17	71	25	74	29	84	60	29	35	85	89	46
19	70	38	54	31	90	76	70	37	76	51	54
23	72	60	45	34	78	52	72	42	77	90	51
26	84	28	62	38	82	60	56	45	79	59	41
27	71	45	68	40	63	48	78	46	84	53	63
30	82	49	91	41	86	72	72	47	87	66	49
32	88	49	42	43	86	37	59				
36	74	59	82	48	84	74	37				
39	77	60	75	49	95	66	52				
44	87	51	57								
50	72	57	40								

每组医院包含的样本量是不同的。有19名护士来自私立医院，有17名护士来自退伍军人管理医院，有14名护士来自大学医院。

如表2.5～表2.7所示，三

Each hospital contains a different number of data points: 19 nurses are from Private Hospitals, 17 nurses are from VA Hospitals, and 14 nurses are from University Hospitals.

According to the following tables, satisfaction

种医院中的护士对工作情况的满意程度是相似的，但是对薪酬和晋升机会的看法差别较大。私立医院有最高的晋升机会满意度，但是薪酬满意度最低。大学医院薪酬满意度最高，但是晋升机会满意度最低。

with work among the three hospitals does not show much difference, but pay and promotion differ a lot. Private Hospitals have the highest promotion satisfaction, but the lowest pay satisfaction. University Hospitals have the highest pay satisfaction, but the lowest promotion satisfaction.

Table 2.5　Outcomes for Private Hospitals

表 2.5　私立医院描述统计分析结果

Private	Work	Pay	Promotion
Mean（均值）	79.32	48.95	62.42
Median（中位数）	82	49	63
Mode（众数）	74	57	62
Std. Deviation（标准差）	8.04	11.53	13.20
Range（极差）	26	41	51
Minimum（最小值）	64	25	40
Maximum（最大值）	90	66	91

Table 2.6　Outcomes for University Hospitals

表 2.6　大学医院描述统计分析结果

University	Work	Pay	Promotion
Mean（均值）	79.71	61.71	52.57
Median（中位数）	78	57.5	51.5
Mode（众数）	*	53	51
Std. Deviation（标准差）	7.27	15.70	19.43
Range（极差）	21	54	76
Minimum（最小值）	69	36	16
Maximum（最大值）	90	90	92

*No value appears more than once.（*表示众数不存在）

Table 2.7　Outcomes for VA Hospitals

表 2.7　退伍军人管理医院描述统计分析结果

VA	Work	Pay	Promotion
Mean（均值）	80.41	54.65	58.94
Median（中位数）	82	56	58
Mode（众数）	72	37	37
Std. Deviation（标准差）	9.70	15.30	15.23
Range（极差）	32	49	57
Minimum（最小值）	63	27	29
Maximum（最大值）	95	76	86

至少在得分最低的方面，医院需要做出改进。比如说，私立医院需要提升护士的薪资水平，大学医院需要改进晋升机制。

At the least, improvements should be made in the aspect which showed the lowest satisfaction. For example, Private Hospitals should improve their salary schemes, and University Hospitals should improve their promotion systems.

步骤4：讨论可以了解和改进工作满意程度的其他描述性统计方法。

Step4: Discuss additional descriptive statistics and insights which can be used to learn about and possibly improve job satisfaction.

下面分别分析三类医院的护士对三个方面的满意度情况（见图2.1～图2.3）。

Use the measurements from the group data to compare the three aspects of satisfaction separately.

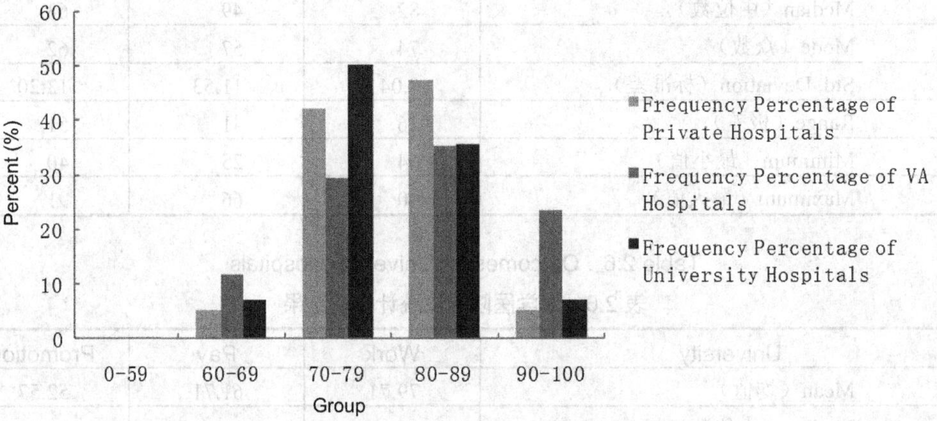

Figure 2.1 Graph for Work

图2.1 工作情况

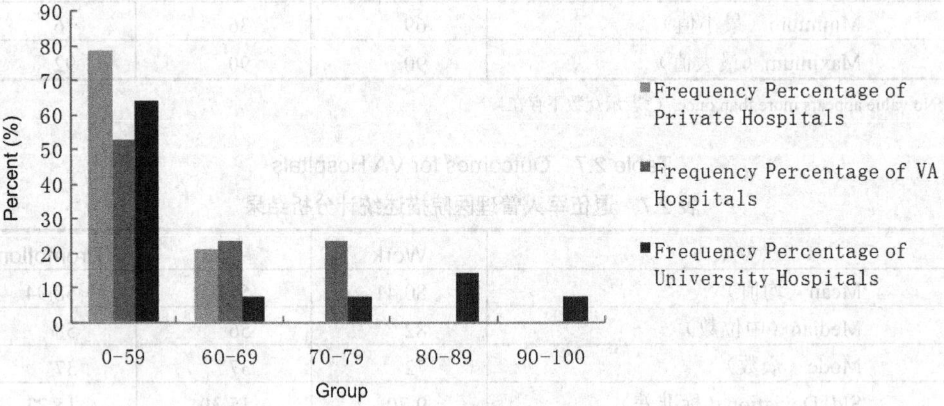

Figure 2.2 Graph for Pay

图2.2 薪酬水平

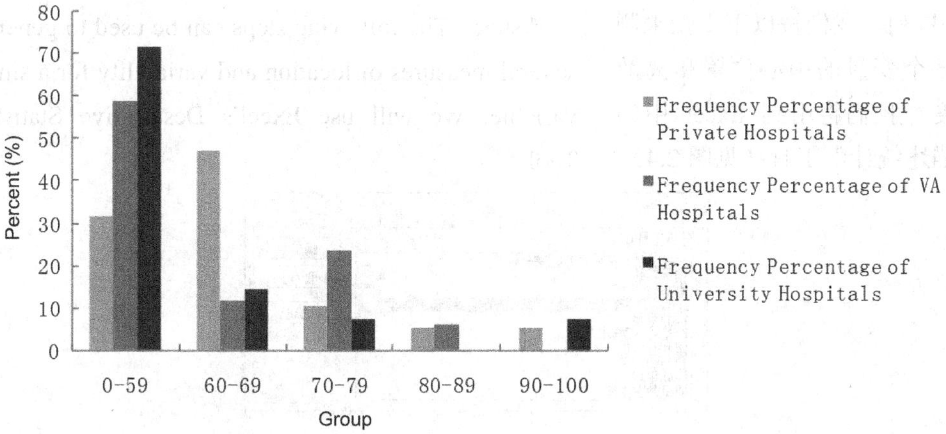

Figure 2.3 Graph for Promotion

图 2.3 晋升机会

对于工作情况来说，表示满意（80～100 分）的人数是差不多的。

In different intervals of work, the hospitals which have the highest satisfaction vary a lot. Scores indicating high satisfaction (80–100) are almost the same among the three types of hospitals.

对于薪酬情况来说，大学医院的护士满意度最高（80～100 分）。

In different intervals of pay, University Hospitals show the highest number of scores indicating satisfaction with pay (80–100).

对于晋升机会来说，私立医院的护士满意度最高（80～100 分）。

In different intervals of promotion satisfaction, Private Hospitals show the highest number of scores indicating satisfaction with promotion (80–100).

总的来说，不同的医院应该在不同方面做出改进：私立医院应该改进护士的薪资水平；大学医院应该改进护士晋升机制；退伍军人管理的医院应该在两个方面都做出一定努力。

In conclusion, improvements should be made in different aspects in different hospitals. Private Hospitals should improve their salary schemes. University Hospitals should improve their promotion of nurses, while VA Hospitals should improve both of these aspects.

Appendix 2.1 Descriptive Statistics Using Excel

附录 2.1 用 Excel 描述性统计分析

Excel 表格中，案例数据在

The data are in columns A to E of an Excel

A～E 列。我们按以下步骤来测定一个变量的中心位置和离散程度。我们将用到 Excel 中的“**描述统计**”工具（见图 2.4）。

worksheet. The following steps can be used to generate several measures of location and variability for a single variable. We will use Excel's Descriptive Statistics Tool.

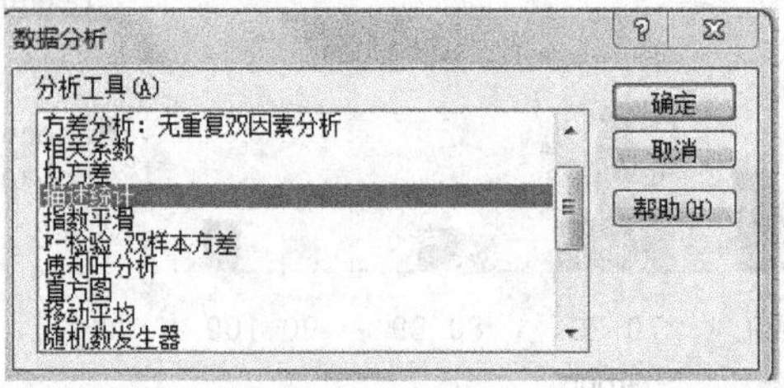

Figure 2.4　Descriptive Statistics from The List Of Analysis Tools

图 2.4　描述性统计分析-1

步骤 1：选择菜单中的“**工具**”。

步骤 2：选择“**数据分析**”。

步骤 3：选择“**分析工具**”中的“**描述统计**”。

步骤 4：当对话框打开时（见图 2.5），在“**输入区域**”中选择 C2:E51，“**分组方式**”选择“**逐列**”，“**输出区域**”选择 G1，选中“**汇总统计**”，单击“**确定**”。统计分析结果如图 2.6 所示。

Step1: Select the **Tools** menu.

Step2: Choose **Data Analysis**.

Step3: Choose **Descriptive Statistics** from the list of **Analysis Tools**.

Step4: When the Descriptive Statistics dialog box appears:

Enter C2:E51 in the **Input Range** box,

Select **Grouped by columns**,

Select **Output Range**,

Enter G1in the **Output Range** box,

Select **Summary Statistics**,

Click **OK**.

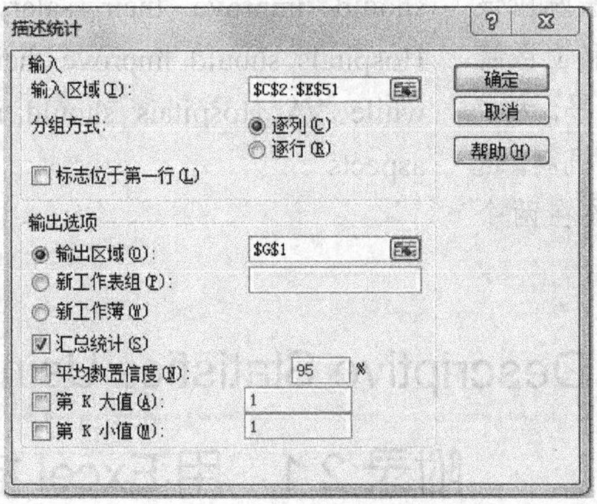

Figure 2.5　Descriptive Statistics from The List Of Analysis Tools

图 2.5　描述性统计分析-2

G	H	I	J	K	L
列1		列2		列3	
平均	79.8	平均	54.46	平均	58.48
标准误差	1.172125	标准误差	2.08556	标准误差	2.262605
中位数	82	中位数	55.5	中位数	58.5
众数	72	众数	60	众数	52
标准差	8.288177	标准差	14.74713	标准差	15.99903
方差	68.69388	方差	217.478	方差	255.969
峰度	-1.04648	峰度	0.083147	峰度	0.41167
偏度	-0.16668	偏度	0.264118	偏度	-0.26232
区域	32	区域	65	区域	76
最小值	63	最小值	25	最小值	16
最大值	95	最大值	90	最大值	92
求和	3990	求和	2723	求和	2924
观测数	50	观测数	50	观测数	50

Figure 2.6　Outcomes of the Data

图 2.6　统计分析结果

Appendix 2.2　Descriptive Statistics Using R

附录 2.2　用 R 语言描述性统计分析

在 R 语言中进行描述性统计分析需要三个步骤。首先，安装并导入数据读取和分析过程需要的程序包。其次，导入数据，将原始数据集转为数据框模式，并将分类型变量设置为因子。最后，调用函数进行描述性统计分析。

There are three steps required to perform descriptive statistical analysis in R. First, install and import packages that needed. Next, import data and turn the original data set into a data frame, set the type variable as a factor. At last, use function to do descriptive statistical analysis.

1．代码

```
#步骤一：安装并导入所需的程序包
install.packages('xlsx')
install.packages('pastecs')
install.packages('psych')
library(xlsx)
library(pastecs)
library(psych)

#步骤二：导入数据，前期数据准备
data=read_excel("Chapter2-National Health Care Association.xls")          #导入数据
data=data.frame(data)                                                      #转换为数据框
data$Hospital=as.factor(data$Hospital)                                     #设置为因子

#步骤三：进行描述性统计分析（表格）
#（1）总体
vars=c("Work","Pay","Promotion")
```

```
stat.desc(data[vars])                                #*总体描述性统计分析，详见函数参数说明

#（2）分组
data_gb=split(data.frame(data),data$Hospital)        #*对原始数据进行分组，详见函数参数说明
describe.by(data[vars],data$Hospital)                #*分组描述性统计分析，详见函数参数说明

#步骤四：进行描述性统计分析(图形)
#（1）数据准备
#对 Work、Pay、Promotion 三个变量进行分箱，断点设置为 0、60、70、80、90、100（左闭右开）
for(i in 1:length(data$Work))
{
  if(data[i,'Work']<60) {data$work_g[i]='0-59'}
  else if(data[i,'Work']<70) {data$work_g[i]='60-69'}
  else if(data[i,'Work']<80) {data$work_g[i]='70-79'}
  else if(data[i,'Work']<90) {data$work_g[i]='80-89'}
  else {data$work_g[i]='90-100'}
}
for(i in 1:length(data$Pay))
{
  if(data[i,'Pay']<60) {data$pay_g[i]='0-59'}
  else if(data[i,'Pay']<70) {data$pay_g[i]='60-69'}
  else if(data[i,'Pay']<80) {data$pay_g[i]='70-79'}
  else if(data[i,'Pay']<90) {data$pay_g[i]='80-89'}
  else {data$pay_g[i]='90-100'}
}
for(i in 1:length(data$Promotion))
{
  if(data[i,'Promotion']<60) {data$promotion_g[i]='0-59'}
  else if(data[i,'Promotion']<70) {data$promotion_g[i]='60-69'}
  else if(data[i,'Promotion']<80) {data$promotion_g[i]='70-79'}
  else if(data[i,'Promotion']<90) {data$promotion_g[i]='80-89'}
  else {data$promotion_g[i]='90-100'}
}

#将分组标识设置为因子
data$work_g=factor(data$work_g)
data$pay_g=factor(data$pay_g)
data$promotion_g=factor(data$promotion_g)

#（2）数据整合与图示
#将原始数据先整理成频数表，再转换为频率表，最后转换为矩阵
m1=as.matrix(prop.table(table(data$Hospital,data$work_g),1))
barplot(m1,beside=T,ylim=c(0,0.6),legend.text=rownames(m1),
        xlab="Group",ylab="Frequency",main="Work")          #*详见函数参数说明
abline(h=0)                                                 #添加水平线

m2=as.matrix(prop.table(table(data$Hospital,data$pay_g),1))
barplot(m2,beside=T,ylim=c(0,0.9)legend.text=rownames(m1),
        xlab="Group",ylab="Frequency",main="Pay")           #*详见函数参数说明
```

```
abline(h=0)                                                    #添加水平线

m3=as.matrix(prop.table(table(data$Hospital,data$promotion_g),1))
barplot(m3,beside=T,ylim=c(0,0.8),legend.text=rownames(m1),
        xlab="Group",ylab="Frequency",main="Promotion")        #*详见函数参数说明
abline(h=0)                                                    #添加水平线
```

2. 具体过程分析

步骤 1：读取文件后缀为.xls 中的数据，需要安装并调用 xlsx 程序包。为进行数据分析，需要安装并调用 pastecs 程序包。为进行图示，需要安装并调用 psych 程序包。

步骤 2：导入数据，并将原数据集转换成数据框形式，并将 Hospital 变量转换为因子。

步骤 3：表格形式呈现分析结果。调用 stat.desc()函数对总体进行描述性统计分析；调用 describe.by()函数对各组进行描述性统计分析，其中以 Hospital 变量作为分组标志。

步骤 4：条形图形式呈现分析结果。先将原始数据整理为频率表，再转换为矩阵，最后绘制条形图。

3. *函数参数说明

```
stat.desc(x,basic=TRUE,desc=TRUE,norm=FALSE,p=0.95,…)
```

- ☑ x：一个数据框或时间序列。
- ☑ basic：逻辑值，默认值为 TRUE，计算其中的所有值，空值，缺失值的数量以及最小值，最大值，值域，合计。
- ☑ desc：逻辑值，默认值为 TRUE，计算中位数，平均数，平均数的标准误差，平均数置信度为 0.95 的置信区间，方差，标准差，以及变异系数。
- ☑ norm：逻辑值，默认值为 FALSE，若设置为 TRUE 则返回正态分布统计量，包括偏度和峰度（以及它们的统计显著程度）和 shapiro-wilk 正态检验结果。
- ☑ p：用来设置计算平均数的置信区间的置信水平，默认值为 0.95。

```
split(x, f, drop = FALSE,…)
```

- ☑ x：一个待分组的向量或者数据框。
- ☑ f：一个 factor 或者 list（如果 list 中元素交互作用于分组中），以此为规则将 x 分组。
- ☑ drop：逻辑值，默认值为 FALSE，如果 f 中的某一个水平没有用上则被弃用。

```
describe.by(x, group=NULL,…)
```

- ☑ x：一个数据框或者矩阵。
- ☑ group：一个分组变量或者一个分组变量列表。

```
barplot(height, legend.text = NULL, beside = FALSE,
        col = NULL, main = NULL, ylim = NULL, xlab = NULL, ylab = NULL,…)
```

- ☑ height：一个向量或者矩阵，条形图对象。

☑ legend.text：图例说明。

☑ beside：逻辑值，默认值为 FALSE，各组之间堆叠排列，若设置为 TRUE，各组间平铺排列。

☑ col：设置条块颜色。

☑ main：设置图标题。

☑ ylim：设置 y 轴范围。

☑ xlab：设置 x 轴标签。

☑ ylab：设置 y 轴标签。

```
abline(h=NULL,⋯)
```

☑ h：水平线的 y 值。

4．分析结果

统计分析结果如表 2.8～表 2.12 和图 2.7～图 2.9 所示。

Table 2.8 Outcomes of Descriptive Statistics

表 2.8 描述统计结果

	Work	Pay	Promotion
nbr.val	50.000 000 0	50.000 000 0	50.000 000 0
nbr.null	0.000 000 0	0.000 000 0	0.000 000 0
nbr.na	0.000 000 0	0.000 000 0	0.000 000 0
min	63.000 000 0	25.000 000 0	16.000 000 0
max	95.000 000 0	90.000 000 0	92.000 000 0
range	32.000 000 0	65.000 000 0	76.000 000 0
sum	3 990.000 000 0	2 723.000 000 0	2 924.000 000 0
median	82.000 000 0	55.500 000 0	58.500 000 0
mean	79.800 000 0	54.460 000 0	58.480 000 0
SE.mean	1.172 125 2	2.085 559 7	2.262 604 6
CI.mean.0.95	2.355 473 8	4.191 089 1	4.546 874 2
var	68.693 877 6	217.477 959 2	255.968 979 6
std.dev	8.288 177 0	14.747 133 9	15.999 030 6
coef.var	0.103 861 9	0.270 788 4	0.273 581 2

Table 2.9 Rearranged Data for National Health Care Association

表 2.9 重组数据

$ Private					
	Nurse	Hospital	Work	Pay	Promotion
1	1	Private	74	47	63
4	4	Private	89	66	62
6	6	Private	85	56	64

续表

	Nurse	Hospital	Work	Pay	Promotion
$ Private					
8	8	Private	88	36	47
10	10	Private	84	42	66
11	11	Private	90	62	66
15	15	Private	64	43	61
16	16	Private	85	57	67
17	17	Private	71	25	74
19	19	Private	70	38	54
23	23	Private	72	60	45
26	26	Private	84	28	62
27	27	Private	71	45	68
30	30	Private	82	49	91
32	32	Private	88	49	42
36	36	Private	74	59	82
39	39	Private	77	60	75
44	44	Private	87	51	57
50	50	Private	72	57	40
$University					
	Nurse	Hospital	Work	Pay	Promotion
3	3	University	75	53	92
5	5	University	69	47	16
7	7	University	89	80	64
9	9	University	88	55	52
12	12	University	72	59	79
14	14	University	90	56	23
18	18	University	71	36	55
33	33	University	74	70	51
35	35	University	85	89	46
37	37	University	76	51	54
42	42	University	77	90	51
45	45	University	79	59	41
46	46	University	84	53	63
47	47	University	87	66	49
$VA					
	Nurse	Hospital	Work	Pay	Promotion
2	2	VA	72	76	37
13	13	VA	82	37	54
20	20	VA	71	49	58
21	21	VA	90	27	67

续表

$VA

	Nurse	Hospital	Work	Pay	Promotion
22	22	VA	73	56	55
24	24	VA	65	42	68
25	25	VA	94	60	52
28	28	VA	72	37	86
29	29	VA	84	60	29
31	31	VA	90	76	70
34	34	VA	78	52	72
38	38	VA	82	60	56
40	40	VA	63	48	78
41	41	VA	86	72	72
43	43	VA	86	37	59
48	48	VA	84	74	37
49	49	VA	95	66	52

Table 2.10 Outcomes for Private Hospitals

表 2.10 私立医院描述性统计分析结果

group: Private

	vars	n	mean	sd	median	trimmed	mad
Work	1	19	79.32	8.04	82	79.59	10.38
Pay	2	19	48.95	11.53	49	49.35	11.86
Promotion	3	19	62.42	13.20	63	62.06	8.90
	min	max	range	skew	kurtosis	se	
Work	64	90	26	−0.22	−1.49	1.84	
Pay	25	66	41	−0.51	−0.82	2.65	
Promotion	40	91	51	0.12	−0.50	3.03	

Table 2.11 Outcomes for University Hospitals

表 2.11 大学医院描述性统计分析结果

group: University

	vars	n	mean	sd	median	trimmed	mad
Work	1	14	79.71	7.27	78.0	79.75	9.64
Pay	2	14	61.71	15.70	57.5	61.50	11.12
Promotion	3	14	52.57	19.43	51.5	52.33	11.86
	min	max	range	skew	kurtosis	se	
Work	69	90	21	0.07	−1.68	1.94	
Pay	36	90	54	0.49	−0.85	4.20	
Promotion	16	92	76	0.06	−0.24	5.19	

Table 2.12 Outcomes for VA Hospitals

表 2.12 退伍军人管理医院描述性统计分析结果

group: VA

	vars	n	mean	sd	median	trimmed	mad
Work	1	17	80.41	9.70	82	80.60	11.86
Pay	2	17	54.65	15.30	56	55.07	20.76
Promotion	3	17	58.94	15.23	58	59.13	14.83
	min	max	range	skew	kurtosis	se	
Work	63	95	32	−0.23	−1.22	2.35	
Pay	27	76	49	−0.10	−1.32	3.71	
Promotion	29	86	57	−0.25	−0.79	3.69	

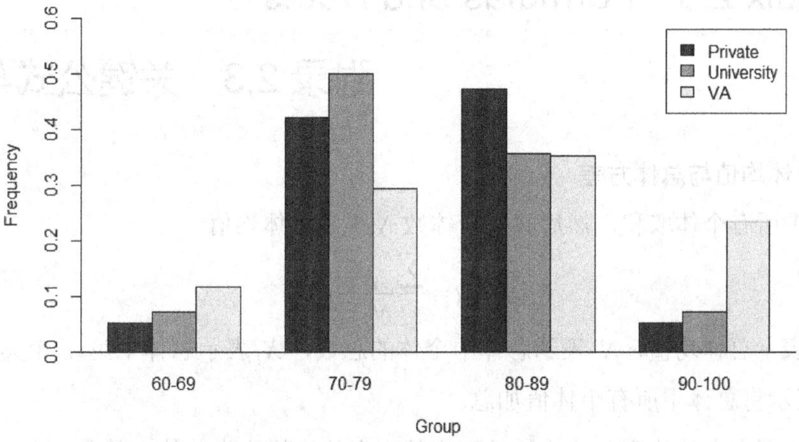

Figure 2.7 Graph for Work

图 2.7 工作情况

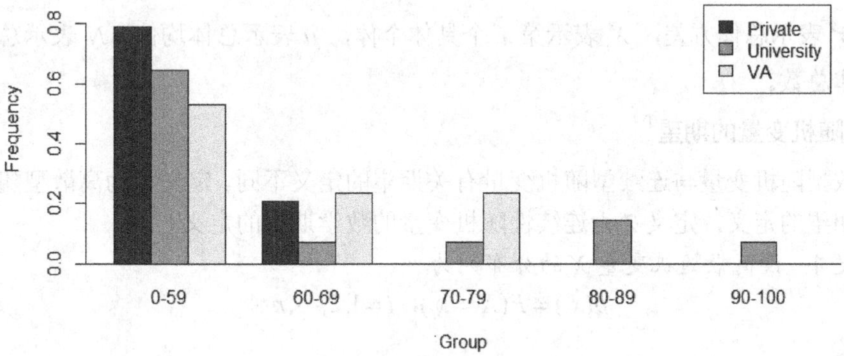

Figure 2.8 Graph for Pay

图 2.8 薪酬水平

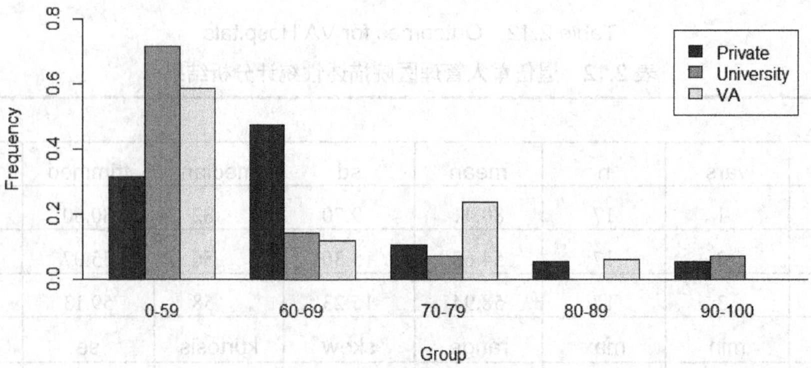

Figure 2.9 Graph for Promotion

图 2.9 晋升机会

Appendix 2.3 Formulas and Notes

附录 2.3 关键公式与注解

1. 总体均值与总体方差

总体中所有个体取和，然后除以个体数 N 得到总体均值。

$$\mu = \frac{\sum_{i=1}^{N} X_i}{N} \tag{2.4}$$

式中：μ 表示总体均值，N 表示总体中个体的总数，X_i 表示总体中第 i 个具体个体，$\sum_{i=1}^{N} X_i$ 表示将总体中所有个体值加总。

总体中所有个体值离总体均值的距离的平方的均值称为总体方差。

$$\sigma^2 = \frac{\sum_{i=1}^{N} (X_i - \mu)^2}{N} \tag{2.5}$$

式中：σ^2 表示总体方差，X_i 表示第 i 个具体个体，μ 表示总体均值，N 表示总体中包含的个体总数。

2. 随机变量的期望①

离散型随机变量与连续型随机变量有关期望的定义不同。定义 1 为离散型随机变量的数学期望的定义，定义 2 为连续性随机变量的数学期望的定义。

定义 1 设离散随机变量 X 的分布列为

$$p(x_i) = P(X = x_i),\ i = 1, 2, \cdots, n\cdots$$

如果

$$\sum_{i=1}^{\infty} |x_i| p(x_i) < \infty$$

① 茆诗松，程依明，濮晓龙．概率论与数理统计教程[M]．2 版．北京：高等教育出版社，2011．

则称

$$E(X)=\sum_{i=1}^{\infty}x_i p(x_i)$$

为随机变量 X 的数学期望，或称为该分布的数学期望，简称期望或均值。若级数 $\sum_{i=1}^{\infty}|x_i|p(x_i)$ 不收敛，则称 X 的数学期望不存在。

定义 2　设连续随机变量 X 的密度函数为 $p(x)$，如果

$$\int_{-\infty}^{\infty}|x|\,p(x)\mathrm{d}x<\infty$$

则称

$$E(x)=\int_{-\infty}^{\infty}xp(x)\mathrm{d}x$$

为 X 的数学期望，或称为该分布的数学期望，简称期望或均值。若 $\int_{-\infty}^{\infty}|x|\,p(x)\mathrm{d}x$ 不收敛，则称 X 的数学期望不存在。

3. 随机变量的方差①

与数学期望相同，连续型随机变量的方差定义与离散型随机变量方差不同。定义 3 为离散型随机变量的方差定义，定义 4 为连续型随机变量的方差定义。

定义 3　设离散随机变量 X 的分布列为

$$p(x_i)=P(X=x_i),\ i=1,2,\cdots,n\cdots$$

如果

$$\sum_{i=1}^{\infty}|x_i-E(x)|^2 p(x_i)<\infty$$

则称

$$D(X)=\sum_{i=1}^{\infty}|x_i-E(x)|^2 p(x_i)$$

为随机变量 X 的方差，或称为该分布的方差。若级数 $\sum_{i=1}^{\infty}|x_i-E(x)|^2 p(x_i)$ 不收敛，则称 X 的方差不存在。

定义 4　设连续随机变量 X 的密度函数为 $p(x)$，如果

$$\int_{-\infty}^{\infty}|x-E(x)|^2\,p(x)\mathrm{d}x<\infty$$

则称

$$D(x)=\int_{-\infty}^{\infty}|x-E(x)|^2\,p(x)\mathrm{d}x$$

为 X 的方差，或称为该分布的方差。

若 $\int_{-\infty}^{\infty}|x-E(x)|^2\,p(x)\mathrm{d}x$ 不收敛，则称 X 的方差不存在。

① 茆诗松，程依明，濮晓龙．概率论与数理统计教程[M]．2 版．北京：高等教育出版社，2011．

Chapter 3

Interval Estimation

第3章　区间估计

Point estimates and interval estimates are two main kinds of estimates of population parameters. A point estimate is a single value derived from a sample which may be used to estimate a population value. Since the parameters are unknown, a point estimate cannot be expected to provide an exact value. An interval estimate is an estimation of a range of values in which we expect the population parameter to occur. The purpose is to provide information about how close the point estimate is to the value of the population parameter with a certain probability.

参数估计通常有两种：点估计和区间估计。点估计是使用样本的一个统计值来估计总体的未知参数的真值。由于参数本身是未知的，估计值免不了有些偏差。区间估计就是估计未知参数所在的可能区间，目的在于观测点估计跟参数值相差多少，并以一定的正确度来保证估计的正确性。

Case Bock Investment Services

案例 伯克投资服务公司周刊简讯的改进研究

1. 案例介绍

伯克投资服务公司（BIS）（以下简称"伯克公司"）的目标是成为南卡罗来纳州货币市场咨询服务的领头羊。为了吸引更多客户并提供更好的服务，伯克公司发行了一份周刊简讯。公司在考虑对周刊增加一项新的内容，用来报告每周对基金经理人的电话调查结果。为了调查提供这项服务的可行性，确定在简讯上增加什么内容，伯克公司进行了一次简单随机抽样调查，挑选了45种货币市场基金。表3.1展示了一部分调查获得的数据，包括资产、最近7天和30天的收益率。在打电话给基金经理们获取各项信息之前，公司决定先对已有数据做一些基本分析。

这个案例主要涉及描述统计和区间估计两种方法，分析资产值和收益率数据，以此来决定哪一项数据真正有价值。

区间估计的计算是用点估计值加上或者减去误差项。点估计是从样本信息得出的用来估计总体参数的统计量。区间估计的目的在于观测点估计跟参数值相差多少。

1. Introduction[①]

The goal of Bock Investment Services (BIS) is to be the leading money market advisory service in South Carolina. To provide better services for their present clients and to attract new clients, BIS developed a weekly newsletter. BIS is considering adding a new feature to the newsletter that will report the results of a weekly telephone survey of fund managers. To investigate the feasibility of offering this service, and to determine what type of information to include in the newsletter, BIS selected a simple random sample of 45 money market funds. A portion of the data obtained is shown in Table 3.1, which reports fund assets and yields for the past 7 and 30 days. Before calling the money market fund managers to obtain additional data, BIS decided to do some preliminary analysis of the data already collected.

In this case, numerical measures and internal estimation are mainly used to analyze the data on assets and yields in order to decide which one is the new feature that BIS really needs.

An internal estimate is often computed by adding and subtracting a value, called the margin of error, to the point estimate. The point estimate is a statistic computed from sample information, which is used to estimate the population parameter. The purpose of an interval estimate is to provide information about how close the point estimate is to the value of the population parameter.

① David R. Anderson, Dennis J. Sweeney, Thomas A. Williams, et al. Statistics for business and economics[M]. Boston: Cengage Learning, 2005.

Table 3.1 Data for Bock Investment Services

表 3.1 BIS 调查数据

Fund（基金）	Assets（资产）	7-day Yield（7 天收益率）	30-day Yield（30 天收益率）	Fund（基金）	Assets（资产）	7-day Yield（7 天收益率）	30-day Yield（30 天收益率）
Amcore	103.9	4.10	4.08	Hanover Cash	794.3	4.32	4.23
Alger	156.7	4.79	4.73	Heritage Cash	1 008.3	4.08	4.00
Arch MM/Trust	496.5	4.17	4.13	Infinity/Alpha	53.6	3.99	3.91
BT Instit Treas	197.8	4.37	4.32	John Hancock	226.4	3.93	3.87
Benchmarrk Div	2 755.4	4.54	4.47	Landmark Funds	481.3	4.28	4.26
Bradford	707.6	3.88	3.83	Liquid Cash	388.9	4.61	4.64
Capital Cash	1.7	4.29	4.22	Market Watch	10.6	4.13	4.05
Cash Mgt Trust	2 707.8	4.14	4.04	Merrill Lynch Money	27 005.6	4.24	4.18
Composite	122.8	4.03	3.91	NCC Funds	113.4	4.22	4.20
Cowen Standby	694.7	4.25	4.19	Nationwide	517.3	4.22	4.14
Cortland	217.3	3.57	3.51	Overland	291.5	4.26	4.17
Declaration	38.4	2.67	2.61	Piermont Money	1 991.7	4.50	4.40
Dreyfus	4 832.8	4.01	3.89	Portico Money	161.6	4.28	4.20
Elfun	81.7	4.51	4.41	Prudential Money Mart	6 835.1	4.20	4.16
FFB Cash	506.2	4.17	4.11	Reserve Primary	1 408.8	3.91	3.86
Federated Master	738.7	4.41	4.34	Schwab Money	10 531.0	4.16	4.07
Fidelity Cash	13 272.8	4.51	4.42	Smith Barney Cash	2 947.6	4.16	4.12
Flex-fund	172.8	4.60	4.48	Stagecoach	1 502.2	4.18	4.13
Fortis	105.6	3.87	3.85	Strong Money	470.2	4.37	4.29
Franklin Money	996.8	3.97	3.92	Transamerica Club	175.5	4.20	4.19
Freedom Cash	1 079.0	4.07	4.01	United Cash	323.7	3.96	3.89
Galaxy Money	801.4	4.11	3.96	Woodward Money	1 330.0	4.24	4.21
Government Cash	409.4	3.83	3.82				

Source: Barron's, October 3,1994

2. 案例分析

步骤 1：使用描述统计分析，总结资产与收益数据的表现。

步骤 2：以 95%的置信水平，做出资产均值以及 7 天收益率和 30 天收益率的置信区间，并针对各个区间估计进行解释。

步骤 3：总结以上结论能够

2. Analytical Procedures

Step1: Use appropriate descriptive statistics to summarize the data on assets and yields for the money market funds.

Step2: Develop a 95% confidence interval estimate of the mean assets, the mean 7-day yield, and the mean 30-day yield for the population of money market funds. Provide a managerial interpretation of each interval estimate.

Step3: Discuss how BIS could use these types of

为伯克公司改进简讯提供哪些信息。

information in preparing their weekly newsletter.

步骤 4：对伯克公司提供更进一步的建议。

Step4: Discuss other types of information further.

以上四个步骤的具体叙述如下。

步骤 1：利用所给数据，进行描述统计分析，以总结资产与收益表现。

Step 1: Use appropriate descriptive statistics to summarize the data on assets and yields for the money market funds.

如表 3.2 所示，资产的极差是 27 003.90，标准差是 4 644.13。两个值都比较大，说明样本的波动程度较明显。从均值和中位数的差异中我们可以看出数据中存在异常值，因为在一般情况下，均值比中位数更易受异常值影响。就 7 天收益率和 30 天收益率来看，标准差相对小很多，说明收益率波动程度较小，而均值、中位数和众数都比较接近。从图 3.1 中不难看出，资产数据存在 5 个异常值。

As the following data on assets shows, the range of assets is 27 003.9 and the standard deviation is 4 644.13. Both of them are quite large according to this sample, which suggests a quality of high variability. Outliers can be found in the data set since the mean value, which is more sensitive in most situations, differs from the median greatly. In terms of the 7-day yield and the 30-day yield, the standard deviation values are comparatively small, which indicates lower variability. The mean, median, and mode values are very close. It is not difficult to see that there are five abnormal values of assets from the box plot which is shown in Figure 3.1.

Table 3.2 Outcomes of Descriptive Statistics

表 3.2 描述性统计分析结果

	Assets（资产）	7-Day Yield（7 天收益率）	30-Day Yield（30 天收益率）
Mean（均值）	1 994.81	4.16	4.10
Median（中位数）	496.50	4.18	4.13
Mode（众数）	*	4.17	4.13
Std. Deviation（标准差）	4 644.13	0.33	0.33
Range（极差）	27 003.90	2.12	2.12
Minimum（最小值）	1.70	2.67	2.61
Maximum（最大值）	27 005.60	4.79	4.73

*None of value appears more than once（*表示众数不存在）

因此可以得出结论，资产值较分散，而 7 天和 30 天收益率较集中。

Therefore the data values for assets are scattered, while the 7-day and 30-day yield values are relatively centralized.

步骤 2：以 95%的置信水平，

Step2: Develop a 95% confidence interval estimate

做出资产均值以及 7 天收益率和 30 天收益率的置信区间，并针对各个区间估计进行解释。

of the mean assets, the mean 7-day yield, and the mean 30-day yield for the population of money market funds. Provide a managerial interpretation of each interval estimate.

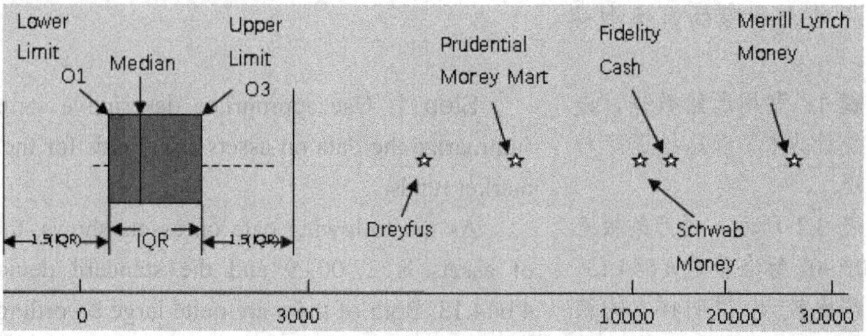

Figure 3.1 Box Plot of Descriptive Statistics

图 3.1 描述性统计：盒型图

本案例样本量 n 为 45，因此在计算中采用正态分布或 t 分布皆可。但是考虑到存在异常值，我们把数据看成 t 分布来进行区间估计。总体标准差未知，在计算中使用样本标准差代替。

Since the sample size is n=45, we can use a normal distribution or a t-distribution in the calculation. However, considering the existence of outliers, we use the t-distribution to compute the interval estimation. The standard deviation of the sample is used in this case because the standard deviation of the population is unknown.

如下为 σ 未知的情况下总体均值的区间估计：

$$\bar{x} \pm t_{\alpha/2}\frac{s}{\sqrt{n}} \quad (3.1)$$

式中：s 是样本标准差，$(1-\alpha)$ 是置信度，$t_{\alpha/2}$ 是自由度为 $(n-1)$ 时 t 分布的上 $\alpha/2$ 分位数。

本案例为总体标准差未知的情况，因此用 t 分布来计算。具体分类见本章“关键公式与注解”的 3。

Internal estimate of a population mean:

σ unknown

$$\bar{x} \pm t_{\alpha/2}\frac{s}{\sqrt{n}} \quad (3.1)$$

where s is the sample standard deviation, $(1-\alpha)$ is the confidence coefficient, and $t_{\alpha/2}$ is the t value, providing an area of $\alpha/2$ in the upper tail of the t distribution with n-1 degrees of freedom.

根据 t 分布表，自由度为 44、置信水平为 95% 时，t 值为 2.015。如表 3.3 所示，区间（599.56,3 390.06）被称为资产的 95%置信区间，表示有 95%的把握基金的资产值在 599.56～

According to the t-distribution table, the t-value is 2.015 with a degree of freedom of 44 and a confidence level of 95%. The interval 599.813 7 to 3 389.804 1 is called the 95% confidence coefficient of assets, which means that we are 95% confident that the assets of the money market fund will range from 599.813 7 to

3 390.06。同样地，我们有 95% 的把握 7 天收益率为 4.064 2～4.260 2，而 30 天收益率为 4.000 5～4.195 9。

3 389.804 1. In the same way, we are 95% confident that the 7-day yield will range from 4.064 2 to 4.260 2, and the 30-day yield values will range from 4.000 5 to 4.195 9. The width of the confidence intervals here are much larger than the others, which indicates that the mean yield values are relatively more accurate.

Table 3.3　Computation of Interval Estimation

表 3.3　置信区间计算结果

	Assets（资产）	7-day Yield（7 天收益率）	30-day Yield（30 天收益率）
Mean（均值）	1 994.81	4.162 2	4.098 2
Standard deviation（标准差）	4 644.125 1	0.326 2	0.325 3
Margin of error（误差项）	1 394.995 2	0.098 0	0.097 7
Upper interval limit（置信区间）	3 389.804 1	4.260 2	4.195 9
Lower interval limit（置信下界）	599.813 7	4.064 2	4.000 5

步骤 3：总结以上结论能够为伯克公司改进简讯提供哪些信息。

Step 3: Discuss how BIS could use these types of information in preparing their weekly newsletter.

根据以上分析，我们给出如下建议。

From our analysis of the data in question, our suggestions are as follows.

资产数这一项信息的价值不如其余两项，置信区间太宽，不利于说明问题。从实际操作上来讲，如摩根斯坦利投资银行和瑞士银行等公司在发布业绩时，往往是公布收益率，而不是资产值。另外，资产值中异常值很多。因此，在简讯上列出资产值的信息并不合适。

The information about assets is less valuable than the other information. The confidence intervals are not small enough. Practically, when companies like Morgan Stanley and the Bank of Switzerland release publicity about their performance, it contains information about yields rather than assets. The asset values may be indicators to the entire market, but for investors this type of information is not much help. Moreover, there are a lot of outliers. Therefore, printing information about assets in the newsletter is not suggested.

考虑到数据轻微波动情况，周刊简讯上可以列出各公司收益率信息，可以使简讯更具可读性。

Considering the lower variability, the information about yields should be shown in the newsletter to make it more readable.

步骤 4：对伯克公司提供更进一步的建议。

Step4: Discuss other types of information further.

对于投资者而言，仅仅有收

As to investors, information about yields only is

益率信息是远远不够的。伯克公司还可以考虑提供以下两方面信息，使周刊更具可读性。

far from enough. We think BIS could also offer the following information to increase the value of its weekly newsletter.

一方面，可以提供长期的投资回报率，如半年收益率。鉴于7天和30天收益率方差都比较小，不妨假设长期收益率的波动也比较小。

On the one hand, long-term returns such as half-year yield rates may be helpful. Considering the low variability of 7-day and 30-day yields, we assume that the long-term yield also has a low variability, and thus the information will be reliable and valuable.

另一方面，公司可以提供净资产增长率数据。这些数值表明基金在一段时期内的增长情况，投资者可据此评估基金的表现。

On the other hand, BIS could also provide information about the growth rate of net assets. This refers to the growth of funds in a certain period of time, and thus investors can assess the performance of funds accordingly.

Appendix 3.1 Interval Estimation Using Excel

附录3.1 Excel区间估计

在初始Excel表格中，资产数据在B列。我们运用以下步骤来计算总体均值区间估计的点估计和误差项。我们要用到Excel中的“描述统计”工具，如图3.2和图3.3所示。

The data about assets are in column B of an Excel worksheet. The following steps can be used to compute the point estimate and the margin of error for an interval estimate of a population mean. We will use Excel's **Descriptive Statistic** tool.

步骤1：选择菜单栏中的“工具”。

步骤2：选择“**数据分析**”。

步骤3：选择分析工具中的“**描述统计**”。

步骤4：当对话框打开时，在“**输入区域**”选择B1～B46，“**分组方式**”选择“**逐列**”，“**输出区域**”选择F1，选中“**汇总统计**”，“**平均数置信度**”选择95，单击“**确定**”。统计分析结果如图3.4所示。

Step 1: Select the **Tools** menu.

Step 2: Choose **Data Analysis**.

Step 3: Choose **Descriptive Statistics** from the list of Analysis Tools.

Step 4: When the Descriptive Statistics dialog box appears:

Enter B1:B46 in the **Input Range** box,

Select **Grouped by columns**,

Select **Output Range**,

Enter F1 in the Output Range box,

Select **Summary Statistics**,

Select **Confidence level for Mean**,

Enter 95 in the confidence level for Mean box,

Click **OK**.

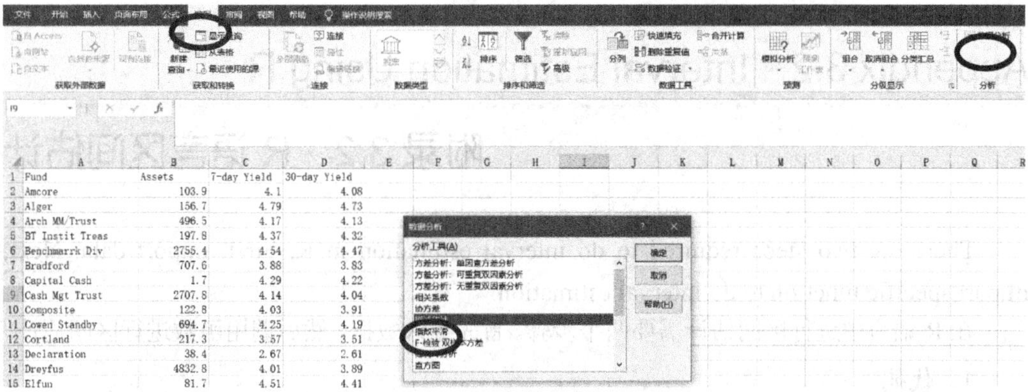

	A	B	C	D
1	Fund	Assets	7-day Yield	30-day Yield
2	Amcore	103.9	4.1	4.08
3	Alger	156.7	4.79	4.73
4	Arch MM/Trust	496.5	4.17	4.13
5	BT Instit Treas	197.8	4.37	4.32
6	Benchmarrk Div	2755.4	4.54	4.47
7	Bradford	707.6	3.88	3.83
8	Capital Cash	1.7	4.29	4.22
9	Cash Mgt Trust	2707.8	4.14	4.04
10	Composite	122.8	4.03	3.91
11	Cowen Standby	694.7	4.25	4.19
12	Cortland	217.3	3.57	3.51
13	Declaration	38.4	2.67	2.61
14	Dreyfus	4832.8	4.01	3.89
15	Elfun	81.7	4.51	4.41

Figure 3.2 Descriptive Statistics

图 3.2 描述性统计-1

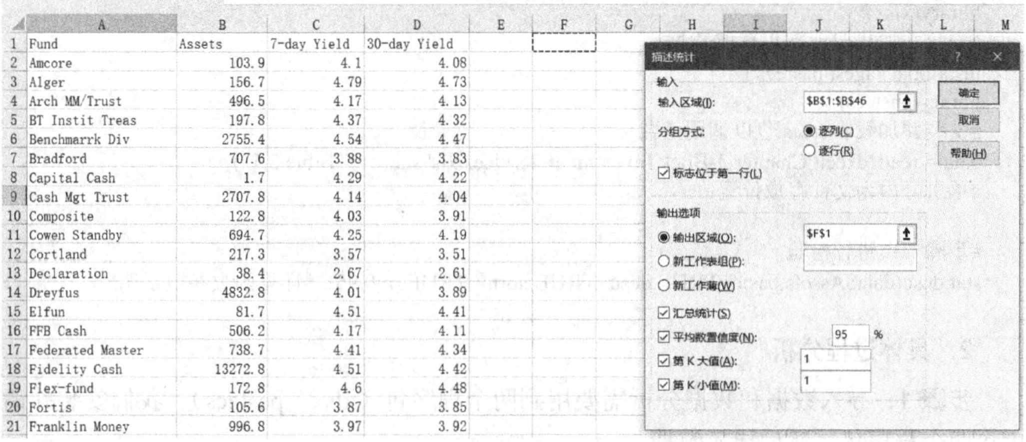

	A	B	C	D
1	Fund	Assets	7-day Yield	30-day Yield
2	Amcore	103.9	4.1	4.08
3	Alger	156.7	4.79	4.73
4	Arch MM/Trust	496.5	4.17	4.13
5	BT Instit Treas	197.8	4.37	4.32
6	Benchmarrk Div	2755.4	4.54	4.47
7	Bradford	707.6	3.88	3.83
8	Capital Cash	1.7	4.29	4.22
9	Cash Mgt Trust	2707.8	4.14	4.04
10	Composite	122.8	4.03	3.91
11	Cowen Standby	694.7	4.25	4.19
12	Cortland	217.3	3.57	3.51
13	Declaration	38.4	2.67	2.61
14	Dreyfus	4832.8	4.01	3.89
15	Elfun	81.7	4.51	4.41
16	FFB Cash	506.2	4.17	4.11
17	Federated Master	738.7	4.41	4.34
18	Fidelity Cash	13272.8	4.51	4.42
19	Flex-fund	172.8	4.6	4.48
20	Fortis	105.6	3.87	3.85
21	Franklin Money	996.8	3.97	3.92

Figure 3.3 Descriptive Statistics

图 3.3 描述性统计-2

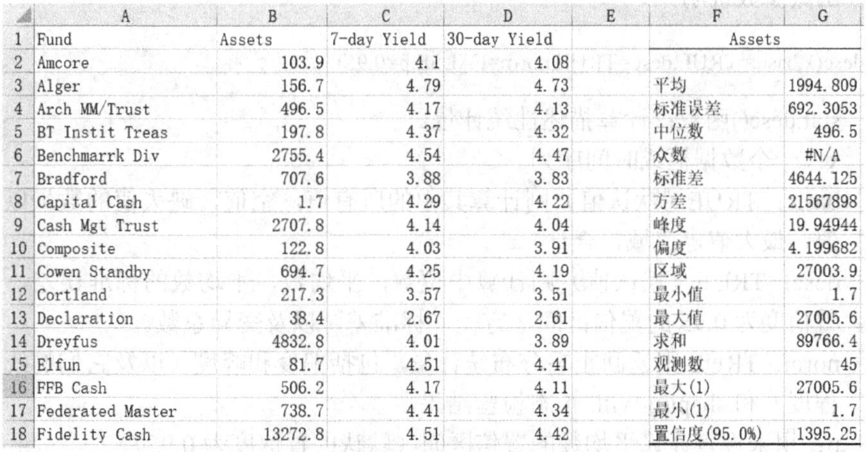

	A	B	C	D	E	F	G
1	Fund	Assets	7-day Yield	30-day Yield		Assets	
2	Amcore	103.9	4.1	4.08			
3	Alger	156.7	4.79	4.73		平均	1994.809
4	Arch MM/Trust	496.5	4.17	4.13		标准误差	692.3053
5	BT Instit Treas	197.8	4.37	4.32		中位数	496.5
6	Benchmarrk Div	2755.4	4.54	4.47		众数	#N/A
7	Bradford	707.6	3.88	3.83		标准差	4644.125
8	Capital Cash	1.7	4.29	4.22		方差	21567898
9	Cash Mgt Trust	2707.8	4.14	4.04		峰度	19.94944
10	Composite	122.8	4.03	3.91		偏度	4.199682
11	Cowen Standby	694.7	4.25	4.19		区域	27003.9
12	Cortland	217.3	3.57	3.51		最小值	1.7
13	Declaration	38.4	2.67	2.61		最大值	27005.6
14	Dreyfus	4832.8	4.01	3.89		求和	89766.4
15	Elfun	81.7	4.51	4.41		观测数	45
16	FFB Cash	506.2	4.17	4.11		最大(1)	27005.6
17	Federated Master	738.7	4.41	4.34		最小(1)	1.7
18	Fidelity Cash	13272.8	4.51	4.42		置信度(95.0%)	1395.25

Figure 3.4 Outcomes of Analysis

图 3.4 统计分析结果

Appendix 3.2 Interval Estimation Using R

附录 3.2 R 语言区间估计

There are two steps required to do interval estimation in R. First, import data. Next, import specific function to do interval estimation.

在 R 语言中进行区间估计需要两个步骤。首先导入数据，然后调用函数进行区间估计。

1. 代码

```
#步骤一：读取数据
install.packages('xlsx')
library(xlsx)
#安装并加载 xlsx 包以读取数据
install.packages('pastecs')
library(pastecs)
#安装并加载 pastecs 包以调用函数
data = read_excel('Chapter 3-Bock Investment Services.xls',sheet = "Table 3.1")
#单引号内为文件存放位置

#步骤二：进行检验
stat.desc(data$Assets,basic=TRUE,desc=TRUE,norm=TRUE,p=0.95)#*详见函数参数说明*
```

2. 具体过程分析

步骤 1： 导入数据和数据分析需要用到两个程序包（xlsx、pastecs）。我们安装并调用这两个程序包，然后导入数据。

步骤 2： 调用 pastecs 包中的 stat.desc()函数进行描述性统计。

3. *函数参数说明

```
stat.desc(x,basic=TRUE,desc=TRUE,norm=FALSE,p=0.95)
```

- ☑ stat.desc()函数：计算描述性统计量。
- ☑ x：一个数据框或时间序列。
- ☑ basic：TRUE（默认值）则计算其中的所有值，空值，缺失值的数量以及最小值，最大值，值域，合计。
- ☑ desc：TRUE（默认值）则计算中位数，平均数，平均数的标准误差，平均数置信度为 0.95 的置信区间，方差，标准差，以及变异系数。
- ☑ norm：TRUE 则返回正态分布统计量，包括偏度和峰度（以及它们的统计显著程度）和 shapiro-wilk 正态检验结果。
- ☑ p：用来设置计算平均数的置信区间（默认的置信度为 0.95）。

4. 分析结果（见图 3.5）

均值 mean 为 1 994.81，CI.mean 是总体均值的 95%置信区间长度的一半，所以总体均值的置信区间为[1 994.81−1 395.25,1 994.81+1 395.25]=[599.56, 3 390.06]。

```
          nbr.val          nbr.null            nbr.na               min               max
45.0000000000000   0.0000000000000   0.0000000000000   1.7000000000000 27005.5999999999985
            range               sum            median              mean           SE.mean
27003.8999999999978 89766.3999999999942 496.5000000000000 1994.8088888888888 692.3052911321112
     CI.mean.0.95               var           std.dev          coef.var          skewness
1395.2496353635065 21567897.7258282825351 4644.1250764625493 2.3281052647852 3.9238512229665
         skew.2SE          kurtosis          kurt.2SE        normtest.W        normtest.p
  5.5463603002796  16.7618279585343  12.0667779978723   0.4420668557961   0.0000000000074
```

Figure 3.5　Outcomes of Analysis

图 3.5　统计分析结果

Appendix 3.3　Formulas and Notes

附录 3.3　关键公式与注解

1. 点估计（point estimate）

用样本的特征值估计总体的对应参数得出一个单一的估计值，称为点估计。具体来说，就是用根据样本信息计算出来的样本统计量，来估计参数的点估计值。

2. 置信区间（interval estimate）

用样本的信息对总体的参数值做出估计，如果估计的结果不是一个点的值，而是一个值的区间，而且我们期望总体参数会依一定的概率落在这个区间内。这样的一个值的区间称为置信区间，这个概率被称为置信水平。

3. 均值的置信区间

设 $x_1,\cdots,x_n$ 是来自 $N(\mu,\sigma^2)$ 的样本，$\bar{x}$ 为样本均值，s 为样本标准差。

在 σ 已知的情况下，总体均值 μ 的置信区间为

$$\left[\bar{x}-\mu_{1-\frac{\alpha}{2}}\sigma/\sqrt{n},\bar{x}+\mu_{1-\frac{\alpha}{2}}\sigma/\sqrt{n}\right]$$

在 σ 未知的情况下，总体均值 μ 的置信区间为

$$\left[\bar{x}-t_{1-\frac{\alpha}{2}}s/\sqrt{n},\bar{x}+t_{1-\frac{\alpha}{2}}s/\sqrt{n}\right]$$

4. 基于总体标准差情况的分类说明

在计算置信区间的过程中，采用正态分布还是 t 分布取决于总体标准差是否已知。如果总体标准差已知，则采用正态分布，若总体标准差未知，且总体可假定为服从正态分布的话，则采用 t 分布。此外，在大样本的情况下，即样本量大于 30 时，也可采用正态分布。

Chapter 4

Hypothesis Tests

第 4 章 假设检验

Hypothesis testing is an important type of statistical inference method, which is different from parameter estimation. Based on the obtained samples, hypothesis testing is to make acceptance or rejection of the null hypothesis formed by a proposition of the overall parameters. For example, if the original hypothesis is $\mu = 30$, then $\mu \neq 30$ can be used as an alternative hypothesis. The purpose of the hypothesis test is to verify that the null hypothesis for the population parameters is correct.

假设检验是一类重要的统计推断方法。区别于参数估计，假设检验是根据所获得的样本对总体参数的某个命题构成的原假设做出接受或拒绝的判断。比如令原假设为“均值等于 30”，即“$\mu = 30$”，那么“$\mu \neq 30$”可以作为一个备择假设。假设检验的目的是验证关于总体参数的原假设是否正确。

And in the second case, we expand the idea of hypothesis testing to two samples. That is, we select random samples from two different populations to determine whether the means or proportions are the same. For example, to make comparisons of the average diameters of the products from two machines, a two-sample test of the hypothesis should be carried out on the basis of two independent samples. The similarity between two-sample and one-sample tests is that we use the same steps.

The differences between them are the hypothesis and testing statistic. In this section, we select a case involving comparison using the means of two populations.

在本章第二节，我们将之前的假设检验思想扩展到两样本的情形，这类假设检验是从两个不同的总体中随机抽取样本，根据样本数据来判断两总体均值或比例是否相等。例如，比较两台机床加工产品的平均直径是否有差异，两样本假设检验是在两样本独立的前提下才能进行的。两样本和单样本假设检验的相同之处是步骤相同，不同之处是假设不同，要用到的检验统计量也不同。在本章中我们以比较两个总体均值的假设检验来具体说明。

Case 4.1 Declining Rates of Credit Card

案例4.1 下降的信用卡利率

1. 案例介绍

1991年，美国信用卡发放者收取的平均利率是18.8%。自那时以来，零售商店、石油公司、校友会、专业体育运动队等发放的信用卡如雨后春笋般地冒了出来。一位金融官员打算研究一下，信用卡市场日益增加的竞争是否会使利率下降。为了进行这个研究，他将要检验一个有关当时美国信用卡发放者收取的平均利率μ的假设。要检验的原假设是$H_0:\mu=18.8\%$，而备择假设是$H_1:\mu<18.8\%$。如果在0.05的显著性水平上拒绝了H_0而支持H_1，这位官员将会得出结论，当时的平均利率低于1991年收取的18.8%的平均利率。为了进行这个假设检验，假设随机地抽取了一个n=15的信用卡样本，并且确认了它们当时的利率（见表4.1）。

1. Introduction①

In 1991, the average interest rate charged by credit card issuers in the United States was 18.8%. Since then, using credit cards has sprung up from retail stores, oil companies, alumni associations, professional sports teams and so on. A financial official once conducted a study on whether the growing competition in the credit card market would reduce interest rates. To do this, he would test a hypothesis about the average interest rate μ charged by U.S. credit card issuers at that time. The original hypothesis to be tested was $H_0:\mu=18.8\%$, while the alternative hypothesis was $H_1:\mu<18.8\%$②. If H_0 was rejected at the significance level of 0.05 in favor of H_1, the official would conclude that the average interest rate at that time was lower than the average interest rate of 18.8% charged in 1991. In order to test the hypothesis, a sample of credit cards with n = 15 were randomly selected, their interest rates confirmed at that time:

Table 4.1 Sample Data

表4.1 样本数据

Rate(%)[利率（%）]							
18.4	15.6	17.8	14.6	17.3	18.7	15.3	16.4
17.6	14.0	19.2	15.8	18.1	16.6	17.0	

① Bruce L.Bowerman, Richard T. O'Connell, J.B.Orris, et al. Essentials of business statistics[M]. 3rd ed. New York: McGraw-Hill Education, 2010.

② 此处采用单侧检验是因为研究目的为判断利率下降。

2．假设检验的步骤

2．The procedures of hypothesis testing

（1）设定原假设和备择假设（见图 4.1）

(1) Set the original hypothesis and alternative hypothesis;

要检验的原假设是 $H_0: \mu = 18.8\%$，而备择假设是 $H_1: \mu < 18.8\%$。

The original hypothesis to be tested is $H_0: \mu = 18.8\%$, while the alternative hypothesis, $H_1: \mu < 18.8\%$.

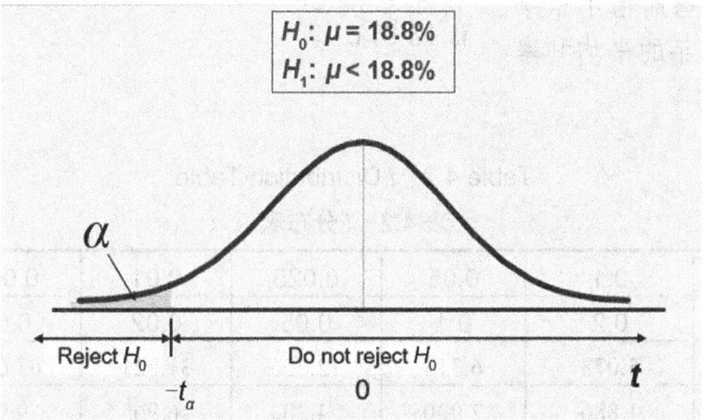

Figure 4.1　Rejection Rule

图 4.1　拒绝规则

（2）选择一个显著性水平

令显著性水平为 $\alpha = 0.05$。

(2) Select a significant level;

Let the significance level be $\alpha = 0.05$.

（3）选择检验统计量

在小样本并且总体方差未知的情况下，假设检验使用到的统计量为 $t = \dfrac{\overline{x} - \mu_0}{s / \sqrt{n}}$。

(3) Select test statistics;

In the case of small sample and unknown population variance, the statistics used in the test is assumed to be $t = \dfrac{\overline{x} - \mu_0}{s / \sqrt{n}}$.

（4）制定拒绝规则（见表 4.2）

该检验为单边假设检验，如果检验统计量 t 的值小于临界值 $-t_{0.05} = -1.761$，应该拒绝 $H_0: \mu = 18.8\%$，这里临界值 $-t_{0.05} = -1.761$ 是基于 $n - 1 = 15 - 1 = 14$ 个自由度得到的。

(4) Formulate rejection rules;

This is a unilateral hypothesis test. If the value of test statistic t is less than the critical value $-t_{0.05} = -1.761$, $H_0: \mu = 18.8\%$ should be rejected. Here, the critical value $-t_{0.05} = -1.761$ is based on $n - 1 = 15 - 1 = 14$ degrees of freedom.

（5）将样本数据代入公式，做出判断得出结论

15 个利率的均值和标准差分别是 $\overline{x} = 16.827$ 和 $s = 1.538$，所以检验统计量为

(5) Substitute the sample data into the formula to make a judgment and draw a conclusion.

The mean and standard deviation of 15 interest rates are $\overline{x} = 16.827$ and $s = 1.538$ respectively, hence the test statistics:

$$t = \frac{16.827 - 18.8}{1.538/\sqrt{15}} = -4.97$$

由于 $t = -4.97$ 小于 $-t_{0.05} = -1.761$，拒绝 $H_0: \mu = 18.8\%$，而支持 $H_1: \mu < 18.8\%$。

可得出结论（在 $\alpha = 0.05$ 的显著性水平下），当时信用卡平均利率低于1991年的平均利率18.8%。

$$t = \frac{16.827 - 18.8}{1.538/\sqrt{15}} = -4.97$$

Because $t = -4.97$ is less than $-t_{0.05} = -1.761$, $H_0: \mu = 18.8\%$ is rejected, while $H_1: \mu < 18.8\%$ is supported. It can be concluded that (at the significance level of $\alpha = 0.05$), the average interest rate of credit card at that time was lower than that of 1991, which is 18.8%.

Table 4.2 *t* Distribution Table

表4.2 *t* 分布表

	One-tailed	0.1	0.05	0.025	0.01	0.005	0.001
Df	Two-tailed	0.2	0.1	0.05	0.02	0.01	0.002
1		3.078	6.314	12.706	31.821	63.657	318.309
2		1.886	2.920	4.303	6.965	9.925	22.327
3		1.638	2.353	3.182	4.541	5.841	10.215
4		1.533	3.132	2.776	3.747	4.604	7.173
5		1.476	2.015	2.571	3.365	4.032	5.893
6		1.440	1.943	2.447	3.143	3.707	5.208
7		1.415	1.895	2.365	2.998	3.499	4.785
8		1.397	1.860	2.306	2.896	3.355	4.501
9		1.383	1.833	2.262	2.821	3.250	4.297
10		1.372	1.812	2.228	2.764	3.169	4.144
11		1.363	1.796	2.201	2.718	3.106	4.025
12		1.356	1.782	2.179	2.681	3.055	3.930
13		1.350	1.771	2.160	2.650	3.012	3.852
14		1.345	1.761	2.145	2.624	2.977	3.787
15		1.341	1.753	2.131	2.602	2.947	3.733

Case 4.2 Hourly Wage Rate in Florida

案例4.2 佛罗里达的小时工资差异

1. 案例介绍

佛罗里达的一个城市规划

1. Introduction[①]

A city planner in Florida wishes to know whether

① Lind, Marchal, Wathen. Statistical techniques in business and economics[M].14th ed. New York: McGrraw-Hill Irwin, 2010: 365.

者想要知道管道工和电工的平均小时工资是否有差别。这样，他就能有更好的想法来以最小的成本规划城市。于是选择了管道工和电工这两个总体。为了比较管道工和电工的平均小时工资，随机抽取了一个含有 40 个管道工和 35 个电工的总样本，分别计算出其中 40 个管道工和 35 个电工的样本均值。表 4.3 就是重复抽取该随机样本 20 次后得到的数据结果。假设两总体的标准差相同。

there is a difference between the mean hourly wage rates of plumbers and electricians in central Florida. In this way, he will have better information about how to plan the city with the lowest cost. To compare the mean hourly wage rates of the two populations, a random sample of 40 plumbers and a random sample of 35 electricians were selected and the mean of each sample was computed. Table 4.3 shows the result of selecting 20 different samples from the 40 plumbers and 35 electricians. Assume the populations have the same standard deviations.

在这个案例中，表 4.3 是 20 个不同的包含 40 个管道工和 35 个电工的数据，我们计算出每个样本的均值并且找出两样本之间的差异。数据是通过重复随机抽样得到的。因为样本中的管道工和电工数都足够大，所以根据中心极限定理，该样本均值分布近似为标准正态分布。在接下来的假设检验中，可以使用适合正态分布的检验统计量。在该例中，我们将进行关于样本均值是否相等的两样本假设检验。总体方差未知，但假定其相等，选取符合以上条件的相关统计量进行检验分析，判定两个总体的均值是否相等，从而可以给予城市规划者相关建议。

In this case, Table 4.3 shows the result of selecting 20 different samples from 40 plumbers and 35 electricians, computing the mean of each sample, and finding the difference between the two sample means. The data is obtained by sampling repeat. Because the sample numbers of plumbers and electricians are big enough, on the basis of the Central Limit Theorem we can determine that the sample of 40 plumbers and 35 electricians approximates a standard normal distribution. So in the next hypothesis test, we can use the test statistic for a normal population. In this case, we will do a two-sample test to examine the difference between two population means.

Table 4.3 Data for Hourly Wage Rate in Florida

表 4.3 佛罗里达的平均小时工资数据

Sample（样本）	Plumbers（$）（管道工）	Electricians（$）（电工）
1	29.8	28.76
2	30.32	29.4
3	30.57	29.94

续表

Sample（样本）	Plumbers（$）（管道工）	Electricians（$）（电工）
4	30.04	28.93
5	30.09	29.78
6	30.02	28.66
7	29.6	29.13
8	29.63	29.42
9	30.17	29.29
10	30.81	29.75
11	30.09	28.05
12	29.35	29.07
13	29.42	28.79
14	29.78	29.54
15	29.6	29.6
16	30.6	30.19
17	30.79	28.65
18	29.14	29.95
19	29.91	28.75
20	28.74	29.21

2. 案例分析

步骤 1：设定一个城市规划者能够比较管道工和电工平均小时工资的假设检验。

步骤 2：分析数据得出假设检验的结果，求出 P 值是多少。

步骤 3：求出每个总体均值的 95%的置信区间，求出两总体均值差的 95%的置信区间。

步骤 4：给出结论和建议，是否有必要进行进一步假设检验？

步骤 1：设定一个城市规划者能够比较管道工和电工平均工资的假设检验。

令 μ_1 代表管道工的平均小

2. Analytical Procedures

Step 1: Formulate a hypothesis test that the city planner could use to compare the mean hourly wage rates of plumbers and electricians.

Step 2: Analyze the data to provide a hypothesis testing conclusion. What is the P-value for your test?

Step 3: What is the 95% confidence interval for the population mean of each sample? What is the 95% confidence interval for the difference between the means of the two populations?

Step 4: Develop conclusions and recommendations. Do you see a need for further testing?

Step 1: Formulate a hypothesis test that the city planner could use to compare the mean hourly wage rates of plumbers and electricians

Let μ_1 denote the population mean hourly wage

时工资，μ_2代表电工的平均小时工资。在不知道哪方的工资较高的情况下，根据题意，原假设应是管道工和电工的平均小时工资相等，备择假设则是这之间是有区别的，即:

$H_0: \mu_1 - \mu_2 = 0$（原假设）

$H_1: \mu_1 - \mu_2 \neq 0$（备择假设）

所以，如果原假设被拒绝，我们就认为管道工和电工的平均小时工资是不同的。

步骤 2：分析数据得出假设检验的结果，求出 P 值是多少。

令$\overline{x}_1$和s_1分别为样本 1 到样本 20 管道工的小时工资的样本平均值和标准差，令$\overline{x}_2$和s_2分别为 20个电工的样本平均值和标准差。然后，使用检验统计量 $t = \dfrac{\overline{x}_1 - \overline{x}_2}{\sqrt{s_p^2\left(\dfrac{1}{n_1}+\dfrac{1}{n_2}\right)}}$，合并样本方差：$s_p^2 = \dfrac{(n_1-1)s_1^2+(n_2-1)s_2^2}{n_1+n_2-2}$ 从表 4.1 可以得到 $\overline{x}_1 = 29.92$，$\overline{x}_2 = 29.24$，$s_1 = 0.544\,7$，$s_2 = 0.544\,8$，$n_1 = 20$，$n_2 = 20$。通过计算得到$s_p^2 = 0.296\,79$，$t = 3.95$。0.05 和 0.01 的显著性水平是最常用的，选择 0.05 作为显著性水平，$H_1: \mu_1 - \mu_2 \neq 0$，$t_{0.025}(38) = 2.024\,4$。拒绝规则为$|t| \geqslant t_{0.025}(38)$，所以拒绝原假设。管道工和电工的样本均值是不同的，P 值为$P(|U| \geqslant |t|) = P(|U| \geqslant 3.95) = 0.000\,078 < 0.05$。

rate of plumbers for the samples of 40 plumbers and 35 electricians (n=20), and let μ_2 denote the population mean hourly wage rate of electricians for the samples of plumbers and electricians (n=20). With no preliminary indication of which wage is higher, we begin by assuming that plumbers and electricians have the same population mean hourly wage rate. Thus, the null hypothesis is $H_0: \mu_1 - \mu_2 = 0$. The alternative hypothesis is $H_1: \mu_1 - \mu_2 \neq 0$. Thus, if the null hypothesis is rejected, we can conclude that the population means of the plumbers and electricians differ.

Step 2: Analyze the data to provide a hypothesis testing conclusion. What is the P-value for your test?

We denote $\overline{x}_1$ and s_1 to be the mean and standard deviations of the hourly wage rate of plumbers from sample 1 to sample 20. Denote $\overline{x}_2$ and s_2 to be the mean and standard deviation of the hourly wage rate of electricians from the 20 samples. Thus, we can use the test statistic $t = \dfrac{\overline{x}_1 - \overline{x}_2}{\sqrt{s_p^2\left(\dfrac{1}{n_1}+\dfrac{1}{n_2}\right)}}$, and we can obtain from the data in Table 4.1 that $\overline{x}_1 = 29.92$, $\overline{x}_2 = 29.24$, $s_1 = 0.544\,7$, $s_2 = 0.544\,8$, $n_1 = 20$ and $n_2 = 20$. We compute $s_p^2 = 0.296\,79$, $t = 3.95$. The 0.05 and 0.01 significance level are the most common; we choose 0.05 as the significance level. $H_1: \mu_1 - \mu_2 \neq 0$, $t_{0.025}(38) = 2.024\,4$, and the rejection principle is $|t| \geqslant t_{0.025}(38)$. In this case $|t| > t_{0.025}(38)$, so we reject H_0. The population means of the plumbers and electricians differ. The P-value is $P(|U| \geqslant |t|) = P(|U| \geqslant 3.95) = 0.000\,078 < 0.05$, so this reaffirms that we should reject H_0.

所以再次确定应该拒绝原假设。

步骤3：求出每个总体均值的95%的置信区间，求出两总体均值差的95%的置信区间。

管道工小时工资的均值95%的置信区间通过计算式可以得出，为[29.67,30.18]。

电工小时工资的均值95%的置信区间通过计算式可以得出，为[28.99, 29.50]。

管道工和电工小时工资的均值差异 95%的置信区间通过计算式可以得出，为[0.506 1, 0.854 9]。

从两个样本小时工资均值差异来看，我们能够推出管道工的小时工资均值比电工的小时工资均值要高。

步骤4：给出结论和建议。是否有必要进行进一步的假设检验？

从假设检验的结果可以得出管道工的平均小时工资与电工的平均小时工资不同。但是哪个更高我们还不确定。所以我们建议，为了得到更确切的两者之间的关系，需要进行进一步的假设检验。在均值差异区间的基础上，我们设定原假设为 $H_0: \mu_1 - \mu_2 \geqslant 0$，备择假设为 $H_1: \mu_1 - \mu_2 < 0$。我们

Step 3: What is the 95% confidence interval for the population mean of each sample? What is the 95% confidence interval for the difference between the means of the two populations?

The 95% confidence interval for the mean of the plumbers is

$$\left[\overline{x}_1 - t_{0.025}(n_1-1)\frac{s_1}{\sqrt{n}}, \overline{x}_1 + t_{0.025}(n_1-1)\frac{s_1}{\sqrt{n}}\right],$$

Entering the data into the formulation, we obtain the values [29.67, 30.18]. The 95% confidence interval for the mean of electricians is

$$\left[\overline{x}_2 - t_{0.025}(n_2-1)\frac{s_2}{\sqrt{n}}, \overline{x}_2 + t_{0.025}(n_2-1)\frac{s_2}{\sqrt{n}}\right],$$

After computing we obtain [28.99, 29.50]. The 95% confidence interval for the difference between the means of the two populations is

$$\left[\overline{x}_1 - \overline{x}_2 - t_{0.025}(38)\frac{s_p}{\sqrt{n_1+n_2}}, \overline{x}_1 - \overline{x}_2 + t_{0.025}(38)\frac{s_p}{\sqrt{n_1+n_2}}\right]$$

After computing we obtain the interval [0.506 1, 0.854 9]. From the difference interval we can generally infer that mean for the plumbers is higher than the mean for the electricians.

Step 4: Develop conclusions and recommendations. Do you see a need for further testing?

From the hypothesis testing above, we can conclude that the means of the two populations differ. The mean hourly wage rates for the plumbers and electricians are different. However, we cannot be sure which is bigger. Thus, the recommendation is that there is a need for further testing; we should do a one-sided hypothesis test. On the basis of the interval for the difference, we can set the null hypothesis $H_0: \mu_1 - \mu_2 \geqslant 0$, and the alternative hypothesis

依然使用统计量：

$$t=\frac{\bar{x}_1-\bar{x}_2}{\sqrt{s_p^2\left(\frac{1}{n_1}+\frac{1}{n_2}\right)}}$$

$t=3.95$，$t_{0.05}(38)=1.686$。如果 $t<-t_{0.05}(38)$，我们拒绝原假设。在该例中，$t>-t_{0.05}(38)$，所以接受原假设。在进一步的检验之后，我们确定管道工的小时工资均值比电工的要高。这个结论可以给城市规划者一些信息。建议城市规划者考虑城市建设成本，在能用电工解决施工上的问题时尽量不用管道工。

$H_1:\mu_1-\mu_2<0$. We can use the same statistic $t=\frac{\bar{x}_1-\bar{x}_2}{\sqrt{s_p^2\left(\frac{1}{n_1}+\frac{1}{n_2}\right)}}$, and after calculation we obtain $t=3.95$, $t_{0.05}(38)=1.686$. If $t<-t_{0.05}(38)$, we reject H_0. In this case, $t>-t_{0.05}(38)$, so we accept H_0. After this further testing, we can be sure that the mean hourly wage rate of the plumbers is higher than that of the electricians. This conclusion provides the required information for the city planner.

Appendix 4.1 Hypothesis Testing Using Excel

附录 4.1 用 Excel 进行假设检验

Excel 并不提供假设检验所需的各统计量的自动生成功能，但是我们可以用 Excel 来处理样本数据，得到我们需要的统计量值，如图 4.2～图 4.5 所示。

Excel does not provide built-in routines for the hypothesis tests presented in this case. But we can use Excel to handle the sample data.

	A	B
1	Rate	
2	15.6%	18.8%
3	17.8%	18.8%
4	14.6%	18.8%
5	17.3%	18.8%
6	18.7%	18.8%
7	15.3%	18.8%
8	16.4%	18.8%
9	18.4%	18.8%
10	17.6%	18.8%
11	14.0%	18.8%
12	19.2%	18.8%
13	15.8%	18.8%
14	18.1%	18.8%
15	16.6%	18.8%
16	17.0%	18.8%

Figure 4.2　Original Data

图 4.2　原始数据

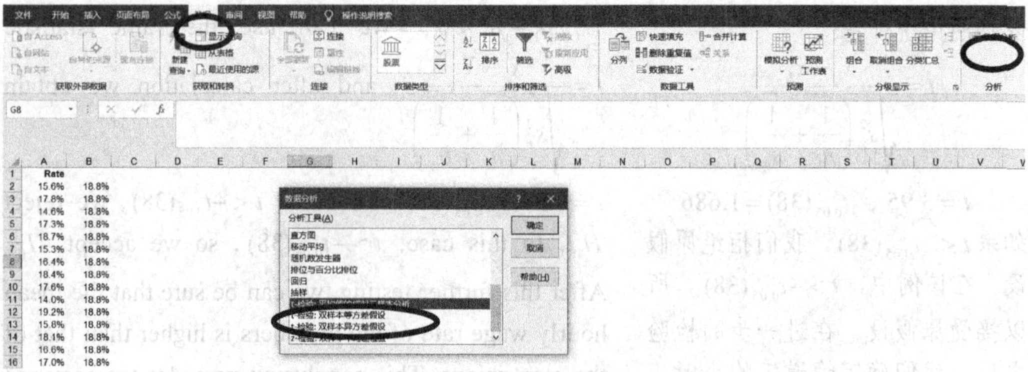

Figure 4.3 Data Analysis

图 4.3 数据分析-1

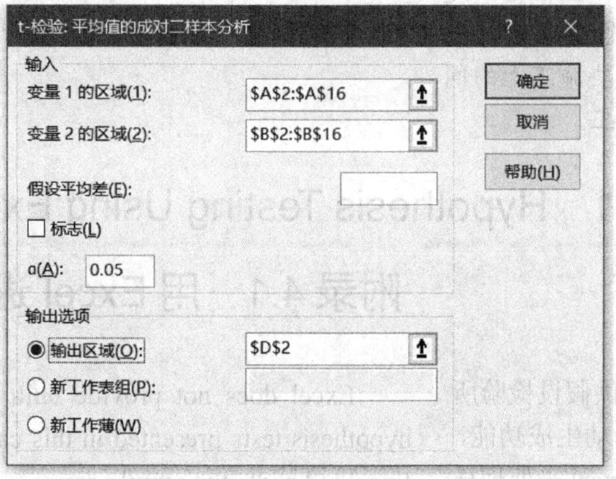

Figure 4.4 Data Analysis

图 4.4 数据分析-2

	A	B	C	D	E	F
1	Rate					
2	15.6%	18.8%		t-检验: 成对双样本均值分析		
3	17.8%	18.8%				
4	14.6%	18.8%			变量 1	变量 2
5	17.3%	18.8%		平均	0.168267	0.188
6	18.7%	18.8%		方差	0.000236	8.25E-34
7	15.3%	18.8%		观测值	15	15
8	16.4%	18.8%		泊松相关系数	2.49E-16	
9	18.4%	18.8%		假设平均差	0	
10	17.6%	18.8%		df	14	
11	14.0%	18.8%		t Stat	-4.96975	
12	19.2%	18.8%		P(T<=t) 单尾	0.000103	
13	15.8%	18.8%		t 单尾临界	1.76131	
14	18.1%	18.8%		P(T<=t) 双尾	0.000206	
15	16.6%	18.8%		t 双尾临界	2.144787	
16	17.0%	18.8%				

Figure 4.5 Outcomes

图 4.5 分析结果

步骤 1：在 F4 单元格中输入“=COUNT()”，然后选择 A2:A31 单元格中的样本数据放置圆括号中，回车得到计算值。在 F5 单元格中输入“=AVERAGE()”，然后同样选择 A2:A31 单元格中的样本数据放置圆括号内，回车即可得到样本均值。

Step 1: Enter the data range A2:A31 into the **=COUNT** cell formula in cell F4, **=AVERAGE** cell formula in cell F5.

步骤 2：在 F6 单元格中输入总体标准差的值 0.21。

Step 2: Enter the population standard deviation 0.21 in cell F6.

步骤 3：在 F8 单元格中输入总体均值 12。

Step 3: Enter the hypothesis value for the population mean 12 in cell F8.

步骤 4：将已知的检验统计量的数值导入计算公式，得到统计量 z 值和 p 值。

Step 4: Compute the test statistic z and p-value.

步骤 5：B2:B31、C2:C31 和 D2:D31 这三个样本的数据处理方式和 A2:A31 一样进行假设检验。

Step 5: The way of handling the data range B2:B31, C2:C31, D2:D31 is the same to the data range A2:A31.

Appendix 4.2 Hypothesis Testing Using R

附录 4.2 用 R 语言假设检验

There are two steps required to make a hypothesis test. First, import data. Next, import specific function to have a t test.

在 R 语言中进行假设检验需要两个步骤。先输入数据，再调用函数进行 t 检验。

1. 单样本假设检验

（1）代码

```
#步骤一：输入数据
data = c(15.6,17.8,14.6,17.3,18.7,15.3,16.4,
         18.4,17.6,14.0,19.2,15.8,18.1,16.6,17.0)                #数据量较小，手动输入数据

#步骤二：进行检验
t.test(x = data, y = NULL,alternative = "less",mu= 18.8,
       paired = FALSE, var.equal = FALSE,conf.level = 0.95)          #*详见函数参数说明*
```

（2）具体过程分析

步骤 1：输入用到的数据。

步骤 2：调用 t.test()函数进行 *t* 检验。

（3）*函数参数说明

```
t.test(x, y = NULL, alternative = c("two.sided", "less","greater"),
       mu= 0, paired = FALSE, var.equal = FALSE, conf.level = 0.95)
```

☑ t.test()函数：做 *t* 检验。

☑ x：唯一的必选参数，一个数值型非空向量，若为单样本检验，那么这里就是那个样本；若为双样本检验，这里就是样本之一。

☑ y：可选参数，单样本检验时可以为空，双样本检验时是样本之一。

☑ alternative：two.sided 为双侧检验，greater 和 less 都是单侧检验，greater 是右侧，less 是左侧。

☑ mu：单样本检验时是样本均值，双样本检验时是样本均值之差，默认值为 0。

☑ paired：是否为配对 *t* 检验，TRUE 为配对 *t* 检验。

☑ var.equal：是否将两个样本的方差视为相等，一般来说如果不能很确定会相等，这里就设置为 FALSE，默认值为 FALSE。

☑ conf.level：置信度，通常设为 0.95。

（4）分析结果（见图 4.6）

```
                One Sample t-test

data:  data
t = -4.9698, df = 14, p-value = 0.0001029
alternative hypothesis: true mean is less than 18.8
95 percent confidence interval:
     -Inf 17.52603
sample estimates:
mean of x
 16.82667
```

Figure 4.6　Outcomes

图 4.6　分析结果

检验的 P 值为 0.000 102 9，远小于 $\alpha = 0.05$，所以拒绝原假设，即得出结论：当时信用卡平均利率低于 1991 年的平均利率 18.8%。

2．两样本假设检验

（1）代码

```
#步骤一：安装并导入所需的程序包，导入数据
install.packages('xlsx')
library(xlsx)
data = read_excel("Chapter 5-Hourly Wage Rate in Florida.xls")

#步骤二：使用内置函数 t.test 进行两独立样本 t 检验
t.test(data$Plumbers,data$Electricians,var.equal=TRUE)
```

（2）具体过程分析

步骤 1：为读取文件后缀为.xls 中的数据，需要安装并调用 xlsx 程序包。

步骤 2：导入数据。

步骤 3：调用 t.test()函数进行假设检验。

（3）*函数参数说明

```
t.test(data$Plumbers,data$Electricians,var.equal=TRUE)
```

☑ data$Plumbers：对 data 中的 Plumbers 数据进行 t 检验。

☑ var.equal: 逻辑值，默认值为 FALSE，表示两总体的方差不相等，若设为 TRUE，则相等。

（4）分析结果（见图 4.7）

```
        Two Sample t-test

data:  data$Plumbers and data$Electricians
t = 3.9503, df = 38, p-value =
0.0003272
alternative hypothesis: true difference in means is not equal to 0
95 percent confidence interval:
 0.3317633 1.0292367
sample estimates:
mean of x mean of y
  29.9235   29.2430
```

Figure 4.7　Outcomes

图 4.7　分析结果

结果表明 P 值<0.05，即在显著性水平为 0.05 时拒绝原假设，认为两样本间的均值存在显著差异。

Appendix 4.3　Formulas and Notes

附录 4.3　关键公式与注解

1. 检验统计量

检验统计量[①]为 $t=\dfrac{\bar{x}_1-\bar{x}_2}{\sqrt{s_p^2\left(\dfrac{1}{n_1}+\dfrac{1}{n_2}\right)}}$，因为总体方差未知，所以我们采用 t 分布，又因为两总体方差假设为相等的，$s_p^2=\dfrac{(n_1-1)s_1^2+(n_2-1)s_2^2}{n_1+n_2-2}$ 为总样本的方差。原假设为 $\mu_1-\mu_2=0$，所以该统计量是 $\bar{x}_1-\bar{x}_2-0$ 除以样本均值差的标准差而得到的，这个标准差是 $\sqrt{s_p^2\left(\dfrac{1}{n_1}+\dfrac{1}{n_2}\right)}$。

① $\bar{x}_1$ 是样本 1 的均值，$\bar{x}_2$ 是样本 2 的均值，n_1 是样本 1 的样本数，n_2 是样本 2 的样本数。s_1^2 是样本 1 的方差，s_2^2 是样本 2 的方差。

2．检验统计量的确定

在一个总体参数的检验中，用到的检验统计量主要有三个：Z统计量，t统计量，χ^2统计量。Z统计量和t统计量常常用于均值和比例的检验，χ^2统计量则用于方差的检验。

选择统计量进行检验需要考虑以下因素。

（1）样本量

在大样本条件下，如果总体为正态分布，样本统计量服从正态分布；如果总体为非正态分布，样本统计量渐进服从正态分布。

检验统计量$Z=\dfrac{\overline{x}-\mu_0}{\sigma/\sqrt{n}}$，服从标准正态分布。

（2）总体标准差σ是否已知

在小样本情况下，如果总体标准差已知，样本统计量将服从正态分布，这时可以采用Z统计量。

如果总体标准差未知，检验统计量$t=\dfrac{\overline{x}-\mu_0}{s/\sqrt{n}}$服从自由度为$n-1$的$t$分布。

当$n<30$时，如果σ未知，必须使用t统计量；在$n\geqslant 30$的条件下，选择t分布还是z分布可以根据使用者的偏爱。

3．检验的P值

在依据临界值进行的判断中，检验都是事先给定显著性水平α，然后通过比较检验统计量的取值和临界值的大小来定是否接受还是拒绝原假设。此外，P值也可以作为接受还是拒绝原假设的依据，若$P\leqslant\alpha$，则拒绝原假设。一般P值都可以通过软件计算得到，P值的计算原理：双侧检验[①] $P=P(|U|\geqslant|u|)$或者$P=P(|U|\geqslant|t|)$；单侧检验$P=P\left(U\geqslant|u|\right)$或者$P=P\left(U\geqslant|t|\right)$。

---

① U是服从标准正态分布的一个统计量，u为根据样本数据代入$u=\dfrac{\overline{x}_1-\overline{x}_2}{\sqrt{\left(\dfrac{\sigma_1^2}{n_1}+\dfrac{\sigma_2^2}{n_2}\right)}}$计算得到的数值，该计算式是在两总体的方差$\sigma_1$、$\sigma_2$已知的条件下成立；$t$为根据样本数据代入$t=\dfrac{\overline{x}_1-\overline{x}_2}{\sqrt{s_p^2\left(\dfrac{1}{n_1}+\dfrac{1}{n_2}\right)}}$计算得到的数值，该式是在两总体的方差未知且假设方差相等的条件下成立的。$t_{\alpha/2}(n-1)$是T分布的临界值，s是样本方差。

Chapter 5

Hypothesis Test: Matched Samples

第5章　假设检验：成对样本情形

Sometimes items or individuals are paired together according to some characteristic of interest when the mean value of two populations are compared. It is not suitable here to use the two-sample t test, as we did in the previous chapter. In comparing the sales of different sales clerks before and after the training, for example, there exists a strong correlation for one salesclerk, even though different salesclerks can have different sales. The conclusion could be misled when the sales of the salesclerk before and after the training are treated as two independent populations. To this paired-wise data, therefore, is introduced paired-wise t test. In this way, the differences of each data could be eliminated by choosing the differences of each pair of data as an indicator, and a one-sample t test is conducted afterward.

在对两个总体的均值进行比较时，有时数据是成对出现的。这时使用第4章的两样本t检验并不合适。例如，比较不同销售人员在培训前后的销售额是否有差异，而销售人员本身销售额就会有差异，每个销售人员在培训前后的销售额有很强的相关性。此时将培训前后销售人员的销售额当作两个独立的总体进行假设检验，得到的结论有可能出现错误。对于这种成对数据，使用每对数据的差值进行单样本t检验可以消除试验单元之间的差别，再进行单样本t检验，这种方法被称为成对数据t检验。

Case Is the training effective

案例 培训是否有效

1. 案例介绍

假定某商店的店员们参加了一个顾客服务技能的培训，培训负责人想要科学评价该培训对于提高店员对客户的服务是否有帮助。为了比较培训前后店员的服务水平是否有提高，收集了 5 个店员在参加培训前后得到的客户抱怨数量（见表 5.1），并假设各个店员在培训前后接待的客户数量及其他条件都相同。

1. Case Introduction[①]

Assume that salesclerk of a shop undertakes customer service ability training, and that the director wants to know whether it works. In order to compare the differences of salesclerks' service ability before and after the training, the director collects the customer complaints of five salesclerks before and after, presuming that other conditions are the same.

Table 5.1 Number of Complaints and Differences Before and After the Training

表 5.1 店员培训前后抱怨数与差值

Salesclerk（店员）	Number of Complaints（抱怨数）		Difference（差值）
	Before（培训前）	After（培训后）	
C.B.	6	4	−2
T.F.	20	6	−14
M.H.	3	2	−1
R.K.	0	0	0
M.O.	4	0	−4

在这个案例中，原始数据是每一个店员参加培训前后的客户抱怨数量，该数据是成对出现的。现将培训前后客户抱怨数相减，得到一个差值，由差值表示培训前后客户抱怨数量的变化，这个两组样本的检验问题被转

In this case, the raw data are the customer complaints before and after the training, which is paired-wise. A difference value is obtained by calculating the differences of the customer complaints before and after, which present the changes in the customer complaints. In so doing, a two-population problem turns to one of one-sample t-test.

① David M. Levine, Timothy C. Krehbiel, Mark L. Berenson. Business statistics[M]. 6th ed. Upper Saddle River, NJ: Pearson, 2012.

换为单样本 t 检验问题。

假设检验的步骤如下。

步骤1：设定原假设和备择假设。

步骤2：选择一个显著性水平。

步骤3：选择检验统计量。

步骤4：制定拒绝准则。

步骤5：将样本数据代入，做出判断，得出结论。

The procedures of hypothesis test:

Step 1: Define the null hypothesis and the alternate hypothesis.

Step 2: Select a significance level.

Step 3: Choose a test statistic.

Step 4: Set rejection rule.

Step 5: Make a judgment and draw a conclusion using the sample data.

2. 案例基本分析

2. Original Case Analysis

步骤1：设定一个店员在培训前后的客户抱怨数是否有差异的原假设和备择假设。假设培训前后店员的客户抱怨数差值服从正态分布，令 μ_D 表示培训前后抱怨数差值的均值，建立如下假设检验。

Step 1: In order to check whether there is a difference of the salesclerk's customer complaints before and after the training, both the null hypothesis and the alternate hypothesis are defined. Assuming that the customer complaint difference is normally distributed, define μ_D as the mean value of the customer complaints the salesclerk receives before and after. A hypothesis test is set as follows.

H_0：培训没有带来显著改变，$\mu_D = 0$

H_1：培训带来了显著变化，$\mu_D \neq 0$

H_0 : No difference occurs after the training, $\mu_D = 0$

H_1 : A difference occurs after the training, $\mu_D \neq 0$

步骤2：选取显著性水平 $\alpha = 0.01$。

Step 2: Select a significance level, $\alpha = 0.01$.

步骤3：本次假设检验使用统计量为

Step 3: Choose a t-statistic:

$$t_{\text{stat}} = \frac{\overline{x} - \mu_0}{S_D / \sqrt{n}}$$

步骤4：根据原假设和备择假设，设立拒绝域为

Step 4: Based on the null hypothesis and the alternate hypothesis, set rejection region as:

$$W = \{t_{stat} < t_{1-\alpha/2}(n-1)\} \cup \{t_{stat} > t_{\alpha/2}(n-1)\},$$

$$W = \{|t_{stat}| > t_{\alpha/2}(n-1)\}, \quad t_{\alpha/2}(n-1) = t_{0.005}(4) = 4.604$$

此假设检验有公式 $p\text{-}value = 2 \cdot P(|t_{stat}| > t(n-1))$。当 $p\text{-}value \leqslant \alpha$ 时，拒绝原假设；当 $p\text{-}value > \alpha$ 时，不拒绝原假设。

In this hypothesis test, $p\text{-}value = 2 \cdot P(|t_{stat}| > t(n-1))$. Reject the null hypothesis when $p\text{-}value \leqslant \alpha$, and when $p\text{-}value > \alpha$, the null hypothesis is not rejected.

步骤5：将样本数据代入，

Step 5: Calculate the test statistic using the

得到检验统计量：

sample data:

$$\bar{x}=\frac{1}{n}\sum x_i=-4.2,\quad S_D^2=\frac{1}{n-1}\sum(x_i-\bar{x})^2=32.15$$

$$t_{stat}=\frac{\bar{x}-\mu_0}{S_D/\sqrt{n}}=-1.66,\quad p\text{-}value=2\cdot P(|t_{stat}|>t(n-1))=0.1733$$

因为 $|t_{stat}|=1.66<4.604=t_{0.005}(4)$，所以在 $\alpha=0.01$ 显著性水平下不拒绝原假设；或者根据 $p\text{-}value=0.1733>0.01$，得出在 0.01 显著性水平下不拒绝原假设，即认为培训没有带来显著改变。

For $|t_{stat}|=1.66<4.604=t_{0.005}(4)$, under the significance level of $\alpha=0.01$, the null hypothesis is not rejected. In another way, based on the fact that $p\text{-}value=0.1733>0.01$, a conclusion could be drawn that the null hypothesis is not rejected, thus no significant change being observed before and after the training.

3. 案例深度分析

3. Deep Analysis

案例基本分析的假设检验认为培训没有带来显著的改变，但直观上根据数据可以看出客户对培训后店员的抱怨数量有明显的减少，这与检验的结果不一致。为了查看该假设检验是否有改进的空间，对假设检验在以下几个方面展开深入分析。

As indicated by the original analysis, there aren't any differences before and after the training. However, no significant reduction is observed after the training, which is opposed to the analysis. To check whether there is any room for the improvement of the test, a deep analysis is made in several aspects.

（1）检验的前提假设

(1) Assumption test

上述 t 检验实质上是方差未知时，单个正态总体均值是否为 0 的检验，而进行该检验的条件是该组数据必须服从正态分布，下面对这个样本进行正态性检验。

H_0：数据服从正态分布

H_1：数据不服从正态分布

Essentially, the t-statistic mentioned above is a test to check whether the mean value of a normal population is zero with variance unknown, which means that the data must be normally distributed. Normality test is made as follows:

H_0: The data is normally distributed.

H_1: The data is not normally distributed.

使用 Shapiro-Wilk 检验（简称 W 检验），得到检验统计量与 $p\text{-}value$ 结果如下：

Shapiro-Wilk test (for short W test), test statistics and $p\text{-}value$ are shown as follows:

$$W=0.781,\quad p\text{-}value=0.0561$$

所以在 0.05 显著性水平下不拒绝原假设，认为数据服从正态分布，进而可以使用 t 检验。

Thus, at the significance level of 0.05, the null hypothesis is not rejected. The data is normally distributed and t-test is suitable here.

（2）检验的形式

(2) The form of test

若考虑本案例假设检验的目的是为了检验培训是否提高了店员的服务水平，也可以使用单侧假设检验。

In order to test whether the salesclerk's service ability is improved, one side test could be used:

H_0：培训没有带来显著改变，$\mu_D = 0$

H_0 : No difference occurs after the training, $\mu_D = 0$

H_1：培训带来了显著变化，$\mu_D < 0$

H_1 : A difference occurs after the training, $\mu_D < 0$

与双侧检验相比（见图 5.1），单侧检验的检验统计量不变，但拒绝域的临界值会变为：$W = \{t_{stat} < t_{1-\alpha}(n-1)\}$；检验的 *p-value* 会缩小一半，$p\text{-}value = P(t_{stat} < t(n-1))$。再次代入数据可以得到：

Compared with two-side test, the test statistic of one-side test is the same, but the critical value of the rejection region is $W = \{t_{stat} < t_{1-\alpha}(n-1)\}$; meanwhile the *p-value* of the hypothesis test would reduce by half, $p\text{-}value = P(t_{stat} < t(n-1))$. The t statistic is calculated using the sample data:

$$t_{stat} = \frac{\bar{x} - \mu_0}{S_D / \sqrt{n}} = -1.66,\quad p-value = P(t_{stat} < t(n-1)) = 0.086\,6$$

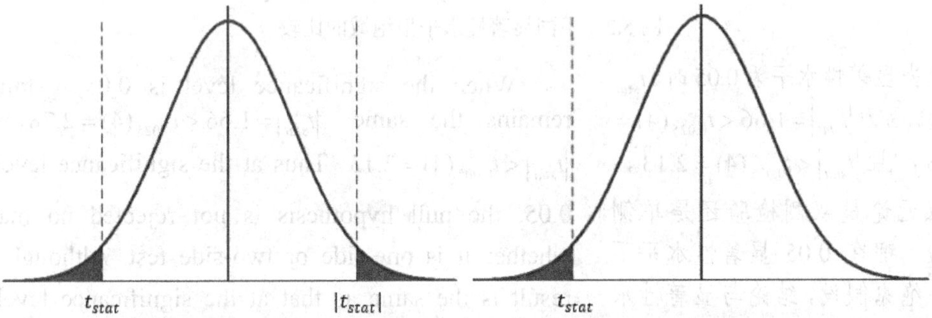

Figure 5.1　Comparison of *p-value* of Two-side and One-side Tests

图 5.1　双侧检验和单侧检验的 *p-value* 比较

由于 $t_{stat} > t_{0.995}(4)$, *p-value* > 0.01，所以单侧检验在 0.01 显著性水平下不拒绝原假设。该结论与双侧检验相同，但是检验统计量与双侧检验相比更加接近拒绝域的临界值，p 值是原来双侧检验的一半。

For $t_{stat} = -1.66 > t_{0.995}(4) = -4.604$, *p-value* > 0.01, at the significance level of 0.01, one side test doesn't reject the null hypothesis. In comparing with the two-side test, the conclusion is the same, but the value of the test statistic is closer to the critical value of the rejection region, the p value reduced by half.

（3）检验的显著性水平

(3) Significance level of the test

在案例基本分析的假设检

In the original case analysis, $|t_{stat}| = 1.66 < t_{0.005}$

验中，计算得到的统计量 $|t_{stat}| = 1.66 < t_{0.005}(4) = 4.604$，所以在0.01显著性水平下不拒绝原假设。0.01显著性水平表示假设检验发生第一类错误的概率是0.01，下面尝试放宽显著性水平到0.05，查看检验结果是否发生改变，如图5.2所示。

$(4) = 4.604$, the null hypothesis is not rejected at the significance level of 0.01, which means that the probability of Type I error of the test is 0.01. Broadening the significance level to 0.05 is to see whether the test result shows a difference.

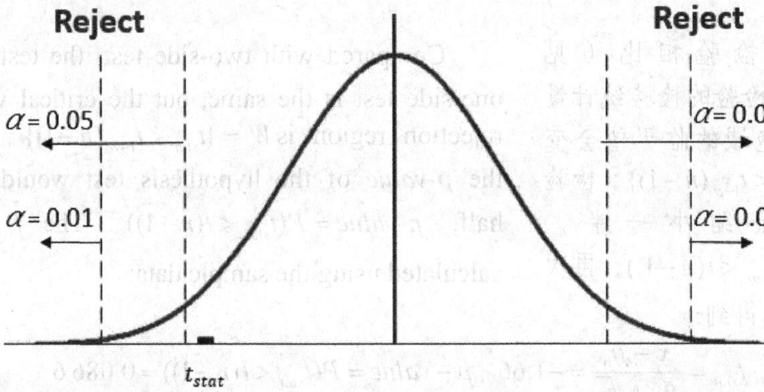

Figure 5.2　Comparison of Rejection Region at Different Significance Levels

图5.2　不同显著性水平拒绝域的比较

当显著性水平为0.05时，t_{stat} 不变。因为 $|t_{stat}| = 1.66 < t_{0.025}(4) = 2.78$，且 $|t_{stat}| < t_{0.005}(4) = 2.13$，所以无论是双侧检验还是单侧检验，都在0.05显著性水平下不拒绝原假设，结论与显著性水平取0.01时相同。虽然结论与0.01显著性水平时相同，但是临界值已经更接近假设检验的统计量。

When the significance level is 0.05, t-statistic remains the same, $|t_{stat}| = 1.66 < t_{0.025}(4) = 2.78$ and $|t_{stat}| < t_{0.005}(4) = 2.13$. Thus at the significance level of 0.05, the null hypothesis is not rejected no matter whether it is one-side or two-side test. Although the result is the same as that at the significance level of 0.01, the critical value is closer to the statistic of the hypothesis test.

通过双侧检验和单侧检验的 *p-value* 可以清楚地得出，在显著性水平 $\alpha \geqslant 0.1733$ 时，就可以拒绝双侧检验的原假设；在显著性水平 $\alpha \geqslant 0.0866$ 时，就可以拒绝单侧检验的原假设。这表明培训带来了显著性改变。

Based on the *p-value* of the one-side test and two-side test, it is obvious to see that the null hypothesis of the two-side test is rejected at the significance level of $\alpha \geqslant 0.1733$, which is true of the null hypothesis of the one-side test at the significance level of $\alpha \geqslant 0.0866$. This suggests that a significant change occurs before and after the training.

（4）原始数据的处理

(4) Raw data processing

① 异常值的处理

① Outlier processing

在假设检验中，极端的数据有可能对假设检验的结果产生巨大影响，此处根据“3σ”原则来判断样本数据是否为异常值：

In the hypothesis test, outliers have a significant impact on the result. The “3σ” rule① is used to judge whether the sample data is outlier.

$$(\hat{\mu}-3\hat{\sigma},\hat{\mu}+3\hat{\sigma})=(\hat{\mu}-3S_D,\hat{\mu}+3S_D)=(-21.2,12.8)$$

查看样本数据，发现只有“−14”没有在以上区间内，被认为是异常值。异常值通常会使得标准差异常大，检验统计量变小，从而对结果产生影响。为了减少异常值的影响，使用平均值“−4.2”来代替异常值。

Among all the sample data, only “-14” is beyond the region, which is considered as outlier. Outliers usually enlarge the deviation, making the test statistic smaller, thus impacting the result. To reduce its impact, the outlier is to be replaced by the mean value “-4.2”.

得到样本数据为（−2,−4.2,−1,0,−4）

The updated data: （−2,−4.2,−1,0,−4）.

重新使用W检验对数据进行正态性检验，结果如下：

W test is used again to test the normality of the data, the result is as follows:

$$W=0.912\,0,\ p\text{-}value=0.479\,6$$

所以在0.05显著性水平下不拒绝原假设，认为数据服从正态分布，继续进行t检验：

Thus under the significance level of 0.05, the null hypothesis is not rejected. The data are normal distributed. And t test is taken as follows:

$$t_{stat}=\frac{\overline{x}-\mu_0}{S_D/\sqrt{n}}=-2.721\,2$$

双侧检验：

Two-side test:

$$p-value=2\cdot P(|t_{stat}|>t(n-1))=0.052\,92$$

单侧检验：

One-side test:

$$p-value=P(t_{stat}<t(n-1))=0.026\,46$$

所以：

Thus:

单侧检验时，在0.05显著性水平拒绝原假设，这表明培训给员工服务带来了显著提高。

In the one-side test, the null hypothesis is rejected at the significance level of 0.05, which suggests that the training does improve the salesclerk’s service ability.

双侧检验时，在0.05显著

In the two-side test, the null hypothesis is not

① “3σ”原则：将距离均值3倍标准差以外的样本数据作为异常值。异常值的常用处理方法：删除含有异常值的记录；用平均值来修正；将异常值视为缺失值，使用缺失值处理方法处理等。

性水平下仍然不拒绝原假设，表明培训没有带来显著效果。

rejected at the significance level of 0.05, which indicates that the training does not improve the service ability.

可以明显看出，减少异常值的影响之后，对检验的结果产生了巨大的影响。虽然双侧检验的检验结果不变，但根据 *p-value*，当显著性水平 $\alpha \geqslant 0.0529$ 时，双侧检验也可以拒绝原假设。由此可以看出，异常值对假设检验的结果有着巨大的影响。在进行假设检验时，非常有必要对样本数据的异常值进行处理。

In view of which, the result can change dramatically after the impact of the outlier is reduced. According to the *p-value*, the null hypothesis could be rejected in the two-side test when the significance level is $\alpha \geqslant 0.0529$, even although its result remains the same. Obviously, outliers can have a significant impact on the test result. In the hypothesis testing, therefore, it is necessary to handle the outliers of the sample data.

② “零值”的处理

② Processing of “zero”

本案例为培训前后员工抱怨数量减少情况，那么选取的样本范围应该为“存在抱怨的员工群体”，而第四个样本 R.K.培训之前就不存在抱怨情况（抱怨为 0），所以这是一个“零值”数据，可以尝试删除该数据（见表 5.2）。

This case is intended to show the differences of the salesclerk’s customer complaints before and after the training, which the sample should range over. Actually, the forth sample, R.K, does not receive any complaint before the training; it is a “zero” data, which should be deleted.

Table 5.2 The Result of Tests after “Zero-Value” Is Removed

表 5.2 删除“零值”后的检验结果

		Outliers not Handled（不处理异常值）	Outliers Handled（处理异常值）
Data（数据）		(−2, −14, −1, −4)	(−2, −5.25, −1,−4)
Shapiro-Wilk normality test（正态性检验）	W-statistic（W 统计量）	0.804 5	0.958 2
	p-value	0.110 5	0.767 8
t-statistic（*t* 检验统计量）		−1.76	−3.19
p-value（*P* 值）	Two-side test（双侧检验）	0.176 6	0.049 6
	One-side test（单侧检验）	0.083 3	0.024 8

删除“零值”数据后重新进

A normality test is taken after the “zero” data

行正态性检验，在 0.05 显著性水平下认为服从正态分布。进行 t 检验，根据 *p-value* 得到：在 0.05 显著性水平下，双侧检验和单侧检验均无法拒绝原假设。结论与原结论相同，并且 *p-value* 与原假设检验的差别不大，说明删除该"零值"对检验结果影响不大。

are deleted, the result of which shows that the data are normally distributed at the significance level of 0.05. After the t test, one-side test and two-side test both couldn't reject the null hypothesis at the significance level of 0.05 based on the *p-value*, which is the same as the previous result. Additionally, not much difference is observed between the *p-value* of each test, which suggests that the "zero" has a weak impact on the test result.

（5）生成其他指标

(5) New indicator generation

本案例的目标是检验培训会不会降低客户对店员的抱怨，即培训有没有效果。以上检验选取的指标是店员在培训前后被顾客抱怨次数的差，接下来尝试将每个店员的客户抱怨数降低率 r 作为指标，查看检验是否仍然可行。假如培训没有效果的话，该比例 r 应当是0，由此建立假设检验：

This case aims to check whether the training works. The chosen indicator is the differences of the customer complaints before and after the training, thus having a new indicator to show the reduction ration r of each salesclerk's customer complaints. If the training has no effect, the ratio should be zero. Accordingly, a new hypothesis test is taken:

双侧检验：$H_0: r=0$ vs $H_1: r\neq 0$

单侧检验：$H_0: r=0$ vs $H_1: r>0$

Two-side test: $H_0: r=0$ vs $H_1: r\neq 0$

One-side test: $H_0: r=0$ vs $H_1: r>0$

再次针对是否删除"零值"数据分别进行假设检验，如表 5.3 所示，得出结论如下。

Another hypothesis test is taken after deleting the "zero" data. The results of both are as follows:

Table 5.3 Complaint Reduction Rate of the Customers

表 5.3 客户抱怨数降低率

Salesclerk（店员）	Number of Complaints（抱怨数）		Difference（差值）	Complaint Reduction Rate（抱怨数降低率 r）	
	Before（培训前）	After（培训后）		"Zero-Value" not Removed（不删除"零值"）	"Zero-Value" Removed（删除"零值"）
C.B.	6	4	−2	0.333	0.333
T.F.	20	6	−14	0.700	0.700
M.H.	3	2	−1	0.333	0.333
R.K.	0	0	0	0.000	—
M.O.	4	0	−4	1.000 0	1.000 0

在不删除“零值”数据R.K.(0)的情况下，进行 t 检验：

Before deleting the “zero” data R.K.(0), a t test is taken as follows:

$$t_{stat} = \frac{\bar{r} - 0}{S_D / \sqrt{n}} = 2.75$$

双侧检验：

Two-side test:

$$p\text{-}value = 2 \cdot P(|t_{stat}| > t(n-1)) = 0.0513$$

单侧检验：

One-side test:

$$p\text{-}value = P(t_{stat} > t(n-1)) = 0.0257$$

所以在0.05显著性水平下，双侧检验不拒绝原假设，认为客户抱怨降低率为0，即培训没有给店员带来显著变化；单侧检验拒绝原假设，认为客户抱怨降低率大于0，培训给店员服务带来了提高。

Thus at the significance level of 0.05, two-side test doesn’t reject the null hypothesis, which suggests that the reduction ratio is zero; to put the point another way, the training has little impact on the salesclerk. However, one-side test indicates that reduction ratio is greater than 0, which suggests that the training does have an impact on the salesclerk.

在删除“零值”数据后，进行 t 检验：

After deleting the “zero” data, another t test is taken as follows:

$$t_{stat} = \frac{\bar{r} - 0}{S_D / \sqrt{n}} = 3.67$$

双侧检验：

Two-side test:

$$p\text{-}value = 2 \cdot P(|t_{stat}| > t(n-1)) = 0.0350$$

单侧检验：

One-side test:

$$p\text{-}value = P(t_{stat} > t(n-1)) = 0.0175$$

所以在0.05显著性水平下，双侧检验和单侧检验都拒绝原假设，分别表明客户抱怨数降低率不为0以及客户抱怨数降低率大于0。

Thus at the significance level of 0.05, both the two-side test and one-side test reject the null hypothesis, the former suggesting that the reduction rate is not zero, and the latter suggesting that the reduction rate is greater than zero.

可以发现，使用客户抱怨数降低率作为指标进行检验时，删除“零值”之后检验的结果发生了巨大的变化。这说明对于同一个问题，使用不同的指标进行假

It is obvious that deleting the “zero” data can have a great influence on the result of the test when the reduction rate is selected as an indicator. This suggests that the impacts of “zero” data can be different when a different indicator is applied to a hypothesis test.

设检验，“零值”的影响大小也不一样，应当在检验中合理地处理“零值”。

（6）案例分析总结

本案例中讨论了当初步的假设检验不符合预期时，如何改进假设检验的几种情况。首先，从表 5.4 中可以看出，无论对数据如何处理以及选取何种检验形式，当显著性水平取 0.01 时就无法拒绝原假设，这很大程度上是因为本案例的样本量太小。其次，在选取抱怨次数的差作为指标时，对异常值的处理对检验结果的影响极大，而删除“零值”对检验结果影响很小；在选取抱怨数降低率作为指标时，删除“零值”又对检验结果具有较大影响。所以，在进行假设检验时，应该注意对数据的异常值和“零值”做合适的处理。

Therefore, it is important that “Zero” data be used appropriately with different indicators.

(6) Summary of hypothesis test results

In this case, we explore how to improve the hypothesis test when the initial hypothesis test does not meet the expectation. As shown in the summary, the null hypothesis is not rejected when the significance level is 0.01, no matter how we deal with the data and how we choose the test form. Behind this the most probable reason is the small sample size of the test. Moreover, the handling of the outliers can have a great influence on the test results when the difference of customer complaints is selected as an indicator, while deleting the “zero” data can hardly impact the test result. When the reduction ratio is selected as an indicator, deleting the “zero” data can impact the result significantly. Thus, it is necessary that we handle the outliers and the “zero” data when conducting a hypothesis test.

Table 5.4 Summary of Hypothesis Test Results

表 5.4 假设检验结果汇总表

Indicator（指标）	Outliers Handled（异常值处理）	Deleting Zero（删除“零值”）	Test Form/Significance level（检验的形式/显著性水平）			
			Two-side（双侧）/0.01	One-side（单侧）/0.01	Two-side（双侧）/0.05	One-side（单侧）/0.05
Number of complaints（抱怨次数差）	No	Yes	×	×	×	×
	Yes	No	×	×	×	√
	No	Yes	×	×	×	×
	Yes	Yes	×	×	√	√
Reduction ratio r（抱怨数降低率 r）	—	No	×	×	×	√
	—	Yes	×	×	√	√

Appendix 5.1 Paired-wise Data Test Using R

附录 5.1 成对数据检验

There are two steps required to perform paired-wise data test in R. First, import raw data, and calculate the difference of the paired-wise data. Next, Perform a two-sided t-test on the processed data. If there are outliers or "zero value" in this data set, perform another two-sided test after dealing with these problems.

在 R 语言中进行成对数据假设检验需要两个步骤。首先导入数据，计算对应数据的差值。其次，对处理后的数据进行双侧 *t* 检验。如果数据存在异常值以及零值问题，使用处理这些问题后的数据再次进行双侧 *t* 检验。

1. 代码

```
#录入原始数据
a <- c(6, 20, 3, 0, 4)
b <- c(4, 6, 2, 0, 0)

#案例基本分析
#步骤一：计算各店员培训前后得到抱怨数的差值
d <- b-a
#步骤二：进行双侧 t 检验
t.test(d, alternative = "two.sided", mu = 0)

#案例深度分析
#W 检验（Shapiro-Wilk 检验）：
shapiro.test(d)
t.test(d, alternative = "less", mu = 0)

#异常值处理后
d1 <- c(-2,-4.2,-1,0,-4)
shapiro.test(d1)
t.test(d1, alternative = "two.sided", mu = 0)
t.test(d1, alternative = "less", mu = 0)

#“零值”处理后
d2 <- c(-2,-14,-1,-4)                                  #未进行异常值处理的数据
shapiro.test(d2)
t.test(d2, alternative = "two.sided", mu = 0)
t.test(d2, alternative = "less", mu = 0)
d3 <- c(-2,-5.25,-1,-4)                                #进行异常值处理后的数据
shapiro.test(d3)
```

```
t.test(d3, alternative = "two.sided", mu = 0)
t.test(d3, alternative = "less", mu = 0)

#生成其他指标
r1 <- c(1/3, 0.7, 1/3, 0, 1)                              #未删除“零值”的数据
shapiro.test(r1)
t.test(r1, alternative = "two.sided", mu = 0)
t.test(r1, alternative = "greater", mu = 0)
r2 <- c(1/3, 0.7, 1/3, 1)                                 #删除“零值”后的数据
shapiro.test(r2)
t.test(r2, alternative = "two.sided", mu = 0)
t.test(r2, alternative = "greater", mu = 0)
```

2. 具体过程分析

步骤 1：录入数据，计算两列抱怨数据的差值。

步骤 2：利用 R 内置的 t.test()函数进行双侧 t 检验。在得到检验结果后，利用 W 检验检验数据是否服从正态分布。之后检查并处理异常值与零值，再次利用 R 内置的 t.test()函数进行双侧 t 检验。

3. *函数参数说明

```
t.test(data, alternative = "two.sided", mu=0)
```

☑ data：表示进行单样本 t 检验的数据。

☑ alternative：控制备择假设是左侧/双侧/右侧。

☑ mu：表示原假设中的均值。

4. 分析结果举例（见图 5.3～图 5.5）

```
> t.test(d, alternative = "two.sided", mu = 0)

        One Sample t-test

data:  d
t = -1.655, df = 4, p-value = 0.1733
alternative hypothesis: true mean is not equal to 0
95 percent confidence interval:
 -11.245828   2.845828
sample estimates:
mean of x
    -4.2
```

Figure 5.3　Outcomes of T-test

图 5.3　t 检验结果-1

p-value = 0.173 3 > 0.05，故在 0.05 显著性水平下不拒绝原假设。

p-value = 0.035 0 < 0.05，故在 0.05 显著性水平下拒绝原假设。

p-value = 0.056 1，故在 0.05 显著性水平下不拒绝原假设，在 0.1 显著性水平下拒绝原假设。

```
> t.test(r2, alternative = "two.sided", mu = 0)

        One Sample t-test

data:  r2
t = 3.6697, df = 3, p-value = 0.03501
alternative hypothesis: true mean is not equal to 0
95 percent confidence interval:
 0.07855831 1.10477503
sample estimates:
mean of x
0.5916667
```

Figure 5.4 Outcomes of *T*-test

图 5.4 *t* 检验结果-2

```
> shapiro.test(d)

        Shapiro-Wilk normality test

data:  d
W = 0.78091, p-value = 0.05612
```

Figure 5.5 Outcomes of *T*-test

图 5.5 *t* 检验结果-3

Appendix 5.2 Formulas and Notes

附录 5.2 关键公式与注解

Shapiro-Wilk 检验（Shapiro-Wilk Test），简称 W 检验，由夏皮诺（Shapiro）和威尔克（Wilk）在 1905 年提出，通常被用于小样本时的正态性检验。

设 $x_1, x_2, \cdots, x_n$ 是样本数据，$x_{(1)} \leqslant x_{(2)} \leqslant \cdots \leqslant x_{(n)}$ 为其次序统计量，对于假设检验：

H_0：总体服从正态分布。

H_1：总体不服从正态分布。

W 统计量定义为

$$W = \frac{\left(\sum_{i=1}^{n} a_i x_{(i)}\right)^2}{\sum_{i=1}^{n}(x_{(i)} - \overline{x})^2}$$

其中，系数 $a_1, a_2, \cdots a_n$ 在样本容量为 n 时有特定的值，可以通过查表得到。检验的拒绝域有形式 $\{W \leqslant W_\alpha\}$，其中 α 分位数 W_α 可以通过查表得到。也可通过编程直接得到检验的 p 值，由此判断是否拒绝原假设。

Chapter 6

Analysis of Variance

第6章 方差分析

In practice, several population means are often analyzed to discover the differences between them and the reasons that cause those differences. The analysis of variance is a hypothesis test that simultaneously handles several population means. It compares the systematic error with the random error among sample observations in order to determine whether there are big differences among those populations. In this chapter we mainly describe the single factor analysis of variance.

在实际生活中，我们往往需要对多个总体的均值进行比较研究，分析它们之间的差异和引起差异的原因。方差分析（ANOVA）是一种假设检验，将同时处理若干个总体均值，对某种因素下各组样本观察值之间可能存在的系统性误差与随机误差进行比较，以此推断各总体间是否存在显著性差异。本章主要介绍单因素方差分析。

Case Bell Grove Medical Center

案例 医疗中心患者流量分析

1. 案例介绍

Gene Dempsey 负责管理Bell Grove 医疗中心的急救中心。她的职责之一是安排足够的护士人手，以便对接踵而来的患者及时处理伤势。即便不是致命伤，病人在长时间的等待中也会很紧张。Dempsey 女士收集了近几个星期以来患者的数量信息（见表 6.1），想从中获取有用的信息。急救中心周末不开放。

1. Introduction[①]

Ms. Gene Dempsey manages the emergency care center at Bell Grove Medical Center. One of her responsibilities is to have enough nurses so that incoming patients needing treatment can be seen promptly. It is stressful for patients to wait a long time for emergency care, even when their care needs are not life-threatening. Ms. Dempsey has observed the number of patients over the last several weeks in order to discover useful information. The center is not open on weekends.

Table 6.1 Data for Bell Grove Medical Center

表 6.1 Bell Grove 医疗中心数据

Date（日期）	Day（工作日）	Patients（患者数量）	Date（日期）	Day（工作日）	Patients（患者数量）
9-29-06	Monday	38	10-13-06	Monday	37
9-30-06	Tuesday	28	10-14-06	Tuesday	29
10-1-06	Wednesday	28	10-15-06	Wednesday	27
10-2-06	Thursday	30	10-16-06	Thursday	28
10-3-06	Friday	35	10-17-06	Friday	35
10-6-06	Monday	35	10-20-06	Monday	37
10-7-06	Tuesday	25	10-21-06	Tuesday	26
10-8-06	Wednesday	22	10-22-06	Wednesday	28
10-9-06	Thursday	21	10-23-06	Thursday	23
10-10-06	Friday	32	10-24-06	Friday	33

这个案例中，我们主要使用方差分析的方法来分析 Bell Grove 医疗中心的数据，以帮助急救中心找出最繁忙的时间段。

In this case, analysis of variance will be used to analyze the Bell Grove Medical Center data in order to help the medical emergency center to identify the busiest days.

方差分析（ANOVA）是将

Analysis of variance (ANOVA) is the simultaneous

① Lind, Marchal, Wathen. Statistical techniques in business and economics[M]. New York: McGraw-Hill Irwin, 2010.

若干个总体均值同时比较的分析方法。涉及的统计量概率分布是 F 分布，使用的总体需假设服从正态分布。ANOVA 在处理回归分析的结果中起到相当重要的作用。

comparison of several population means. The probability distribution used here is the F-distribution. The populations studied with this method must follow a normal distribution. ANOVA is of considerable importance in analyzing the results of regression analysis.

2. 分析步骤

2. Analytical Procedures

步骤 1：使用所给数据进行方差分析，构造所用的假设检验。在一周不同的日子里，前来就诊的患者数量是否有差异？

Step 1: Use analysis of variance on the data set. State the hypothesis being tested. Does it appear that there are any differences in the numbers of patients treated by the day of the week?

步骤 2：如果有差异，那么，哪些日子更为忙碌呢？

Step 2: If there are differences, which days seem to be the busiest?

步骤 3：对本次研究做进一步分析。

Step 3: Discuss extensions of this study.

以上三个步骤具体实施过程如下。

步骤 1：使用所给数据（见表 6.2）进行方差分析，构造所用的假设检验。在一周不同的日子里，前来就诊的患者数量是否有差异？

Use analysis of variance on the data set. State the hypothesis being tested. Does it appear that there are any differences in the numbers of patients treated by the day of the week?

Table 6.2 Rearranged Data

表 6.2 重组后的数据

Monday（周一）	Tuesday（周二）	Wednesday（周三）	Thursday（周四）	Friday（周五）
38	28	28	30	35
35	25	22	21	32
37	29	27	28	35
37	26	28	23	33

现用五个步骤进行假设检验。

Use the five-step hypothesis testing procedure.

第一步：建立原假设和备择假设。

Step 1: State the null hypothesis and the alternate hypothesis.

原假设为每个工作日来医疗中心就诊的患者人数的均值

The null hypothesis is that the means are the same for all the days of the week.

相同。

$$H_0: \mu_1 = \mu_2 = \mu_3 = \mu_4 = \mu_5$$

备择假设为至少有两个工作日的患者人数的均值不同。

The alternate hypothesis is that at least two of the means are different.

H_1: The means are not all equal.

第二步：选择显著性水平。

Step 2: Select the level of significance.

一般情况下选 0.05 作为显著性水平。

We select the 0.05 significance level as it is the most common level in many situations.

第三步：确定检验统计量。

Step 3: Determine the test statistic.

本案例中，检验统计量服从 F 分布。图 6.1 即为 F 分布。分子自由度为 4，分母自由度为 15。

The test statistic follows the F-distribution. Here is a graph of the F-distribution. The degree of freedom in the numerator is 4, and the degree of freedom in the denominator is 15.

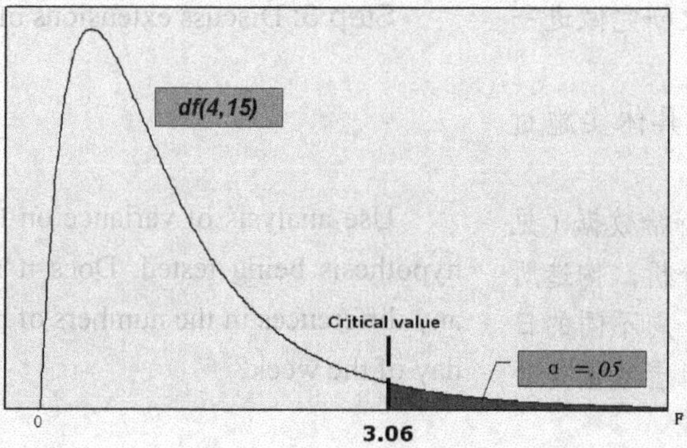

Figure 6.1　F-Distribution

图 6.1　F 分布

第四步：确定检验规则。

Step 4: Formulate the decision rule.

如图 6.1 所示，临界值为 3.06，也就是说，如果 F 统计量的值超过 3.06，就拒绝原假设。

According to the graph above, the critical value is 3.06, which means H_0 will be rejected if the computed F exceeds 3.06.

第五步：根据方差分析表所得结果做出决定。

Step 5: Use an ANOVA table to make a decision.

根据计算，F 值为 15.54，比临界值 3.06 大，因此我们拒绝原假设。

The computed value of F is 15.54, which is greater than the critical value of 3.06, so the null hypothesis is rejected.

表 6.3 的结果显示，不同工作日前来就诊的患者人数是有差别的。

According to Table 6.3, there is a difference in the number of patients treated according to the day of the week.

Table 6.3 Outcomes of ANOVA

表 6.3 方差分析结果

Source of Variation（方差来源）	Sum of Squares（平方和）	Degrees of Freedom（自由度）	Mean Square（均方）	*F*（*F* 值）
Treatments（因素）	411.3	4	102.83	15.54
Error（误差）	99.25	15	6.62	
Total（总和）	510.55	19		

步骤 2：如果有差异，那么，哪些日子显得比较忙碌呢？

我们通过构造置信区间来分析这个问题。

根据表 6.4 和表 6.5，周二、周三和周四之间有重合部分，而周二、周三、周四和周一、周五这两组之间并无重合部分。周二、周三、周四的均值之间没有明显差异，而周一与周五的均值均大于其他三个工作日。因此，可以说周一和周五最为忙碌。

2. If there are differences, which days seem to be the busiest?

The method of analyzing confidence intervals is used to solve this problem.

According to Table 6.4,Table 6.5, there are overlaps between Tuesday, Wednesday, and Thursday, and there is no common area between the group (Tuesday, Wednesday, Thursday) and the group (Monday, Friday). Although there does not seem to be much difference between the means on Tuesday, Wednesday, and Thursday, the fact is that the means on Monday and Friday are larger. As a result, Monday and Friday seem to be busiest.

Table 6.4 Outcomes of Confidence Interval

表 6.4 置信区间结果

	Upper 95%（95%置信下限）	Lower 95%（95%置信上限）
Monday	33.947 81	39.552 19
Tuesday	24.197 81	29.802 19
Wednesday	23.447 81	29.052 19
Thursday	22.697 81	28.302 19
Friday	30.947 81	36.552 19

Table 6.5 Outcomes of Confidence Interval

表 6.5 置信区间结果示意

	N（样本个数）	Mean（样本均值）	Standard Deviation（样本标准差）	----+---------+---------+---------+-----
Monday	4	36.750	1.258	(-----*----)
Tuesday	4	27.000	1.826	(----*----)
Wednesday	4	26.250	2.872	(-----*----)

续表

	N（样本个数）	Mean（样本均值）	Standard Deviation（样本标准差）	----+---------+---------+---------+-----
Thursday	4	25.500	4.203	(----*----)
Friday	4	33.750	1.500	(-----*----)
				----+---------+---------+---------+----- 25.0 30.0 35.0 40.0

步骤3：对本次研究做进一步分析。

3. Discuss extensions of this study.

为了证实以上结论，我们对数据分组，进行方差分析。

Additional ANOVA may be carried out to verify the conclusions to the problems above.

首先，分析周二至周四的数据（见表 6.6），并对它们进行计算。

First, an analysis of the data for Tuesday, Wednesday, and Thursday is computed.

Table 6.6 Rearranged Data for Three Days

表 6.6 三天数据

Tuesday	Wednesday	Thursday
28	28	30
25	22	21
29	27	28
26	28	23

如表 6.7 所示，F 值为 0.23，小于临界值 4.26，因此不能拒绝原假设，说明周二、周三和周四这三个工作日的均值没有明显差异。

The computed value of F is 0.23, which is smaller than the critical value of 4.26, so the null hypothesis is not rejected, which means there is no significant difference among the means for Tuesday, Wednesday, and Thursday.

Table 6.7 Outcomes of ANOVA

表 6.7 三天方差分析结果

Source of Variation（方差来源）	Sum of Squares（平方和）	Degrees of Freedom（自由度）	Mean Square（均方）	F（F 值）
Treatments（因素）	4.5	2	2.25	0.23
Error（误差）	87.75	9	9.75	
Total（总和）	92.25	11		

加入周五的数据（见表 6.8）

The same analysis is performed when the data for

进行类似分析。如表6.9所示，F值为7.33，大于临界值3.49，因此拒绝原假设，说明在周二、周三、周四和周五中至少有两天的均值有显著差异。

Monday or Friday are added. When Friday is added, the computed value of F is 7.33, which is larger than the critical value of 3.49, so the null hypothesis is rejected, which means there is a significant difference among the means for Tuesday, Wednesday, Thursday, and Friday.

Table 6.8 Rearranged Data for Four Days

表6.8 四天数据

Tuesday	Wednesday	Thursday	Friday
28	28	30	35
25	22	21	32
29	27	28	35
26	28	23	33

Table 6.9 Outcomes of ANOVA

表6.9 四天方差分析结果

Source of Variation（方差来源）	Sum of Squares（平方和）	Degrees of Freedom（自由度）	Mean Square（均方）	F（F值）
Treatments（因素）	173.25	3	57.75	7.33
Error（误差）	94.5	12	7.88	
Total（总和）	267.75	15		

加入周一的数据（见表6.10）进行类似分析，如表6.11所示，F值为14.50，也大于临界值3.49，因此拒绝原假设，说明在周一、周二、周三和周四这四天中至少有两天的均值有显著差异。

When the data for Monday is added, the computed value of F is 14.50, which is also larger than the critical value of 3.49. Again the null hypothesis is rejected, which means there is a significant difference among the means for Monday, Tuesday, Wednesday, and Thursday.

Table 6.10 Rearranged Data for Four Days

表6.10 加入周一的四天数据

Monday	Tuesday	Wednesday	Thursday
38	28	28	30
35	25	22	21
37	29	27	28
37	26	28	23

Table 6.11 Outcomes of ANOVA

表6.11 加入周一的四天方差分析结果

Source of Variation（方差来源）	Sum of Squares（平方和）	Degrees of Freedom（自由度）	Mean Square（均方）	*F*（*F*值）
Treatments（因素）	335.25	3	111.75	14.45
Error（误差）	92.5	12	7.71	
Total（总和）	427.75	15		

方差分析显示一旦加入周一或周五的数据，均值就会有明显差异。这个结果证实了我们前一步的结论，周一和周五前来急救中心就诊的患者比较多。

Both ANOVA tables show that the means are not all equal once the data for Monday or Friday are added to the analysis. The results verify our previous conclusion that more patients visit the medical center on Mondays and Fridays.

因此，我们可以以95%的概率认为一周之内，不同工作日就诊的患者人数是有差异的，其中差异主要来自周一和周五。造成这种情况的原因之一可能是医疗中心周六和周日不接待患者。

In conclusion, we are 95% confident that there is a difference in the number of patients treated according to the day of the week. Furthermore, Monday and Friday are the source of difference. One of the reasons might be because the center is not open on weekends.

建议 Bell Grove 医疗中心在周一和周五加派护士人手，以适应患者的需要，使进入急救中心的患者可以及时得到救治。

We recommend that Bell Grove Medical Center should arrange for additional nurses on these two days to meet the needs of patients, so that incoming patients can be handled promptly.

Appendix 6.1 Analysis of Variance with Excel

附录6.1 用Excel进行方差分析

在初始Excel表格中，患者人数在A～E列。我们运用以下步骤来进行单因素方差分析。

The data about Bell Grove Medical Center are in an Excel worksheet. The following steps can be used to obtain the ANOVA table for single-factor observational studies.

步骤1：选择菜单栏中的“工具”。

Step 1: Select the **Tools** menu.

步骤2：选择“数据分析”。

Step 2: Choose **Data Analysis**.

步骤3：选择分析工具中的

Step 3: Choose **ANOVA: Single-Factor** from the

“方差分析：单因素方差分析”（见图 6.2），单击“确定”。

list of Analysis Tools and click **OK**.

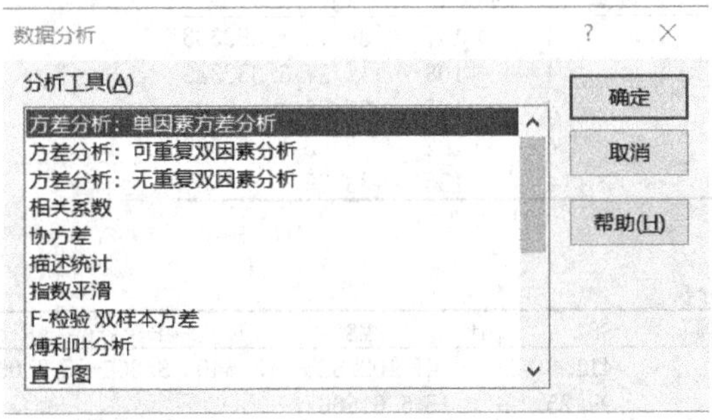

Figure 6.2　ANOVA from the List of Analysis Tools

图 6.2　数据分析中的方差分析选项

步骤 4：当对话框打开时，如图 6.3 所示，在“**输入区域**”中选择 A2 至 E5，分组方式选择“**列**”，选中“**标志位于第一行**”，“**输出区域**”选择 A7，单击“**确定**”。

Step 4: When the ANOVA: Single-Factor dialog box appears, enter A2:E5 in the **Input Range** box.

Select **Columns**.

Select **Labels in First Row**.

Select **Output Range** box and enter A7 in the box.

Click **OK**.

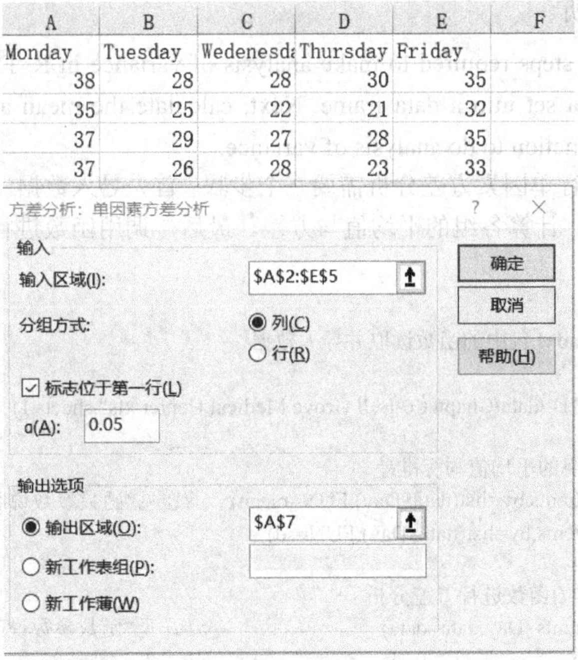

Figure 6.3　ANOVA from the List of Analysis Tools

图 6.3　方差分析对话框

方差分析结果如图 6.4 所示。

方差分析：单因素方差分析						
SUMMARY						
组	观测数	求和	平均	方差		
列 1	4	147	36.75	1.583333		
列 2	4	108	27	3.333333		
列 3	4	105	26.25	8.25		
列 4	4	102	25.5	17.66667		
列 5	4	135	33.75	2.25		
方差分析						
差异源	SS	df	MS	F	P-value	F crit
组间	411.3	4	102.825	15.5403	3.26E-05	3.055568
组内	99.25	15	6.616667			
总计	510.55	19				

Figure 6.4 Outcomes of ANOVA

图 6.4 方差分析结果

Appendix 6.2 Analysis of Variance with R

附录 6.2 用 R 语言代码进行方差分析

单因素方差分析

There are there steps required to make analysis of variance in R. First, import data and turn the original data set into a data frame. Next, calculate the mean and variance of each group. At last, use function to do analysis of variance.

在 R 语言中进行单因素方差分析需要三个步骤。首先导入数据，将原始数据集转为数据框模式。其次，计算各组的平均值与方差。最后，调用函数进行单因素方差分析。

1. 代码

```
#步骤一：利用 readxl 包中的函数读取并导入数据
library(readxl)
data <- read_excel("D:/data/Chapter 6-Bell Grove Medical Center.xls",sheet=1)

#步骤二：计算各组的平均值与标准差
aggregate(data$Patients,by=list(data$Day),FUN=mean)      #详见*函数参数说明
aggregate(data$Patients,by=list(data$Day),FUN=sd)

#步骤三：利用 aov()函数进行方差分析
score_lm<-aov(Patients~Day,data=data)                    #详见*函数参数说明
summary(score_lm)
```

2. 具体过程分析

步骤 1：为读取文件后缀为.xls 中的数据，需要安装并调用 xlsx 程序包。

步骤2：利用R内置的aggregate()函数计算各组的均值与标准差。

步骤3：利用R内置的aov()函数进行方差分析。

3. *函数参数说明

```
aggregate(data$Patients,by=list(data$Day),FUN=mean)
```

☑ data$Patients：指data数据框中Patients那一列的数据。

☑ by=list(data$Day)：在aggregate函数中依据Day列的值进行分组。

☑ FUN=mean：表示计算均值，若为sd则为计算标准差。

```
score_lm<-aov(Patients~Day,data=data)
```

☑ Patients~Day：指Patients按照因子Day对应因素水平的取值

4. 分析结果

将R语言输出结果进行整理，具体结果如表6.12和表6.13所示。

Table 6.12 Mean and Standard Deviation

表6.12 原始数据的均值标准差

组	观测数	平均值	标准差
Monday	4	36.75	1.26
Tuesday	4	27.00	1.82
Wednesday	4	26.25	2.87
Thursday	4	25.50	4.20
Friday	4	33.75	1.50

Table 6.13 Outcomes of ANOVA

表6.13 方差分析结果

差异源	SS	df	MS	F	P-value
组间	411.3	4	102.82	15.54	3.26e-05
组内	99.2	15	6.62		

Appendix 6.3 Formulas and Notes

附录6.3 关键公式与注解

1. 方差分析

通过检验各总体的均值是否相等来判断分类型自变量对数值型因变量是否有显著影响。在方差分析中，所要检验的对象称为因素或因子。因素的不同表现称为水平或处理。每个因子水平下得到的样本数据称为观测值。

2．组内误差与组件误差

组内误差是来自水平内部的数据误差。它反映一个样本内部数据的离散程度，只含有随机误差。

组间误差是来自不同水平之间的数据误差，组间误差是随机误差和系统误差的总和，反映不同样本之间数据的离散程度。

3．总平方和（*SST*）、组内平方和（*SSE*）、组间平方和（*SSR*）

总平方和是反映全部数据误差大小的平方和，它反映全部观测值的离散状况。

组内平方和是反映组内误差大小的平方和，它反映每个样本内各观测值的总离散情况。

组间平方和是反映组间误差大小的平方和，它反映样本均值之间的差异程度。

4．方差分析的三个基本假定

（1）每个总体都应服从正态分布。

（2）每个总体的方差 σ^2 都相同。

（3）观测值是独立的。

5．方差分析中假设检验的一般提法

设因素有 k 个水平，每个水平的均值分别用 $\mu_1,\mu_2,\cdots,\mu_k$ 表示，要检验 k 个水平的均值是否相等，需要提出如下假设：

$$H_0:\mu_1=\mu_2=\cdots=\mu_k$$

（自变量对因变量没有显著影响）

$$H_1:\mu_1,\mu_2,\cdots,\mu_k \text{ 不全相等}$$

（自变量对因变量有显著影响）

Chapter 7

Simple Linear Regression

第 7 章　一元线性回归

Simple linear regression analysis is a regression analysis of the relationship between two variables, involving one independent variable and one dependent variable. The relationship between the variables is approximated by a straight line. We can develop a mathematical equation to estimate the value of one variable based on the known value of another by regression analysis. When researching the practical problems, we usually need to find the relationship of a phenomenon and the important factor by simple linear regression.

一元线性回归是对两个变量间线性关系的一种回归分析，其中一个是自变量，另一个是因变量，这两个变量的关系在坐标平面上几乎呈一条直线的趋势。通过回归分析可以得到一个模型表达式，使用该等式，在其中一变量已知时可以估计另一变量的值。在研究实际问题时，我们经常需要研究某一现象与影响它的某一重要因素之间的关系，这就需要用到一元线性回归。

Case Alumni Donation

案例 校友捐赠额影响因素分析

1. 案例介绍

校友捐赠是大学重要的收入来源。如果管理者能够判定出影响校友捐赠率增长的因素，那么他们就能采取一些相应措施来增加学校收入。调查研究表明，那些更满意与老师沟通交流的学生更容易毕业。所以，可以得出一个结论：更小的班级和更低的师生比率会带来更高的毕业生满意度，随之也可能带来更高的校友捐赠率。表 7.1 给出了 48 所国立大学的数据（《美国最好的大学》，2000 年版）。“% of class under 20”列显示的是少于 20 个学生的班级占全校班级的百分比。“Student/Faculty Ratio”列显示的是学生数量与老师数量的比率，即生师比。最后，“Alumni Giving Rate”列是捐赠的校友的百分比。

1. Introduction①

Alumni donation is important source of revenue for colleges and universities. If administrators could determine the factors that influence increases in the percentage of alumni who make a donation, they might be able to implement policies that could lead to increased revenues. Research shows that students who are satisfied with their contact with teachers are more likely to graduate. As a result, one might suspect that smaller class sizes and lower student-faculty ratios might lead to a higher percentage of satisfied graduates, which in turn might lead to increases in the percentage of alumni who make a donation. Table 7.1 shows data for 48 national universities (*America's Best Colleges*, Year 2000 Edition). The column labeled "Student/Faculty Ratio" is the number of students enrolled divided by the total number of faculty. Finally, the column labeled "Alumni Giving Rate" shows the percentage rate of alumni that made a donation to the university.

Table 7.1 Data for 48 National Universities

表 7.1 美国国立大学的相关数据

School（大学名称）	% of Classes Under 20（小班占比）	Student/Faculty Ratio(%)（生师比）	Alumni Giving Rate(%)（校友捐赠率）
Boston College 波士顿大学	39	13	25
Brandeis University 布兰代斯大学	68	8	33
Brown University 布朗大学	60	8	40

① David R. Anderson, Dennis J. Sweeney, Thomas A. Williams, et al. Statistics for business and economics[M]. Boston: Cengage Learning, 2005.

续表

School （大学名称）	% of Classes Under 20 （小班占比）	Student/Faculty Ratio(%) （生师比）	Alumni Giving Rate(%) （校友捐赠率）
California Inst. of Technology 加州理工学院	65	3	46
Carnegie Mellon University 卡内基·梅隆大学	67	10	28
Case Western Reserve University. 凯斯西储大学	52	8	31
College of William and Mary 威廉玛丽大学	45	12	27
Columbia University 哥伦比亚大学	69	7	31
Cornell University 康奈尔大学	72	13	35
Dartmouth College 达特茅斯大学	61	10	53
Emory University 埃默里大学	65	7	37
Duke University 杜克大学	68	8	45
Georgetown University 乔治城大学	54	10	29
Harvard University 哈佛大学	73	8	46
John Hopkins University 约翰斯·霍普金斯大学	64	9	27
Lehigh University 利哈伊大学	55	11	40
Massachusetts Inst. of Technology 麻省理工学院	65	6	44
New York University 纽约大学	63	13	13
Northwestern University 西北大学	66	8	30
Pennsylvania State University. 宾夕法尼亚州立大学	32	19	21
Princeton University 普林斯顿大学	68	5	67
Rice University 莱斯大学	62	8	40

续表

School （大学名称）	% of Classes Under 20 （小班占比）	Student/Faculty Ratio(%) （生师比）	Alumni Giving Rate(%) （校友捐赠率）
Stanford University 斯坦福大学	69	7	34
Tufts University 塔夫茨大学	67	9	29
Tulane University 杜兰大学	56	12	17
U. of California – Berkeley 加州伯克利大学	58	17	18
U. of California – Davis 加州戴维斯大学	32	19	7
U. of California – Irvine 加州大学欧文分校	42	20	9
U. of California – Los Angeles 加州大学洛杉矶分校	41	18	13
U. of California – San Diego 加州大学圣地亚哥分校	48	19	8
U. of California – Santa Barbara 加州大学圣巴巴拉分校	45	20	12
U. of Chicago 芝加哥大学	65	4	36
U. of Florida 佛罗里达大学	31	23	19
U. of Illinois – Urbana Champaign 伊利诺伊大学厄巴纳-香槟分校	29	15	23
U. of Michigan – Ann Arbor 密歇根州安阿大学	51	15	13
U. of North Carolina-Chapel Hill 北卡罗来纳大学教堂山分校	40	16	26
U. of Notre Dame 圣母大学	53	13	49
U. of Pennsylvania 宾夕法尼亚大学	65	7	41
U. of Rochester 罗切斯特大学	63	10	23
U. of Southern California 南加州大学	53	13	22
U. of Texas – Austin 得克萨斯大学奥斯汀分校	39	21	13

续表

School（大学名称）	% of Classes Under 20（小班占比）	Student/Faculty Ratio(%)（生师比）	Alumni Giving Rate(%)（校友捐赠率）
U. of Virginia 弗吉尼亚大学	44	13	28
U. of Washington 华盛顿大学	37	12	12
U. of Wisconsin – Madison 威斯康星大学麦迪逊分校	37	13	13
Vanderbilt University 范德比特大学	68	9	31
Wake Forest University 维克森林大学	59	11	38
Washington University – St. Louis 华盛顿大学（圣路易斯）	73	7	33
Yale University 耶鲁大学	77	7	50

一元线性回归是最简单的回归分析。我们可以先进行相关性分析，看这两个变量之间的关系是否紧密，使用一元线性回归模型建模，然后用最小二乘估计方法来估计模型参数，得到估计的回归方程，最后进行 t 检验和 F 检验。若通过检验，则该模型拟合得较好，可以用来表达两变量之间的关系以及实际用来估计和预测。

Simple linear regression is the simplest type of regression. We can first study the correlation between the two variables by correlation between the two variables by correlation analysis to see how strong the relationship between variables is. Then set a linear regression model, estimate the parameters using least squares estimation, and finally, determine whether the equation passes t test and F test[①]. If the equation passes all the tests, the model fits well and therefore, we can use the equation to present the relationship of two variables, estimate and forecast the dependent variables.

2. 案例分析

步骤 1：对所给的数据进行描述统计分析。

步骤 2：根据 20 人班级百分比这一变量值，用回归分析得出可预测校友捐赠率的回归估计方程。

2. Analytical Procedures

Step 1: Develop numerical descriptive summaries of the data.

Step 2: Use regression analysis to develop an estimated regression equation that could be used to predict the alumni giving rate given the percentage of classes with fewer than 20 students.

① t 检验、F 检验详见本章“关键公式与注解”。

步骤3：根据生师比这一变量值，用回归分析得出可预测校友捐赠率的回归估计方程。

Step 3: Use regression analysis to develop an estimated regression equation that could be used to predict the alumni giving rate given the student -faculty ratio.

步骤4：这两个回归方程哪个更合适呢？选出更合适的一个回归方程，对其进行残差分析。

Step 4: Which of the two estimated regression equations provides the best fit? For this estimated regression equation, perform an analysis of the residuals and discuss your findings and conclusions.

步骤5：从这一分析中得出结论和建议。

Step 5: Develop conclusions and recommendations from further analysis.

以上5个步骤具体介绍如下。

Analytical procedures are described in detail as follows.

步骤1：对所给的数据进行统计分析。

Step 1: Develop numerical summaries of the data.

从表 7.2 可以看出，变量“% of classes under 20”的取值极差为 48，方差为 174.1。变量“alumni giving rate”和变量“% of classes under 20”的情况相似，它们和变量“student/faculty ratio”相比，都有着较大的波动性。

We can see from the table 7.2, the range of “% of classes under 20” is 48.0 and the variance is 174.1. The data of “alumni giving rate” shows a similar situation as the “% of classes under 20”. Compared to the variable of student faculty ration, both of them are large which presents a high variability. In terms of student/faculty ratio, the range and the variance are relatively small, which means a lower variability.

所以，变量“student/faculty ratio”的值相对集中，变量“alumni giving rate”和变量“% of classes under 20”的值则比较分散。

Therefore, the data values for “student/faculty ratio” are relatively centralized, while the data values for “% of classes under 20” and “alumni giving” rate are more scattered.

Table 7.2 Outcomes of Descriptive Statistics

表7.2 各变量描述性统计量

Variable（变量）	N（样本数）	Mean（均值）	Sd（标准差）	Median（中位数）
% of Classes Under 20（小班占比）	48	55.73	13.19	59.5
Student/Faculty Ratio（生师比）	48	11.54	4.85	10.5
Alumni Giving Rate（校友捐赠率）	48	29.27	13.44	29.0
% of Classes Under 20（小班占比）	29	77	48	
Student/Faculty Ratio（生师比）	3	23	20	
Alumni Giving Rate（校友捐赠率）	7	67	60	

步骤 2：根据 20 人班级百分比这一变量值，用回归分析得出可预测校友捐赠率的回归估计方程。

我们选择"alumni giving rate"作为因变量 y，"% of classes under 20"作为自变量 x。再将两列数据导入 R 软件中进行一元线性回归，得到如表 7.3～表 7.5 所示结果。

Step 2: Use regression analysis to develop an estimated regression equation that could be used to predict the alumni giving rate given the percentage of classes with fewer than 20 students.

We choose "alumni giving rate" as the dependent variable y, and "% of classes under 20" as the independent variable x. We can input the two columns' data using R, which is a very useful statistical software to do simple linear regression analysis. We obtain the result as follows:

Table 7.3　Model Summary

表 7.3　模型总结

Residual standard error（残差标准差）	10.38	Multiple R-squared（样本决定系数）	0.416 9
Adjusted R-squared（调整后的样本决定系数）	0.404 2		

Table 7.4　Analysis of Variance for Simple Linear Regression

表 7.4　方差分析

Analysis of Variance					
Source（方差来源）	DF（自由度）	Sum of Squares（平方和）	Mean Square（均方）	*F*-statistic（*F* 值）	*p*-value（*p* 值）
Model（回归）	1	3 539.795 9	3 539.795 9	32.88	7.228e-07
Error（剩余）	46	4 951.683 3	107.645 3		
Corrected Total（总和）	47	8 491.479 2			

Table 7.5　Coefficients

表 7.5　系数

Parameter Estimates				
Variable（变量）	Estimate（参数估计）	Std. Error（标准误）	*t* value（*t* 值）	*Pr*(>|*t*|)（*p* 值）
(Intercept)	-7.386 1	6.565 5	-1.125	0.266
% of Classes Under 20（小班占比）	0.657 8	0.114 7	5.734	7.23e-07

从表 7.3 可以看出，R^2 值是

We can see from Table 7.3 that the R Square is

0.416 9，不够大，所以以“% of classes under 20”为自变量、“alumni giving rate”为因变量的一元线性回归模型拟合得不够好。实际上，表 7.4 是一个方差分析表，我们可以根据这个表进行 F 检验。一元线性回归的模型为 $y=\beta_0+\beta_1 x+\varepsilon$，原假设为 $H_0:\beta_1=0$，备择假设为 $H_1:\beta_1\neq 0$，统计量 F 值为 32.88，在 $\alpha=0.05$ 的前提下，F 的临界值 $F_\alpha(1,46)=4.08$，显然，$F>F_{0.05}(1,46)$，所以我们拒绝原假设。

同样的，P 值小于 α，再次证明应该拒绝原假设，该模型通过了 F 检验，说明变量“% of classes”对“alumni giving rate”是有显著影响的。最后，从表 7.5 可得出一元线性回归模型的方程为

y=0.658x−7.386

0.4169, which is not large enough, so the model fit is not good enough. Actually, Table 7.4 is an analysis of variance table by which we can complete F test. The simple linear regression model is $y=\beta_0+\beta_1 x+\varepsilon$. We can have the null hypothesis $H_0:\beta_1=0$, the alternate hypothesis $H_1:\beta_1\neq 0$ The statistic F is 32.88, we refer to the table of F distribution that $F_\alpha(1,46)=4.08$ given $\alpha=0.05$. Apparently, $F>F_{0.05}(1,46)$, so we reject H_0. At the same time, we can obtain the p-value which is less than 0.0001 from the Table 7.4 at the last column. P-value$<\alpha$, we can prove the judgement is right again. So this model has passed F test, showing the impact of x corresponding to y is significant. Finally, we can get the simple linear regression equation: y=0.658x-7.386 from Table 7.5.

步骤 3：根据生师比这一变量值，用回归分析得出可预测校友捐赠率的回归估计方程。

Step 3: Use regression analysis to develop an estimated regression equation that could be used to predict the alumni giving rate given the student -faculty ratio.

我们选择变量“alumni giving rate”作为因变量 y，变量“student-faculty ratio”作为自变量 x。然后将这两个变量的两列数据可以导入 R 中进行回归分析，相应的输出结果如表 7.6～表 7.8 所示。

We choose alumni giving rate as the dependent variable y and student-faculty ratio as the independent variable x. Then the two columns' data can be input to R. After a regression analysis, corresponding results would be output as follows.

Table 7.6 Model Summary

表 7.6 模型总结

Residual standard error（残差标准差）	9.103	Multiple R-squared（样本决定系数）	0.551 2
Adjusted R-squared（调整后的样本决定系数）	0.541 4		

Table 7.7 Analysis of Variance for Simple Linear Regression

表 7.7 方差分析

Analysis of Variance					
Source（方差来源）	DF（自由度）	Sum of Squares（平方和）	Mean Square（均方）	*F*-statistic（*F* 值）	*p*-value（*p* 值）
Model（回归）	1	4 680.112 7	4 680.112 7	56.49	1.544e-09
Error（剩余）	46	3 811.366 5	82.855 8		
Corrected Total（总和）	47	8 491.479 2			

Table 7.8 Coefficients

表 7.8 系数

Parameter Estimates				
Variable（变量）	Estimate（参数估计）	Std. Error（标准误）	*t* value（*t* 值）	*Pr*(>|*t*|)（*p* 值）
(Intercept)	53.013 8	3.421 5	15.49 5	< 2e-16
% of Classes Under 20（小班占比）	−2.057 2	0.273 7	−7.516	1.54e-09

我们可以从表 7.6 得出 R^2 值仅为 0.551 2。以“student / faculty ratio”为自变量，“alumni giving rate”为因变量的一元线性回归拟合得不够好。但要优于步骤 2 中的回归拟合度。按表 7.7，进行 *F* 检验。

We can see from Table 7.6 that R Square is 0.5512, again not large enough, so we can say the mode fit is not very good. However, compared to the first regression model, this one is better. From Figure 7.7, we can do an *F* test.

与步骤 2 的 *F* 检验类似，统计量 *F* 的值为 56.49，根据 *F* 分布表，*F* 临界值 $F_{0.05}(1,46)=4.08$，显然 $F>F_{0.05}(1,46)$，所以拒绝原假设。同时，在表 7.7 中显示的 P 值 $<\alpha$，我们可以证明，之前拒绝原假设的判断是正确的。

Similar to the above *F* test, here the statistic *F* is 56.49. Referring to the table of *F* distribution, $F_{0.05}(1,46)=4.08$ given $\alpha=0.05$. Apparently, $F>F_{0.05}(1,46)$, so we reject H_0. Also the *p*-value presenting at the last column of Table 7.7 is <0.0001, *p*-value $<\alpha$, we can prove the judgement is right again. So the model has passed *F* test, which means a

该回归模型通过了 t 检验和 F 检验，说明变量“student-faculty ratio”是有显著影响的。最后，由表 7.8 可得这个一元线性回归模型方程为

$$y=-2.057x+53.014$$

significant relationship exists between the alumni giving rate and student-faculty ratio. At last, we can get the simple linear regression equation: $y = -2.057x+ 53.014$ from Table 7.8.

步骤 4：这两个回归方程哪个更合适呢？选出更合适的一个回归方程，对其进行残差分析。

Step 4: Which of the two estimated regression equations provides the best fit? For this estimated regression equation, perform an analysis of the residuals and discuss your findings and conclusions.

经过回归分析可以总结出，这两个模型方程都通过了 F 检验。自变量和因变量之间都有显著的线性关系。最后，经过比较，我们认为 $y = -2.057x + 53.014$ 拟合得更好，因为在两个模型同样都通过了显著性检验的情况下，它的 R^2 值更大，为 0.551 2。接下来，我们要对这个选定的模型进行残差分析，而通过画残差图来分析是最直观有效的方式。图 7.1 是标准化残差图。

After regression analysis, we can conclude that the two equations both pass F test and have significant relationship between independent variable and dependent variable. But the equation of alumni giving rate and student-faculty ration has higher R square of 0.551 2. Therefore, we think $y = -2.057x + 53.014$ provides the best fit. Next, we perform a residual analysis of this regression equation. Residual graph is the most intuitive way to understand. Below is the plot.

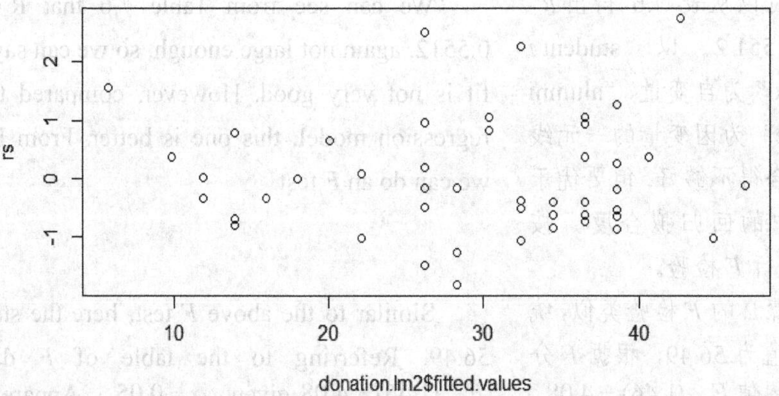

Figure 7.1 Plot of the Standardized Residuals Against The Dependent Variable Y

图 7.1 标准化残差图

从残差图中可以看出，各点都落在 $|r|\leqslant 2$ 这个区间内，

We can define r-standardized residual, $\hat{y}$ -the predicted values of alumni giving rate.

并且是无趋势、无规律地分布在坐标平面中，表明回归模型 $y = -2.057x + 53.013$ 地方差齐性。

标准化残差可以用来判断异常点。任何一个观测点的标准化残差绝对值 $|r| > 2$，则为一个异常点。从图 7.1 所示的残差图可以看出，有 3 个点的标准化残差的绝对值是大于 2 的（见表 7.9）。

We can see from the scatter plot that points generally fall into $|r| \leqslant 2$ level in-bands and don't present any trend. As the figure shows, these points distribute irregularly, so the model is appropriate.

The standardized residuals can be used to identify outliers. Any observation with $|r| > 2$ is an unusual observation. We can see from the figure above that three points' standardized residuals are greater than 2.

Table 7.9 Outliers

表 7.9 异常点

School（学校）	Standardized residual（标准化残差）
Dartmouth College（达特茅斯学院）	2.285
Princeton University（普林斯顿大学）	2.749
U. of Notre Dame（圣母大学）	2.526

然后，我们通过杠杆值 h_i 来判断第 i 个观测值是否是强影响点。当 $h_i > 6/n$ 时，则为强影响点。此处有一个强影响点（见表 7.10）：

Then, we can use the leverage of the i_{th} observation, denoted h_i, to identify influential observations. If $h_i > 6/n$, the i_{th} observation has large influence. There is one influential observation,

$$h_i = 0.138 > \frac{6}{48} = 0.125$$

Table 7.10 Influential Observations

表 7.10 强影响点

School（学校）	h_i（杠杆值）
U. of Florida（佛罗里达大学）	0.139 552 4

步骤 5：从这一分析中得出结论和建议。

由于两个一元回归做出的效果都不是很满意，我们需要进一步改进模型。这里我们剔除异常点和强影响点之后再进行回归分析（见表 7.11～表 7.13）。

Step 5: Develop conclusions and analysis.

From step 4, we can see that there are several outliers and influential observations in the data. The model may be improved if we eliminate these points. The result of analysis is:

Table 7.11 Model Summary

表 7.11 模型总结

Residual standard error（残差标准差）	6.827	Multiple R-squared（样本决定系数）	0.668
Adjusted R-squared（调整后的样本决定系数）	0.660 1		

Table 7.12 Analysis of Variance for Simple Linear Regression

表 7.12 简单线性回归的方差分析

Analysis of Variance					
Source（方差来源）	DF（自由度）	Sum of Squares（平方和）	Mean Square（均方）	*F*-statistic（*F* 值）	*p*-value（*p* 值）
Model（回归）	1	3 938.406 3	3 983.406 3	84.50	1.302e-11
Error（剩余）	42	1 957.480 0	46.606 7		
Corrected Total（总和）	43	5 895.886 4			

Table 7.13 Coefficients

表 7.13 系数

Parameter Estimates				
Variable（变量）	Estimate（参数估计）	Std. Error（标准误）	*t* value（*t* 值）	*Pr*(>|*t*|)（*p* 值）
(Intercept)	51.225 0	2.762 5	18.543	< 2e-16
% of Classes Under 20（小班占比）	−2.061 4	0.224 2	−9.193	1.3e-11

我们可以得出将这些异常点和强影响点剔除之后，模型得到改进的结论。R^2 的值已经从 0.551 2 增加到 0.668。并且这个模型通过了 F 检验和 t 检验，所以这个模型比步骤 4 中得到的模型要拟合得更好。该模型方程为 $y = -2.061x+51.225$。

所以，我们可以建议大学的教务管理者采取相关措施，减少师生比来增加学校的校友捐赠收入。建立一个以少于 20 名学生数的班级百分比和师生比为自变量的多元回归模型对校友捐赠率的预测会更准确。

或者，我们可以找到其他更

We can conclude that after eliminating these points, the model has been improved. The value of R Square has increased from 0.551 2 to 0.668. And the model has passed the F test and t test. So it is more suitable than the one in step 4. The model is $y = -2.061x + 51.225$. Therefore, we can give some suggestion that if administrators of college want to implement some policies to increase revenues, they can take measures to reduce student-faculty ratio. It may be more descriptive to develop an estimated multiple regression equation with the percentage of classes with fewer than 20 students and the student-faculty ratio as the independents to predict the alumni giving rate. But this involves multiple regression.

Also, we can find more variables which influence

多的影响校友捐赠率的变量。方向可以大致定为三个方面：捐赠意向、捐赠能力和捐赠渠道。

the alumni giving rate. It can be set about from three dimensions, which are intension to donate, ability to donate, and channel to donate.

Appendix 7.1　Linear Regression Using R

附录 7.1　R 语言一元线性回归

There are four steps required to perform linear regression in R. First, import data. Then, perform statistical analysis of each variable. Next, perform linear regression. Last, carry out regression diagnosis, and deal with problems.

在 R 语言中进行简单线性回归需要四个步骤。首先，导入数据。其次，对各变量进行统计分析。然后，进行一元线性回归。最后，进行回归诊断，对模型存在的问题进行处理。

1．代码

```
#步骤一：设置工作空间并读取数据
path<-setwd("E:/chpt7_donation")
getwd()                                  #设置工作空间
list.files()                             #列出所设工作空间内的文件，判断是否设置正确
install.packages("readxl")
library(readxl)                          #安装并加载 readxl 包以读取数据
donation<- read_excel ("Chapter 7-Alumni Donation.xls")  #引号内为文件存放位置
dim(donation)                            #获取数据维度信息

#步骤二：对各变量进行统计分析
install.packages("psych")
library(psych)                           #安装并调用 psych 程序包以进行统计分析
describe(donation[,-1])                  #计算各变量的基本统计量

#步骤三：一元线性回归
#因变量：Alumni.Giving.Rate；自变量：% of.Classes.Under.20
donation.lm1<-lm(`Alumni Giving Rate`~`% of Classes Under 20`,data=donation)
                                         #使用函数 lm()进行一元线性回归
                                         #一般用法*详见函数参数说明*
summary(donation.lm1)                    #查看回归结果
#因变量：Alumni.Giving.Rate；自变量：Student.Faculty.Ratio
donation.lm2<-lm(`Alumni Giving Rate`~`Student/Faculty Ratio`,data=donation)
summary(donation.lm2)

#步骤四：回归诊断
rs<-rstandard(donation.lm2)              #计算标准化残差
plot(rs~donation.lm2$fitted.values)      #绘制残差图
donation.rs<-data.frame(donation$School,rs)
donation.rs[which(rs>2),]                #找出标准化残差大于 2 的异常点
hat<-hatvalues(donation.lm2)             #计算杠杆值
```

```
donation.hat<-data.frame(donation$School,hat)
donation.hat[which(hat>6/nrow(donation)),]                #找出强影响点

#步骤五：剔除异常点与强影响点后再次进行回归
r<-which(rs>2)
h<-which(hat>6/nrow(donation))
donation.rh<-donation[-c(r,h),]                           #剔除异常点与强影响点
nrow(donation.rh)                                         #检查剔除后的观测数
donation.lm3<-lm(`Alumni Giving Rate`~`Student/Faculty Ratio`,data=donation.rh)
summary(donation.lm3)                                     #剔除后重新进行回归
```

2. 具体过程分析

步骤 1：设置工作空间，为读取文件后缀为.xls 中的数据，需要安装并调用 readxl 程序包。然后导入数据，并了解其维度。

步骤 2：安装并调用 psych 程序包，利用 describe()函数对各变量进行统计分析。

步骤 3：调用 lm()函数分别以 20 人以下班级比和师生比作为自变量，建立一元线性回归模型，并查看模型拟合效果及显著性检验结果。比较两模型效果，选出较好的模型。

步骤 4：对效果较好的模型进行回归诊断：绘制残差图，计算标准化残差与杠杆值以判断异常点与强影响点。

步骤 5：去掉异常点与强影响点后重新进行一元线性回归，观察回归效果并进行显著性检验。

3. *函数参数说明

```
lm(formula, data, …)
```

☑ lm()函数：建立线性回归模型。

☑ formula：所要建立的线性回归模型的公式形式，写法为 y~x1+x2+⋯，其中 y 代表因变量，x1,x2,⋯代表各个自变量。

☑ data：指定数据所在的数据集名。

4. 分析结果

（1）对各变量进行统计分析

变量“% of classes under 20”的极差为 48，标准差为 13.19；变量“student/faculty ratio”的极差为 20，标准差为 4.85；变量“alumni giving rate”的极差为 60，标准差为 13.44。比较分析可总结出：变量“student/faculty ratio”的值相对比较集中、稳定，而变量“% of classes under 20”和“alumni giving rate”的值波动较大。

（2）一元线性回归

以“alumni giving rate”作为因变量，“% of classes under 20”作为自变量进行一元线性回归（见表 7.14）。R^2 为 0.416 9，模型拟合效果不够好。$F = 32.88$，p-value = 7.228×10^{-7}，即 F 检验结果为拒绝原假设，方程通过显著性检验。$t = 5.734$，相应 p-value = 7.23×10^{-7}，即变量通过了显著性检验。

Table 7.14　Regression Results

表 7-14　回归结果

```
Call:
lm(formula = `Alumni Giving Rate` ~ `% of Classes Under 20`,
    data = donation)

Residuals:
     Min        1Q     Median       3Q       Max
  -21.053    -7.158    -1.660     6.734    29.658

Coefficients:
                            Estimate   Std. Error   t value     Pr(>|t|)
(Intercept)                 -7.386 1    6.565 5     -1.125      0.266
`% of Classes Under 20`      0.657 8    0.114 7      5.734      7.23e-07 ***
---
Signif. codes:   0 '***' 0.001 '**' 0.01 '*' 0.05 '.' 0.1 ' ' 1

Residual standard error: 10.38 on 46 degrees of freedom
Multiple R-squared:   0.4169,      Adjusted R-squared:   0.4042
F-statistic: 32.88 on 1 and 46 DF,   p-value: 7.228e-07
```

以“alumni giving rate”作为因变量，“student/faculty ratio”作为自变量进行一元线性回归（见表 7.15）。R^2 为 0.551 2，模型拟合效果不够好但优于上一步中的模型。$F = 56.49$，p-value = 1.544×10^{-9}，即 F 检验结果为拒绝原假设，方程通过显著性检验。$t = -7.516$，相应 p-value = 1.54×10^{-9}，即变量通过了显著性检验。

Table 7.15　Regression Results

表 7.15　回归结果

```
Call:
lm(formula = `Alumni Giving Rate` ~ `Student/Faculty Ratio`,
    data = donation)

Residuals:
     Min        1Q    Median       3Q       Max
  -16.328   -5.692   -1.471     4.058    24.272

Coefficients:
                            Estimate   Std. Error   t value    Pr(>|t|)
 (Intercept)                53.013 8     3.421 5    15.495     < 2e-16 ***
`Student/Faculty Ratio`     -2.057 2     0.273 7    -7.516     1.54e-09 ***
---
Signif. codes:   0   '***'   0.001   '**'   0.01   '*'   0.05 '.'   0.1   ' '   1

Residual standard error: 9.103 on 46 degrees of freedom
Multiple R-squared:   0.5512, Adjusted R-squared:   0.5414
F-statistic: 56.49 on 1 and 46 DF,   p-value: 1.544e-09
```

（3）回归诊断

绘制标准化残差图（见图 7.2），各点大致无趋势无规律地分布在[−2,2]区间内，表明回归模型不存在异方差问题。

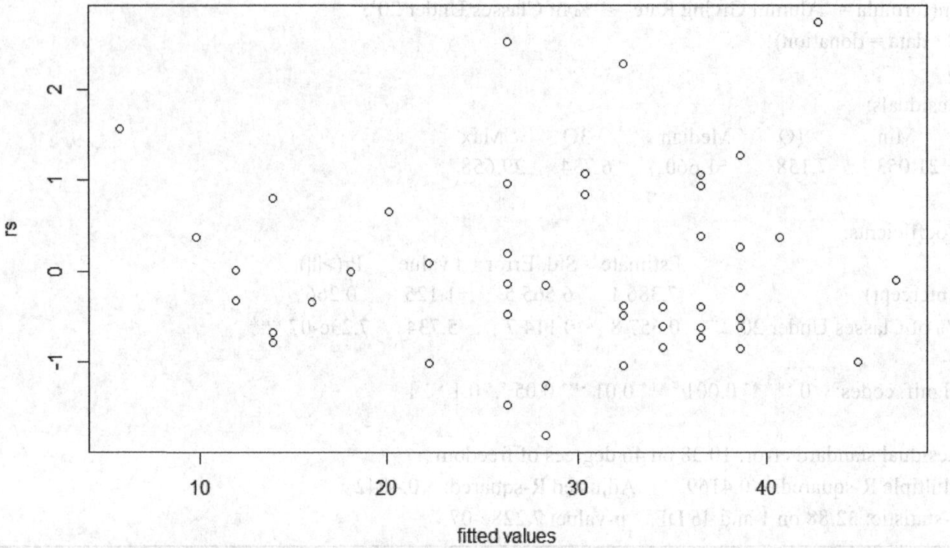

Figure 7.2 Residual Plot

图 7.2 残差图

计算标准化残差，有三个点的标准化残差大于 2，认为其为异常点。这三个点的行号分别为 10，21，37（见表 7.16）。

Table 7-16 Outliers

表 7.16 异常点

	donation.School	rs
10	Dartmouth College	2.284 9
21	Princeton University	2.749 61
37	U. of Notre Dame	2.525 9

计算杠杆值，发现行号为 33 的点的杠杆值为 0.14>6/48，认为其为强影响点（见表 7.17）。剔除异常点与强影响点后再次进行回归（见表 7.18）。

Table 7.17 Influential Observations

表 7.17 强影响点

	donation.School	hat
33	U. of Florida	0.139 552 4

新模型的 R^2 提高到了 0.668，说明模型在剔除一些异常点之后得到了改进。

Table 7.18　Regression Results

表 7.18　回归结果

```
Call:
lm(formula = `Alumni Giving Rate` ~ `Student/Faculty Ratio`,
    data = donation.rh)

Residuals:
    Min       1Q   Median      3Q     Max
 -14.488  -4.227  -1.058   5.085  13.205

Coefficients:
                          Estimate  Std. Error  t value  Pr(>|t|)
(Intercept)               51.225 0    2.762 5    18.543  < 2e-16 ***
`Student/Faculty Ratio`   -2.061 4    0.224 2    -9.193  1.3e-11 ***
---
Signif. codes:  0 '***' 0.001 '**' 0.01 '*' 0.05 '.' 0.1 ' ' 1

Residual standard error: 6.827 on 42 degrees of freedom
Multiple R-squared:  0.668, Adjusted R-squared:  0.6601
F-statistic:  84.5 on 1 and 42 DF,  p-value: 1.302e-11
```

Appendix 7.2　Formulas and Notes

附录 7.2　关键公式与注解

1．线性关系检验（F 检验）

（1）提出假设

$$H_0: \beta_1 = 0$$

（两个变量之间的线性关系不显著）

$$H_1: \beta_1 \neq 0$$

（两个变量之间的线性关系显著）

（2）计算检验的统计量 F

$$F = \frac{SSR/1}{SSE/(n-2)} \sim F(1, n-2)$$

（3）做出决策

给定显著性水平 α，根据分子自由度 1 以及分母自由度 $n-2$，查 F 分布表得 F_α。

若$F>F_{\alpha}$，则拒绝原假设；若$F\leqslant F_{\alpha}$，则不拒绝原假设。

2．回归系数检验（t检验）

（1）提出假设

$$H_0:\beta_1=0,\ H_1:\beta_1\neq 0$$

（2）计算检验得统计量t

$$t=\frac{\widehat{\beta_1}}{s_{\widehat{\beta_1}}}\sim t(n-2)$$

式中，$s_{\widehat{\beta_1}}$是回归系数$\widehat{\beta_1}$的抽样分布的标准差，即$s_{\widehat{\beta_1}}=\dfrac{s_e}{\sqrt{\sum x_i^2-\frac{1}{n}\left(\sum x_i\right)^2}}$

（3）做出统计决策

给定显著性水平α，根据自由度$n-k-1$查t分布表，得$t_{\alpha/2}$的值。若$|t|>t_{\alpha/2}$，则拒绝原假设；若$|t|>t_{\alpha/2}$，则不拒绝原假设。

3．拟合优度

拟合优度是多元回归中回归平方和占总平方和的比例。即

$$R^2=\frac{SSR}{SST}=1-\frac{SSE}{SST}$$

拟合优度取值范围为0～1，越大表明回归平方和占总平方和的比例越大，回归直线与各点观测值越接近，用x的变化来解释y值变差的部分就越多，回归直线的拟合程度就越好。反之，拟合优度越接近于0，回归直线的拟合程度就越差。

Chapter 8

Multiple Regression

第 8 章　多元回归

Chapter 7 focuses on the simple linear regression model that uses one numerical independent variable to predict the value of a numerical dependent one. The fact is that you can often make a better prediction by using more than one independent variable. In this chapter, you will learn how to develop a multiple regression model to determine the simultaneous effects of several independent variables on a dependent one.

The two following cases are intended to provide you with a facilitating guide to the multiple regression analysis. You will learn how to develop a multiple regression model to interpret the regression coefficients, how to determine what independent variables to include in the model, how to make a regression diagnosis, and additionally how to deal with the influence of multicollinearity.

在第 7 章中，我们学习了用一个数值型解释变量去预测一个数值型被解释变量的一元线性回归模型。一般而言，使用多于一个的解释变量可能取得更好的预测效果。这就需要使用本章介绍的多元回归模型，揭示若干个解释变量如何同时对被解释变量产生影响。

本章的两个案例将提供多元回归的简单指导。我们将探讨如何建立多元回归模型和解释回归系数的含义，如何进行变量选择、模型诊断和处理多重共线性的影响。

Case 8.1 Sales of Cotton Fabric

案例 8.1 棉织物销量影响因素分析

1. 案例介绍

在生活中，棉织物随处可见。本案例尝试通过建立模型来预测棉织物的销量。首先，根据经济理论，价格影响销量，价格越高，棉织物销量就越少。另外，还有一些因素也会对其销量产生影响。棉织物的进口量会减少国内对织品的需求，出口则会增加需求。进口与出口对商品的需求量产生相反的作用。随着纺织服装产业的迅速发展，销量随着时间也会发生变化，因此也要考虑时间因素。表 8.1 为棉织物数据。其中，6 个变量分别表示季度、年份、棉织物销量、销售价格指数、织物进口量以及织物出口量。

1. Introduction①

Cotton fabric can be seen everywhere around us. Here we try to build a model to predict sales of cotton fabric. First of all, economic theory tells us that price has an important effect on sales, which means that increased price reduces the quantity of cotton required. In addition, there are likely to be other variables that influence the quantity of cotton fabric required. We find that the quantity of cotton fabric imported may reduce the demand for domestic fabric, and that the quantity of cotton fabric exported may increase demand. Imports and exports of fabric shift the demand function. Since the textile and garment industry have developed significantly, sales may also change over time, and we should take this into consideration. Table 8.1 shows a set of data related to cotton fabric. The variables stand for quarter of year, year of observation, sales of cotton fabric, wholesale price index, quantity of imported fabric, and quantity of exported fabric, respectively.

Table 8.1 Cotton Fabric Data

表 8.1 棉织物数据

Quarter（季度）	Year（年份）	Cottonq（棉织物产量）	Whoprice（销售价格指数）	Impfab（织物进口量）	Expfab（织物出口量）
1	66	2 274	98	9.3	256
2	66	2 287	98.1	3.7	189
3	66	2 083	98.4	16	277
4	66	2 181	98.7	4.7	477
1	67	2 221	99.3	5.7	439
2	67	2 131	99.5	8.3	334.3
3	67	1 891	100.3	25.3	249.7
4	67	2 035	100.9	17.3	301.3

① Paul Newbold, William L. Carlson, Betty M. Thorne. Statistics for business and economics[M]. Harlow: Pearson Education, Inc., 2013.

续表

Quarter（季度）	Year（年份）	Cottonq（棉织物产量）	Whoprice（销售价格指数）	Impfab（织物进口量）	Expfab（织物出口量）
1	68	2 035	102	5.3	452.3
2	68	1 930	102.9	27	355.3
3	68	1 712	104	22	277.3
4	68	1 792	105	1.3	204.3
1	69	1 824	106.1	1.3	80
2	69	1 810	106.6	4.7	375
3	69	1 608	108.2	2	188.7
4	69	1 733	108.8	6.7	115.7
1	70	1 654	109.6	5	317.7
2	70	1 810	110.4	3.7	292
3	70	1 467	111.1	3	119.7
4	70	1 560	111.8	1.3	264.7
1	71	1 607	112.2	5.7	186
2	71	1 609	112.2	2.7	367
3	71	1 405	113.6	3	228.7
4	71	1 527	113.8	1.3	294.7
1	72	1 511	114	12	392
2	72	1 475	114.3	6	195
3	72	1 277	115.2	3.7	83.7
4	72	1 384	115.8	2.7	359

2．案例分析

（1）选择合适的回归变量和模型形式

确定一组潜在的自变量以及模型的数学形式，这个过程被称为模型的设定。这是建立多元回归模型的第一步。

正如本案例介绍中提到的，选择了四个变量，包括系数应该为负数的价格变量、系数为正的出口量、系数为负的进口量以及时间变量。考虑到时间的特殊形式，需要对其进行变换（如下所示），以便简化模型的拟合过程。

Time=Year+0.25×Quarter

模型设定部分的第二个步骤是检测变量之间的线性关系。

2. Analytical Procedures

(1) Select appropriate variables and form for the model

The process of determining a set of potential predictor variables and the mathematical form of the model is known as model specification. It is the first step in building a multiple regression model.

For reasons discussed in the introduction, we choose four variables, including price with a negative coefficient, exported fabric with a positive coefficient, imported fabric with a negative coefficient, and a time variable. Since time is presented as a combination of year and quarter, we use a transformation to simplify the data, as follows:.

Time=Year+0.25×Quarter

The next step is to examine the linear relationships between the variables. The correlation matrix calculated

可以通过 R 软件的 cor()函数得到变量的相关性矩阵。如表 8.2 所示，棉织物销量、价格指数和时间之间有明显的线性关系。作为解释变量，价格指数与时间之间的相关性会使回归系数的估计值不稳定，引起多重共线性的问题。本书将在本章第二个案例中具体介绍多重共线性。从表 8.2 也可以看出，其他解释变量之间并不存在明显的线性关系。

by R can help us a lot. As shown in Table 8.2, there are strong relationships among cottonq, whoprice, and time. The correlation between the independent variables time and whoprice will lead to a high variance for the coefficient estimators and cause multicollinearity. Details can be found in Case 8.2. There are no other strong relationships between the potential predictor variables.

Table 8.2 Coefficients Matrix

表 8.2 相关系数矩阵

	Cottonq	Whoprice	Impfab	Expfab	Time
Cottonq	1.000 000 0	−0.949 859 6	0.291 105 6	0.370 196 6	−0.949 673 7
Whoprice	−0.949 859 6	1.000 000 0	−0.439 266 3	−0.284 970 5	0.992 283 1
Impfab	0.291 105 6	−0.439 266 3	1.000 000 0	0.180 696 8	−0.391 550 4
Expfab	0.370 196 6	−0.284 970 5	0.180 696 8	1.000 000 0	−0.238 190 4
Time	−0.949 673 7	0.992 283 1	−0.391 550 4	−0.238 190 4	1.000 000 0

另外，有必要进行各变量的描述性统计分析。如表 8.3 所示，从各变量的描述统计量中可以了解模型取值的区间范围。

In addition, a statistical description of the variables is also necessary. The values of the descriptive statistics shown in Table 8.3 indicate the potential region of the model.

Table 8.3 Descriptive Statistics

表 8.3 描述性统计量

variable（变量）	Cottonq	Whoprice	Impfab	Expfab	Time
n（样本数）	28	28	28	28	28
mean（均值）	1 779.8	106.8	7.5	274	69.6
sd（标准差）	290.5	6.1	7.3	107.7	2.1
median（中位数）	1 762.5	107.4	4.9	277.2	69.6
min（最小值）	1 277	98	1.3	80	66.25
max（最大值）	2 287	115.8	27	477	73
range（组距）	1 010	17.8	25.7	397	6.75
skew（偏度）	0.214	−0.097	1.441	−0.034	0
kurtosis（峰度）	−1.176 5	−1.575 5	0.864 7	−0.849 8	−1.329 1
se（标准误）	54.89	1.16	1.38	20.35	0.39

基于上述分析，模型的初始形式如下所示：

$$y_i = \beta_0 + \beta_1 x_{1i} + \beta_2 x_{2i} + \beta_3 x_{3i} + \beta_4 x_{4i} + \varepsilon_i$$

式中：x_1 表示物价指数；x_2 表示进口棉织物的数量；x_3 表示出口棉织物的数量；x_4 表示时间值。

（2）估计回归方程来预测棉织物销量

运用 R 软件构建多元回归模型。经济理论表明，棉织物的销量与价格和进口量呈一定的相反关系。以棉织物销量为被解释变量，价格指数、进口量、出口量和时间作为解释变量建立模型，如表 8.4 所示。价格指数和时间变量的 t 值的绝对值都比较小，两者 P 值也都大于 0.05，说明这两个变量不显著。看来应该把两个变量都去掉。但是，时间和价格指数有明显的相关关系，不进一步分析就删去这两个变量并不合适。

Based on the study above, the initial model has the form:

$$y_i = \beta_0 + \beta_1 x_{1i} + \beta_2 x_{2i} + \beta_3 x_{3i} + \beta_4 x_{4i} + \varepsilon_i$$

where x_1 is the wholesale price, x_2 is the quantity of imported fabric, x_3 is the quantity of exported fabric, and x_4 represents time.

(2) Develop an estimated regression equation to predict the quantity of cotton fabric

We generate the first multiple regression model with R. Economic theory suggests that the quantity of cotton fabric produced should be inversely related to price and the amount of fabric imported. Select cottonq as the dependent variable and whoprice, impfab, expfab, and time as the independent variables. The multiple regression analysis is shown in Table 8.4. The absolute t values of whoprice and time seem to be quite small. Both of the P values are larger than 0.05, which means that whoprice and time are not significant. It seems that we should remove both of them. However, time and whoprice are correlated strongly, as we mentioned above. It is therefore not appropriate to remove the variables without further analysis.

Table 8.4　Multiple Regression Analysis

表 8.4　多元回归分析：以四个变量作为解释变量

Coefficients（系数）	Estimate（估计值）	Std. Error（标准误）	*t* value（*t* 值）	*Pr*(>|*t*|)（*P* 值）	
(Intercept)	8 875.740 0	2 294.628 8	3.868	0.000 78	***
Whoprice	−24.305 7	24.452 8	−0.994	0.330 57	
Impfab	−5.565 2	2.527 3	−2.202	0.037 96	*
Expfab	0.375 8	0.159 5	2.355	0.027 40	*
Time	−65.506 4	70.238 3	−0.933	0.360 70	

Residual standard error: 78.91 on 23 degrees of freedom
（在自由度为 23 的残差标准差）

Multiple R-squared: 0.937 1, Adjusted R-squared: 0.926 2
（多重 R 平方）

F-statistic: 85.69 on 4 and 23 DF,　*p*-value: 1.795e-13
[在自由度为（4,23）下的 *F* 统计量]　（*P* 值）

注：*表示在 5%的显著性水平下该变量显著，***表示 0.1%的显著性水平下该变量显著。

删除变量需要同时考虑经济理论和统计方法。从经济理论方面看，当要预测供需数量时，价格变量是必不可少的。从统计的角度看，应该删除 t 值的绝对值最小的变量，即本案例中的时间变量。两方面一起考虑，结果是一致的。在经济供需模型中，一般遵循经济规律，保留价格变量，除非统计结果与做出的判断有相当严重的冲突。

鉴于以上原因，本案例中去掉时间变量，另外建立了一个模型，如表 8.5 所示。从表中可以看出，价格指数高度显著，R^2 系数与第一个模型基本相同。价格指数的回归系数的标准差大幅度下降，从 24.45 减少为 2.84。其余两个变量与时间没有明显的相关性，因此系数标准差没有较大变化。

The rule for removing variables is based on a combination of economic theories for the model and statistical methods. In terms of economic theory, a price variable is absolutely necessary when we predict quantity produced or quantity demanded. As for the statistical rule, the variable with the smallest absolute t should be dropped. In this case, that is time. Both rules lead to the same conclusion. In economic demand or supply models, we should follow economic theory and keep price as a regressor unless the statistical results are very strongly against our judgement.

In view of the above, we develop another regression model with time excluded. From Table 8.5 we can see that whoprice is highly significant and R-square is essentially the same in the first regression model. The standard deviation of the whoprice coefficient decreased from 24.45 to 2.84—a large margin. The standard errors for the other two coefficients have not changed substantially because their correlations with time were not obvious.

Table 8.5 Multiple Regression Analysis after removing time variable

表 8.5 多元回归分析：删除时间变量

Coefficients（系数）	Estimate（估计值）	Std. Error（标准误）	*t* value（*t* 值）	*Pr*(>|t|)（*P* 值）	
(Intercept)	6 757.009 3	322.156 9	20.974	< 2e-16	***
Whoprice	−46.956 4	2.835 4	−16.561	1.23e-14	***
Impfab	−6.517 5	2.305 6	−2.827	0.009 33	**
Expfab	0.319 0	0.147 1	2.169	0.040 21	*
Residual standard error: 78.7 on 24 degrees of freedom（在自由度为 24 的残差标准差）					
Multiple R-squared: 0.934 7, Adjusted R-squared: 0.926 6（多重 R 平方）					
F-statistic: 114.6 on 3 and 24 DF, *p*-value: 2.331e-14 [在自由度为（3,24）下的 *F* 统计量]（*P* 值）					

注：*表示在 5%的显著性水平下该变量显著，**表示在 1%的显著性水平下该变量显著，***表示在 0.1%的显著性水平下该变量显著。

（3）检查模型残差，看模型拟合的情况

在这个部分，将通过残差图来检测模型拟合的情况以及模

(3) Examine the residuals to see if the model fits the data well

In this part, we will check how the model actually fits the data and the regression assumptions using

型是否符合回归的一系列假定。残差的计算公式为

$$e_i = y_i - \hat{y}_i$$

是真实值与拟合值的差。

将残差图和响应变量的预测值作图，如图8.1所示。本案例中残差有正有负，呈随机形态分布。散点是分散的，没有明显的模式。因此，可以得出结论，残差与拟合值之间不相关，没有理由拒绝线性假设，模型的误差是比较稳定的。

residual plots. The residuals are computed as follows:

$$e_i = y_i - \hat{y}_i$$

Consider a plot of the residuals versus the predicted value of the dependent variable. which is Figure 8.1 here. In this case the residual plot shows a random distribution of positive and negative values across the entire range. The points are scattered and there is no obvious pattern. We can draw the conclusion that the residuals and predicted values are not correlated. There is no reason to reject the linearity assumption, and the model errors are stable over the range.

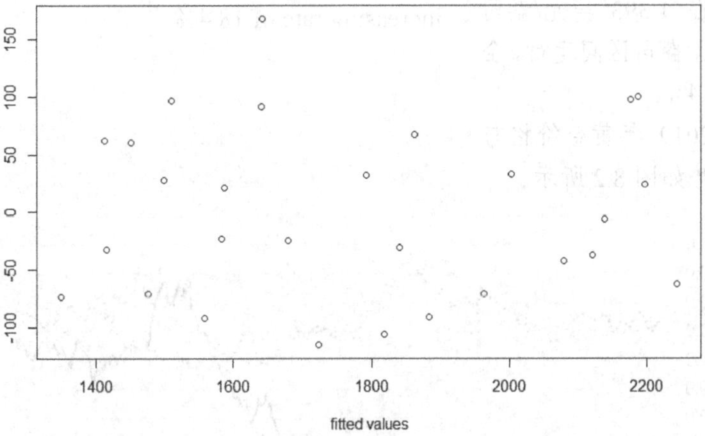

Figure 8.1 Residual Plot

图 8.1 残差—拟合值散点图

Case 8.2 Main Influential Factors of Gold Price

案例 8.2 黄金价格主要影响因素分析

1. 案例介绍

黄金作为贵金属之首，历来受到人们的喜爱与追捧。它兼具商品属性与货币属性，不仅是投资市场上的重要一员，也是国际储备不可或缺的组成部分。

世界黄金协会的数据显示，2019 年前三季度，土耳其央行增持 132.03 吨黄金，俄罗斯央行增持 128.83 吨黄金，波兰央行增持 100.12 吨黄金，我国央行也增持了 95.79 吨黄金。2019 年国际金价在 1 393 美元/盎司至 1 546 美元/盎司区间运行，全年涨幅达 18.4%。

1990—2019 年黄金价格与美元指数趋势如图 8.2 所示。

1. Introduction

Gold, known as the first precious metal, has been almost cherished across the world. Thanks to its two attributes of commodity and currency, gold functions as an important member of the investment market and an indispensable part of international reserves as well.

According to World Gold Council, during the first three quarters of 2019, Turkey increased its gold holdings by 132.03 tons; Russia, by 128.83 tons; Poland, by 100.12 tons; China, by 95.79 tons. During 2019, the international gold price had risen from 1 393 USD/ounce to 1 546 USD/ounce, with a yearly increasing rate of 18.4%.

Figure 8.2 Gold Price and Us Dollar Index Of Year 1990-2019

图 8.2 1990—2019 年黄金价格与美元指数走势图[①]

1944 年，西方主要国家代表商定了布雷顿森林体系，确立了以美元和黄金为基础的金汇兑本位制。20 世纪 70 年代以前，

In 1944, the representatives of major western countries agreed on the Bretton Woods system to establish the gold exchange standard based on the US dollar and gold. Before the 1970s, the price of gold was

① 数据来源：wind。新兴市场国家国际储备结构的调整，尤其是黄金储备的增持备受关注，而近期金价的大涨同样引起了各界的注意。

黄金价格基本由各国政府及中央银行决定，因此国际金价比较稳定。20 世纪 70 年代初期，布雷顿森林体系解体，黄金价格的影响因素日益增多，波动也逐渐加大。

basically determined by governments and central banks; thus it was relatively stable. In the early 70s, the Bretton Woods system disintegrated. As the number of the factors affecting gold price was escalating, the fluctuation was increasing.

研究人员很早就开始关注黄金市场行为及其与现货市场的关系。多数研究认为国际金价的变动与汇率、利率、通货膨胀、证券市场及石油价格的变化有密切关系。

Researchers have long focused on the behavior of gold market and its relationship with the spot market. In most of their studies, they believe that the change of international gold price is closely related to the change of exchange rate, interest rate, inflation, securities market and oil price①.

本案例采集了 1990 年 1 月至 2019 年 6 月（共计 354 个月）的数据构建模型。其中金价为将国际黄金现货日价格进行算术平均后获得的月度价格（US$/ounce）；美元指数采用以 1 973 为基期的美元对其主要贸易国货币的指数；美国消费者价格指数以 1983 年 6—7 月的数据为基期；道琼斯指数指道琼斯 30 种工业股票在每个月最后一个交易日的平均价格编制而得的指数；石油价格为西德克萨塞中质原油现货价格；美国联邦基准利率月度数据来自美国联邦基金储备委员会网站。部分数据如表 8.6 所示，全部金价数据见附录 A.12。

In this case, the data are collected from January 1990 to June 2019 (354 months in all) to build the model. In detail, the gold price is the monthly price (US$/ounce) obtained after the arithmetic average of the international gold spot day price. The US dollar index adopts the US dollar index against the currencies of its major trading countries based on 1973; US consumer price index is based on the data of June-July 1983. Dow Jones index refers to the average price index of 30 industrial stocks of Dow Jones on the last trading day of each month; oil price, to the spot price of WTI. The monthly data of US Federal benchmark interest rate is derived from the website of US Federal Fund Reserve Committee. Table 8.1 shows the selected list, and Appendix A.12, the whole list.

① 已有许多学者证实了大宗商品价格、通货膨胀水平等重要经济、金融变量对金价和美元汇率均会产生显著影响。Levin & Wright（2006）、刘曙光、胡再勇（2008）、Wang et al.（2011）等学者研究得出发现黄金价格变动受到联邦基金利率和美国物价水平的影响。而 Baur & McDermott（2010）和 Baur & Lucey（2010）等分析认为黄金对股票市场具有一定的避险能力。2012 年，Lee et al.研究发现黄金期货价格与油价之间存在着协整和因果关系；Benhmad 验证了美元的汇率与原油价格间的因果关系。2013 年，Wang and Chueh 的研究表明，黄金价格、原油价格、美元、利率之间存在着短期或长期的动态传导关系；杨楠运用滚动 VAR 模型分析得出，标准普尔指数、国际原油价格、美国 CPI 指数和美国联邦基金利率对黄金抗美元贬值避险能力的影响具有时变性。

Table 8.6 Selected Data of Gold Price

表8.6 原始数据（部分节选）

Date（日期）	lnGP（黄金价格）	lnUSDX（美元指数）	lnCPI（价格指数）	lnIR（利率）	lnDJI（道琼斯指数）	lnWTI（石油价格）
Jan-90	6.015	4.526	0.242	−2.497	7.860	3.129
Feb-90	6.033	4.527	0.247	−2.496	7.874	3.096
Mar-90	5.974	4.547	0.252	−2.491	7.904	3.015
Apr-90	5.925	4.547	0.254	−2.494	7.885	2.914
May-90	5.911	4.533	0.256	−2.503	7.964	2.901
Jun-90	5.865	4.533	0.262	−2.490	7.966	2.815
Jul-90	5.893	4.505	0.265	−2.507	7.974	2.915
Aug-90	5.978	4.479	0.275	−2.510	7.869	3.307
Sep-90	5.964	4.466	0.283	−2.501	7.805	3.512
Oct-90	5.942	4.436	0.289	−2.512	7.801	3.585
Nov-90	5.945	4.428	0.291	−2.550	7.848	3.476
Dec-90	5.932	4.444	0.291	−2.616	7.876	3.306

多重共线性是指模型的解释变量间存在线性关系。现实中，在建立回归模型时，往往很难在众多因素中找到一组既互不相关又对响应变量存在显著影响的解释变量，所选的一组解释变量不可避免地会存在一定程度上的相关性。尤其在实际经济问题中，常常由于经济变量间共同的变化趋势、滞后变量的引入或样本资料的限制等问题导致多重共线性。多重共线性是存在于计量经济学模型中的一个普遍问题。

当模型的解释变量间存在多重共线性时，参数估计值的方差会变大，这会影响模型的可靠性以及后续推断，影响主要体现在以下三个方面。首先，参数估计量有时不存在或非有效，导致无法正确判断解释变量对因变量的影响程度，有时会出现一些

Multicollinearity is the condition that there exists a linear relationship between the explanatory variables of the model. In practice, it is difficult to select a set of completely unrelated variables which all have a significant effect on the dependent one when building a model. Several of the independent variables are unavoidably correlated, to some degree. Especially in the economical field, multicollinearity exists due to the same trend of the economical variables, introduction of lag variables and limits of the data set. Multicollinearity is a common problem in econometric models.

When there exists a multicollinearity in a model, the variance of parameter estimate will increase, which would impact the stability and forecast ability of the model in three aspects. Firstly, the condition of multicollinearity present among the variables will cause the instability of the regression coefficients, which may lead to misjudgment of the effects that the independent variables have on the dependent one. some of the coefficients may have an unexpected sign, thus making it impossible to explain the meaning. Secondly,

反常的现象（如回归系数的符号不合理），导致无法对估计量的经济意义做出解释。其次，重要的解释变量可能会被剔除在外，这是由于参数估计值方差的变大，容易使 T 统计量的值小于临界值，误导出参数为 0 的推断。最后，预测可能会失去意义，这是因为变大的方差造成区间预测的“区间”变大。总而言之，多重共线性的存在使得普通最小二乘估计法得出的系数并不准确，无法为推断提供可靠的信息。

important explanatory variable may be excluded. The value of t-statistic is probably lower than critical value due to the increase of the variance of the parameter estimate, which could mislead the conclusion that the parameter is 0. At last, forecasting become meaningless because of the increased variance. Therefore, multicollinearity could make the coefficients obtained by the ordinary least square estimation method not accurate, and couldn`t provide stable information.

2. 案例分析

本章将以探索黄金价格的影响因素为例介绍模型中多重共线性的鉴别与处理方法。

（1）初步建立模型

将黄金价格（lnGP）作为响应变量，其余 5 个变量作为解释变量，建立多元线性回归模型，建模结果如表 8.7 所示。根据表 8.7 中的结果，F 检验结果为拒绝原假设（F=670.3，p-value< 22×10^{-16}），即回归方程通过显著性检验，表明至少有一个解释变量对响应变量 lnGP 有影响。拟合优度为 0.904 6，表明方程可以解释响应变量（lnGP）90.46% 的方差，各变量均通过了 t 检验（p 值均小于 0.05）。初步看来，模型结果是较好的。为了保证模型的可靠性，进一步对模型进行回归诊断，接下来进行多重共线性检测。

2. Analytical Procedures

In this case, an introduction is made to the ways to check the multiple linear regression models for multicollinearity and to deal with the problem.

(1) Build the Model

Take gold price as a dependent variable and the other five as independent variables. According to Table 8.2, the value of F-statistic is statistically significant (F=670.3) indicating that at least one of the explanatory variables influences lnGP.[①] The R-square is 0.9046, which means that the regression model can explain 90.46% of the variation in lnGP. All of the variables pass the t-test. Later we will present the ways to check the multiple linear regression models for the problem of multicollinearity.

① F 检验、t 检验以及拟合优度详见本章“关键公式与注解”。

Table 8.7 Outcomes of Regression Procedure

表 8.7 多元线性回归模型结果

Coefficients（系数）	Estimate（估计值）	Std. Error（标准误）	*t* value（*t* 值）	*Pr*(>|*t*|)（*P* 值）	
(Intercept)	17.300	0.865	19.999	< 2e-16	***
lnUSDX	−1.578	0.183	−8.639	< 2e-16	***
lnCPI	4.679	0.299	15.668	< 2e-16	***
lnIR	−0.027	0.012	−2.220	0.0271	*
lnDJI	−0.688	0.074	−9.279	< 2e-16	***
lnWTI	−0.184	0.046	−4.028	6.91e-05	***
Residual standard error: 0.1957 on 348 degrees of freedom（在自由度为 348 下的残差标准差）					
Multiple R-squared: 0.905 9, Adjusted R-squared: 0.904 6（多重 R 平方）					
F-statistic: 670.3 on 5 and 348 DF, p-value: < 2.2e-16					
[在自由度为（5,38）下的 *F* 统计量]（*P* 值）					

注：*表示在 5%的显著性水平下该变量显著，***表示 0.1%的显著性水平下该变量显著。

（2）多重共线性的识别

这里介绍两种常用的方差扩大因子法和条件数判别法，来鉴别模型中的多重共线性。

① 方差扩大因子法

使用方差扩大因子法（简称 VIF）检测模型的多重共线性，结果如表 8.8 所示。一般认为，若 VIF 小于 5，则解释变量间不存在多重共线性关系。若 VIF 大于 10，则解释变量间存在严重的多重共线性关系。若 VIF 为 5～10，则解释变量间存在中等程度的多重共线性关系。根据这一准则，结合表 8.8，发现美国消费者价格指数（lnCPI）和道琼斯指数（lnDJI）这两个变量的 VIF 均大于 10，因此认为模型中存在严重的多重共线性。

(2) Recognition of multicollinearity

Here we introduce two common methods, variance inflation and condition index, to identify multicollinearity.

① Variance Inflation (VIF)

If the VIFs are smaller than 5, it indicates that the explanatory variables are not correlated. If any VIF exceeds 10, it is generally believed that the independent variable has a serious linear association with the others. If the value is between 5 and 10, it is thought that there exists multicollinearity moderately. As indicated in Table 8.8, the VIF of lnCPI and lnDJI is larger than 10; consequently, the variables are closely correlated in this model.

Table 8.8 Outcomes of Multicollinearity Diagnostics (VIF)

表 8.8 多重共线性检测结果

Variable（变量名）	lnUSDX	lnCPI	lnIR	lnDJI	lnWTI
VIF	3.759 022	32.353 579	3.293 949	18.456 687	7.848 436

② 条件数判别法

使用条件数检测模型的多重共线性，结果如图 8.3 所示。条件数越大表明多重共线性越严重。一般认为，若条件数小于 10，则解释变量间不存在多重共线性关系。若条件数大于 100，则解释变量间存在严重的多重共线性关系。若条件数为 10～100，则解释变量间存在中等程度或较强的多重共线性关系。结合图 8.3 可得，所构建模型的条件数为 177.541 1。根据这一准则，认为模型中存在严重的多重共线性。

② Condition Index.

Furthermore, multicollinearity can be measured in terms of the ratio of the largest to the smallest eigenvalue, which is called the condition index. To be precise, the condition number of its eigenvalue is derived from the following formula:

$$k_i = \sqrt{\frac{\lambda_m}{\lambda_i}}, i = 0,1,2,\cdots,p \tag{8.1}$$

where λ_m is the largest eigenvalue .

Large condition index indicates serious multicollinearity. Generally speaking, if the values are smaller than 10, the explanatory variables are not correlated. If any condition number exceeds 100, it indicates that the independent variable has a quite strong linear association with the others. If the value is between 10 and 100, it is thought that there exists multicollinearity moderately. As indicated in Figure 8.3, the variables are closely correlated, since the value is 177.5411 in this model.

```
> XX<-cor(Chpt8[2:6])
> kappa(XX,exact=TRUE)
[1] 177.5411
```

Figure 8.3 Outcomes of Multicollinearity Diagnostics (Condition Index)

图 8.3 多重共线性检测结果（条件数）

上述两种方法均表明构建的多元线性回归模型中存在严重的多重共线性，因此需要采取必要的措施来处理这一问题。

Both of the rules show the importance of taking measures to address the problem. In this regression model, some of the variables are closely related.

（3）多重共线性的处理

针对多重共线性问题，处理

(3) Approaches to the Multicollinearity

The general approach to multicollinearity is as

的思路一般为：如果变量的数量不是太少，当存在多重共线性时，应该考虑删除一些不重要的变量，可以根据逐步回归来选择需要的变量，然后再次检查共线性，看结果是否得到改善。若删除一些变量后仍存在多重共线性，则可考虑用有偏估计方法来建立岭回归模型。

follows: If the variables are not too less, consider some ways of deleting some unimportant variables including stepwise selection. If the multicollinearity still exists after some variables are deleted, then consider using a biased estimation method to build the model of ridge regression.

① 逐步回归

逐步回归的基本思想是，将变量逐个引入，引入变量的条件是其偏回归平方和经检验是显著的。同时每引入一个新变量后，对已选入的变量要进行逐个检验，将不显著变量剔除，直到没有应选入的也没有应剔除的变量为止，这样保证最后引入的所有变量均是显著的。

① Stepwise Selection

The concept of stepwise selection is to enter variables one by one. It is imperative that only those be chosen which have a significant partial regression sum of squares. Once a new one is selected, test every variable in the model and remove insignificant ones to make sure that all the explanatory variables are statistically significant. Repeat the procedures until there is no more to be added or removed.

在 R 中进行逐步回归，以 AIC 信息量为准则，通过选择最小的 AIC 信息量，来进行变量的取舍。逐步回归结果如图 8.4 所示。由图 8.4 可知，初始时，全部变量进入回归方程中，AIC 值为-1 148.78。同时可知，当不删除任何变量时，AIC 取值最小，为-1 148.78。这表明在本案例中，在 AIC 准则下的逐步回归并不能剔除任何变量，无法改善模型中的多重共线性问题，所以接下来采取岭回归的方法处理多重共线性问题。

Perform the stepwise regression in R, with the AIC criterion. Choose the smallest AIC value to select variables, hence the results of the stepwise regression (Figure 8.4). As indicated in Figure 8.4, at the beginning all variables enter the regression equation, the AIC value being -1148.78. It's easy to see that when all variables are kept, the AIC value is the smallest (-1148.78). In this case, the stepwise regression under the AIC criterion cannot eliminate the multicollinearity; therefore, the ridge regression method is to be adopted to address the problem of multicollinearity.

② 岭回归

岭回归是对最小二乘估计法进行改进后的有偏估计方法，它通过牺牲估计量的无偏性来换取模型估计量的稳定性。当模

② Ridge Regression

As a biased estimation method, ridge regression makes an alteration to Least Squares Method by adding a Ridge parameter to the model to reduce the variance of the estimated regression coefficient. When multicollinearity

型中存在多重共线性时，参数估计值的方差会变大，岭回归估计加入岭参数进行调整，以减少回归系数的方差。实际应用中，可以根据岭迹曲线的变化形状来确定适当的岭参数值及筛选变量。

exists, ridge regression is used to accept a slight deviation of the parameter estimation, thereby eliminating the model instability in return. In practice, the ridge trace is a procedure for choosing the shrinkage parameter.

```
Start:  AIC=
                 Df   Sum of Sq      RSS        -1 148.78
lnGP ~ lnUSDX + lnCPI + lnIR + lnDJI + lnWTI
AIC
<none>                             13.333      -1 148.78
- lnIR           1    0.188 8      13.522      -1 145.81
- lnWTI          1    0.621 6      13.955      -1 134.65
- lnUSDX         1    2.859 4      16.192      -1 082.00
- lnDJI          1    3.299 0      16.632      -1 072.52
- lnCPI          1    9.405 2      22.738        -961.82
```

Figure 8.4 Outcomes of Stepwise Selection

图 8.4 逐步回归过程

借助岭迹图选取岭参数需使得：

- ☑ 各回归系数的岭估计基本稳定。
- ☑ 用普通最小二乘估计得到符号不合理的回归系数，在岭估计下变得合理。
- ☑ 残差平方和增大不太多。

The criteria of selecting ridge parameter k via the ridge trace graph are as follows:

- ☑ All the ridge estimation of each parameter becomes stable basically.
- ☑ The regression coefficients with an unreasonable sign once appear when using Least Squares Method becomes reasonable in the approach of ridge regression.
- ☑ The sum of squares due to residual doesn't expand too much.

一般情况下，取岭迹图中的平稳拐点处作为参数 k 的估计值。

In general, it is necessary that the stable changing point be chosen as the estimator of k.

借助岭迹选择变量的基本原则：

- ☑ 剔除岭回归系数比较稳定且绝对值比较小的解释变量。
- ☑ 剔除岭回归系数不稳

The criteria of independent variable selection via ridge trace graph are as follows:

- ☑ Remove the variables whose values of k are stable, but close to zero.
- ☑ Remove the variables whose values of k are

定且随岭参数的增加迅速趋于零的变量。

☑ 去掉一个或若干个具有不稳定岭回归系数的解释变量。

在进行岭回归之前需要对数据进行标准化处理。对标准化后的数据进行岭回归，画出岭迹图，如图 8.5 所示。根据岭迹图，可以看到 lnCPI（三角形）与 lnDJI（X 号）系数的和比较稳定，可以考虑剔除一个，进一步做出各变量间的相关系数矩阵，如表 8.9 所示，发现 lnCPI 与 lnGP 的相关系数为 0.855 3，要高于 lnDJI 与 lnGP 的相关系数 0.651 7，故剔除变量 lnDJI。同理，变量 lnIR（+号）与 lnWTI（正方形）系数的和比较稳定，考虑到 lnWTI 与 lnGP 的相关系数（0.837 1）要高于 lnIR 与 lnGP 的相关系数（−0.798 6），故剔除变量 lnIR。

not stable, and close to zero soon as *k* increases.

☑ Remove the variables whose values of k change rapidly.

Take the standardized form of the raw data and apply the Ridge Regression approach. As indicated in Figure 8.5, the ridge traces are displayed; the sum of lnCPI and lnDJI is quite stable and one of them may be deleted. Furthermore, the correlation coefficient between lnCPI and lnDJI is 0.855 3, much bigger than 0.651 7, which is the correlation coefficient between lnDJI and lnGP (Table 8.9). Therefore, lnDJI is the one to be deleted. For the same reason, the sum of lnIR and lnWTI is quite stable and the correlation coefficient between lnWTI and lnGP is 0.837 1, much bigger than −0.798 6, the correlation coefficient between lnIR and lnGP; therefore, lnIR is deleted.

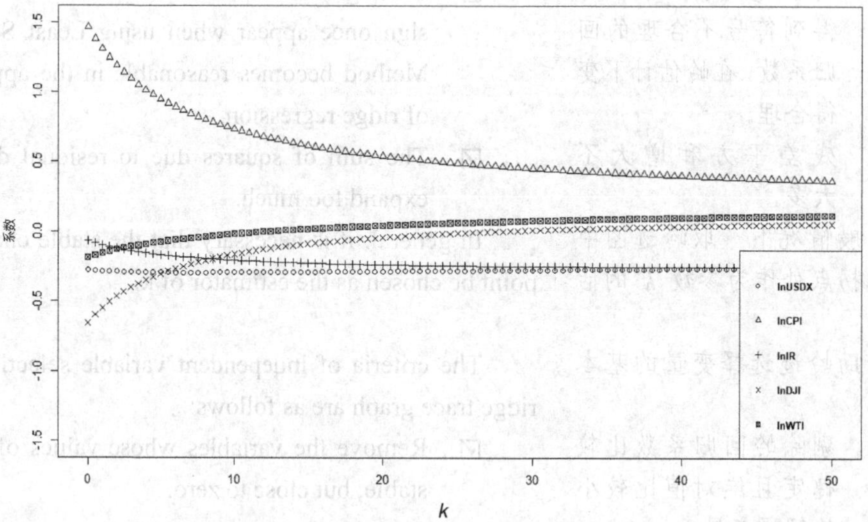

Figure 8.5 Outcomes of Ridge Traces

图 8.5 5 个解释变量的岭迹图

Table 8.9 Outcomes of Correlation Analysis

表 8.9 相关矩阵表

	lnGP	lnUSDX	lnCPI	lnIR	lnDJI	lnWTI
lnGP	1.000 000 0	−0.661 986 0	0.855 298 8	−0.798 575 8	0.651 695 6	0.837 135 4
lnUSDX	−0.661 986 0	1.000 000 0	−0.387 914 7	0.526 054 2	−0.130 064 9	−0.708 056 6
lnCPI	0.855 298 8	−0.387 914 7	1.000 000 0	−0.714 283 0	0.929 609 4	0.834 153 8
lnIR	−0.798 575 8	0.526 054 2	−0.714 283 0	1.000 000 0	−0.508 041 5	−0.679 764 1
lnDJI	0.651 695 6	−0.130 064 9	0.929 609 4	−0.508 041 5	1.000 000 0	0.670 644 9
lnWTI	0.837 135 4	−0.708 056 6	0.834 153 8	−0.679 764 1	0.670 644 9	1.000 000 0

将 lnGP 与保留的三个自变量 lnUSDX、lnCPI、lnWTI 再次进行岭回归，画出岭迹图，如图 8.6 所示。发现当 k 大于 30 时，各变量的系数趋于稳定，此处选取 k 值为 30，此时各变量的系数如表 8.10 所示。

Repeat the Ridge Regression approach again with the three independent variables left, lnUSDX, lnCPI, and lnWTI. The ridge traces show that the regression coefficients tend to be stable when k is larger than 30 (Figure 8.6). Furthermore, the Root MSE increases slightly compared with the value when the least square method is adopted. Thus, the ideal number of 30 is chosen for k, with the corresponding coefficients shown (Table 8.10).

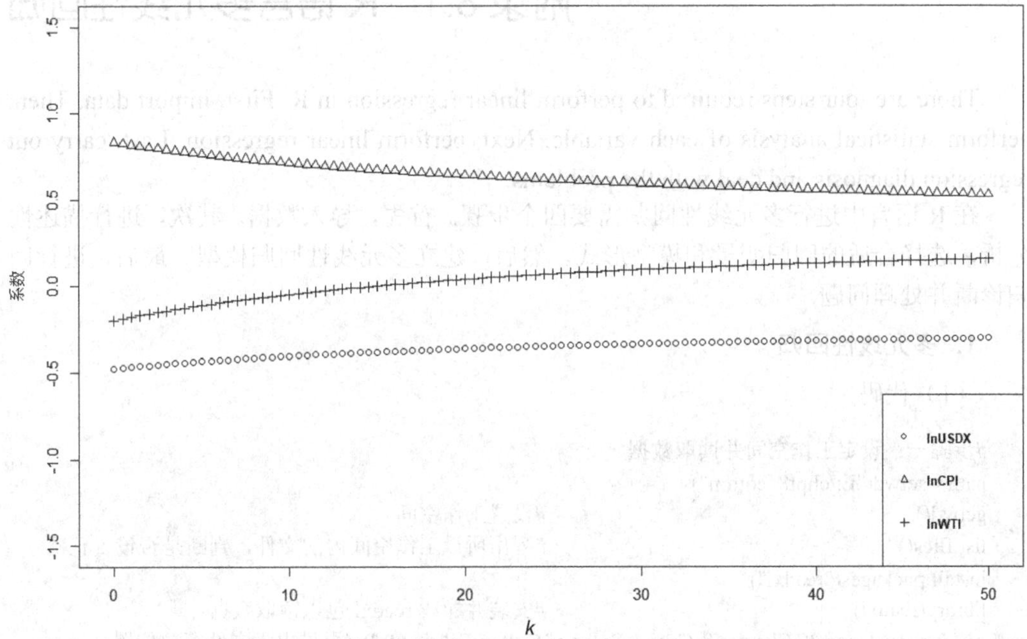

Figure 8.6 Outcomes of Ridge Traces (Finally)

图 8.6 3 个解释变量的岭迹图

Table 8.10 Outcomes of Coefficients

表 8.10 岭回归回归系数

Variable（变量名）	lnUSDX	lnCPI	lnWTI
Coefficient（系数）	−0.334 949 01	0.594 860 71	0.094 569 56

最终可以得到如下岭回归方程：

The standardized ridge regression equation is as follows:

$$\frac{\ln GP-6.387\,2}{0.633\,6}=-\frac{0.334\,9(\ln USDX-4.464\,1)}{0.110\,6}+\frac{0.594\,9(\ln CPI-0.635\,5)}{0.198\,4}+\frac{0.094\,6(\ln WTI-3.665\,4)}{0.637\,8}$$

整理得更为直观的形式：

Sort it into a more explicable form as follows:

$$\ln GP=13.400\,6-1.918\,6\ln USDX+1.899\,7\ln CPI+0.093\,9\ln WTI$$

若已知美元指数、消费者价格指数和国际油价数据，我们就可以估计黄金价格。

Based on this, we can estimate the gold price if we know the U.S. Dollar Index, Consumer Price Index and oil price.

Appendix 8.1 Multiple Linear Regression with R

附录 8.1 R 语言多元线性回归

There are four steps required to perform linear regression in R. First, import data. Then, perform statistical analysis of each variable. Next, perform linear regression. Last, carry out regression diagnosis and deal with the problems.

在 R 语言中进行多元线性回归需要四个步骤。首先，导入数据。其次，进行描述性分析，选择合适的回归变量和模型形式。然后，建立多元线性回归模型。最后，进行回归诊断并处理问题。

1. 多元线性回归

（1）代码

```
#步骤一：设定工作空间并读取数据
path<-setwd("E:/chpt8_cotton")
getwd()                                    #设置工作空间
list.files()                               #列出所设工作空间内的文件，判断是否设置正确
install.packages("readxl")
library(readxl)                            #安装并加载 readxl 包以读取数据
cotton<-read_excel("Chapter 8-Case 1-Sales of Cotton Fabric.xls") #引号内为文件存放位置
dim(cotton)                                #了解数据维度

#步骤二：变量准备及描述性分析
cotton$Time<-cotton$Year+0.25*cotton$Quarter    #将季节与年份变量转换为变量 Time
```

```
cotton.t<-cotton[,c(3:7)]                           #去掉第 1、2 列变量 Quarter、Year
correlation<-cor(cotton.t)                           #计算相关矩阵
install.packages("psych")
library(psych)                                       #安装并调用 psych 程序包以进行统计分析
describe(cotton.t)                                   #计算各变量的基本统计量

#步骤三：多元线性回归
#因变量：Cottonq，自变量：Whoprice，Impfab，Expfab，Time
cotton.lm1<-lm(Cottonq~Whoprice+Impfab+Expfab+Time,data=cotton.t)
                                                     #使用 lm()函数进行多元线性回归
                                                     #一般用法*详见函数参数说明*
summary(cotton.lm1)                                  #查看回归结果及显著性检验结果

cotton.lm2<-lm(Cottonq~Whoprice+Impfab+Expfab,data=cotton.t)
summary(cotton.lm2)                                  #去掉时间变量 Time，重新建立模型

#步骤四：绘制残差—拟合值散点图
plot(cotton.lm2$residuals~cotton.lm2$fitted.values)
```

（2）具体过程分析

步骤 1：设置工作空间，为读取文件后缀为.xls 中的数据，需要安装并调用 readxl 程序包。然后导入数据，并了解其维度。

步骤 2：安装并调用 psych 程序包，利用 describe()函数对各变量进行统计分析。

步骤 3：调用 lm()函数建立多元线性回归模型，并查看模型拟合效果及显著性检验结果。由于变量 Time 对因变量影响不显著，故将其删除，重新建立多元线性回归模型。

步骤 4：绘制残差图，对所建立的模型进行回归诊断。

（3）*函数参数说明

```
lm(formula, data, …)
```

☑ lm()函数：建立线性回归模型。

☑ formula：所要建立的线性回归模型的公式形式，写法为 y~x1+x2+…，其中 y 代表因变量，x1, x2, …代表各个自变量。

☑ data：指定数据所在的数据集名。

（4）分析结果

① 对各变量进行统计分析

计算各变量间的相关系数，棉织物销量、价格指数和时间两两之间的相关系数绝对值均超过 0.9（见图 8.7），表明有明显的线性关系。作为解释变量，价格指数与时间之间的相关性会使回归系数的估计值不稳定，引起多重共线性的问题。

② 建立多元线性回归模型

以棉织物销量为被解释变量，价格指数、进口量、出口量和时间作为解释变量建立模型（见图 8.8）。R^2 为 0.937 1，模型拟合效果较好。但发现价格指数和时间变量 t 检验的 p 值都大于 0.05，未通过 t 检验，表明这两个变量的影响不显著。综合考虑经济理论和统计方法，认为从模型中删除时间变量较为合理。

	Cottonq	Whoprice	Impfab	Expfab	Time
Cottonq	1.000 000 0	−0.949 859 6	0.291 105 6	0.370 196 6	−0.949 673 7
Whoprice	−0.949 859 6	1.000 000 0	−0.439 266 3	−0.284 970 5	0.992 283 1
Impfab	0.291 105 6	−0.439 266 3	1.000 000 0	0.180 696 8	−0.391 550 4
Expfab	0.370 196 6	−0.284 970 5	0.180 696 8	1.000 000 0	−0.238 190 4
Time	−0.949 673 7	0.992 283 1	−0.391 550 4	−0.238 190 4	1.000 000 0

Figure 8.7 Outcomes of Correlation Analysis

图 8.7 相关矩阵表

```
Call:
lm(formula = Cottonq ~ Whoprice + Impfab + Expfab + Time, data = cotton.t)

Residuals:
     Min        1Q    Median       3Q      Max
 −128.574   −50.661   0.436     58.629   146.672

Coefficients:
              Estimate    Std. Error   t value   Pr(>|t|)
(Intercept)  8 875.740 0  2 294.628 8   3.868    0.000 78 ***
Whoprice      −24.3057     24.452 8    −0.994    0.330 57
Impfab         −5.5652      2.527 3    −2.202    0.037 96 *
Expfab          0.3758      0.159 5     2.355    0.027 40 *
Time          −65.5064     70.238 3    −0.933    0.360 70
---
Signif. codes:  0  '***'  0.001  '**'  0.01  '*'  0.05  '.'  0.1  ' '  1

Residual standard error: 78.91 on 23 degrees of freedom
Multiple R-squared:   0.9371,     Adjusted R-squared:   0.9262
F-statistic: 85.69 on 4 and 23 DF,   p-value: 1.795e-13
```

Figure 8.8 Outcomes of Regression

图 8.8 回归结果

删除时间变量后重新建立模型。R^2 为 0.934 7，与删除前相比变化不大。但价格指数这一变量通过了 t 检验，即认为其显著，其回归系数的标准差也大幅度下降，从 24.45 减少为 2.84（见图 8.9）。

③ 回归诊断

将残差值和响应变量的预测值作图，观察发现残差有正有负，呈随机形态分布（见图 8.10）。散点是分散的，没有明显的模式。因此，可以得出结论，残差与拟合值之间不相关，没有理由拒绝线性假设，模型是比较稳定的。

```
Call:
lm(formula = Cottonq ~ Whoprice + Impfab + Expfab, data = cotton.t)


Residuals:
     Min        1Q   Median        3Q       Max
 -115.48    -64.96   -14.81     60.65    167.95


Coefficients:
                Estimate    Std. Error    t value     Pr(>|t|)
(Intercept)   6 757.009 3    322.156 9    20.974    < 2e-16 ***
Whoprice        -46.956 4      2.835 4   -16.561    1.23e-14 ***
Impfab           -6.517 5      2.305 6    -2.827    0.009 33 **
Expfab            0.319 0      0.147 1     2.169    0.04 021 *
---
Signif. codes:  0  '***'  0.001  '**'  0.01  '*'  0.05  '.'  0.1  ' '  1


Residual standard error: 78.7 on 24 degrees of freedom
Multiple R-squared:  0.9347,    Adjusted R-squared:  0.9266
F-statistic: 114.6 on 3 and 24 DF,   p-value: 2.331e-14
```

Figure 8.9　Outcomes of Regression

图 8.9　回归结果

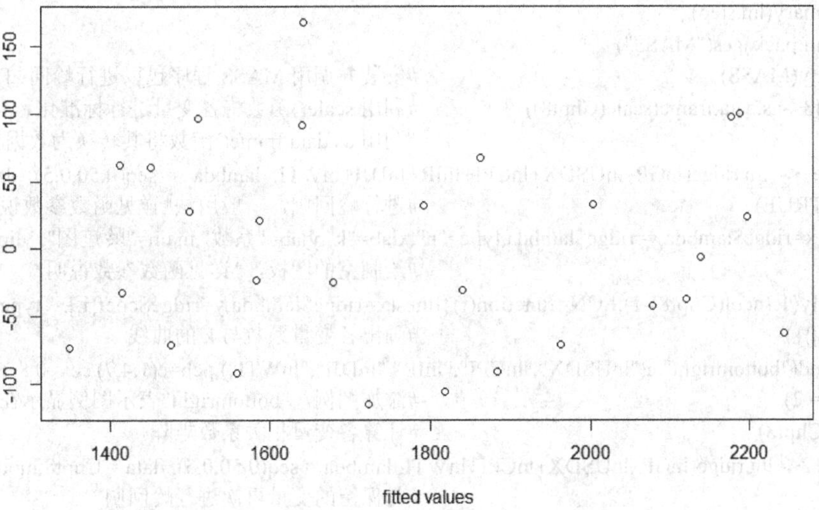

Figure 8.10　Outcomes of Regression Diagnosis

图 8.10　回归诊断结果

2. 多重共线性及其处理方式

在 R 语言中处理本章黄金价格案例的多重共线性问题需要四个步骤。首先，导入数据，对数据进行初步的观察了解。其次，建立多元线性回归模型。然后，对模型进行多重共线性诊断，判断是否存在多重共线性。最后，若存在多重共线性，需对其进行处理。

（1）代码

```
#步骤一：读取数据
install.packages("readxl")
library(readxl)                                  #安装并加载readxl包以读取数据
Gold<- read_excel ("E: /Gold.xls")               #引号内为文件存放位置
dim(Gold)                                        #获取数据维度信息
head(Gold)                                       #观察所读入数据的前几行，检查读入是否正确
Chpt8<-Gold[,-1]                                 #去掉日期变量Date

#步骤二：多元线性回归
lm<-lm(lnGP~lnUSDX+lnCPI+lnIR+lnDJI+lnWTI,Chpt8)
                                                 #使用lm()函数进行多元线性回归
                                                 #一般用法*详见函数参数说明*
summary(lm)                                      #利用summary()函数查看结果

#步骤三：多重共线性诊断
install.packages("car")
library(car)                                     #安装并调用car程序包以用VIF法进行检验
vif(lm)                                          #计算各自变量的方差膨胀因子
XX<-cor(Chpt8[2:6])                              #cor()计算各自变量间的相关系数矩阵
kappa(XX,exact=TRUE)                             #计算条件数

#步骤四：处理多重共线性
lm.step<-step(lm)                                #调用step()函数进行逐步回归
summary(lm.step)
install.packages("MASS")
library(MASS)                                    #安装并调用MASS程序包以进行岭回归
Chpt8<-as.data.frame(scale(Chpt8))               #利用scale()函数将各变量进行标准化
                                                 #利用as.data.frame()函数将其转换为数据框格式
ridge <- lm.ridge(lnGP~lnUSDX+lnCPI+lnIR+lnDJI+lnWTI, lambda = seq(0,50,0.5), data = Chpt8,
model = TRUE)                                    #进行岭回归，一般用法*详见函数参数说明*
plot(x=ridge$lambda,y=ridge$lambda,type="n",xlab="k",ylab="系数",main="岭迹图", ylim=c(-1.5,1.5))
                                                 #绘制空的图板，*详见函数参数说明*
lapply(1:(ncol(Chpt8)-1),FUN=function(i){lines(x=ridge$lambda,y=ridge$coef[i,], type="p", pch=
c(1:4,7)[i])})                                   #画出各变量系数与k的曲线
legend("bottomright",c("lnUSDX","lnCPI","lnIR","lnDJI","lnWTI"),pch=c(1:4,7),cex=0.8, text.width =5,
text.font = 2)                                   #添加图例，"bottomright"表示图例显示在图的右下方
cor(Chpt8)                                       #计算各变量相关系数矩阵
ridge2<- lm.ridge(lnGP~lnUSDX+lnCPI+lnWTI, lambda = seq(0,50,0.5), data = Chpt8,model = TRUE)
                                                 #与保留的变量再次进行岭回归
plot(x=ridge2$lambda,y=ridge2$lambda,type="n",xlab="k",ylab="系数",main="岭迹图",ylim=c(-1.5,1.5))
                                                 #绘制空的图板
lapply(1:3, FUN = function(i){lines(x = ridge2$lambda, y= ridge2$coef[i, ], type = "p",
pch=i)})                                         #画出各变量系数与k的曲线
legend("bottomright", c("lnUSDX","lnCPI","lnWTI"), pch = 1:3, cex = 0.8,
```

```
text.width =5,text.font = 2)                    #添加图例
ridge2$coef[,which(ridge2$lambda==30)]          #显示各变量系数
```

（2）具体过程分析

步骤 1：为读取文件后缀为.xls 中的数据，需要安装并调用 readxl 程序包，然后导入数据。读入后判断数据是否正确读入并了解其维度。由于原数据中的日期在后续分析中并未用到，故直接将其删除。

步骤 2：调用 lm()函数初步建立多元线性回归模型，并查看模型拟合效果及显著性检验结果。

步骤 3：分别利用方差膨胀因子法与条件数法诊断模型的多重共线性。使用方差膨胀因子法：需安装并调用 car 程序包，然后调用 vif()函数计算方差膨胀因子，再结合相应判断标准进行判断。使用条件数法：调用 kappa()函数计算条件数，再结合相应判断标准进行判断。

步骤 4：处理多重共线性。首先考虑采用逐步回归，由于在本案例中逐步回归的方法并不能解决多重共线性，所以选择采用岭回归方法进行有偏估计，具体过程如下。

① 将所有变量标准化。

② 所有自变量进入模型进行岭回归。

③ 绘制岭迹图，依据变量选择原则选择自变量。

④ 将所保留的自变量与因变量再次进行岭回归。

⑤ 重复执行③、④，直至所有自变量的系数均稳定。

（3）*函数参数说明

```
lm(formula, data, …)
```

☑ lm()函数：建立线性回归模型。

☑ formula：所要建立的线性回归模型的公式形式，写法为 y~x1+x2+⋯，其中 y 代表因变量，x1, x2, ⋯代表各个自变量。

☑ data：指定数据所在的数据集名。

```
lm.ridge(formula, data, lambda=0,model=FALSE, …)
```

☑ lm.ridge()函数：进行岭回归。

☑ formula，data 的含义同 lm()函数。

☑ lambda：岭参数，可以为标量或矢量，默认为 0。本例中设置为 seq(0,50,0.5)，表示 0～50 的常数，间隔为 0.5。

☑ model：逻辑值，表示结果是否返回模型框架。

```
plot(x,y,type="p", xlim=NULL, ylim=NULL, main=NULL, xlab=NULL, ylab=NULL, pch=1, …)
```

☑ plot()函数：绘图函数，可绘制散点图、曲线图等。

☑ x：横坐标变量。

☑ y：纵坐标变量。

☑ type：绘图类型。默认值为 p，表示点，本案例中所用 n 表示绘制空图。
☑ xlim：横轴取值范围。
☑ ylim：纵轴取值范围。
☑ main：图的标题。
☑ xlab：横轴标签。
☑ ylab：纵轴标签。
☑ pch：点的样式。

（4）分析结果

① 初步建立模型

初步建立多元线性回归方程，结果如图 8.11 所示。拟合优度 R^2 为 0.904 6。F=670.3，p-value < 2.2×10^{-16}，即 F 检验结果为拒绝原假设，方程通过显著性检验。对各变量系数进行 t 检验，相应 p 值均小于 0.05，即各变量均通过了 t 检验。

```
Call:
lm(formula = lnGP ~ lnUSDX + lnCPI + lnIR + lnDJI + lnWTI, data = Chpt8)


Residuals:
     Min        1Q     Median        3Q       Max
 -0.41988   -0.10327   0.01433    0.11475   0.64001

Coefficients:
             Estimate    Std. Error t  value   Pr(>|t|)
(Intercept)  17.300 42     0.865 07   19.999   < 2e-16 ***
lnUSDX       -1.578 07     0.182 67   -8.639   < 2e-16 ***
lnCPI         4.678 78     0.298 62   15.668   < 2e-16 ***
lnIR         -0.027 39     0.012 34   -2.220   0.0271 *
lnDJI        -0.687 97     0.074 14   -9.279   < 2e-16 ***
lnWTI        -0.184 32     0.045 76   -4.028   6.91e-05 ***
---
Signif. codes:  0  '***'  0.001  '**'  0.01  '*'  0.05  '.'  0.1  ' '  1

Residual standard error: 0.1957 on 348 degrees of freedom
Multiple R-squared:   0.9059,    Adjusted R-squared:   0.9046
F-statistic: 670.3 on 5 and 348 DF,   p-value: < 2.2e-16
```

Figure 8.11　Outcomes of Regression

图 8.11　回归结果

② 检验多重共线性

计算各自变量的方差扩大因子，结果如图 8.12 所示。lnCPI 和 lnDJI 这两个变量的

VIF 均大于 10，因此认为模型中存在严重的多重共线性。

lnUSDX	lnCPI	lnIR	lnDJI	lnWTI
3.759 022	32.353 579	3.293 949	18.456 687	7.848 436

Figure 8.12　Outcomes of VIF Test

图 8.12　方差扩大因子检验结果

计算条件数，结果如图 8.13 所示，大小为 177.541 1，认为模型中存在严重的多重共线性。

```
[1] 177.541 1
```

Figure 8.13　Outcomes of Condition Index Tests

图 8.13　条件数检验结果

③ 处理多重共线性

进行逐步回归（见图 8.14），未能删除变量，无法解决多重共线性问题。

```
Start:   AIC=-1148.78
lnGP ~ lnUSDX + lnCPI + lnIR + lnDJI + lnWTI

           Df Sum of Sq    RSS       AIC
<none>                    13.333   −1 148.78
- lnIR      1    0.188 8  13.522   −1 145.81
- lnWTI     1    0.621 6  13.955   −1 134.65
- lnUSDX    1    2.859 4  16.192   −1 082.00
- lnDJI     1    3.299 0  16.632   −1 072.52
- lnCPI     1    9.405 2  22.738     −961.82
```

Figure 8.14　Outcomes of Stepwise Regression

图 8.14　逐步回归结果

所有变量进入模型，进行岭回归，绘制岭迹图（见图 8.15）。观察发现 lnCPI（三角形）与 lnDJI（X 号）系数的和比较稳定，可以考虑剔除一个，考虑到 lnCPI 与 lnGP 的相关系数为 0.855 3，要高于 lnDJI 与 lnGP 的相关系数为 0.651 7，故剔除变量 lnDJI。同理，变量 lnIR（+号）与 lnWTI（正方形）系数的和比较稳定，考虑到 lnWTI 与 lnGP 的相关性（相关系数为 0.837 1）要强于 lnIR 与 lnGP 的相关性（相关系数为−0.798 6），故剔除变量 lnIR。

将 lnGP 与保留的三个自变量 lnUSDX、lnCPI、lnWTI 再次进行岭回归，画出岭迹图，如图 8.16 所示。发现当 k 大于 30 时，各变量的系数趋于稳定，故选取 k 值为 30。

选取岭参数 k 为 30 后，岭回归所得各自变量的系数如图 8.17 所示。变量 lnUSDX 的系数为−0.334 9，变量 lnCPI 的系数为 0.594 9，变量 lnWTI 的系数为 0.094 6。

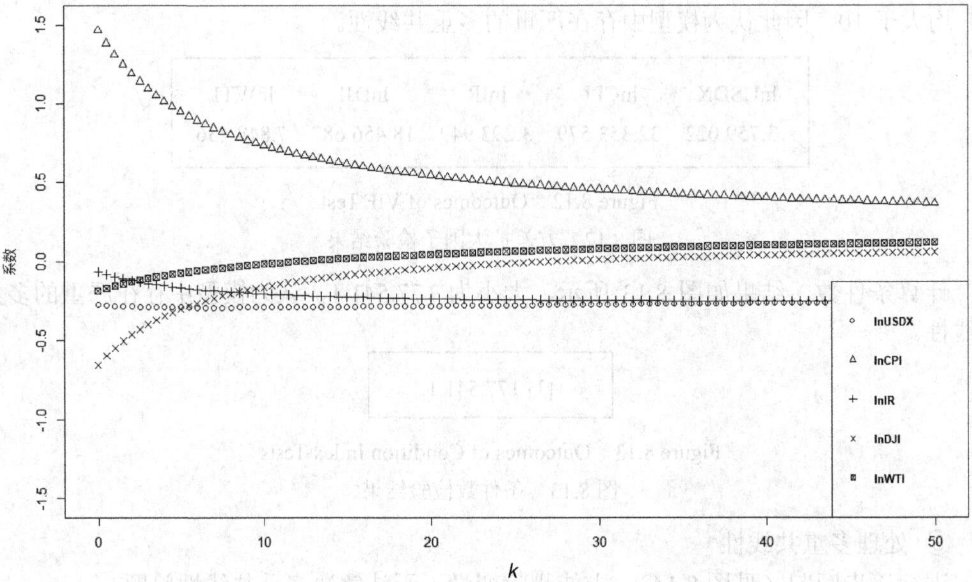

Figure 8.15 Ridge Trace Diagram

图 8.15 岭迹图-1

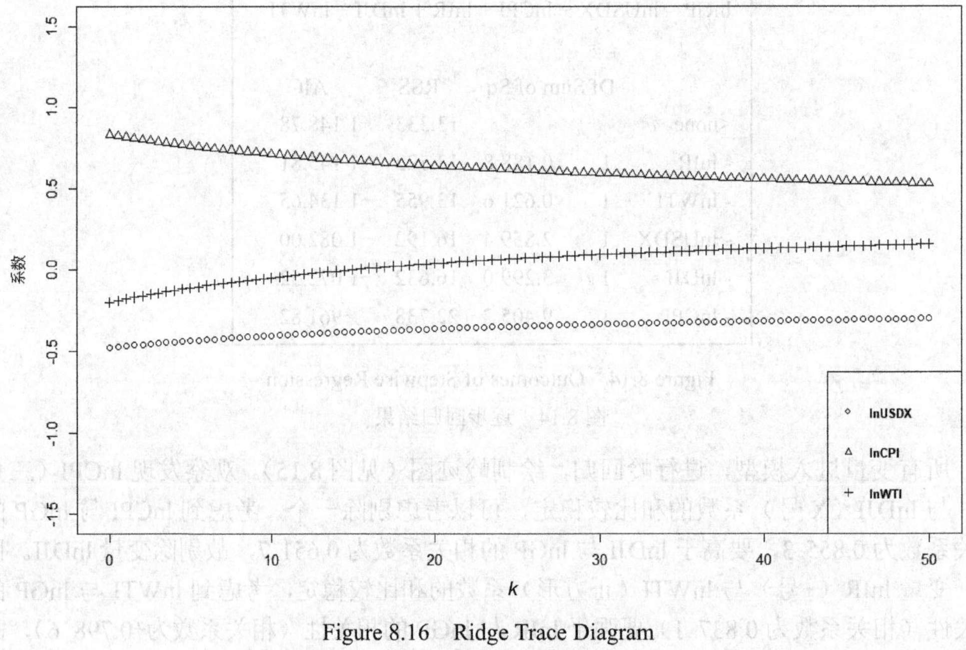

Figure 8.16 Ridge Trace Diagram

图 8.16 岭迹图-2

lnUSDX	lnCPI	lnWTI
−0.334 949 01	0.594 860 71	0.094 569 56

Figure 8.17 Outcomes of Ridge Regression

图 8.17 岭回归结果

Appendix 8.2　Formulas and Notes

附录 8.2　关键公式与注解

1. F 检验

F 检验是检验因变量 y 与 k 个自变量之间的关系是否显著，也称为总体显著性检验。检验的具体步骤如下。

（1）提出假设

$H_0:\beta_1=\beta_2=\cdots=\beta_k=0$

$H_1:\beta_1,\beta_2,\cdots,\beta_k$ 至少有一个不等于 0

（2）计算检验的统计量 F

$$F=\frac{SSR/k}{SSE/(n-k-1)}\sim F(k,n-k-1)$$

（3）做出统计决策

给定显著性水平 α，根据分子自由度 k 以及分母自由度 $n-k-1$，查 F 分布表得 F_α。若 $F>F_\alpha$，则拒绝原假设；若 $F<F_\alpha$，则不拒绝原假设。

2. t 检验

（1）提出假设

对应任意参数 $\beta_i(i=1,2,\cdots,k)$，有

$H_0:\beta_i=0$，$H_1:\beta_i\neq 0$

（2）计算检验统计量 t

$$t=\frac{\widehat{\beta_i}}{s_{\widehat{\beta_i}}}\sim t(n-k-1)$$

式中，$s_{\widehat{\beta_i}}$ 是回归系数 $\widehat{\beta_i}$ 的抽样分布的标准差，即 $s_{\widehat{\beta_i}}=\dfrac{s_e}{\sqrt{\sum x_i^2-\frac{1}{n}\left(\sum x_i\right)^2}}$。

（3）做出统计决策

给定显著性水平 α，根据自由度 $n-k-1$ 查 t 分布表，得 $t_{\alpha/2}$ 的值。若 $|t|>t_{\alpha/2}$，则拒绝原假设；若 $|t|>t_{\alpha/2}$，则不拒绝原假设。

3. 拟合优度

拟合优度是多元回归中回归平方和占总平方和的比例。即

$$R^2=\frac{SSR}{SST}=1-\frac{SSE}{SST}$$

拟合优度取值范围为 0～1，越大说明模型拟合程度越高。

Chapter 9

Nonparametric Methods

第 9 章　非参数方法

Nonparametric tests are designed to have desirable statistical properties when few assumptions can be made about the underlying distribution of the data. In other words, when the data are obtained from a non-normal distribution or one containing outliers, a nonparametric test is often a more powerful statistical tool than its parametric "normal theory" equivalent.

The following example will provide you with an easy guide to several nonparametric tests. We will explore the use of both the sign test and the Wilcoxon signed-rank test to find out whether there is an overall tendency for the customers to prefer one product to the other. The result can serve as a useful reference in decision-making.

当对于数据的分布知之甚少时，可以考虑使用非参数检验。当对非正态分布总体或包含异常值的情形，相较于参数检验，非参数检验更具优势。

本章案例将提供几种非参数检验的简易指南。我们将探讨符号检验和 Wilcoxon 符号秩检验的使用，以找出顾客对产品的偏好是否存在一个整体趋势，为最终决策提供参考。

Case　Product Preference

案例　购买产品时的选择偏好

1．案例介绍

Frick's 是一个家族餐饮连锁企业，主要分布于美国东南部。它提供了一份完整的晚餐菜单，特色菜是鸡肉。最近，其所有者和创始人 Bernie Frick 发明了一种新的辛辣味的面糊用来烹饪鸡肉。在更换目前的味道之前，他想要做一些测试，以确保顾客更喜欢辛辣口味。

首先，他挑选了由 15 名顾客组成的随机样本。每个采样顾客会得到一份当前的鸡肉小块，并被要求对其整体风味在 1～20 分内进行评分。评分值接近 20 说明参与者喜欢这个味道，而评分值接近 0 则说明他们不喜欢。然后，让同样的 15 名参与者品尝味道更辛辣的新的鸡肉样品，并再次让他们在 1～20 分内对味道评分，结果如表 9.1 所示。得到辛辣口味更受欢迎的结论是否合理呢？使用 0.05 的显著性水平进行检验。

1．Introduction①

Frick's is a family restaurant chain located primarily in the southeastern part of the United States. It offers a full dinner menu, but its specialty is chicken. Recently Bernie Frick, the owner and founder, developed a new spicy flavor for the batter in which the chicken is cooked. Before replacing the current flavor, he wants to conduct some tests to be sure that patrons will like the spicy flavor better.

To begin, Bernie selects a random sample of 15 customers. Each sampled customer is given a small piece of the current chicken and asked to rate its overall taste on a scale of 1 to 20. A value near 20 indicates the participant liked the flavor, whereas a score near 0 indicates they did not like the flavor. Next, the same 15 participants are given a sample of the new chicken with the spicier flavor and again asked to rate its taste on a scale of 1 to 20. The results are reported below. Is it reasonable to conclude that the spicy flavor is preferred? Use the 0.05 significance level.

Table 9.1　Flavor Rating for Current and Spicy Flavors

表 9.1　对现有口味和辛辣口味的评分

No. 序号	Participant 参与者	Spicy Score 辣味评分	Current Score 现有口味评分	No. 序号	Participant 参与者	Spicy Score 辣味评分	Current Score 现有口味评分
1	Arquette	14	12	3	Fish	6	2
2	Jones	8	16	4	Wagner	18	4

① Lind, Marchal, Wathen. Statistical techniques in business and economics[M]. New York: McGraw-Hill Irwin, 2010.

续表

No. 序号	Participant 参与者	Spicy Score 辣味评分	Current Score 现有口味评分	No. 序号	Participant 参与者	Spicy Score 辣味评分	Current Score 现有口味评分
5	Badenhop	20	12	11	Miller	16	13
6	Hall	16	16	12	Peterson	18	2
7	Fowler	14	5	13	Boggart	4	13
8	Virost	6	16	14	Hein	7	14
9	Garcia	19	10	15	Whitten	16	4
10	Sundar	18	10				

基于上述数据和信息，两样本间差值的总体分布不遵循正态分布，所以，应采用非参数统计方法。由于该研究采集的对两个不同产品的评分数据来源于同一组顾客，所以两个样本为相关样本。在本案例中，数据的测量水平为**间隔量表**，那么对于判断两个间隔量表的相关指标总体分布是否具有显著性差异的问题，哪些非参数方法是合适的呢？

Based on the given data and information, we believe that the difference between the samples doesn't follow a normal distribution. Therefore, a nonparametric test must be used instead of a parametric test. Since the research collected the rating scores on two different products from the same group of customers, the samples are dependent pairs. Therefore, what kind of nonparametric tests are appropriate for two dependent samples with interval scaling①?

我们将分别使用符号检验和 Wilcoxon 符号秩检验方法，最后再比较两次检验的结果，找出它们之间的相似性和差异。

We will introduce the use of the two nonparametric tests that are appropriate for two dependent samples, the sign test and the Wilcoxon signed-rank test. First, we will conduct a sign test using the binomial and standard normal distributions as the test statistics. Then, we will employ the Wilcoxon signed-rank test using its regular test statistics and normal approximated test statistics. Finally, we will compare the results of the two tests to find the similarities and differences between them.

符号检验是最简单的非参数检验，它基于两个相关观测值间差值的符号。符号检验的基本思路是分析正号和负号的数量，以确定两个相关的观测值是否显著不同。首先去掉观测值相同

The sign test is the simplest nonparametric test to carry out. It is based on the sign of the difference between the values of two related observations. We usually designate a plus sign for a positive difference and a minus sign for a negative difference. The basic idea underlying the sign test is to analyze the frequency

① 间隔量表是变量测量水平的一种，具有顺序量表的特征，且量表中任意两个数的距离为已知大小。

的样本对，然后将实验组样本的观测值减去对照组样本的观测值。差值为正，记为“+”；差值为负，记为“-”。正号和负号的数量记为 S 和 $n-S$，其中 n 为非零样本对的数量。这里的 S 即为符号检验的检验统计量。

设符号为“+”的概率为 P，则检验 S 和 $n-S$ 是否相同的问题就转化为一个检验 P 值是否为0.5的二项分布检验。建立原假设：

$$H_0: P = 0.5$$

在确定了原假设和备择假设，并找到检验统计量之后，下一步要确定 p 值，然后依据判定准则做出决策。为了计算 p 值，当样本量 $n \leqslant 20$ 时，应使用二项分布确定概率计算法；当样本量 $n > 20$ 时，常利用二项分布的正态近似。

在大样本下，正号个数的样本分布近似服从正态分布，原假设为 $p = 0.5$。

均值：$\mu = 0.5n$ （9.1）

标准差：$\sigma = \sqrt{0.25n}$ （9.2）

检验统计量：$Z = \dfrac{S^* - \mu}{\sigma}$ （9.3）

其中，S^* 是经过连续性修正的检验统计量。

of the plus and minus signs to determine whether they are significantly different. The sign test is used to test

$$H_0: P = 0.5$$

where P is the proportion of non-zero observations in the population that are positive. *The test statistic S for the sign test* for paired samples is simply

S = the number of pairs with a positive difference

where S has a binomial distribution with $p = 0.5$ and n = the number of non-zero differences.

After determining the null and alternative hypotheses and finding the test statistic, the next step is to determine the p-value and draw conclusions based on a decision rule. Since the test statistic is expected to follow a binomial distribution, the standard binomial test is used to calculate significance. The normal approximation to the binomial distribution can be used for large sample sizes.

Normal distribution of the sampling distribution of the number of plus signs when H_0: $p = 0.5$

Mean: $\mu = 0.5n$ (9.1)

Standard Deviation: $\sigma = \sqrt{0.25n}$ (9.2)

The test statistic is $Z = \dfrac{S^* - \mu}{\sigma}$ (9.3)

where S^* [①] is the test statistic corrected for continuity.

① 双侧检验：当 $S < \mu$ 时，$S^* = S + 0.5$；当 $S > \mu$ 时，$S^* = S - 0.5$。

上单尾检验：$S^* = S - 0.5$；下单尾检验：$S^* = S + 0.5$。

值加或减的0.5是连续性修正因子，目的是为了将连续分布应用到近似的离散型分布。

Wilcoxon 符号秩检验是当总体分布无法满足正态假设时用于代替配对样本t检验的非参数方法，它既考虑了正、负号，又利用了差值大小。假设两配对样本差值的总体分布是对称的，并且要检验的原假设为该分布集中在0。首先去除差值为零的样本对，我们将剩下的n个差值绝对值数据（n为配对样本量）按升序排列，并求出相应的秩（若存在同分秩，则需要同分修正）。然后，分别计算出正号秩总和R^+和负号秩总和R^-，其中较小的一个就是**Wilcoxon 符号秩统计量**T，即：

$$T=\min(R^+,R^-) \quad (9.4)$$

其中：R^+为正号秩总和；
R^-为负号秩总和；
n为非零差异样本对。

当$n<25$时，应根据附录A.18 Wilcoxon 临界值下界表判断否定域；但当样本中的非零差异样本对个数n为大样本（$n\geqslant 25$）时，可以将Wilcoxon统计量T在原假设（即总体差异集中在0）成立下的分布近似于正态分布。当这个假设为真时，该分布的均值和方差为

均值：$$\mu_T=\frac{n(n+1)}{4} \quad (9.5)$$

方差：$$\sigma_T{}^2=\frac{n(n+1)(2n+1)}{24} \quad (9.6)$$

检验统计量：$$Z=\frac{T-\mu_T}{\sigma_T} \quad (9.7)$$

通常来讲，Wilcoxon 符号秩检验比符号检验有更高的统计效率，但是如果数据中包含离群

As to the *Wilcoxon signed-rank test*, it can be used as an alternative to the paired Student's t-test when the population cannot be assumed to be normally distributed. Like the paired sample t-test, the Wilcoxon signed-rank test involves comparisons of differences between measurements. Assume that the population distribution of the differences in these paired samples is symmetric, and that we want to test the null hypothesis that this distribution is centered at 0. Discarding pairs for which the difference is 0, we rank the remaining n absolute differences in ascending order with ties assigned the average of the ranks they occupy. The sums of the ranks corresponding to positive and negative differences are calculated, and the smaller of these sums is the *Wilcoxon signed rank statistics T* – that is,

$$T=\min(R^+,R^-) \quad (9.4)$$

where R^+ = Sum of the positive ranks
R^- = Sum of the negative ranks
n = Number of non-zero differences

When the number n of non-zero differences in the sample is large ($n\geqslant 25$), the normal distribution provides a good approximation to the distribution of the Wilcoxon statistic T under the null hypothesis that the population differences are centered on 0. When this hypothesis is true, the mean and variance of this distribution are given by

Mean: $$\mu_T=\frac{n(n+1)}{4} \quad (9.5)$$

Variance: $$\sigma_T{}^2=\frac{n(n+1)(2n+1)}{24} \quad (9.6)$$

The test statistic is $$Z=\frac{T-\mu_T}{\sigma_T} \quad (9.7)$$

In general, the Wilcoxon signed-rank test has more statistical power than the sign test, but if the data include outliers or are obtained from a heavy-tailed

值或从一个重尾分布中获得，则符号检验的统计效力更高。

distribution, the sign test will have the most statistical power.

在下面分析中，我们将在两种方法中使用五步假设检验步骤。

In the following analysis, we will use the five-step hypothesis-testing procedure in both methods.

2. 分析步骤

2. Analytical Procedures

步骤1：建立原假设和备则假设。

Step 1: State the null and alternate hypotheses.

步骤2：设定显著性水平。

Step 2: Select a level of significance.

步骤3：计算检验统计量。

Step 3: Compute the test statistics.

步骤4：制定判定规则。

Step 4: Formulate a decision rule.

步骤5：对原假设做出统计决策。

Step 5: Make a decision regarding the null hypothesis.

（1）符号检验基本步骤

（1）Sign Test

① 建立原假设和备则假设

① State the null and alternative hypotheses

表9.2显示了每位品尝者评分分值的差异以及差异的符号。如果偏好新的辣风味，则得到一个“+”；如果偏好现在的风味，则得到一个“–”；如果两个分数相同，则为“0”。

Table 9.2 shows the differences in the scores for every taster and the signs of the differences. Thus, a + is assigned if the new spicy flavor is preferred, a – if the current flavor is preferred, and 0 if the two products are rated equally.

Table 9.2 Taster Ratings for New and Current Flavors

表9.2 品尝者对于新的和现在的风味的评分

No. 序号	Taster 品尝者	RATING（评分）		Difference（差值）	
		New Product 新产品	Current Product 现有产品	(New-Current) 差值（新-现在）	Sign of Difference 差值的符号
1	Arquette	14	12	2	+
2	Jones	8	16	−8	–
3	Fish	6	2	4	+
4	Wagner	18	4	14	+
5	Badenhop	20	12	8	+
6	Hall	16	16	0	0
7	Fowler	14	5	9	+
8	Virost	6	16	−10	–
9	Garcia	19	10	9	+
10	Sundar	18	10	8	+
11	Miller	16	13	3	+
12	Peterson	18	2	16	+

续表

No. 序号	Taster 品尝者	RATING（评分）		Difference（差值）	
		New Product 新产品	Current Product 现有产品	(New-Current) 差值（新-现在）	Sign of Difference 差值的符号
13	Boggart	4	13	−9	−
14	Hein	7	14	−7	−
15	Whitten	16	4	12	+

原假设可以这样设：总体差异的中位数为 0。如果原假设成立，那么正差值和负差值的序列可以看作是从取“+”和“−”概率都是 0.5 的总体中抽出的随机样本。也就是说，观察值可以组成一个来自取“+”概率为 0.5 的二项分布总体的随机样本。假设 p 代表“+”在总体中的实际比例（即偏好新的辛辣口味的实际比例），那么原假设为

$$H_0: p = 0.5$$

对新旧风味的偏好没有整体的倾向。

一个单侧检验用于决定偏好辛辣口味的鸡肉是否存在整体倾向。备择假设为，在总体中大多数偏好新产品。这种备则假设表示为

$$H_1: p > 0.5$$

大多数偏好辛辣口味（或少于 50%的人偏好现有口味）。

② 设定显著性水平

案例规定显著性水平为0.05。

③ 计算检验统计量

原假设为总体中对风味的偏好没有整体趋势。在分析这个假设时，我们比较表达偏好的数据，去除了那些两次评分一致的数据。在这个特殊的案例中，10 个品尝者偏好新的辛辣口味鸡

The null hypothesis can be viewed as the hypothesis that the population median of the differences is 0. If the null hypothesis was true, our sequence of + and – differences could be regarded as a random sample from a population in which the probabilities for + and – were each 0.5. In that case, the observations would constitute a random sample from a binomial population in which the probability of + was 0.5. Thus, if p denotes the true proportion of +s in the population (that is, the true proportion of the population that prefers the new spicy chicken), the null hypothesis is simply

$$H_0: p = 0.5$$

(there is no overall tendency to prefer one flavor over the other)

A one-tailed test is used to determine if there is an overall tendency to prefer the new spicy chicken to the current one. The alternative of interest is that in the population the majority of preferences are for the new product. This alternative is expressed as

$$H_1: p > 0.5$$

(a majority prefers the new spicy flavor, or fewer than 50% prefer the current flavor)

② Select a level of significance

We chose the 0.05 level which is required by the case.

③ Compute the test statistics

The null hypothesis of interest is that in the population at large there is no overall tendency to prefer one flavor over the other. In assessing this hypothesis, we compare the numbers expressing a preference for each product, discarding those who rated the products equally. In this particular experiment, ten tasters

肉，4 个品尝者偏好现有口味的鸡肉，1 个名叫 Hall 的品尝者的评分相同，而在进一步的分析中，Hall 被排除了。这样，有效样本容量就减少为 14。

我们在检验中唯一使用的样本信息是 14 位品尝者中那 10 位偏好辛辣口味产品的品尝者。因此，检验统计量 $S=10$。检验统计量 S 服从二项分布，因为符号检验满足二项分布的所有假设。具体如下：

- ☑ 每次试验只有两种结果："成功"或"失败"。一名品尝者要么偏好辛辣口味（"成功"），要么不喜欢辛辣口味。
- ☑ 每次试验成功的概率假设为 0.50，因此，每次试验（即品尝者）的成功概率是一样的。
- ☑ 试验的总数是固定的（在此试验中总数是 14）。
- ☑ 每个试验是独立的。比如，Arquette 的偏好与 Jones 的偏好是不相关的。

④ 制定判定准则

下一步，计算在原假设成立的情况下，和观察样本结果一样极端或比它更极端的概率值。这一值即为该检验的 p 值。如果把在 $n=14$ 次、每次成功概率为 0.5 的贝努利实验中成功 x 次的概率记为 $P(x)$，那么成功 10 次及 10 次以上的累计二项分布概率可以通过二项分布公式、二项分布表或者 Excel 软件获得。计算 P 值的公式为

preferred the new chicken and four the current; one taster Humed Hall rated them equal. Thus, the values for the taster named Hall are omitted from the subsequent analysis and the effective sample size is reduced to n=14.

The only sample information on which our test is based is that ten of the fourteen tasters preferred the new spicy product. Hence, the test statistic is $S=10$. The test statistic follows the binomial probability distribution. It is appropriate because the sign test meets all the binomial assumptions, namely:

- ☑ There are only two outcomes: a "success" and a "failure". A taster either preferred the new spicy flavor (a success) or they did not.
- ☑ For each trial the probability of success is assumed to be 0.50. Thus, the probability of a success is the same for all trials (tasters in this case).
- ☑ The total number of trials is fixed (14 in this experiment).
- ☑ Each trial is independent. This means, for example, that Arquette's preference is unrelated to Jones's preference.

④ Formulate a decision rule

Next, we find the probability of classifying a sample result as extreme as or more extreme than that found if the null hypothesis was, in fact, true. This value is the *p-value* of the test. If we denote by $P(x)$ the probability of observing x "successes" (+s) in $n=14$ binomial trials, each with probability of success 0.5, then the cumulative binomial probability of observing 10 or more +s can be obtained using the binomial formula, a binomial table, or computer software such as Microsoft Excel. The *p-value* is found with Equation to be

P值 $= P(x \geqslant 10)$
$= P(x=10)+\cdots+P(x=14)$
$= 0.000\,06+0.000\,85+0.005\,55+0.022\,22+0.061\,10$
$= 0.089\,78$

之前我们选定了 0.05 的显著性水平，为了得到该问题的判定准则，可以查找表 9.3 中列 3 的累计概率。从下往上读取，直到累计概率值最接近但不超过显著性水平 0.05。此时第一列的累计概率为 0.028 69，与其相应的成功个数（“+”个数）为 11。所以，**判定准则为**：

如果样本中“+”个数为 11 或更多，则拒绝原假设，接受备则假设。

P-value $= P(x \geqslant 10)$
$= P(x=10)+\cdots+P(x=14)$
$= 0.000\,06+0.000\,85+0.005\,55+0.022\,22+0.061\,10$
$= 0.089\,78$

Recall that we selected the 0.05 level of significance. To arrive at the decision rule for this problem, we go to the cumulative probabilities shown in Table 9.3, column 3. We read up from the bottom until we come to the cumulative probability nearest to but not exceeding the level of significance (0.05). That cumulative probability is 0.028 69. The number of successes (plus signs) corresponding to 0.028 69 in column 1 is 11. Therefore, the **decision rule** is:

If the number of pluses in the sample is 11 or more, the null hypothesis is rejected and the alternative hypothesis accepted.

Table 9.3 Binomial Probability Distribution for n=14, p=0.50

表 9.3 二项概率分布，n=14，p=0.50

Number of Successes（成功个数）	Probability of Successes（成功概率）		Cumulative Probability（累计概率）	
0	0.000 06		1.000 00	
1	0.000 85		0.999 94	
2	0.005 55		0.999 08	
3	0.022 22		0.993 53	
4	0.061 10		0.971 31	
5	0.122 19		0.910 22	
6	0.183 29		0.788 02	
7	0.209 47		0.604 74	
8	0.183 29		0.395 26	
9	0.122 19		0.211 98	
10	0.061 10	↑	0.089 78 ←	0.000 06+0.000 85+
11	0.022 22		0.028 69	0.005 55+0.022 22+
12	0.005 55		0.006 47	0.061 10
13	0.000 85		0.000 92	
14	0.000 06	Add up	0.000 06	
	1.000 00			

重复一遍：我们把概率值从下往上加总，因为不等号的方向向右，表明拒绝域在上尾。如果样本中的加号数量为 11 或更多，则拒绝原假设（见图 9.1）；否则，无法拒绝原假设。

To repeat: we add the probabilities up from the bottom because the direction of the inequality (>) is toward the right, indicating that the region of rejection is in the upper tail. If the number of plus signs in the sample is 11 or more, we reject the null hypothesis; otherwise, we do not reject H_0. The region of rejection is portrayed in Figure 9.1.

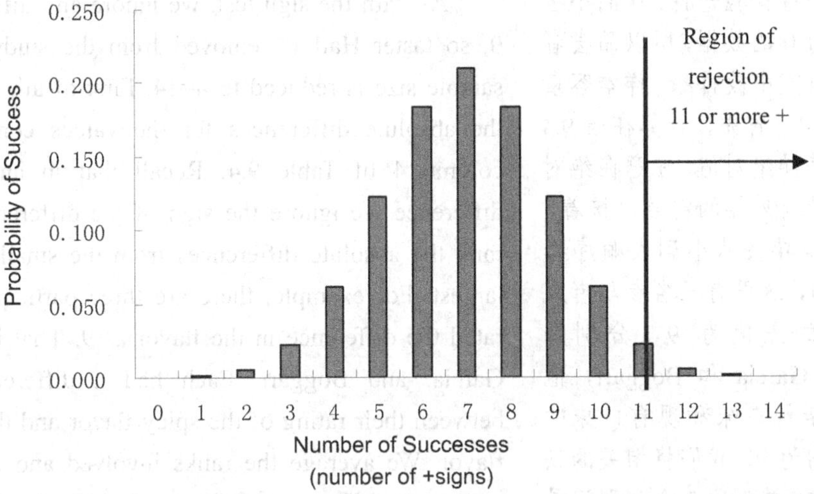

Figure 9.1 Binomial Distribution n=14, P=0.5

图 9.1 二项分布图，n=14，p=0.5

⑤ 对原假设做出统计决策

之前计算得到 p 值为 0.089 78，由于 0.089 78>0.05，不能拒绝原假设，并得出结论没有充分理由说明参与者对新产品有所偏好。同样地，14 名品尝者中有 10 名偏好辛辣口味，数字 10（<11）不在拒绝域中，拒绝域从 11 开始，所以不能拒绝原假设 H_0。再次得出结论，用该数据建议在特色鸡中改变口味没有统计学意义。

⑤ Make a decision regarding the null hypothesis

Recall that the p-value of this test is 0.08978. With a p-value this large we are unable to reject the null hypothesis, and we conclude the data are not sufficient to suggest that the participants have a preference for the new product. Similarly, ten out of fourteen tasters preferred the new spicy flavor. The number 10 (<11) is not in the rejection region, which starts at 11, so H_0 cannot be rejected. Again we must conclude that the data are not statistically significant to recommend a flavor change in the restaurant's specialty chicken.

（2）Wilcoxon 检验基本步骤

(2) Wilcoxon Signed Rank Test

① 建立原假设和备则假设

$H_0: p = 0.5$，对新旧口味

① State the null and alternative hypotheses

$H_0: p = 0.5$, There is no overall tendency to

的偏好没有整体的倾向。

$H_1: p > 0.5$，大多数偏好辛辣口味（或少于 50%的人偏好现有口味）。

② 设定显著性水平

案例规定显著性水平为 0.05。

③ 计算检验统计量

和符号检验一样，我们不考虑差异为 0 的数据，所以品尝者 Hall 从研究中被排除，样本容量缩小为 14。首先，计算在表 9.4 列 4 中差异绝对值。注意在绝对差异中没有差异的符号。接着，对绝对差异按从小到大顺序排秩。例如，这里有三名参与者风味评分的差值为 9，分别是 Fowler、Garcia 和 Boggart，他们对于辛辣口味和现有口味的评分值均为 9。我们将相关的秩进行平均，并为这 3 个分别记录平均秩。由于这里涉及秩 8、9 和 10，所以这三名参与者的秩均为 9。其他的差值都是按相似方法进行排秩。

prefer one flavor to the other.

$H_1: p > 0.5$, A majority prefers the new spicy flavor (or fewer than 50% prefer the current flavor).

② Select a level of significance

It is 0.05, as stated in the problem.

③ Compute the test statistics

As with the sign test, we ignore any difference of 0, so taster Hall is removed from the study and the sample size is reduced to n=14. First of all, determine the absolute differences for the values computed in column 4 of Table 9.4. Recall that in an absolute difference we ignore the sign of the difference. Next, rank the absolute differences from the smallest to the largest. For example, there are three participants who rated the difference in the flavor as 9. That is Fowler, Garcia, and Boggart. Each had a difference of 9 between their rating of the spicy flavor and the current flavor. We average the ranks involved and report the average rank for each. This situation involves the ranks 8, 9, and 10, so all three participants are assigned the rank of 9. The other differences are ranked in a similar manner.

Table 9.4 Computations of Absolute Difference and Rank

表 9.4 绝对值差和排秩计算

No.（序号）	Taster（品尝者）	Difference(New-Current) [差值（新-现在）]	Absolute Difference（绝对差值）	Rank（评秩）
1	Arquette	2	2	1
2	Jones	−8	8	6
3	Fish	4	4	3
4	Wagner	14	14	13
5	Badenhop	8	8	6
6	Hall	*	*	*
7	Fowler	9	9	9
8	Virost	−10	10	11
9	Garcia	9	9	9
10	Sundar	8	8	6

续表

No. （序号）	Taster （品尝者）	Difference(New-Current) [差值（新-现在）]	Absolute Difference （绝对差值）	Rank （评秩）
11	Miller	3	3	2
12	Peterson	16	16	14
13	Boggart	−9	9	9
14	Hein	−7	7	4
15	Whitten	12	12	12

在表 9.5 中，列 3 的秩会得到和原来差异一样的符号，其结果显示在列 5 中。然后，R^+ 和 R^- 的列都会被加总。正号的秩和为 75，负号的秩和为 30。将两个秩和中较小的那个作为检验统计量，记为 T。

$$T=\min(R^+,R^-)$$

这样，我们最后就得到检验统计量 T=30。

In Table 9.5, each assigned rank in column 3 of the table is then given the same sign as the original difference, and the results are reported in column 5. For example, the second participant Jones has a difference score of -8 and a rank of 6. This value is located in the R^- section of column 5. Then, the R^+ and R^- columns are totaled. The sum of the positive ranks is 75 and the sum of the negative ranks is 30. The smaller of the two rank sums is used as the test statistic and referred to as T. Therefore, we finally obtain T=30.

Table 9.5 Calculations of Wilcoxon Test Statistics for Taste Preference Data

表 9.5 口味偏好数据的 Wilcoxon 检验统计量计算

No. （序号）	Taster （品尝者）	Rank （评秩）	Sign of Difference （差值的符号）	Signed Rank（符号秩） R^+	 R^-
1	Arquette	2.5	+	1	
2	Jones	11	−		6
3	Fish	6.5	+	3	
4	Wagner	19	+	13	
5	Badenhop	11	+	6	
6	Hall	*	*	*	*
7	Fowler	14.5	+	9	
8	Virost	17	−		11
9	Garcia	14.5	+	9	
10	Sundar	11	+	6	
11	Miller	5	+	2	
12	Peterson	20	+	14	
13	Boggart	14.5	−		9
14	Hein	9	−		4
15	Whitten	18	+	12	
		Rank Sum（秩和）		75	30
Wilcoxon signed rank statistic T=minimum (75,30)=30					

④ 制定判定准则

由于 $n = 14 (< 25)$，应根据附录 A.18 Wilcoxon 符号秩检验临界值表来判断否定域。α 行用于单侧检验，2α 行用于双侧检验。在此案例中，我们想显示顾客更喜欢辣味，这是一个单侧检验，所以选择 α 行。我们选定了显著性水平为 0.05，所以在表中向右移至标为 0.05 的那一列。从那列往下看，直到 n 为 14 的那一行停下。（回忆一下在研究中有一个人给两种口味的评分相同，因而从研究中被除去，使得有效样本量为 14。）

表中交叉处的值为 25，所以临界值为 25。判定准则为

如果较小的秩和为 25 或更小，则拒绝原假设。

从附录 A.18 得到的值是拒绝域中最大的值。

④ Formulate the decision rule

The critical values for the Wilcoxon signed-rank test are located in Appendix 18. The α row is used for one-tailed tests and the 2α row for two-tailed tests. In this case we want to show that customers like the spicy taste better, which is a one-tailed test, so we select the α row. We chose the 0.05 significance level, so move to the right to the column headed 0.05. Go down that column to the row where n is 14. (Recall that one person in the study rated the chicken flavors the same and was dropped from the study, making the usable sample size 14.) The value at the intersection is 25, so the critical value is 25. The decision rule is to reject H_0 if the smaller of the rank sums is 25 or less. The value obtained from Appendix 18 is the largest value in the rejection region.

⑤ 对原假设做出统计决策

在此案例中，较小秩和为 30，所以不能拒绝原假设，即不能说明对现有口味和辛辣口味的评分间存在显著差异。Frick 先生没有显示出顾客更喜欢新的口味。他可能仍然保留现有口味，不会更改成辛辣口味的。

⑤ Make a decision regarding the null hypothesis

In this case, the smaller rank sum is 30, so the decision is not to reject the null hypothesis. We cannot conclude there is a difference in the flavor ratings between the current recipe and the spicy flavor. Mr. Frick has not shown that customers prefer the new flavor. He should probably stay with the current flavor of chicken and not change to the spicier flavor.

（3）探讨与结论

上述符号检验和 Wilcoxon 符号秩检验达成了一致的结论。他们的检验结果表明，在 0.05 显著性水平下没有充分理由拒绝原假设。

然而，Wilcoxon 符号秩检验的结果通常更受研究者的青睐。青睐的原因是符号检验只考虑

(3) Conclusion and Further Discussion

The sign test and the Wilcoxon signed-rank test above both reached a consistent conclusion. Their results show that it is not possible to reject the null hypothesis at the 0.05 significance level.

However, results from the Wilcoxon signed-rank test are generally preferred by researchers. The reason for this preference is that the sign test takes into

到非常有限的信息，即差异的符号。比如，在表 9.2 中，符号检验仅仅记录了哪个产品受偏爱，却忽略了偏爱的程度。当样本量小时，可能会因此怀疑该检验的可信度。不同于符号检验，Wilcoxon 符号秩检验提供了一种方法来吸收配对样本间差异大小的信息。因此，Wilcoxon 符号秩检验比符号检验可以提供更多信息，它往往能够得出更好地反映数据真实性质的结论。

account only a very limited amount of information, namely the signs of the differences. For example, in Table 9.2 the sign test simply records which product is preferred, ignoring the strengths of the preferences. When the sample size is small, it might therefore be expected that the test would not be very powerful. The Wilcoxon signed-rank test, unlike the sign test, provides a method to incorporate information about the magnitude of the differences between matched pairs. Thus, the Wilcoxon signed-rank test uses more information than the sign test does. It tends to yield conclusions that better reflect the true nature of the data.

根据检验结果，得出辛辣味道更受欢迎的结论是不合理的。Frick's 餐厅的老板 Frick 先生应该继续保留当前的鸡肉味道，而不是使其变得更辣。其他提高鸡味评分的替代方法包括调制辛辣口味和开发新的配方。请记住要事先进行类似的研究，以测试顾客的喜好。

According to the test results, it is unreasonable to conclude that the spicy flavor is preferred. Mr. Frick, the owner of Frick's Restaurant, should be advised to stay with the current flavor of chicken and not make a change to the spicier flavor. Other alternative methods to improve the rating scores of different chicken flavors might include modifying the spicy flavor and developing new recipes. However, he should remember to conduct similar research in advance to test the patrons' preferences.

Appendix 9.1 Nonparametric Methods Using R

附录 9.1 R 语言非参数方法

1. 符号检验

There are three steps required to do sign test in R. First, import data and turn the original data set into a data frame. Next, prepare for hypothesis testing . At last, use function to perform Binomial distribution hypothesis test.

在 R 语言中进行符号检验需要三个步骤。首先，导入数据，将原始数据集转为数据框模式。然后，对假设检验进行相应的准备工作。最后，调用函数进行二项分布假设检验。

（1）代码

```
#步骤一：读取数据
install.packages("readxl")
```

```
library(readxl)
#安装并加载 readxl 包以读取数据
setwd('')
#单引号内为文件存放位置
data=read_excel("Chapter 9-Product Preference.xls")
#read_excel()函数读取文件
data=data.frame(data)
#转换为数据框格式

#步骤二：假设检验准备工作
dif=as.vector(data$Spicy.Score-data$Current.Score)
#配对数据做差
n=length(dif)
# length()取作差后的数据长度，本例中即共有多少人给出评分
n1=0
n2=n
for(i in 1:n)
  if(as.integer(dif[i])>0)
    n1=n1+1
#循环，n1 统计差值为正的个数
for(i in 1:n)
  if(as.integer(dif[i])==0)
    n2=n2-1
#循环，n2 统计差值不为 0 的个数

#步骤三：进行检验
binom.test(n1,n2,p=0.5,alternative="greater",conf.level=0.95) #*详见函数参数说明*
```

（2）具体过程分析

步骤 1：为读取文件后缀为.xls 中的数据，需要安装并调用 readxl 程序包。然后导入数据，并将原数据集转成数据框形式。

步骤 2：进行假设检验前的准备工作，包括：

① 计算实验组与对照组的差值；

② 统计差值为正的样本数量（n1）；

③ 统计差值不为 0 的样本数量（n2）。

步骤 3：调用 binom.test()函数进行二项分布假设检验。

（3）*函数参数说明

```
binom.test(n1,n2,p=0.5,alternative="greater",conf.level=0.95)
```

☑ binom.test()函数：做二项分布假设检验。

☑ n1：样本中正例的个数。

☑ n2：样本个数。

☑ p：二项分布中随机变量为正的概率，本例中为原假设给出的值。

☑ alternative：控制备择假设是左侧/双边/右侧。

☑ conf.level：置信度。

（4）分析结果（见图 9.2）

```
        Exact binomial test

data:  n1 and n2
number of successes = 10, number of trials = 14, p-value = 0.08978
alternative hypothesis: true probability of success is greater than 0.5
95 percent confidence interval:
 0.4599946 1.0000000
sample estimates:
probability of success
             0.7142857
```

Figure 9.2 Outcomes of Sign Test

图 9.2 符号检验结果

p-value=0.089 78>0.05，故不能拒绝原假设。

2. Wilcoxon 符号秩检验

There are three steps required to do Wilcoxon sign test in R. First, import data and turn the original data set into a data frame. Next, prepare for hypothesis testing . At last, use function to perform Wilcoxon sign test.

在 R 语言中进行 Wilcoxon 符号秩检验在本例中可以分为三个步骤。首先，导入数据，将原始数据集转为数据框模式。然后，对假设检验进行相应的准备工作。最后，调用函数进行 Wilcoxon 符号秩检验。

（1）代码

```
#步骤一：读取数据
install.packages("readxl")
library(readxl)
#安装并加载 readxl 包以读取数据
setwd('')
#单引号内为文件存放位置
data=read_excel("Chapter 9-Product Preference.xls")
#read_excel()函数读取文件
data=data.frame(data)
#转换为数据框格式

#步骤二：假设检验准备工作
i=which(data$Spicy.Score==data$Current.Score)
#用 i 标记两次评分相等的位置
x=data$Spicy.Score[-i]
y=data$Current.Score[-i]
#去掉差值为 0 的数据对
z=runif(length(x),0,0.000001)
x=x+z
#给 x 加上一个服从 N(0,0.000001)的扰动

#步骤三：进行检验
wilcox.test(x, y, alternative="greater", paired=TRUE, conf.level=0.95) #*详见函数参数说明*
```

（2）具体过程分析

步骤 1：为读取文件后缀为.xls 中的数据，需要安装并调用 readxl 程序包。然后导入数据，并将原数据集转成数据框形式。

步骤 2：进行假设检验前的准备工作，包括：

① 去掉差值为 0 的数据对；

② 为使差值的绝对值有所区分，给 x 的每个分量加上一个很小的随机扰动。

步骤 3：调用 wilcox.test()函数进行 Wilcoxon 符号秩检验。

（3）*函数参数说明

```
wilcox.test(x, y, alternative="greater", paired=TRUE, conf.level=0.95)
```

☑ wilcox.test()函数：做 Wilcoxon 符号秩检验。

☑ x：本例中为原口味的评分。

☑ y：本例中为新口味的评分。

☑ alternative：控制备择假设是左侧/双边/右侧。

☑ paired：x、y 是否为配对数据，本例中为 TURE。

☑ conf.level：置信度。

（4）分析结果（见图 9.3）

```
            Wilcoxon signed rank test

data:  x and y
V = 77, p-value = 0.06763
alternative hypothesis: true location shift is greater than 0
```

Figure 9.3 Outcomes of Wilcoxon Signed Rank Test

图 9.3 Wilcoxon 符号秩检验结果

p-value=0.067 63>0.05，故不能拒绝原假设。

Appendix 9.2 Formulas and Notes

附录 9.2 关键公式与注解

1. 非参数方法（nonparametric methods）

非参数方法是指对总体的概率分布假设以及测量尺度没有限制或者限制很少的统计方法。在能够得到名义或定序数据时，我们可以使用这些方法。

2. 符号检验（sign test）

这是一种非参数统计检验方法，它以对名义数据的分析为基础来判断两个总体间的差异。

大样本情形下：均值：$\mu = 0.50n$

标准差：$\sigma = \sqrt{0.25n}$

3．Wilcoxon 符号秩检验（Wilcoxon signed-rank test）

这是一种非参数统计检验方法，它以对相互匹配或成对样本的分析为基础来判断两个总体间的差异。

大样本情形：均值：$\mu_T = \dfrac{n(n+1)}{4}$

标准差：$\sigma_T = \sqrt{\dfrac{n(n+1)(2n+1)}{24}}$

4．曼-惠特尼-威尔科克森检验（Mann-Whitney-Wilcoxon test）

这是一种非参数统计检验方法，它以对两个独立样本的分析为基础来判断两个总体间的差异。

大样本情形下：均值：$\mu_T = n_1 n_2 / 2$

标准差：$\sigma_T = \sqrt{n_1 n_2 (n_1 + n_2 + 1)/12}$

5．克鲁斯卡尔-沃利斯检验（Kruskal-Wallis test）

这是一种用于确定三个或三个以上总体间差异的非参数检验方法。

$$W = \left[\frac{12}{n_T(n_T+1)} \sum_{i=1}^{k} \frac{R_i^2}{n_i} \right] - 3(n_T+1) \tag{9.8}$$

6．斯皮尔曼秩相关系数（Spearman rank-correlation coefficient）

这是对两个变量排秩数据之间的相关关系的一种度量。

$$r_s = 1 - \frac{6\sum_{i=1}^{n} d_i^2}{n(n^2-1)} \tag{9.9}$$

Chapter 10

Time Series Forecasting

第10章 时间序列预测

In this chapter we introduce basic methods for time series analysis and forecasting. A time series is a sequence of data points, typically measured at successive times spaced at uniform time intervals. Examples of time series include the daily closing value of the Dow Jones index, monthly UK average interest rates, quarterly Microsoft Corporation sales, or the annual production of Toyota cars. The objective of time series analysis methods is to discover a pattern in the historical data and then extrapolate the pattern into the future.

This case deals with the use of a restaurant's monthly sales data to forecast future sales. First, we assume the separate components comprising a time series. Then, we employ some seasonally adjusted techniques to identify a trend. Finally, we forecast monthly sales for next year, thus provide appropriate strategies in advance.

本章我们将介绍时间序列分析和预测的基本方法。时间序列通常是按连续时间顺序和相同时间间隔测量的一组数字序列。时间序列数据的例子很多，如道琼斯指数每日收盘价，英国每月平均利率，微软公司每个季度销售额，以及丰田汽车年产量。时间序列分析可以在历史资料中发现规律性的轨迹，然后将这个轨迹外推到未来。

本章案例通过对一餐厅的月销售数据进行处理来预测未来的销售额。首先，使用移动平均法把时间序列分解为长期趋势、季节变动和不规则变动三种独立因素。然后，使用一些季节性调整技术，用以识别趋势。最后，预测下一年的各月销售额，从而提前制定出合适的战略。

Case　Forecasting Food and Beverage Sales

案例　预测食品和饮料的销售额

1. 案例介绍

Vintage 餐厅位于靠近佛罗里达州迈尔斯堡的卡普蒂瓦岛上，由 Karen Payne 拥有并经营，到目前已持续 3 年。在此期间，Karen 一直致力于将该餐厅打造成一个具有海鲜特色的高档餐厅。通过 Karen 及其员工的努力，她的餐厅已成为岛上最好的且营业额增长最快的餐厅之一。

Karen 认为为了做好餐厅未来的发展计划，她需要建立一个系统以提前一年预测食品和饮料的每月销售额。Karen 整理了 3 年里关于食品和饮料的销售总额（千美元）数据，如表 10.1 所示。

1. Introduction①

The Vintage Restaurant, on Captiva Island near Fort Myers, Florida, is owned and operated by Karen Payne. The restaurant just completed its third year of operation. During that time, Karen sought to establish a reputation for the restaurant as a high-quality dining establishment that specializes in fresh seafood. Through the efforts of Karen and her staff, her restaurant has become one of the best and fastest-growing restaurants on the island.

Karen believes that to plan for the growth of the restaurant in the future, she needs to develop a system that will enable her to forecast food and beverage sales by month for up to one year in advance. Karen compiled the following data (in thousands of dollars) on total food and beverage sales for the three years of operation.

Table 10.1　Data for Vintage Food and Beverage Sales

表 10.1　Vintage 餐厅食品和饮料的销售额数据

单位：千美元

Month（月）	First Year（第一年）	Second Year（第二年）	Third Year（第三年）	Month（月）	First Year（第一年）	Second Year（第二年）	Third Year（第三年）
January	242	263	282	July	145	157	166
February	235	238	255	August	152	161	174
March	232	247	265	September	110	122	126
April	178	193	205	October	130	130	148
May	184	193	210	November	152	167	173
June	140	149	160	December	206	230	235

① David R. Anderson, Dennis J. Sweeney, Thomas A. Williams, et al. Statistics for business and economics[M]. Boston: Cengage Learning, 2005.

在本案例中，我们将展示如何预测一个既有**长期趋势**（T）又有**季节变动因素**（S）的销售额时间序列。由于 Vintage 餐厅的食品和饮料销售额根据季节变化而变化（见表 10.1），所以提前一年的月度预测对经营者 Karen 制订出良好计划是必不可少的。对于过去三年销售额季节波动的分析将帮助 Karen 评估过去和现在的销售水平和年度增长，也可以使 Karen 将自己的餐厅与行业规范相比较。它还能帮助 Karen 轻松地监控价格和运营成本以保证利润，发觉存在的问题，防患于未然。

This case provides an introduction to the basic methods of time series analysis and forecasting. In this example we show how to forecast a sales time series that has both a *trend* (T) and *seasonal components* (S). Since the food and beverage sales of Vintage Restaurant vary according to the season (see Figure 10.1), a forecast one year in advance, by month, is essential for the owner Karen to be able to schedule effectively. An analysis of seasonal fluctuations over the past three years can also help Karen to evaluate past and current sales levels and annual growth, and allow her to compare her company with industry norms. It will also help her to establish her policies so that she can easily monitor prices and operating costs to guarantee profits, making her aware of minor problems before they become major ones.

从一个时间序列中识别出季节效应的影响是很重要的。经过这一步后，月与月之间的比较才更有意义，能帮助 Karen 识别销售额是否存在趋势。在此案例中我们采取的这个方法适用于只有季节变动存在或者季节变动和长期趋势因素都存在的情况。第一步是计算 12 个月的**季节指数**，并用它们来消除数据的季节变动影响。接下来，如果长期趋势在消除季节变动影响的数据中明显存在，那么我们使用回归分析来估计它。最后，我们使用 12 个月的季节指数来调整下一年销售额的预测值。

Removing the seasonal effect from a time series is known as *deseasonalizing the time series*. After we do this, month-to-month comparisons are more meaningful and can help Karen to identify whether a sales trend exists. The approach we take in this case is appropriate in situations when only seasonal effects are present, or in situations when both seasonal and trend components are present. The first step is to compute twelve monthly *seasonal indexes* and use them to deseasonalize the data. Then, if a trend is apparent in the deseasonalized data, we use regression analysis on the deseasonalized data to estimate the trend component. Finally, we use the twelve monthly seasonal indexes to adjust the sales forecasts for next year.

除了上面提到的**长期趋势**（T）和**季节变动因素**（S）之外，在此案例中，我们假设销售额的时间序列中还包括**不规则变动因素**（I）。使用 T_t，S_t，I_t 来确定在时间 t 时的长期趋势、季节

In addition to the trend component (T) and seasonal component (S) mentioned above, we will assume, in this case, that the time series of sales involves an irregular component (I). Using T_t, S_t, and I_t to identify the trend, seasonal, and irregular components at time t, we will assume that the time

变动因素和不规则变动因素，我们假设销售额的时间序列值（记为 Y_t ）可以描述为以下**时间序列乘法模型**:

$$Y_t = T_t \times S_t \times I_t \qquad (10.1)$$

我们将使用表 10.1 和图 10.1 中的月度数据，来分析由趋势、季节和不规则成分组成的乘法模型的应用。这些数据显示了 Vintage 餐厅在过去三年的运营中食品和饮料的销售额（千美元）。我们从如何确定时间序列中的季节变动因素开始分析。

2．分析步骤

步骤 1：使用**移动平均法**计算出每个月的季节指数。

步骤 2：消除时间序列的季节影响。

步骤 3：使用回归分析来估计消除季节影响的时间序列的趋势成分。

步骤 4：使用步骤 3 的趋势来预测第 4 年 1～12 月的销售额时间序列的趋势成分。

步骤 5：使用每个月的季节指数调整趋势预测值。

步骤 6：进一步讨论其他信息。

（1）计算季节指数

图 10.1 描绘了 Vintage 餐厅在过去三年内的月度销售额。观察销售额的季节性变动，每年 1 月份的销售额最高，9 月份的销售额最低。同时，销售额年年稳步上升。比如，在过去三年中，1 月份的销售额不断增长。如果在脑海里把这些点连接起来，你

series value of sales, denoted by Y_t, can be described by the following *multiplicative time series model*:

$$Y_t = T_t \times S_t \times I_t \qquad (10.1)$$

We will illustrate the use of the multiplicative model with trend, seasonal, and irregular components by working with the monthly data in Table 10.1 and Chart 10-1. These data show the Vintage food and beverage sales (in thousands of dollars) over the three years of operation. We begin by showing how to identify the seasonal component of the time series.

2. Analytical Procedures

Step 1: Using the **Moving Average Method** to Calculate the 12 Monthly Seasonal Indexes

Step 2: Deseasonalizing the Time Series

Step 3: Using Regression Analysis on the Deseasonalized Data to Identify Trend

Step 4: Using the Results of Step 3 to Develop a Monthly Forecast of Sales for the Fourth Year Based on Trend

Step 5: Adjust the Trend Projection with 12 Monthly Seasonal Indexes

Step 6: Discuss other types of information further.

(1) Calculating the Seasonal Indexes

Figure 10.1 depicts the monthly sales for Vintage Restaurant over the three-year period. Notice the seasonal nature of the sales. For each year the January sales are the largest and the September sales are the smallest. Also, there's a moderate increase from one year to the next. To observe this feature, look only at the three January sales figures. Over the three-year period, the sales in January increased. If you connect

可以想象第四年 1 月份销售额增长的情形。

these points in your mind, you can visualize the January sales increasing for the fourth year.

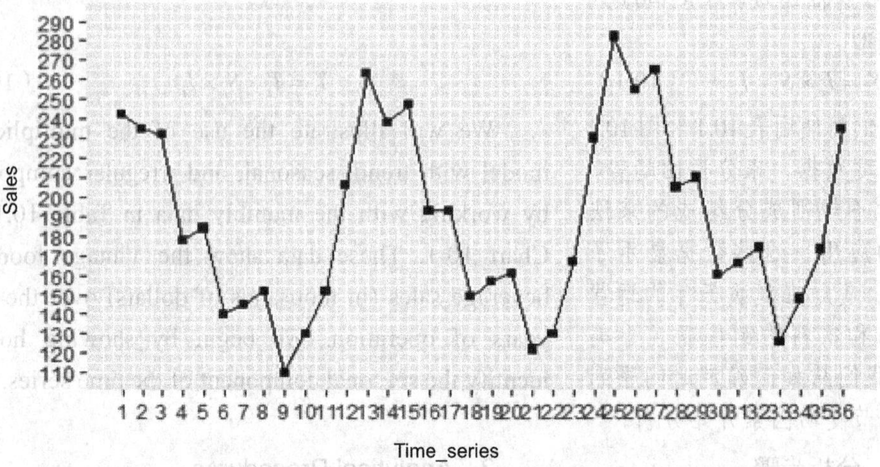

Figure 10.1 Monthly Vintage Food and Beverage Sales Time Series

图 10.1 Vintage 餐厅食品和饮料月度销售额时间序列

确定每月季节变动的影响从计算移动平均值开始，把合并的季节变动因素 S_t、不规则变动因素 I_t 与趋势变动因素 T_t 相分离。由于我们处理的是月度序列，所以在每次的移动平均计算中使用 12 个数据值。例如，对于前 12 个月的食品和饮料销售额的移动平均计算值是 175.500，记为 M_1，计算过程如下：

$$M_1 = \frac{242 + 235 + \cdots + 206 + 263}{12}$$
$$= 175.500$$

The computational procedure used to identify each month's seasonal influence begins by computing a moving average to separate the combined seasonal and irregular components, S_t and I_t, from the trend component T_t. Because we are working with a monthly series, we will use twelve data values in each moving average. For example, the moving average calculation for the first twelve months of food and beverage sales data is 175.500, denoted by M_1 and found by

$$M_1 = \frac{242 + 235 + \cdots + 206 + 263}{12}$$
$$= 175.500$$

继续上面移动平均值的计算，我们可以得到其他的移动平均值，如表 10.2 所示。由于前面计算的移动平均值没有直接对应于时间序列的原始月份，所以使用连续移动平均值的中点与原始月份一一对应。得到的结

Continuing the moving average calculations, we can find other moving averages as Table 10.2 shows.

Because the moving average values we computed do not correspond directly to the original months of the time series, we use the midpoints between successive moving average values. The result is called a *Centered Moving Average*①. For example, 175.500 corresponds

① 在移动平均数的计算过程中，如果数据的个数是奇数，则没有必要再中心化移动平均。

果称为**中心化移动平均值**。例如，对于 175.500 对应于第 7 个月的前一半，177.250 对应于第 7 个月的后一半，那么第 7 个月的中心化移动平均值就是 176.375，记为 C_1，计算过程如下：

$$C_1 = \frac{175.500 + 177.250}{2} = 176.375$$

表 10.2 显示了完整的食品和饮料销售额数据的中心化移动平均值计算过程。

to the first half of month 7 and 177.250 corresponds to the last half of month 7, so the centered moving average calculation for month 7 is 176.375, denoted by C_1 is found by

$$C_1 = \frac{175.500 + 177.250}{2} = 176.375$$

Table 10.2 shows a complete summary of the centered moving average calculations for the food and beverage sales data.

Table 10.2 Centered Moving Average Calculations for the Vintage Food and Beverage Sales Time Series

表 10.2 Vintage 餐厅食品和饮料销售额时间序列的中心化移动平均计算

Year（年）	Month（月）	Sales (1000d) [销售额（千美元）]	12-Month Moving Average [12 个月移动平均值（千美元）]	Centered Moving Average [中心化移动平均值（千美元）]
1	1	242		
	2	235		
	3	232		
	4	178		
	5	184		
	6	140		
			175.500	
	7	145		176.375
			177.250	
	8	152		177.375
			177.500	
	9	110		178.125
			178.750	
	10	130		179.375
			180.000	
	11	152		180.375

续表

Year（年）	Month（月）	Sales (1000d) [销售额（千美元）]	12-Month Moving Average [12 个月移动平均值（千美元）]	Centered Moving Average [中心化移动平均值（千美元）]
			180.750	
	12	206		181.125
			181.500	
2	1	263		182.000
			182.500	
	2	238		182.875
			183.250	
	3	247		183.750
			184.250	
	4	193		184.250
			184.250	
	5	193		184.875
			185.500	
	6	149		186.500
			187.500	
	7	157		188.292
			189.083	
	8	161		189.792
			190.500	
	9	122		191.250
			192.000	
	10	130		192.500
			193.000	
	11	167		193.708
			194.417	
	12	230		194.875
			195.333	
3	1	282		195.708
			196.083	
	2	255		196.625
			197.167	
	3	265		197.333
			197.500	
	4	205		198.250
			199.000	
	5	210		199.250
			199.500	

续表

Year（年）	Month（月）	Sales (1000d) [销售额（千美元）]	12-Month Moving Average [12 个月移动平均值（千美元）]	Centered Moving Average [中心化移动平均值（千美元）]
	6	160		199.708
			199.917	
	7	166		
	8	174		
	9	126		
	10	148		
	11	173		
	12	235		

图 10.2 是实际时间序列值和中心化移动平均值的折线图。通过比较中心化移动平均值和原始的时间序列，可以明显地看出中心化移动平均值消除了时间序列中的季节变动和不规则变动。

Figure 10.2 is a plot of the actual time series values and the centered moving average values. By comparing the centered moving average with the original time series, we can clearly see the centered moving average values "smooth out" both the seasonal and irregular fluctuations in the time series.

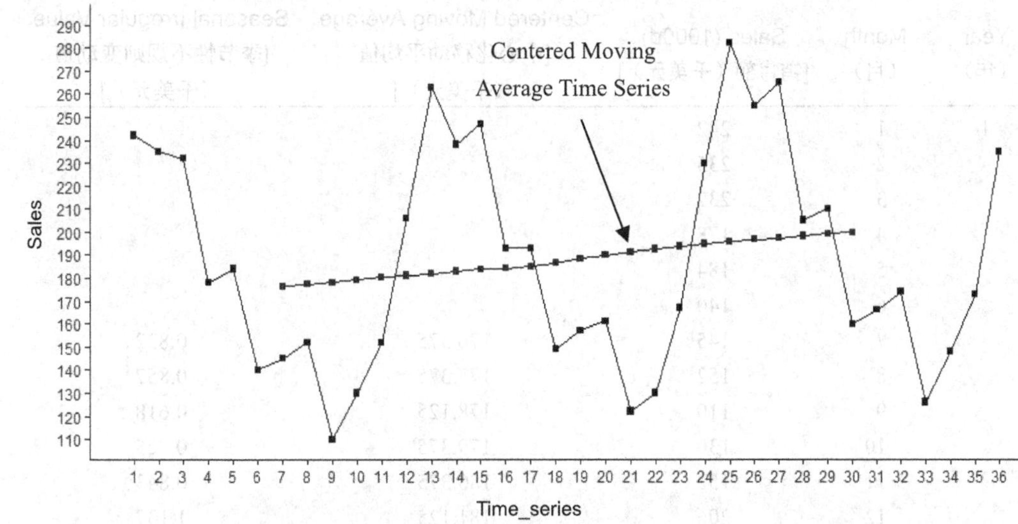

Figure 10.2　Monthly Vintage Food and Beverage Sales Time Series and Centered Moving Average

图 10.2　Vintage 餐厅月度销售额时间序列实际值及其中心化移动平均值

通过将原始观察值除以相对应的中心化移动平均值，可以确定时间序列中的季节变动和不规则变动效应。例如，将第 7 个月的实际销售值除以相对应的中心化移动平均值，可以得到它的季节性不规则变动值，记为 S_7I_7，计算过程如下：

$$S_7I_7 = 145 \div 176.375 = 0.822$$

表 10.3 列出了整个时间序列的季节性不规则值。

由于年与年之间季节不规则变动因素的波动主要是由于不规则变动因素引起的，故可将每月季节指数的计算值平均化，以消除不规则因素的影响，并分别得到各月季节效应的估计值。例如，5 月份的季节变动效应（记为 S_5）是 1.049，计算过程为：

$$S_5 = \frac{1.044 + 1.054}{2} = 1.049$$

By dividing each time series observation by the corresponding centered moving average, we can identify the seasonal irregular effect in the time series. For example, the actual sales value of month 7 divided by its corresponding centered moving average value yields its seasonal irregular value S_7I_7:

$$S_7I_7 = 145 \div 176.375 = 0.822$$

Table 10.3 summarizes the seasonal irregular values for the entire time series. With the year-to-year fluctuations in the seasonal irregular value attributable primarily to the irregular component, we can average the computed values to eliminate the irregular influence and obtain an estimate of 12-month seasonal influences respectively. For instance, the seasonal effect in May, denoted by S_5, is 1.049, and is found by

$$S_5 = \frac{1.044 + 1.054}{2} = 1.049$$

Table 10.3 Seasonal Irregular Values for the Vintage Food and Beverage Sales Time Series

表 10.3 Vintage 餐厅食品和饮料销售额时间序列的季节性不规则变动因素

Year（年）	Month（月）	Sales (1000d) [销售额（千美元）]	Centered Moving Average [中心化移动平均值（千美元）]	Seasonal Irregular Value [季节性不规则变动值（千美元）]
1	1	242		
	2	235		
	3	232		
	4	178		
	5	184		
	6	140		
	7	145	176.375	0.822
	8	152	177.375	0.857
	9	110	178.125	0.618
	10	130	179.375	0.725
	11	152	180.375	0.843
	12	206	181.125	1.137
2	1	263	182.000	1.445
	2	238	182.875	1.301

续表

Year（年）	Month（月）	Sales (1000d) [销售额（千美元）]	Centered Moving Average [中心化移动平均值（千美元）]	Seasonal Irregular Value [季节性不规则变动值（千美元）]
	3	247	183.750	1.344
	4	193	184.250	1.047
	5	193	184.875	1.044
	6	149	186.500	0.799
	7	157	188.292	0.834
	8	161	189.792	0.848
	9	122	191.250	0.638
	10	130	192.500	0.675
	11	167	193.708	0.862
	12	230	194.875	1.180
3	1	282	195.708	1.441
	2	255	196.625	1.297
	3	265	197.333	1.343
	4	205	198.250	1.034
	5	210	199.250	1.054
	6	160	199.708	0.801
	7	166		
	8	174		
	9	126		
	10	148		
	11	173		
	12	235		

因此，5 月份的典型季节指数为 1.049。在表 10.4 中，我们总结了涉及计算销售额时间序列的典型季节指数的运算数据。

Hence, the typical seasonal index for May is 1.049. In Table 10.4 we summarize the calculations involved in computing the typical seasonal indexes for sales time series.

Table 10.4 12 Monthly Typical Seasonal Index Calculations for the Vintage Food and Beverage Sales Time Series

表 10.4 Vintage 餐厅食品和饮料销售额时间序列的月度季节指数计算

Month（月）	Seasonal Irregular Component Values [季节性不规则变动因素值（S_tI_t）]		Typical Seasonal Index [典型季节指数（S_t）]
1	1.445	1.441	1.443
2	1.301	1.297	1.299
3	1.344	1.343	1.344
4	1.047	1.034	1.041
5	1.044	1.054	1.049
6	0.799	0.801	0.800

续表

Month（月）	Seasonal Irregular Component Values [季节性不规则变动因素值（S_tI_t）]		Typical Seasonal Index [典型季节指数（S_t）]
7	0.834	0.822	0.828
8	0.848	0.857	0.853
9	0.638	0.618	0.628
10	0.675	0.725	0.700
11	0.862	0.843	0.852
12	1.180	1.137	1.159

这 12 个月的算术平均(1.443, 1.229,1.344,1.041,1.049,0.800,0.828, 0.853,0.628,0.700,0.852,1.159) 在理论上总和为 12.00，因为其理论平均值设定为 1.0。然而，这 12 个月度均值总和可能由于四舍五入不完全等于 12.00。在这个案例中，这 12 个均值的总和为 11.995。因此，我们应该对每个均值使用**修正因子**，使得它们总和为 12.00。这个修正因子记为 *CF*。

The twelve monthly arithmetic means (1.443, 1.229,1.344,1.041,1.049,0.800,0.828,0.853,0.628, 0.700,0.852,1.159) should theoretically total 12.00, because the average is set at 1.0. The total of the twelve monthly means may not exactly equal to 12.00 because of rounding. In this case, the twelve means total 11.995. Thus, we should apply a *correction factor* to each of the twelve means to force them to total 12.00. The correction factor is denoted by *CF*.

在这个案例中，

$$CF = \frac{12.00}{11.995} = 1.000\,416$$

In this case,

$$CF = \frac{12.00}{11.995} = 1.000\,416$$

例如，调整后的 1 月份的季节指数是 $1.443 \times 1.000\,416 = 1.444$。由于修正因子大于 1.00，每个均值都向上调整，使得这 12 个月度均值的总和为 12.00。同样，我们可以得到其他月份的调整后的季节指数，如表 10.5 所示。

For example, the adjusted January monthly index is, therefore $1.443 \times 1.000\,416 = 1.444$. Because the correction factor is larger than 1.00, each of the means is adjusted upward so that the total of the twelve monthly means is 12.00. Similarly, we can obtain adjusted seasonal indexes for the other months as shown in Table 10.5 below.

Table 10.5 12 Monthly Adjusted Seasonal Index Calculations for the Vintage Food and Beverage Sales Time Series

表 10.5 Vintage 餐厅食品和饮料销售额时间序列的 12 个月份调整后季节指数计算

Month（月）	Seasonal Index [季节指数（S_t）]	Correction Factor（修正因子）	Adjusted Seasonal Index [调整后的季节指数（Adjusted S_t）]
1	1.443	1.000 416	1.444
2	1.299	1.000 416	1.300
3	1.344	1.000 416	1.344
4	1.041	1.000 416	1.041

续表

Month（月）	Seasonal Index [季节指数（S_t）]	Correction Factor（修正因子）	Adjusted Seasonal Index [调整后的季节指数（Adjusted S_t）]
5	1.049	1.000 416	1.049
6	0.800	1.000 416	0.800
7	0.828	1.000 416	0.828
8	0.853	1.000 416	0.853
9	0.628	1.000 416	0.628
10	0.700	1.000 416	0.700
11	0.852	1.000 416	0.858
12	1.159	1.000 416	1.159

从图 10.3 中的 12 个月调整后的季节指数图形可以看出，Vintage 餐厅的每月食品和饮料销售额有明显的季节效应。在这个案例中，1 月季节指数最大，说明 1 月食品和饮料销售额在一年中是最高的；相反，9 月季节指数最小，说明 9 月的食品和饮料销售额最低。4 月的季节指数接近平均值，比 1 大了仅仅 0.41%。这就说明 4 月食品和饮料销售额与过去三年运营中的每年平均水平几乎相同。

From the plot of the 12-month adjusted seasonal indexes above, simply by visual inspection we can see that the seasonal effect of sales is very obvious. In this case, the January seasonal index is the largest, indicating that food and beverage sales in January are the highest throughout the year, while the September seasonal index is the smallest, showing that food and beverage sales in September are the lowest. Closest to the average, the April seasonal index is larger than 1 by only 0.41%. That is to say, food and beverage sales in April are almost the same as the annual average level over the past three years of operation.

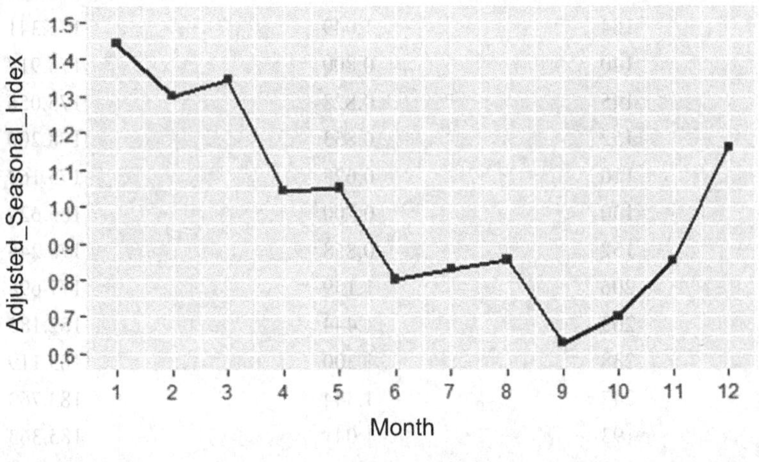

Figure 10.3　12-Month Seasonal Indexes of Vintage Food and Beverage Sales

图 10.3　Vintage 餐厅食品和饮料销售的 12 个月调整后的季节指数

（2）消除时间序列的季节影响

上一步已经得到月季节指数，可用来将季节效应从时间序列中移除，以研究趋势成分。

利用乘法模型的表示法，得到

$$Y_t = T_t \times S_t \times I_t \qquad (10.2)$$

通过将每个时间序列观察值除以相应的季节指数，可以把季节变动效应从实际销售额时间序列中移除。这一过程称为**消除时间序列的季节变动影响**。表 10.6 总结了消除季节变动影响的 Vintage 餐厅食品和饮料销售额时间序列。

(2) Deseasonalizing the Time Series

Now that we have monthly seasonal indexes, we can use them to remove the seasonal effects from the sales time series so that the trend can be studied. This process is referred to as *deseasonalizing* the time series. Using the notation of the multiplicative model, we have

$$Y_t = T_t \times S_t \times I_t \qquad (10.2)$$

By dividing each time series observation by the corresponding seasonal index, we can remove the effect of season from the actual sales time series. The deseasonalized time series for Vintage food and beverage sales is summarized in Table 10.6.

Table 10.6 Deseasonalized Values for the Vintage Food and Beverage Sales Time Series

表 10.6 Vintage 餐厅食品和饮料销售额消除季节性影响的时间序列

Year（年）	Month（月）	Sales(Y_t)[销售额（千美元）]	Adjusted Seasonal Index（调整后的季节指数）	Deseasonalized ($Y_t / S_t = T_t I_t$)（消除季节影响的值）
1	1	242	1.444	167.638
	2	235	1.300	180.811
	3	232	1.344	172.604
	4	178	1.041	170.956
	5	184	1.049	175.341
	6	140	0.800	174.917
	7	145	0.828	175.056
	8	152	0.853	178.200
	9	110	0.628	175.163
	10	130	0.700	185.629
	11	152	0.858	178.245
	12	206	1.159	177.698
2	1	263	1.444	182.185
	2	238	1.300	183.119
	3	247	1.344	183.763
	4	193	1.041	185.363
	5	193	1.049	183.917
	6	149	0.800	186.161
	7	157	0.828	189.543

续表

Year（年）	Month（月）	Sales(Y_t)[销售额（千美元）]	Adjusted Seasonal Index（调整后的季节指数）	Deseasonalized ($Y_t / S_t = T_t I_t$)（消除季节影响的值）
	8	161	0.853	188.751
	9	122	0.628	194.272
	10	130	0.700	185.629
	11	167	0.858	195.835
	12	230	1.159	198.400
3	1	282	1.444	195.347
	2	255	1.300	196.199
	3	265	1.344	197.155
	4	205	1.041	196.888
	5	210	1.049	200.117
	6	160	0.800	199.905
	7	166	0.828	200.409
	8	174	0.853	203.992
	9	126	0.628	200.641
	10	148	0.700	211.331
	11	173	0.858	202.871
	12	235	1.159	202.714

浏览表 10.6 列 5 的消除季节变动的销售额，可以看到在过去三年中，Vintage 餐厅的食品和饮料销售额呈现稳步增长的长期趋势。图 10.4 显示了实际销售额以及消除季节变动后的销售额。很显然，通过消除季节效应使我们能够专注于整体长远趋势上。

Scanning the deseasonalized sales in column 5 of Table 10.6, we see that the sales of food and beverages showed a moderate increase over the three-year period. Figure 10.4 shows both the actual sales and the deseasonalized sales. It is clear that removing the seasonal factor allows us to focus on the overall long-term trend of sales.

（3）使用消除季节影响后的时间序列来识别趋势

(3) Using the Deseasonalized Data to Identify Trend

在图 10.5 中描绘的消除季节影响后的数据似乎遵循一条直线。因此，根据这些数据用线性最小二乘法建立趋势的回归方程是合理的。

The deseasonalized data depicted in Figure 10.5 seems to follow a straight line. Hence, it is reasonable to develop a linear least squares trend equation based on these data.

为识别趋势，使用 R 软件得到回归方程。输出如下，包括一个实际观察值和消除季节变动影响销售额的散点图以及回

To identify the trend, we use R to find the regression equation. The output follows. The output includes a scatter diagram of the coded time periods and the deseasonalized sales as well as the regression

归直线。长期趋势线的方程为

$$\hat{Y} = 169.350 + 1.0213x$$

line.

The equation for the trend line is

$$\hat{Y} = 169.350 + 1.0213x$$

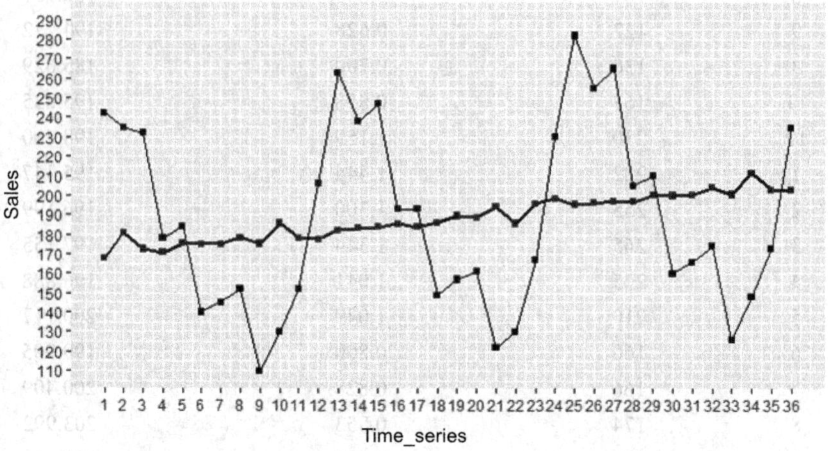

Figure 10.4 Actual and Deseasonalized Sales Time Series for Vintage

图 10.4 真实的和消除季节影响后的 Vintage 餐厅销售额的时间序列

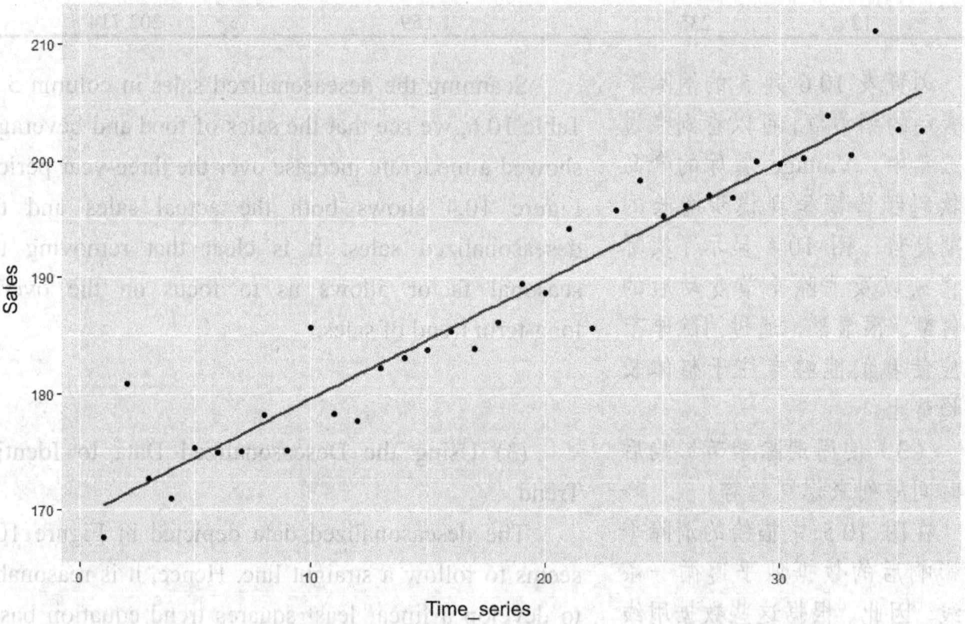

Figure 10.5 Fit Line Plot of Deseasonalized Sales Time Series For Vintage

图 10.5 Vintage 餐厅消除季节影响的销售额时间序列的线性拟合图

所以，$T_t = 169.350 + 1.0213t$ 是该时间序列的线性长期趋势因素的表达形式。斜率 1.021 3 表明在过去 36 个月里，Vintage

Therefore, $T_t = 169.350 + 1.0213t$ is the expression for the linear trend component of the time series.

The slope of 1.021 3 indicates that over the past 36 months, Vintage Restaurant averaged deseasonalized

餐厅消除季节变动影响后的销售额平均增长额为每月 1 021.3 美元。值 169.350 是趋势线在 Y 轴上的截距（当 $t=0$ 时取到）。R 软件同时也输出**决定系数**。该值称为 R^2，为 91.81%。由于这些数据不是样本信息，理论上不能使用 R^2 来判断这里的回归方程的好坏。但是，这将有助于快速评估消除季节影响的销售额数据的线性拟合程度。在此例中，由于拟合优度相当大，接近于1，所以回归方程的拟合效果很好，说明 Vintage 餐厅消除季节效应后的销售数据可以有效地被这条线性趋势方程解释。

growth in sales of about 1 021.3 dollars per month. The value of 169.350 is the intercept of the trend line on the Y-axis (i.e., for t=0).The R system also outputs the coefficient of determination. This value, called R^2, is 91.81 percent. Because this is not sample information, technically we should not use R^2 for judging a regression equation. However, it will serve to quickly evaluate the fit of the deseasonalized sales data. In this case, because R^2 is rather large with a value close to 1, we conclude that the deseasonalized sales of Vintage Restaurant are effectively explained by the linear trend equation.

（4）基于步骤 3 的趋势进行预测

(4) Develop a Forecast Based on Trend

如果假设过去三年的运作是今后相当不错的预测指标，那么这个方程可用于预测第四年的时间序列的趋势组成部分。例如，如表 10.7 所示，对应于第四年第一个月的 t 值为 37，所以那时的长期趋势预测值为 207.137。计算过程如下：

$$T_{37}=169.350+1.0213\times37$$
$$=207.137$$

If we assume that the past three-year operation is a reasonably good indicator of the future, this equation can be used to project the trend component of the time series for the fourth year. For example, for the first month of the fourth year the value of t is 37 and the trend forecast of that period is 207.137, found by

$$T_{37}=169.350+1.0213\times37=207.137$$

Table 10.7 Monthly Trend Projections for the Vintage Food and Beverage Sales Time Series

表 10.7 Vintage 餐厅食品和饮料销售额时间序列的月度长期趋势预测

Year（年）	t value（时间 t 值）	Month（月）	Trend Forecast[①]（长期趋势预测值）
4	37	1	207.137
	38	2	208.159
	39	3	209.180
	40	4	210.201
	41	5	211.223

① 上面得到的是销售额的趋势预测值，然后才考虑季节性因素的影响。

续表

Year（年）	t value（时间 t 值）	Month（月）	Trend Forecast（长期趋势预测值）
	42	6	212.244
	43	7	213.265
	44	8	214.287
	45	9	215.308
	46	10	216.329
	47	11	217.350
	48	12	218.372

因此，通过长期趋势因素得到来年 1 月的销售额预测值为 207.137 美元。上面得到的是销售额的趋势预测值，然后还需考虑季节性因素的影响。同样地，利用趋势成分可以分别得到其他月份的销售额预测值。

Thus, the trend component yields a sales forecast of 207.137 thousand dollars for January in the coming year. This is the sales trend forecast, before we consider the effects of seasonality. Similarly, the trend component produces sales forecasts in other months respectively.

（5）使用每个月的季节指数调整趋势预测值

(5) Seasonal Adjustments of Trend Projection

上一步得到了未来 12 个月的趋势预测值，接下来需要对它们进行季节性调整。例如，由于 1 月份调整后的季节指数为 1.444（见表 10.5），所以可以将第四年 1 月份的趋势预测值调整为

$$207.137 \times 1.444 = 299.021$$

Now that we have the trend forecasts for the next twelve-month period in the fourth year, we can seasonally adjust them. The adjusted seasonal index for January is 1.444, so we can seasonally adjust the forecast for January of the fourth year by

$$207.137 \times 1.444 = 299.021$$

使用相同的算法，确定出第四年每个月的月度预测值（见表 10.8）。R 软件输出如下。

We use the same procedure and a R spreadsheet to determine a monthly forecast for each month of the fourth year. The R output follows.

Table 10.8 Monthly Forecasts for the Vintage Food and Beverage Sales Time Series

表 10.8 Vintage 餐厅食品和饮料销售额时间序列的月度预测值

Year（年）	Month（月）	Trend Forecast（长期趋势预测值）	Seasonal Index（季节指数）	Monthly Forecast（月份预测值）
4	1	207.137	1.444	299.021
	2	208.159	1.300	270.544
	3	209.180	1.344	281.163
	4	210.201	1.041	218.862

续表

Year（年）	Month（月）	Trend Forecast（长期趋势预测值）	Seasonal Index（季节指数）	Monthly Forecast（月份预测值）
	5	211.223	1.049	221.654
	6	212.244	0.800	169.876
	7	213.265	0.828	176.649
	8	214.287	0.853	182.781
	9	215.308	0.628	135.211
	10	216.329	0.700	151.500
	11	217.350	0.853	185.348
	12	218.372	1.159	253.152

最后，我们得到季节调整后的第四年月销售预测值。在表 10.7 第 5 列中的下一年销售预测值将成为 Vintage 餐厅自我评估的有效工具，然后调整预算以增加来年的利润。

Finally, we have the adjusted monthly sales forecast for the fourth year of Vintage Restaurant. The resulting sales forecast for the next year's performance in column 5 of Table 10.7 is an effective self-assessment tool for Vintage Restaurant to adjust budgets so as to increase profits for the coming year.

（6）探讨与结论

(6) Discuss other types of information further

对于 Vintage 餐厅老板 Karen 而言，光对过去 3 年销售业绩以及未来销售预测进行大致评价是远远不够的。Karen 还应该考虑以下几个方面信息。

For Karen, the owner of Vintage Restaurant, it is far from satisfactory to make only a general assessment of the sales performance of the past three years and sales forecasts for the future. The following types of information should also be considered.

第一，要考虑影响销售和顾客的内部服务。Karen 应该结合过去 3 年各月销售额，客观分析包括订单流程、批发成本、食物储存、食品定价、员工招聘与培训、顾客服务质量等运营过程中存在的问题，积极采取解决方案，提高 Vintage 饭店的食品和服务质量。

Firstly, we can consider internal services relating to sales and customers. By combining monthly sales over the past three years, Karen could objectively analyze existing problems within the operation, including the ordering process, wholesale costs, food storage, food pricing, staff recruitment and training, and customer service quality. It is necessary to take active steps to improve the food and service quality of Vintage Restaurant.

第二，需获得竞争对手的表现的信息。Karen 应将 Vintage 之前的销售表现与其竞争对手

Second, information on the performance of its competitors is needed. Karen should compare Vintage's previous sales performance with those of its

以及行业平均水平做同期比较，分析差距原因从而改进经营状况。值得注意的是，Karen应借鉴竞争对手在销售淡季增加利润的措施，比如，除了海鲜高档正餐之外，推出另一款当季食品以抵消季节效应。这是将企业固定成本分摊到整一年而不是几个月的有效方法。

competitors and industrial average levels over the same period, and then analyze the reasons for discrepancies to improve her operating conditions. It is noteworthy that Karen should learn from competitors' measures to boost profits in off-season periods. For instance, in addition to the high-end seafood dinner, another in-season food is put forward on sale to offset the seasonal effect. This is an effective way to apportion the fixed costs of the enterprise over the entire year instead of over several months.

第三，结合以上两个方面，建议Karen做SWOT市场分析，确定企业本身的竞争优势、竞争劣势、机会和威胁，同时考虑整个行业的现状及发展趋势，从而将企业的发展战略与企业内部资源、外部环境有机结合。

Third, it is recommended that Karen should do a SWOT market analysis based on the above-mentioned two aspects. By doing this, she can discover competitive advantages and disadvantages, opportunities and threats. Meanwhile, the industry's status quo and development trend should be also taken into account in order to dynamically combine the enterprise's strategies with its' internal resources and external environment.

第四，随着第四年的到来，Karen应该实时追踪实际销售额与预期销售额的误差原因，监控企业销售价格和成本变动，这样可以在大问题发生前及时调整企业预算，缩减额外开支，以保证预期利润的顺利实现。

Finally, at the start of the fourth year Karen should undertake real-time tracking of the reasons for any discrepancies between real sales and expected ones, monitoring sales price and cost changes. In this way, she can adjust her budget in a timely manner and reduce additional costs before big problems occur, thus ensure the smooth realization of her anticipated profits.

Appendix 10.1 Forecasting Using Excel

附录10.1 用Excel进行预测

对于存在长期趋势和季节变动的时间序列，可通过以下步骤来进行预测。

The following steps can be used to forecast a time series that has both trend(T) and seasonal components(S).

1．移动平均法的操作步骤（见图 10.6～图 10.11）

1．Moving Averages

步骤 1：单击“文件”，在左侧菜单栏选择**“选项”**。

Step 1: Click File and select **Options** on the left menu.

步骤 2：单击**“加载项”**选项，再单击屏幕下方的**“转到”**。

Step 2: Click the **Add-ons** option, then click **Go to** at the bottom of the screen.

步骤 3：在弹出窗口中选中**“分析工具库”**和**“分析工具库-VBA”**，并单击**“确定”**。

Step 3: Click **Analysis Tool Library** and **Analysis Tool Library-VBA** in the pop-up window, and click **OK**.

步骤 4：单击**“数据”**，选择**“数据分析”**。

Step 4: Click Data and select **Data Analysis**.

步骤 5：选择**“移动平均”**，单击**“确定”**。

Step 5: Select **Moving Average** and click **OK**.

步骤 6：把数据按图所示排好，在输入区域输入 **B2:B37**，在间隔输入 **12**，在输出区域输入 **C2**，单击**“确定”**。调整数据最终结果，使得数据的前六项与后六项为#N/A。

Step 6: Arrange the data as shown in the figure. Enter **B2: B37** in the input area, enter **12** in the interval, and enter **C2** in the output area and click OK.

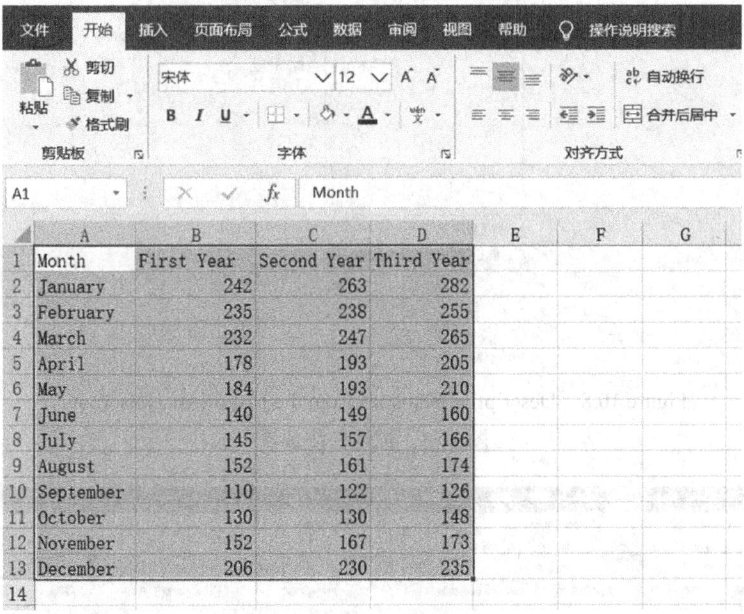

Figure 10.6　Descriptive Statistics from the List of Analysis Tools

图 10.6　描述性统计-1

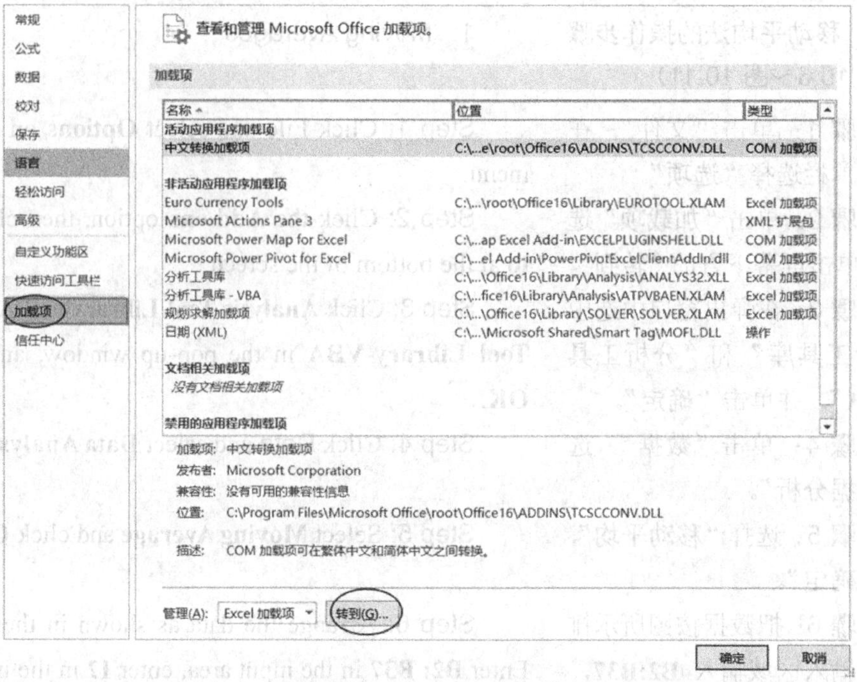

Figure 10.7 Descriptive Statistics from the List of Analysis Tools

图 10.7 描述性统计-2

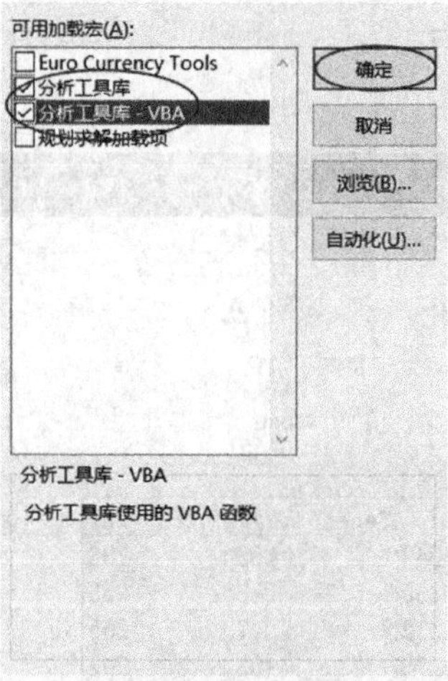

Figure 10.8 Descriptive Statistics from the List of Analysis Tools

图 10.8 描述性统计-3

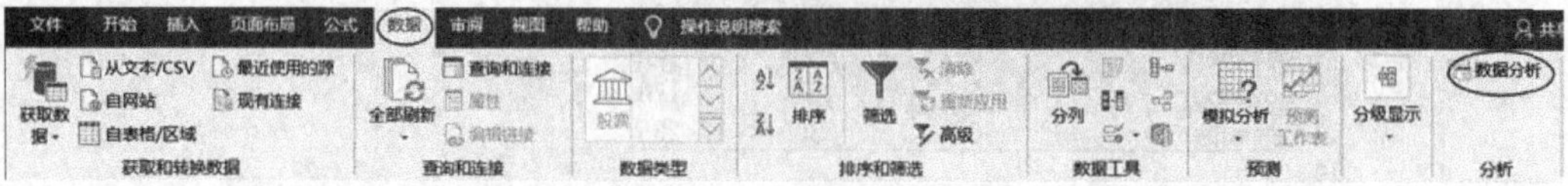

Figure 10.9 Descriptive Statistics from the List of Analysis Tools

图 10.9 描述性统计-4

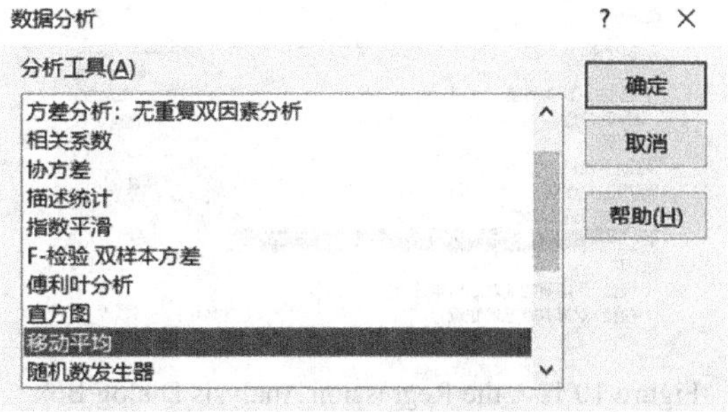

Figure 10.10 the Moving Average Dialog Box

图 10.10 移动平均-1

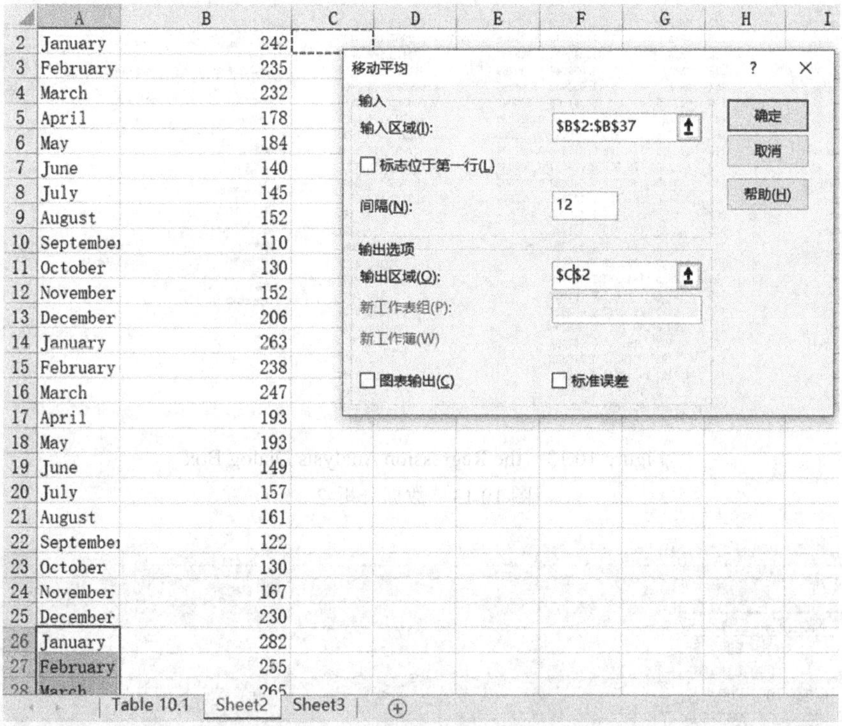

Figure 10.11 the Moving Average Dialog Box

图 10.11 移动平均-2

2．趋势识别的操作步骤（见图 10.12～图 10.14）

步骤 1：选择“数据分析”，选择“回归”，单击“确定”。

步骤 2：在 Y 值输入区域输入 J2:J37，在 X 值输入区域输入 A2:A37，单击“确定”。

2. Identifying Trend

Step 1: Select **Data Analysis**, select **Regression** and click **OK**.

Step 2: Enter **J2:J37** in the Y value input area, **A2: A37** in the X value input area, click **OK**.

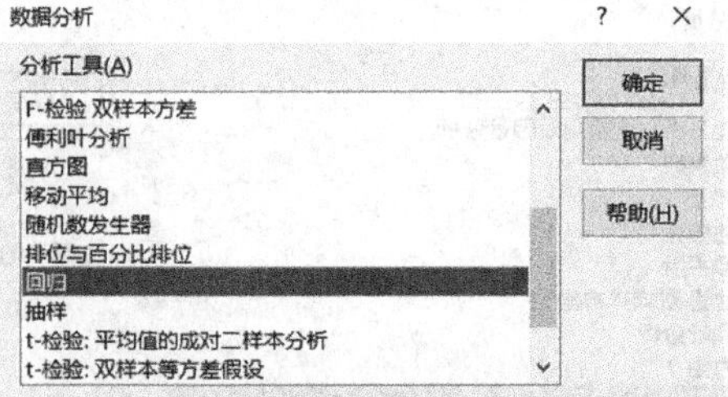

Figure 10.12　the Regression Analysis Dialog Box

图 10.12　数据分析-1

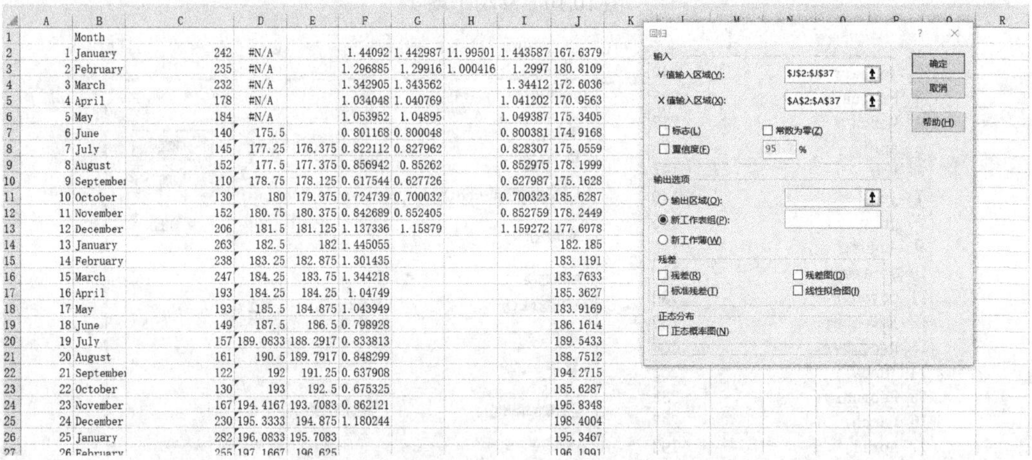

	A	B	C	D	E	F	G	H	I	J
1		Month								
2	1	January	242	#N/A		1.44092	1.442987	11.99501	1.443587	167.6379
3	2	February	235	#N/A		1.296885	1.29916	1.000416	1.2997	180.8109
4	3	March	232	#N/A		1.342905	1.343562		1.34412	172.6036
5	4	April	178	#N/A		1.034048	1.040769		1.041202	170.9563
6	5	May	184	#N/A		1.053952	1.04895		1.049387	175.3405
7	6	June	140	175.5		0.801168	0.800048		0.800381	174.9168
8	7	July	145	177.25	176.375	0.822112	0.827962		0.828307	175.0559
9	8	August	152	177.5	177.375	0.856942	0.85262		0.852975	178.1999
10	9	Septembe	110	178.75	178.125	0.617544	0.627726		0.627987	175.1628
11	10	October	130	180	179.375	0.724739	0.700032		0.700323	185.6287
12	11	November	152	180.75	180.375	0.842689	0.852405		0.852759	178.2449
13	12	December	206	181.5	181.125	1.137336	1.15879		1.159272	177.6978
14	13	January	263	182.5	182	1.445055				182.185
15	14	February	238	183.25	182.875	1.301435				183.1191
16	15	March	247	184.25	183.75	1.344218				183.7633
17	16	April	193	184.25	184.25	1.04749				185.3627
18	17	May	193	185.5	184.875	1.043949				183.9169
19	18	June	149	187.5	186.5	0.798928				186.1614
20	19	July	157	189.0833	188.2917	0.833813				189.5433
21	20	August	161	190.5	189.7917	0.848299				188.7512
22	21	Septembe	122	192	191.25	0.637908				194.2715
23	22	October	130	193	192.5	0.675325				185.6287
24	23	November	167	194.4167	193.7083	0.862121				195.8348
25	24	December	230	195.3333	194.875	1.180244				198.4004
26	25	January	282	196.0833	195.7083					195.3467
27	26	February	255	197.1667	196.625					196.1991

Figure 10.13　the Regression Analysis Dialog Box

图 10.13　数据分析-2

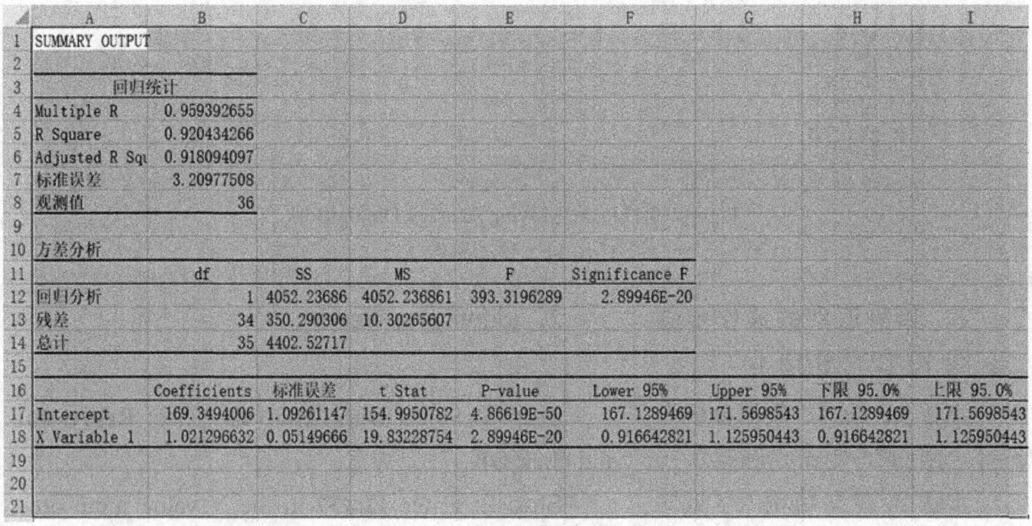

	A	B	C	D	E	F	G	H	I
1	SUMMARY OUTPUT								
2									
3	回归统计								
4	Multiple R	0.959392655							
5	R Square	0.920434266							
6	Adjusted R Squ	0.918094097							
7	标准误差	3.20977508							
8	观测值	36							
9									
10	方差分析								
11		df	SS	MS	F	Significance F			
12	回归分析	1	4052.23686	4052.236861	393.3196289	2.89946E-20			
13	残差	34	350.290306	10.30265607					
14	总计	35	4402.52717						
15									
16		Coefficients	标准误差	t Stat	P-value	Lower 95%	Upper 95%	下限 95.0%	上限 95.0%
17	Intercept	169.3494006	1.09261147	154.9950782	4.86619E-50	167.1289469	171.5698543	167.1289469	171.5698543
18	X Variable 1	1.021296632	0.05149666	19.83228754	2.89946E-20	0.916642821	1.125950443	0.916642821	1.125950443
19									
20									
21									

Figure 10.14　Outcomes from Excel

图 10.14　分析结果

3．预测

由回归模型进行预测，并计算上季节指数得到最终预测值（见图 10.15）。

3．Forecast

Forecast by regression model and calculate the seasonal index to get the final forecast value.

	A	B	C	D	E	F	G	H	I	J	K	L	M
28	27	March	265	197. 5	197. 3333					197. 155			
29	28	April	205	199	198. 25					196. 8879			
30	29	May	210	199. 5	199. 25					200. 1169			
31	30	June	160	199. 9167	199. 7083					199. 9049			
32	31	July	166	#N/A						200. 4089			
33	32	August	174	#N/A						203. 992			
34	33	Septembe	126	#N/A						200. 641			
35	34	October	148	#N/A						211. 3311			
36	35	November	173	#N/A						202. 8708			
37	36	December	235	#N/A						202. 7135			
38	37										169. 3494	207. 1374	299. 0209
39	38										1. 021297	208. 1587	270. 5439
40	39											209. 18	281. 163
41	40											210. 2013	218. 8619
42	41											211. 2226	221. 6542
43	42											212. 2439	169. 8759
44	43											213. 2652	176. 649
45	44											214. 2865	182. 7809
46	45											215. 3077	135. 2105
47	46											216. 329	151. 5002
48	47											217. 3503	185. 3475
49	48											218. 3716	253. 1521
50													
51													
52													
53													

Table 10.1 | Sheet1 | Sheet2 | Sheet3

Figure 10.15　Final Outcomes of Forecast from Excel

图 10.15　预测结果

Appendix 10.2　Forecasting Using R

附录 10.2　时间序列预测

There are six steps required to perform forecasting in R. 1. Import data and draw a basic plot. 2. Calculate seasonal index of every month in moving average methods. 3. Eliminate seasonal effects of time series. 4. Build regression equation in linear least square test. 5. Forcast with regression equation. 6. Adjust the forecast with the seasonal index of each month.

在 R 语言中进行时间序列预测需要六个步骤：一是导入数据，做基础图像。二是使用移动平均法计算出每个月的季节指数。三是消除时间序列的季节影响。四是用线性最小二乘法建立趋势的回归方程。五是利用回归方程进行预测。六是利用每个月的季节指数调整预测值。

1．代码

```
#步骤一：读取数据并作图
install.packages("ggplot2")
```

```
library(ggplot2)
#加载并安装 ggplot2 包
install.packages("readxl")
library(readxl)
#安装并加载 readxl 包以读取数据
rm(list=ls())
#清空工作环境
data<-read_excel("Chapter 10-Forecasting Food and Beverage Sales.xls")
data1<-transform(data,list=rep(1:36))
ggplot(data1,aes(x=Time_series,y=Sales))+geom_line(size=0.5,color="blue")+geom_point(size=1.5,color="black",shape=15)+scale_y_continuous(limits=c(110,290),breaks=seq(110,290,10))+scale_x_continuous(limits=c(1,36),breaks=seq(1,36,1))
#读入数据并观察
#ggplot()是 R 中用来作图的函数，aes、geom_line、geom_path、geom_point、scale_y_continuous、scale_x_continuous 用来调整作图的细节，后不再赘述

#步骤二：使用移动平均法计算出每个月的季节指数
data<-transform(data,Months_Moving_Average=filter(data$Sales/12,rep(1,12),sides = 2))
data<-transform(data,Centered_Moving_Average=filter(data$Months_Moving_Average/2,rep(1,2),sides = 1))
data
data1<-transform(data,Time_series=rep(1:36))
ggplot(data1,aes(x=Time_series,y=Sales))+geom_line(size=0.5,color="blue")+
geom_path(x=data1$Time_series,y=data1$Centered_Moving_Average,size=0.5,color="black")+
geom_point(size=1.5,color="black",shape=15)+
geom_point(x=data1$Time_series,y=data1$Centered_Moving_Average,size=1.5,color="red",shape=15)+
scale_y_continuous(limits=c(110,290),breaks=seq(110,290,10))+
scale_x_continuous(limits=c(1,36),breaks=seq(1,36,1))

data<-transform(data,Seasonal_Irregular_Value=Sales/Centered_Moving_Average)
#计算季节不规则值
data[is.na(data)] <- 0
#将数据中 NA 转变为 0，方便处理数据
Month<-array(1:12)
#定义变量，准备进行季节指数平均化
SI1<-array(0,12)
SI2<-array(0,12)
for(j in 1:12){
    for(i in 1:nrow(data)){
        if(identical(Month[j],data[i,1])&(data[i,5]!=0)){
          if( identical(SI1[j],0)){
            SI1[j]=data[i,5]} else {SI2[j]=data[i,5]}
        }
    }
}
#循环，将两年的季节不规则值分别放入 SI1、SI2 中
d<-data.frame(Month=rep(1:12))
#建立数据框，将所得数据置入其中
```

```
d<-transform(d,SI_1=SI1)
d<-transform(d,SI_2=SI2)
d
d<-transform(d,Typical_Seasonal_Index=(SI_1+SI_2)/2)
#将每月季节指数的计算值平均化
d

CF<-12/sum(d[4])
#计算修正因子
d<-transform(d,Adjusted_Seasonal_Index=Typical_Seasonal_Index*CF)
#调整每月的季节指数
d
ggplot(d,aes(x=Month,y=Adjusted_Seasonal_Index))+
geom_line(size=0.8,color=" black" )+
geom_point(size=1.5,color="red",shape=15)+
scale_y_continuous(limits=c(0.6,1.5),breaks=seq(0.6,1.5,0.1))+
scale_x_continuous(limits=c(1,12),breaks=seq(1,12,1))

#步骤三：消除时间序列的季节影响
Adjusted_SeasonalIndex<-rep(d[,5],3)
#消除时间序列季节影响
data<-transform(data,Adjusted_Seasonal_Index=Adjusted_SeasonalIndex)
data<-transform(data,Deseasonalized=Sales/Adjusted_Seasonal_Index)
data
data1<-transform(data,Time_series=rep(1:36))
ggplot(data1,aes(x=Time_series,y=Sales))+
geom_line(size=0.5,color="blue")+
geom_path(x=data1$Time_series,y=data1$Deseasonalized,size=0.8,color="black")+
geom_point(size=1.5,color="black",shape=15)+
geom_point(x=data1$Time_series,y=data1$Deseasonalized,size=1.5,color="red",shape=15)+
scale_y_continuous(limits=c(110,290),breaks=seq(110,290,10))+
scale_x_continuous(limits=c(1,36),breaks=seq(1,36,1))

#步骤四：用线性最小二乘法建立回归方程
x<-data1$Time_series
y<-data1$Deseasonalized
lm.SI<-lm(y~1+x)  #*详见函数参数说明*
summary(lm.SI)

#步骤五：使用回归方程进行预测
data2<-data.frame(
      t_value=c(37:48),
      Month=c(1:12),
      Trend_Forecast=predict(lm.SI,data.frame(x=c(37:48))) #*详见函数参数说明*
)
data2
```

```
#步骤六：使用每个月的季节指数调整预测值
data2<-transform(data2,Seasonal_Index=d$Adjusted_Seasonal_Index)
data2<-transform(data2,Monthly_Forecast=Trend_Forecast*Seasonal_Index)
data2
```

2．具体过程分析

步骤 1：为实现高级作图，需要安装并调用 ggplot 程序包。以.csv 形式读入数据并做出散点图。

步骤 2：使用移动平均法计算出每个月的季节指数，包括：

（1）计算移动平均数以及中心化移动平均数；

（2）计算平均化季节指数；

（3）调整每月的季节指数，使其总和等于 12。

步骤 3：消除时间序列的季节影响。

步骤 4：用线性最小二乘法建立趋势的回归方程。

步骤 5：使用步骤 4 的趋势来预测第 4 年 1～12 月的销售额时间序列的趋势成分。

步骤 6：使用每个月的季节指数调整趋势预测值。

3．*函数参数说明

```
lm(y~1+x)
```

☑ lm(formula)函数：拟合广义线性模型。

☑ formula：给出要拟合的模型信息，y~1+x 代表要拟合的模型是一元线性模型。

```
predict(lm.SI,data.frame(x=c(37:48))
```

☑ predict(object,data)函数：进行预测。

☑ object：给定模型。

☑ data：给定要预测的月份。

4．分析结果（见表 10.9）

Table 10.9 Outcomes of Analysis

表 10.9 分析结果

Year（年）	Month（月）	Trend Forecast（趋势预测）	Seasonal Index（季节指数）	Monthly Forecast（月度预测）
4	1	207.137	1.444	299.021
	2	208.159	1.300	270.544
	3	209.180	1.344	281.163
	4	210.201	1.041	218.862
	5	211.223	1.049	221.654
	6	212.244	0.800	169.876
	7	213.265	0.828	176.649

续表

Year（年）	Month（月）	Trend Forecast（趋势预测）	Seasonal Index（季节指数）	Monthly Forecast（月度预测）
	8	214.287	0.853	182.781
	9	215.308	0.628	135.211
	10	216.329	0.700	151.500
	11	217.350	0.853	185.348
	12	218.372	1.159	253.152

*最终的预测销售额在最后一列给出。

Appendix 10.3　Formulas and Notes

附录 10.3　关键公式与注解

1．长期趋势（Trend）

长期趋势是指时间序列观测值的长期移动或者波动。

2．季节变动因素（Seasonal Component）

季节变动因素是时间序列分解的因素之一，它显示在一年或一年以内的具有周期性规律的变动。

3．不规则变动因素（Irregular Component）

不规则变动因素是时间序列分解的因素之一，它反映时间序列的数值在剔除了长期趋势、季节和循环因素之外的随机变动。

4．移动平均法（Moving Average）

移动平均法又称滑动平均法，它使用时间序列中最近 n 期数据值的平均数作为下一时期的预测值。其公式为

$$\text{移动平均数} = \frac{\text{最近 } n \text{ 期数据值之和}}{n}$$

5．消除季节影响的时间序列（Deseasonalized Time Series）

这是用时间序列每一个原始观测值除以相应的季节指数后得到的一个时间序列。

6．时间序列乘法模型（Multiplicative Time Series Model）

这是将时间序列的独立成分乘在一起来确定时间序列实际值的一种模型。如果假设中有趋势、循环、季节和不规则四种成分，得到 $Y_t = T_t \times C_t \times S_t \times I_t$；如果假设中有趋势、季节和不规则三种成分，得到 $Y_t = T_t \times C_t \times S_t \times I_t$。

References

参考文献

[1] 袁卫，庞皓，曾五一．统计学[M]．北京：高等教育出版社，2009．

[2] 吴喜之．统计学：从数据到结论[M]．北京：中国统计出版社，2006．

[3] 茆诗松，程依明，濮晓龙．概率论与数理统计教程[M]．2 版．北京：高等教育出版社，2011．

[4] 盛骤，谢式千，潘承毅．概率论与数理统计[M]．4 版．北京：高等教育出版社，2008．

[5] 何晓群，刘文卿．应用回归分析[M]．北京：中国人民大学出版社，2007．

[6] 王星．非参数统计[M]．北京：中国人民大学出版社，2005．

[7] 刘顺忠，荣丽敏，景丽芳．非参数统计和 SPSS 软件应用[M]．武汉：武汉大学出版社，2008．

[8] 陈颖．SAS 数据分析系统教程[M]．上海：复旦大学出版社，2008．

[9] 王黎明，陈颖，杨楠．应用回归分析[M]．2 版．上海：复旦大学出版社，2018．

[10] Bruce L. Bowerman．商务统计基础[M]．韩小亮，译．3 版．北京：清华大学出版社，2012．

[11] 孙允午．统计学——数据的搜集、整理和分析[M]．上海：上海财经大学出版社，2006．

[12] Ron Larson，Betsy Farber．基础统计学（英文版第 4 版）[M]．刘超，改编．北京：中国人民大学出版社，2010．

[13] B. S. Everitt．剑桥统计学辞典[M]．钱晓明，译．上海：上海财经大学出版社，2010．

[14] 刘曙光，胡再勇．黄金价格的长期决定因素稳定性分析[J]．世界经济研究，2008（2）：35-41．

[15] 杨楠，邱丽颖．我国国际储备资产的最优结构研究——基于时变 Copula 及 VaR 的投资组合模型分析[J]．财经研究，2012，38（05）：15-27．

[16] 杨楠，何皆易．黄金抗通胀功能的阶段性变化及影响因素分析[J]．上海财经大学学报，2011，13（06）：80-88．

[17] 杨楠，方茜．黄金抗美元贬值避险能力的动态分析[J]．国际金融研究，2013（3）：58-67．

[18] Lind, Marchal, Wathen. Statistical techniques in business and economics[M]. New York: McGraw-Hill Irwin, 2010.

[19] David R. Anderson, Dennis J. Sweeney, Thomas A. Williams, et al. Statistics for business and economics[M]. Boston: Cengage Learning, 2005.

[20] Paul Newbold, William L. Carlson, Betty M. Thorne. Statistics for business and economics[M]. Harlow: Pearson Education, Inc., 2013.

[21] Jessica M. Utts. Seeing through statistics[M]. North Sciute: Duxbury Press, 2004.

[22] Dennis D. Wackerly, William Mendenhall III, Richard L. Scheaffer. Mathematical statistics with application[M]. Belmont, CA: Thomson Brooks/Cole, 2008.

[23] Raymond H.Myers. Classical and modern regression with applications[M]. 2nd ed. Beijing: Higher Education Press, 2008.

[24] Levin E J, Wright R E. Short-run and long-run determinants of the price of gold[R]. World gold council research study, 2006(32).

[25] Baur D, Lucey B. Is gold a hedge or a safe haven? An analysis of stocks, bonds and gold[J]. The financial review, 2010 (45): 217-229.

[26] Baur D, McDermott T. Is gold a safe haven? international evidence[J]. Journal of banking and finance, 2010(34): 1886-1898.

[27] Wang K M, Lee Y M, Thi N T B. Time and place where gold acts as an Inflation hedge: an application of long-run and short-run threshold model[J]. Economic modelling, 2011(28): 806-819.

[28] Benhmad F. Modeling nonlinear granger causality between the oil price and U.S. dollar: a wavelet based approach[J]. Economic modelling, 2012 (29): 1505-1514.

[29] Lee Y H, Huang Y L, Yang H J. The asymmetric long-run relationship between crude oil and gold futures[J]. Global journal of business research, 2012(6): 9-15.

[30] Wang Y S, Chueh Y L. Dynamic transmission effects between the interest rate, the US dollar, and gold and crude oil prices[J]. Economic modelling, 2013(30): 792-798.

参考网站

[1] http://www.gold.org

[2] http://www.federalreserve.gov

[3] http://www.dol.gov

[4] http://finance.yahoo.com

[5] http://www.eia.doe.gov

[6] https://www.bls.gov

[7] https://fred.stlouisfed.org

[8] http://report.iresearch.cn

Appendix A

附录 A

A.1 Data Set – School's Out

A.1 数据集——年轻人暑期工作情况分析

Table A.1 Percentage of Summer School Attendance,1985—2010

表 A.1 暑期学校的参加率

July, of year	Percentage of Summer School Attendance	
year	16 to 24 years	20 to 24 years
1986	9.8	8.4
1987	10.6	8.6
1988	11.7	10.7
1989	12.3	10.5
1990	13.3	11.4
1991	13.3	12
1992	12.6	11.9
1993	12.6	11.6
1994	16.3	13.8
1995	18	14.8
1996	18.5	15.5
1997	19.3	15.3
1998	20.4	16.4
1999	21.5	16.8
2000	21.2	16.2
2001	24.4	18.7
2002	25.9	19.7
2003	25.5	19.3
2004	28.9	21.7
2005	27.8	20.7
2006	28.5	21.1
2007	31.5	23.2
2008	32	23.9
2009	33.6	24.4
2010	34.9	26.3

Table A.2 Unemployment Rate, Persons 16 to 24 Years of Age, by Sex, Race, and Hispanic or Latino Ethnicity, not Seasonally Adjusted, July, 2007—2010

表 A.2 2007—2010 年每年 7 月 16～24 岁青年人的失业率

（按年龄、性别、种族划分，未经季节性调整）

Sex, race, and ethnicity	2007	2008	2009	2010
16 to 24 years of age, total	10.8	14	18.5	19.1
Women	10.4	12.8	17.3	17.5
Men	11.1	15	19.7	20.5
White	9.3	12.3	16.4	16.2
Hispanic or Latino ethnicity	11.8	16	21.7	22.1
Black or African American	20.5	24.8	31.2	33.4

Table A.3 Data for Employed Persons, Aged 16～24, by Industry and Sex, July 2010

表 A.3 2010 年 7 月调查得到的 16～24 岁青年人的就业数据（按性别、行业划分）

Industry	Men 16～19	Men 20～24	Women 16～19	Women 20～24
Accommodation and food services	726 000	1 032 000	859 000	1 229 000
Retail trade	540 000	1 312 000	622 000	1 244 000
Education and health services	149 000	537 000	338 000	1 802 000
Professional and business services	212 000	718 000	105 000	540 000
Manufacturing	148 000	634 000	77 000	192 000
Arts, entertainment, and recreation	260 000	326 000	267 000	196 000
Construction	192 000	690 000	2 000	33 000
Other services	90 000	318 000	145 000	285 000
Financial activities	57 000	319 000	53 000	380 000
Transportation and utilities	55 000	257 000	17 000	80 000
Public administration	42 000	137 000	22 000	197 000
Information	55 000	163 000	62 000	107 000
Agriculture and related	117 000	164 000	24 000	67 000
Wholesale trade	35 000	200 000	13 000	53 000
Mining, quarrying, and oil and gas extraction	2 000	50 000	3 000	12 000
Total	2 680 000	6 857 000	2 609 000	6 418 000

A.2 Data Set – Fitness
A.2 数据集——我国健身人群画像

Table A.4 Age of the Fitness Crowd

表 A.4 健身人群的年龄分布

Age	Proportion
<20	5.7%
20～30	31.5%
31～40	41.7%
41～50	14.7%
>51	6.5%

Table A.5 Reasons for Fitness

表 A.5 锻炼的原因

Reasons	Proportion
Stay Healthy	66.8%
Strengthen Body	58.4%
Stress Relief	44.8%
Enjoy Exercise	37.7%
Improve Confidence	34.7%
Enhance Willpower	34.6%
Gain Pleasure	31.1%

Table A.6 Fitness Time

表 A.6 健身时间

Time	Proportion
<10 min	0.00%
11～20 min	2.1%
21～30 min	16.8%
31～40 min	32.5%
41～50 min	29.0%
1～1.5 h	16.2%
>1.5 h	3.3%

Table A.7 The Consumption Structure of Fitness People

表 A.7 健身人群的消费结构

Consumption	Courses	Sports	Shoes and Clothes
Proportion	20.8%	24.6%	54.7%

资料来源：2019 年中国运动健身行业发展趋势白皮书，http://report.iresearch.cn/report/201903/3345.shtml.

A.3 Data Set – Forbes 400 Richest Americans
A.3 数据集——福布斯全美 400 富豪榜

Table A.8 Selected Data from the Forbes 400 Richest Americans

表 A.8 福布斯全美 400 富豪榜

Rank	English name	Net worth($)	Age	Residence	Source
1	Jeff Bezos	$114 B	55	Washington	Amazon
2	Bill Gates	$106 B	64	Washington	Microsoft
3	Warren Buffett	$80.8 B	89	Nebraska	Berkshire Hathaway
4	Mark Zuckerberg	$69.6 B	35	California	Facebook
5	Larry Ellison	$65 B	75	California	software
6	Larry Page	$55.5 B	46	California	Google
7	Sergey Brin	$53.5 B	46	California	Google
8	Michael Bloomberg	$53.4 B	77	New York	Bloomberg LP
9	Steve Ballmer	$51.7 B	63	Washington	Microsoft
10	Jim Walton	$51.6 B	71	Arkansas	Walmart
11	Alice Walton	$51.4 B	70	Texas	Walmart
12	Rob Walton	$51.3 B	75	Arkansas	Walmart
13	Charles Koch	$41 B	83	Kansas	Koch Industries
14	Julia Koch & family	$41 B	57	New York	Koch Industries
15	MacKenzie Bezos	$36.1 B	49	Washington	Amazon.com
16	Phil Knight & family	$35.9 B	81	Oregon	Nike
17	Sheldon Adelson	$34.5 B	86	Nevada	casinos
18	Michael Dell	$32.3 B	54	Texas	Dell computers
19	Jacqueline Mars	$29.7 B	80	Virginia	candy, pet food
20	John Mars	$29.7 B	84	Wyoming	candy, pet food
21	Jim Simons	$21.6 B	81	New York	hedge funds
22	Laurene Powell Jobs & family	$21.3 B	55	California	Apple, Disney
23	Elon Musk	$19.9 B	48	California	Tesla Motors, SpaceX
24	Rupert Murdoch & family	$19.1 B	88	New York	newspapers, TV network
25	Leonard Lauder	$18.8 B	82	New York	Estee Lauder
26	Ray Dalio	$18.7 B	70	Connecticut	hedge funds
27	Len Blavatnik	$18.3 B	62		diversified
28	Lukas Walton	$18.1 B	33	Wyoming	Walmart
29	Stephen Schwarzman	$17.7 B	72	New York	investments

续表

Rank	English name	Net worth($)	Age	Residence	Source
30	Carl Icahn	$17.6 B	83	New York	investments
31	Thomas Peterffy	$17.5 B	75	Florida	discount brokerage
32	Donald Bren	$17 B	87	California	real estate
33	Eric Schmidt	$14.2 B	64	California	Google
34	Abigail Johnson	$14 B	57	Massachusetts	money management
35	Steve Cohen	$13.6 B	63	Connecticut	hedge funds
36	Pierre Omidyar	$13.1 B	52	Hawaii	eBay, PayPal
37	Donald Newhouse	$12.8 B	90	New York	media
38	Ken Griffin	$12.7 B	51	Illinois	hedge funds
39	David Tepper	$12 B	62	Florida	hedge funds
40	Dustin Moskovitz	$11.6 B	35	California	Facebook
41	Philip Anschutz	$11.5 B	79	Colorado	investments
42	Thomas Frist, Jr. & family	$11.5 B	81	Tennessee	hospitals
43	John Menard, Jr.	$11.5 B	79	Wisconsin	home improvement stores
44	Charles Ergen	$10.8 B	66	Colorado	satellite TV
45	David Duffield	$10.7 B	79	Nevada	business software
46	Gordon Moore	$10.3 B	90	California	Intel
47	Jan Koum	$10.1 B	43	California	WhatsApp
48	Andrew Beal	$9.8 B	66	Texas	banks, real estate
49	Carl Cook	$9.7 B	57	Indiana	medical devices
50	Stanley Kroenke	$9.7 B	72	Texas	sports, real estate
51	Jim Kennedy	$9.6 B	71	Georgia	media, automotive
52	Blair Parry-Okeden	$9.6 B	69		media, automotive
53	Hank & Doug Meijer	$9.5 B		Michigan	supermarkets
54	Stewart and Lynda Resnick	$9 B		California	agriculture, water
55	Harold Hamm & family	$8.8 B	73	Oklahoma	oil & gas
56	Jerry Jones	$8.6 B	77	Texas	Dallas Cowboys
57	George Soros	$8.6 B	89	New York	hedge funds
58	Christy Walton	$8.5 B	70	Wyoming	Walmart
59	Micky Arison	$8.1 B	70	Florida	Carnival Cruises
60	David Geffen	$7.9 B	76	California	movies, record labels
61	Shahid Khan	$7.8 B	69	Florida	auto parts
62	Tom & Judy Love	$7.8 B	82	Oklahoma	retail & gas stations
63	Leon Black	$7.7 B	68	New York	private equity
64	Ronald Perelman	$7.7 B	76	New York	leveraged buyouts
65	Charles Schwab	$7.7 B	82	California	discount brokerage

续表

Rank	English name	Net worth($)	Age	Residence	Source
66	Stephen Ross	$7.6 B	79	New York	real estate
67	John Doerr	$7.5 B	68	California	venture capital
68	Richard Kinder	$7.5 B	75	Texas	pipelines
69	Ann Walton Kroenke	$7.5 B	70	Texas	Walmart
70	David Green & family	$7.4 B	77	Oklahoma	retail
71	Marijke Mars	$7.4 B	55	California	candy, pet food
72	Pamela Mars	$7.4 B	59	Virginia	candy, pet food
73	Valerie Mars	$7.4 B	60	New York	candy, pet food
74	Victoria Mars	$7.4 B	62	Pennsylvania	candy, pet food
75	John Malone	$7.3 B	78	Colorado	cable television
76	David Shaw	$7.3 B	68	New York	hedge funds
77	James Goodnight	$7.2 B	76	North Carolina	software
78	Herbert Kohler, Jr. & family	$7.2 B	80	Wisconsin	plumbing fixtures
79	Diane Hendricks	$7 B	72	Wisconsin	roofing
80	Edward Johnson, III.	$7 B	89	Massachusetts	money management
81	George Kaiser	$7 B	77	Oklahoma	oil & gas, banking
82	Robert Kraft	$6.9 B	78	Massachusetts	New England Patriots
83	Steven Rales	$6.9 B	68	California	manufacturing
84	Eli Broad	$6.8 B	86	California	investments
85	Jim Davis & family	$6.7 B	76	Massachusetts	New Balance
86	Nancy Walton Laurie	$6.7 B	68	Nevada	Walmart
87	J. Christopher Reyes	$6.7 B	65	Florida	food distribution
88	Jude Reyes	$6.7 B	64	Florida	food distribution
89	John A. Sobrato & family	$6.7 B	80	California	real estate
90	Patrick Soon-Shiong	$6.7 B	67	California	pharmaceuticals
91	Israel Englander	$6.6 B	71	New York	hedge funds
92	Reinhold Schmieding	$6.6 B	64	Florida	medical devices
93	Marc Benioff	$6.5 B	55	California	business software
94	Daniel Gilbert	$6.5 B	57	Michigan	Quicken Loans
95	James Chambers	$6.4 B	62	New York	media, automotive
96	Bernard Marcus	$6.4 B	90	Georgia	Home Depot
97	Robert Pera	$6.4 B	41	California	wireless networking gear
98	Katharine Rayner	$6.4 B	74	New York	media, automotive
99	Margaretta Taylor	$6.4 B	77	New York	media, automotive
100	Dannine Avara	$6.3 B	55	Texas	pipelines
101	Scott Duncan	$6.3 B	36	Texas	pipelines

续表

Rank	English name	Net worth($)	Age	Residence	Source
102	Milane Frantz	$6.3 B	50	Texas	pipelines
103	Pauline MacMillan Keinath	$6.3 B	85	Missouri	Cargill
104	Ralph Lauren	$6.3 B	80	New York	Ralph Lauren
105	Dennis Washington	$6.3 B	85	Montana	construction, mining
106	Randa Duncan Williams	$6.3 B	58	Texas	pipelines
107	George Lucas	$6.2 B	75	California	Star Wars
108	John Overdeck	$6.1 B	49	New Jersey	hedge funds
109	George Roberts	$6.1 B	76	California	private equity
110	David Siegel	$6.1 B	58	New York	hedge funds
111	Ronda Stryker	$6.1 B	65	Michigan	medical equipment
112	Henry Kravis	$6 B	75	New York	private equity
113	Martha Ingram & family	$5.8 B	84	Tennessee	book distribution, transportation
114	Bubba Cathy	$5.7 B	65	Georgia	Chick-fil-A
115	Dan Cathy	$5.7 B	66	Georgia	Chick-fil-A
116	Ernest Garcia, II.	$5.7 B	62	Arizona	used cars
117	Tamara Gustavson	$5.7 B	57	Kentucky	self storage
118	Tom Gores	$5.6 B	55	California	private equity
119	Arthur Blank	$5.5 B	77	Georgia	Home Depot
120	Edward Roski, Jr.	$5.5 B	80	California	real estate
121	Robert Rowling	$5.5 B	66	Texas	hotels, investments
122	David Sun	$5.5 B	68	California	computer hardware
123	John Tu	$5.5 B	78	California	computer hardware
124	Sam Zell	$5.5 B	78	Illinois	real estate, private equity
125	Charles Dolan & family	$5.3 B	93	New York	cable television
126	Bruce Kovner	$5.3 B	74	New York	hedge funds
127	Ray Lee Hunt	$5.2 B	76	Texas	oil, real estate
128	Ted Lerner & family	$5.1 B	94	Maryland	real estate
129	Whitney MacMillan	$5.1 B	90	Florida	Cargill
130	Isaac Perlmutter	$5.1 B	76	Florida	Marvel comics
131	Rocco Commisso	$5 B	69	New Jersey	telecom
132	Paul Tudor Jones, II.	$5 B	65	Florida	hedge funds
133	Karen Pritzker	$5 B	61	Connecticut	hotels, investments
134	Jeff Skoll	$5 B	54	California	eBay
135	Robert F. Smith	$5 B	56	Texas	private equity
136	Harry Stine	$5 B	77	Iowa	agriculture
137	Daniel Ziff	$5 B	47	New York	investments

续表

Rank	English name	Net worth($)	Age	Residence	Source
138	Dirk Ziff	$5 B	55	Florida	investments
139	Robert Ziff	$5 B	53	New York	investments
140	Robert Bass	$4.9 B	71	Texas	oil, investments
141	Tilman Fertitta	$4.9 B	62	Texas	Houston Rockets, entertainment
142	Charles B. Johnson	$4.9 B	86	Florida	money management
143	Terrence Pegula	$4.9 B	68	Florida	natural gas
144	Leonard Stern	$4.8 B	81	New York	real estate
145	John Brown	$4.7 B	85	Georgia	medical equipment
146	Stanley Druckenmiller	$4.7 B	66	New York	hedge funds
147	Howard Schultz	$4.7 B	66	Washington	Starbucks
148	Henry Samueli	$4.6 B	65	California	semiconductors
149	Sheldon Solow	$4.6 B	91	New York	real estate
150	Stephen Bisciotti	$4.5 B	59	Maryland	staffing, Baltimore Ravens
151	Chase Coleman, III.	$4.5 B	44	New York	hedge fund
152	Walter Scott, Jr. & family	$4.5 B	88	Nebraska	utilities, telecom
153	Tim Sweeney	$4.5 B	48	North Carolina	video games
154	Jack Dangermond	$4.4 B	74	California	mapping software
155	Joshua Harris	$4.4 B	54	New York	private equity
156	Mitchell Rales	$4.4 B	63	Maryland	manufacturing, investments
157	Julian Robertson, Jr.	$4.4 B	87	New York	hedge funds
158	Les Wexner & family	$4.4 B	82	Ohio	retail
159	David Filo	$4.3 B	53	California	Yahoo
160	Jeremy Jacobs, Sr. & family	$4.3 B	79	New York	food service
161	Jane Lauder	$4.3 B	46	New York	Estée Lauder
162	Ronald Lauder	$4.3 B	75	New York	Estee Lauder
163	Igor Olenicoff	$4.3 B	77	Florida	real estate
164	Robert Rich, Jr.	$4.3 B	78	Florida	frozen foods
165	Alejandro Santo Domingo	$4.3 B	42	New York	beer
166	Andres Santo Domingo	$4.3 B	41	New York	beer
167	Kelcy Warren	$4.3 B	63	Texas	pipelines
168	Bert Beveridge	$4.2 B	57	Texas	vodka
169	Margot Birmingham Perot	$4.2 B	85	Texas	computer services, real estate
170	Nathan Blecharczyk	$4.2 B	36	California	Airbnb
171	Rick Caruso	$4.2 B	60	California	real estate
172	Brian Chesky	$4.2 B	38	California	Airbnb
173	Barry Diller	$4.2 B	77	New York	online media

续表

Rank	English name	Net worth($)	Age	Residence	Source
174	Dagmar Dolby & family	$4.2 B	78	California	Dolby Laboratories
175	Jack Dorsey	$4.2 B	42	California	Twitter, Square
176	Joe Gebbia	$4.2 B	38	California	Airbnb
177	Jensen Huang	$4.2 B	56	California	semiconductors
178	John Paulson	$4.2 B	63	New York	hedge funds
179	Neal Blue & family	$4.1 B	84	California	defense
180	Mark Cuban	$4.1 B	61	Texas	online media
181	Richard LeFrak & family	$4.1 B	74	New York	real estate
182	Henry Nicholas, III.	$4.1 B	60	California	semiconductors
183	Sumner Redstone	$4.1 B	96	California	media
184	Eric Smidt	$4.1 B	59	California	hardware stores
185	Jeff Sutton	$4.1 B	59	New York	real estate
186	Steven Udvar-Hazy	$4.1 B	73	California	aircraft leasing
187	Dan Friedkin	$4 B	54	Texas	Toyota dealerships
188	Rupert Johnson, Jr.	$4 B	79	California	money management
189	Ken Langone	$4 B	84	New York	investments
190	Janice McNair	$4 B	83	Texas	energy, sports
191	Gwendolyn Sontheim Meyer	$4 B	58	California	Cargill
192	Thomas Pritzker	$4 B	69	Illinois	hotels, investments
193	Jerry Speyer	$4 B	79	New York	real estate
194	Jon Stryker	$4 B	61	New York	medical equipment
195	Neil Bluhm	$3.9 B	81	Illinois	real estate
196	Ken Fisher	$3.9 B	68	Washington	money management
197	Tom Golisano	$3.9 B	77	Florida	payroll services
198	Jeff Greene	$3.9 B	64	Florida	real estate, investments
199	Thomas Hagen	$3.9 B	83	Pennsylvania	insurance
200	H. Fisk Johnson	$3.9 B	61	Wisconsin	cleaning products
201	S. Curtis Johnson	$3.9 B	64	Wisconsin	cleaning products
202	Helen Johnson-Leipold	$3.9 B	62	Wisconsin	cleaning products
203	Winifred Johnson-Marquart	$3.9 B	60	Virginia	cleaning products
204	Joe Mansueto	$3.9 B	63	Illinois	investment research
205	Russ Weiner	$3.9 B	49	Florida	energy drinks
206	Anthony Wood	$3.9 B	53	California	Roku
207	Ben Ashkenazy	$3.8 B	50	New York	real estate
208	Judy Faulkner	$3.8 B	76	Wisconsin	health IT
209	Rakesh Gangwal	$3.8 B	66	Florida	airline

续表

Rank	English name	Net worth($)	Age	Residence	Source
210	Jeffery Hildebrand	$3.8 B	60	Texas	oil
211	Min Kao & family	$3.8 B	70	Kansas	navigation equipment
212	Douglas Leone	$3.8 B	62	California	venture capital
213	John Morris	$3.8 B	71	Missouri	sporting goods retail
214	Richard Schulze	$3.8 B	78	Florida	Best Buy
215	Fred Smith	$3.8 B	75	Tennessee	FedEx
216	Donald Sterling	$3.8 B	85	California	real estate
217	David Bonderman	$3.7 B	76	Texas	private equity
218	Marian Ilitch	$3.7 B	86	Michigan	Little Caesars
219	Michael Milken	$3.7 B	73	California	investments
220	Bobby Murphy	$3.7 B	31	California	Snapchat
221	Trevor Rees-Jones	$3.7 B	68	Texas	oil & gas
222	Gary Rollins	$3.7 B	75	Georgia	pest control
223	Frank VanderSloot	$3.7 B	71	Idaho	nutrition, wellness products
224	Meg Whitman	$3.7 B	63	California	eBay
225	Austen Cargill, II.	$3.6 B	68	Montana	Cargill
226	James Cargill, II.	$3.6 B	70	Wisconsin	Cargill
227	Jay Chaudhry	$3.6 B	60	California	security software
228	Jonathan Gray	$3.6 B	49	New York	investments
229	Amos Hostetter, Jr.	$3.6 B	82	Massachusetts	cable television
230	James Leprino	$3.6 B	81	Colorado	cheese
231	Marianne Liebmann	$3.6 B	66	Montana	Cargill
232	Rodger Riney & family	$3.6 B	73	Missouri	discount brokerage
233	Randall Rollins	$3.6 B	87	Georgia	pest control
234	Marc Rowan	$3.6 B	57	New York	private equity
235	John Sall	$3.6 B	71	North Carolina	software
236	Lynsi Snyder	$3.6 B	37	California	In-N-Out Burger
237	Evan Spiegel	$3.6 B	29	California	Snapchat
238	Steven Spielberg	$3.6 B	72	California	movies
239	Charles Cohen	$3.5 B	67	New York	real estate
240	Scott Cook	$3.5 B	67	California	software
241	Reed Hastings	$3.5 B	59	California	Netflix
242	Travis Kalanick	$3.5 B	43	California	Uber
243	Mary Alice Dorrance Malone	$3.5 B	69	Pennsylvania	Campbell Soup
244	Michael Moritz	$3.5 B	65	California	venture capital
245	Gabe Newell	$3.5 B	56	Washington	videogames

续表

Rank	English name	Net worth($)	Age	Residence	Source
246	Jay Paul	$3.5 B	72	California	real estate
247	Anthony Pritzker	$3.5 B	58	California	hotels, investments
248	Paul Singer	$3.5 B	75	New York	hedge funds
249	David Steward	$3.5 B	68	Missouri	IT provider
250	Allan Goldman	$3.4 B	76	New York	real estate
251	Jane Goldman	$3.4 B	64	New York	real estate
252	Amy Goldman Fowler	$3.4 B	65	New York	real estate
253	Peter Kellogg	$3.4 B	77	New Jersey	investments
254	Diane Kemper	$3.4 B	74	New York	real estate
255	J.B. Pritzker	$3.4 B	54	Illinois	hotels, investments
256	Bernard Saul, II.	$3.4 B	87	Maryland	banking, real estate
257	Lynn Schusterman	$3.4 B	80	Oklahoma	oil & gas, investments
258	Herb Simon	$3.4 B	85	Indiana	real estate
259	Charles Simonyi	$3.4 B	71	Washington	Microsoft
260	Ronald Wanek	$3.4 B	78	Florida	furniture
261	John Arnold	$3.3 B	45	Texas	hedge funds
262	John Middleton	$3.3 B	64	Pennsylvania	tobacco
263	Arturo Moreno	$3.3 B	73	Arizona	billboards, Anaheim Angels
264	Patrick Ryan	$3.3 B	82	Illinois	insurance
265	Mark Shoen	$3.3 B	68	Arizona	U-Haul
266	Romesh T. Wadhwani	$3.3 B	72	California	software
267	Mark Walter	$3.3 B	59	Illinois	finance
268	Leon G. Cooperman	$3.2 B	76	Florida	hedge funds
269	Edward Johnson, IV.	$3.2 B	54	Massachusetts	money management
270	Elizabeth Johnson	$3.2 B	56	Massachusetts	money management
271	Daniel Och	$3.2 B	58	New York	hedge funds
272	Jean (Gigi) Pritzker	$3.2 B	57	California	hotels, investments
273	Don Vultaggio & family	$3.2 B	67	New York	beverages
274	Denise York & family	$3.2 B	69	Ohio	San Francisco 49ers
275	Sid Bass	$3.1 B	77	Texas	oil, investments
276	Gayle Benson	$3.1 B	72	Louisiana	pro sports teams
277	William Conway, Jr.	$3.1 B	70	Virginia	private equity
278	Daniel D'Aniello	$3.1 B	73	Virginia	private equity
279	John Paul DeJoria	$3.1 B	75	Texas	hair products, tequila
280	Noam Gottesman	$3.1 B	58	New York	hedge funds
281	Don Hankey	$3.1 B	76	California	auto loans

续表

Rank	English name	Net worth($)	Age	Residence	Source
282	David Rubenstein	$3.1 B	70	Maryland	private equity
283	Richard Sands	$3.1 B	68	New York	liquor
284	Donald Trump	$3.1 B	73	District of Columbia	real estate
285	Herbert Wertheim	$3.1 B	80	Florida	investments
286	Steve Wynn	$3.1 B	77	Nevada	casinos, hotels
287	Orlando Bravo	$3 B	49	California	private equity
288	Jim Davis	$3 B	59	Maryland	staffing & recruiting
289	Johnelle Hunt	$3 B	87	Arkansas	trucking
290	James Irsay	$3 B	60	Indiana	Indianapolis Colts
291	Thai Lee	$3 B	60	Texas	IT provider
292	Joseph Liemandt	$3 B	51	Texas	Software
293	Ira Rennert	$3 B	85	New York	investments
294	Thomas Siebel	$3 B	66	California	business software
295	William Wrigley, Jr.	$3 B	55	Florida	chewing gum
296	Jimmy Haslam	$2.9 B	65	Tennessee	gas stations, retail
297	Vincent McMahon	$2.9 B	74	Connecticut	entertainment
298	Jeff Rothschild	$2.9 B	64	California	Facebook
299	Michael Rubin	$2.9 B	47	Pennsylvania	online retail
300	Haim Saban	$2.9 B	75	California	TV network, investments
301	Robert Sands	$2.9 B	61	New York	liquor
302	Pat Stryker	$2.9 B	63	Colorado	medical equipment
303	Glen Taylor	$2.9 B	78	Minnesota	printing
304	Ty Warner	$2.9 B	75	Illinois	real estate, plush toys
305	Mortimer Zuckerman	$2.9 B	82	New York	real estate, media
306	Clifford Asness	$2.8 B	53	Connecticut	money management
307	Bennett Dorrance	$2.8 B	73	Arizona	Campbell Soup
308	Archie Aldis Emmerson & family	$2.8 B	90	California	timberland, lumber mills
309	B. Wayne Hughes	$2.8 B	86	Kentucky	self storage
310	James Jannard	$2.8 B	70	Washington	sunglasses
311	William Lauder	$2.8 B	59	New York	Estee Lauder
312	Eric Lefkofsky	$2.8 B	50	Illinois	Groupon
313	Daniel Loeb	$2.8 B	57	New York	hedge funds
314	Stephen Mandel, Jr.	$2.8 B	63	Connecticut	hedge funds
315	Richard Peery	$2.8 B	81	California	real estate
316	Penny Pritzker	$2.8 B	60	Illinois	hotels, investments
317	Antony Ressler	$2.8 B	57	California	finance

续表

Rank	English name	Net worth($)	Age	Residence	Source
318	Alan Trefler	$2.8 B	63	Massachusetts	software
319	John Catsimatidis	$2.7 B	71	New York	oil, real estate
320	Edward DeBartolo, Jr.	$2.7 B	72	Florida	shopping centers
321	Peter Gassner	$2.7 B	54	California	software
322	John Henry	$2.7 B	70	Florida	sports
323	Aerin Lauder	$2.7 B	49	New York	cosmetics
324	Jeffrey Lurie	$2.7 B	68	Pennsylvania	Philadelphia Eagles
325	Sean Parker	$2.7 B	39	California	Facebook
326	Bob Parsons	$2.7 B	68	Arizona	web hosting
327	Phil Ruffin	$2.7 B	84	Nevada	casinos, real estate
328	Thomas Secunda	$2.7 B	65	New York	Bloomberg LP
329	E. Joe Shoen	$2.7 B	70	Arizona	U-Haul
330	Mark Stevens	$2.7 B	59	California	venture capital
331	John Tyson	$2.7 B	66	Arkansas	food processing
332	Oprah Winfrey	$2.7 B	65	California	TV shows
333	William Berkley	$2.6 B	73	Florida	insurance
334	Timothy Boyle	$2.6 B	70	Oregon	Columbia Sportswear
335	Jim Coulter	$2.6 B	59	California	private equity
336	W. Herbert Hunt	$2.6 B	90	Texas	oil
337	Drayton McLane, Jr.	$2.6 B	83	Texas	Walmart, logistics
338	John Pritzker	$2.6 B	66	California	hotels, investments
339	J. Joe Ricketts & family	$2.6 B	78	Wyoming	TD Ameritrade
340	Dan Snyder	$2.6 B	54	Maryland	Washington Redskins
341	Jerry Yang	$2.6 B	50	California	Yahoo
342	Brian Acton	$2.5 B	47	California	WhatsApp
343	George Argyros & family	$2.5 B	82	California	real estate, investments
344	John Arrillaga	$2.5 B	82	California	real estate
345	Riley Bechtel & family	$2.5 B	67	California	engineering, construction
346	Stephen Bechtel, Jr.	$2.5 B	94	California	engineering, construction
347	Norman Braman	$2.5 B	87	Florida	art, car dealerships
348	Jim Breyer	$2.5 B	58	California	venture capital
349	John Fisher	$2.5 B	58	California	Gap
350	Joseph Grendys	$2.5 B	57	Illinois	poultry processing
351	C. Dean Metropoulos	$2.5 B	73	Florida	investments
352	Daniel Pritzker	$2.5 B	60	California	hotels, investments
353	Warren Stephens	$2.5 B	62	Arkansas	investment banking

续表

Rank	English name	Net worth($)	Age	Residence	Source
354	David Walentas	$2.5 B	81	New York	real estate
355	Bill Austin	$2.4 B	77	Texas	hearing aids
356	Ron Baron	$2.4 B	76	New York	money management
357	George Bishop	$2.4 B	82	Texas	oil & gas
358	Doris Fisher	$2.4 B	88	California	Gap
359	Brad Kelley	$2.4 B	62	Tennessee	tobacco
360	Phillip T. (Terry) Ragon	$2.4 B	70	Massachusetts	health IT
361	T. Denny Sanford	$2.4 B	83	South Dakota	banking, credit cards
362	Evan Williams	$2.4 B	47	California	Twitter
363	Ray Davis	$2.3 B	77	Texas	pipelines
364	Gerald Ford	$2.3 B	75	Texas	banking
365	Ernest Garcia, III.	$2.3 B	37	Arizona	used cars
366	David Gottesman	$2.3 B	93	New York	investments
367	Clayton Mathile	$2.3 B	78	Ohio	pet food
368	Stewart Rahr	$2.3 B	73	New York	drug distribution
369	Peter Thiel	$2.3 B	52	California	Facebook, Palantir
370	Edward Bass	$2.2 B	74	Texas	oil, investments
371	Lee Bass	$2.2 B	63	Texas	oil, investments
372	Aneel Bhusri	$2.2 B	53	California	business software
373	Chuck Bundrant	$2.2 B	77	Washington	fishing
374	Ben Chestnut	$2.2 B	45	Georgia	email marketing
375	Todd Christopher	$2.2 B	57	Florida	hair care products
376	James Dinan	$2.2 B	60	New York	hedge funds
377	Bruce Karsh	$2.2 B	64	California	private equity
378	Jim Kavanaugh	$2.2 B	57	Missouri	IT provider
379	Randal J. Kirk	$2.2 B	65	Florida	pharmaceuticals
380	Dan Kurzius	$2.2 B	47	Georgia	email marketing
381	Howard Marks	$2.2 B	73	New York	private equity
382	H. Ross Perot, Jr.	$2.2 B	60	Texas	real estate
383	Nicholas Pritzker	$2.2 B	75	California	hotels, investments
384	Brian Sheth	$2.2 B	43	Texas	investments
385	Kavitark Ram Shriram	$2.2 B	62	California	venture capital, Google
386	Vincent Viola	$2.2 B	63	New York	electronic trading
387	Jon Yarbrough	$2.2 B	62	Tennessee	video games
388	James Clark	$2.1 B	75	Florida	Netscape, investments
389	Gordon Getty	$2.1 B	85	California	Getty Oil

续表

Rank	English name	Net worth($)	Age	Residence	Source
390	Alec Gores	$2.1 B	66	California	private equity
391	Jeffrey Gundlach	$2.1 B	60	California	investments
392	Stanley Hubbard	$2.1 B	86	Minnesota	DirecTV
393	Bradley Jacobs	$2.1 B	63	Connecticut	logistics
394	Vinod Khosla	$2.1 B	64	California	venture capital
395	Chris Larsen	$2.1 B	59	California	cryptocurrency
396	Henry Laufer	$2.1 B	74	Florida	hedge funds
397	Chad Richison	$2.1 B	49	Oklahoma	payroll processing
398	Julio Mario Santo Domingo, III.	$2.1 B	34	New York	beer
399	Ted Turner	$2.1 B	80	Georgia	cable television
400	Elaine Wynn	$2.1 B	77	Nevada	casinos, hotels

A.4 Data Set – National Health Care Association
A.4 数据集——全美护士工作满意度调查研究

Table A.9 Data for National Health Care Association

表 A.9 全美医疗保健协会调查数据

Nurse	Hospital	Work	Pay	Promotion
1	Private	74	47	63
2	VA	72	76	37
3	University	75	53	92
4	Private	89	66	62
5	University	69	47	16
6	Private	85	56	64
7	University	89	80	64
8	Private	88	36	47
9	University	88	55	52
10	Private	84	42	66
11	Private	90	62	66
12	University	72	59	79
13	VA	82	37	54
14	University	90	56	23
15	Private	64	43	61
16	Private	85	57	67

续表

Nurse	Hospital	Work	Pay	Promotion
17	Private	71	25	74
18	University	71	36	55
19	Private	70	38	54
20	VA	71	49	58
21	VA	90	27	67
22	VA	73	56	55
23	Private	72	60	45
24	VA	65	42	68
25	VA	94	60	52
26	Private	84	28	62
27	Private	71	45	68
28	VA	72	37	86
29	VA	84	60	29
30	Private	82	49	91
31	VA	90	76	70
32	Private	88	49	42
33	University	74	70	51
34	VA	78	52	72
35	University	85	89	46
36	Private	74	59	82
37	University	76	51	54
38	VA	82	60	56
39	Private	77	60	75
40	VA	63	48	78
41	VA	86	72	72
42	University	77	90	51
43	VA	86	37	59
44	Private	87	51	57
45	University	79	59	41
46	University	84	53	63
47	University	87	66	49
48	VA	84	74	37
49	VA	95	66	52
50	Private	72	57	40

A.5 Data Set – Bock Investment Services
A.5 数据集——伯克投资服务公司周刊简讯的改进研究

Table A.10 Data for Bock Investment Services
表 A.10 BIS 调查数据

Fund	Assets	7-day Yield	30-day Yield
Amcore	103.9	4.10	4.08
Alger	156.7	4.79	4.73
Arch MM/Trust	496.5	4.17	4.13
BT Instit Treas	197.8	4.37	4.32
Benchmarrk Div	2 755.4	4.54	4.47
Bradford	707.6	3.88	3.83
Capital Cash	1.7	4.29	4.22
Cash Mgt Trust	2 707.8	4.14	4.04
Composite	122.8	4.03	3.91
Cowen Standby	694.7	4.25	4.19
Cortland	217.3	3.57	3.51
Declaration	38.4	2.67	2.61
Dreyfus	4 832.8	4.01	3.89
Elfun	81.7	4.51	4.41
FFB Cash	506.2	4.17	4.11
Federated Master	738.7	4.41	4.34
Fidelity Cash	13 272.8	4.51	4.42
Flex-fund	172.8	4.60	4.48
Fortis	105.6	3.87	3.85
Franklin Money	996.8	3.97	3.92
Freedom Cash	1 079.0	4.07	4.01
Galaxy Money	801.4	4.11	3.96
Government Cash	409.4	3.83	3.82
Hanover Cash	794.3	4.32	4.23
Heritage Cash	1 008.3	4.08	4.00
Infinity/Alpha	53.6	3.99	3.91
John Hancock	226.4	3.93	3.87
Landmark Funds	481.3	4.28	4.26
Liquid Cash	388.9	4.61	4.64
Market Watch	10.6	4.13	4.05
Merrill Lynch Money	27 005.6	4.24	4.18
NCC Funds	113.4	4.22	4.20
Nationwide	517.3	4.22	4.14

续表

Fund	Assets	7-day Yield	30-day Yield
Overland	291.5	4.26	4.17
Piermont Money	1991.7	4.50	4.40
Portico Money	161.6	4.28	4.20
Prudential Money Mart	6 835.1	4.20	4.16
Reserve Primary	1 408.8	3.91	3.86
Schwab Money	10 531.0	4.16	4.07
Smith Barney Cash	2 947.6	4.16	4.12
Stagecoach	1 502.2	4.18	4.13
Strong Money	470.2	4.37	4.29
Transamerica Club	175.5	4.20	4.19
United Cash	323.7	3.96	3.89
Woodward Money	1 330.0	4.24	4.21

Source: Barron's, October 3,1994

A.6 Data Set – Declining Rates of Credit Card
A.6 数据集——下降的信用卡利率

Table A.11 Sample Data

表 A.11 样本数据

Rate(%)							
18.4	15.6	17.8	14.6	17.3	18.7	15.3	16.4
17.6	14.0	19.2	15.8	18.1	16.6	17.0	

A.7 Data Set – Hourly Wage Rate in Florida
A.7 数据集——佛罗里达的小时工资差异

Table A.12 Data for Hourly Wage Rate in Floride

表 A.12 佛罗里达的平均小时工资数据

Sample	Plumbers	Electricians	Sample	Plumbers	Electricians
1	29.8	28.76	6	30.02	28.66
2	30.32	29.4	7	29.6	29.13
3	30.57	29.94	8	29.63	29.42
4	30.04	28.93	9	30.17	29.29
5	30.09	29.78	10	30.81	29.75

续表

Sample	Plumbers	Electricians	Sample	Plumbers	Electricians
11	30.09	28.05	16	30.6	30.19
12	29.35	29.07	17	30.79	28.65
13	29.42	28.79	18	29.14	29.95
14	29.78	29.54	19	29.91	28.75
15	29.6	29.6	20	28.74	29.21

A.8 Data Set – Is the Training Effective
A.8 数据集——培训是否有效

Table A.13 Number of Complaints and Differences Before and After the Training

表 A.13 店员培训前后抱怨数与差值

Salesclerk	Number of Complaints		Difference
	Before	After	
C.B.	6	4	−2
T.F.	20	6	−14
M.H.	3	2	−1
R.K.	0	0	0
M.O.	4	0	−4

A.9 Data Set – Bell Grove Medical Center
A.9 数据集——医疗中心患者流量分析

Table A.14 Date for Bell Grove Medical Center

表 A.14 Bell Grove 医疗中心数据

Date	Day	Patients	Date	Day	Patients
9-29-06	Monday	38	10-13-06	Monday	37
9-30-06	Tuesday	28	10-14-06	Tuesday	29
2010/1/6	Wednesday	28	10-15-06	Wednesday	27
2010/2/6	Thursday	30	10-16-06	Thursday	28
2010/3/6	Friday	35	10-17-06	Friday	35
2010/6/6	Monday	35	10-20-06	Monday	37
2010/7/6	Tuesday	25	10-21-06	Tuesday	26
2010/8/6	Wednesday	22	10-22-06	Wednesday	28
2010/9/6	Thursday	21	10-23-06	Thursday	23
2010/10/6	Friday	32	10-24-06	Friday	33

A.10 Data Set – Alumni Donation
A.10 数据集——校友捐赠额影响因素分析

Table A.15 Date for 48 National Universities

表 A.15 国立大学的相关数据

School	% of Classes Under 20	Student/Faculty Ratio	Alumni Giving Rate
Boston College	39	13	25
Brandeis University	68	8	33
Brown University	60	8	40
California Institute of Technology	65	3	46
Carnegie Mellon University	67	10	28
Case Western Reserve Univ.	52	8	31
College of William and Mary	45	12	27
Columbia University	69	7	31
Cornell University	72	13	35
Dartmouth College	61	10	53
Duke University	68	8	45
Emory University	65	7	37
Georgetown University	54	10	29
Harvard University	73	8	46
John Hopkins University	64	9	27
Lehigh University	55	11	40
Massachusetts Inst. of Technology	65	6	44
New York University	63	13	13
Northwestern University	66	8	30
Pennsylvania State Univ.	32	19	21
Princeton University	68	5	67
Rice University	62	8	40
Stanford University	69	7	34
Tufts University	67	9	29
Tulane University	56	12	17
U. of California-Berleley	58	17	18
U. of California-Davis	32	19	7
U. of California-Irvine	42	20	9
U. of California-Los Angeles	41	18	13
U. of California-San Diego	48	19	8

续表

School	% of Classes Under 20	Student/Faculty Ratio	Alumni Giving Rate
U. of California-Santa Barbara	45	20	12
U. of Chicago	65	4	36
U. of Florida	31	23	19
U. of Illinois-Urbana Champaign	29	15	23
U. of Michigan-Ann Arbor	51	15	13
U. of North Carolina-Chapel Hill	40	16	26
U. of Notre Dame	53	13	49
U. of Pennsylvania	65	7	41
U. of Rochester	63	10	23
U. of Southern California	53	13	22
U. of Texas-Austin	39	21	13
U. of Virginia	44	13	28
U. of Washington	37	12	12
U. of Wisconsin-Madison	37	13	13
Vanderbuilt University	68	9	31
Wake Forest University	59	11	38
Washington University-St. Louis	73	7	33
Yale University	77	7	50

A.11 Data Set – Sales of Cotton Fabric

A.11 数据集——棉织物销量影响因素分析

Table A.16 Cotton Fabric Data

表 A.16 棉织物数据

Quarter	Year	Cottonq	Whoprice	Impfab	Expfab
1	66	2 274	98	9.3	256
2	66	2 287	98.1	3.7	189
3	66	2 083	98.4	16	277
4	66	2 181	98.7	4.7	477
1	67	2 221	99.3	5.7	439
2	67	2 131	99.5	8.3	334.3
3	67	1 891	100.3	25.3	249.7
4	67	2 035	100.9	17.3	301.3
1	68	2 035	102	5.3	452.3
2	68	1 930	102.9	27	355.3
3	68	1 712	104	22	277.3
4	68	1 792	105	1.3	204.3

续表

Quarter	Year	Cottonq	Whoprice	Impfab	Expfab
1	69	1 824	106.1	1.3	80
2	69	1 810	106.6	4.7	375
3	69	1 608	108.2	2	188.7
4	69	1 733	108.8	6.7	115.7
1	70	1 654	109.6	5	317.7
2	70	1 810	110.4	3.7	292
3	70	1 467	111.1	3	119.7
4	70	1 560	111.8	1.3	264.7
1	71	1 607	112.2	5.7	186
2	71	1 609	112.2	2.7	367
3	71	1 405	113.6	3	228.7
4	71	1 527	113.8	1.3	294.7
1	72	1 511	114	12	392
2	72	1 475	114.3	6	195
3	72	1 277	115.2	3.7	83.7
4	72	1 384	115.8	2.7	359

A.12 Data Set – Gold Price
A.12 数据集——黄金价格主要影响因素分析

Table A.17 Data of Gold Price

表 A.17 原始数据

Date	GP	USDX	CPI	IR	DJI	WTI
1-90	409.61	92.406 9	127.4	8.23	2 590.54	22.86
2-90	416.81	92.449 0	128.0	8.24	2 627.25	22.11
3-90	393.06	94.312 7	128.7	8.28	2 707.21	20.39
4-90	374.24	94.308 0	128.9	8.26	2 656.76	18.43
5-90	369.05	93.017 6	129.2	8.18	2 876.66	18.20
6-90	352.33	93.005 4	129.9	8.29	2 880.69	16.70
7-90	362.53	90.468 0	130.4	8.15	2 905.20	18.45
8-90	394.73	88.177 5	131.6	8.13	2 614.36	27.31
9-90	389.32	87.021 1	132.7	8.20	2 452.48	33.51
10-90	380.74	84.419 1	133.5	8.11	2 442.33	36.04
11-90	381.72	83.772 6	133.8	7.81	2 559.65	32.33
12-90	376.95	85.098 1	133.8	7.31	2 633.66	27.28
1-91	383.64	85.012 7	134.6	6.91	2 736.39	25.23

续表

Date	GP	USDX	CPI	IR	DJI	WTI
2-91	363.83	83.773 2	134.8	6.25	2 882.18	20.48
3-91	363.33	88.176 0	135.0	6.12	2 913.86	19.90
4-91	358.38	89.869 9	135.2	5.91	2 887.87	20.83
5-91	356.95	90.482 7	135.6	5.78	3 027.50	21.23
6-91	366.72	92.285 8	136.0	5.90	2 906.75	20.19
7-91	367.68	92.087 8	136.2	5.82	3 024.82	21.40
8-91	356.30	90.905 7	136.6	5.66	3 043.60	21.69
9-91	348.74	89.146 5	137.2	5.45	3 016.77	21.89
10-91	358.69	88.263 9	137.4	5.21	3 069.10	23.23
11-91	360.17	86.700 1	137.8	4.81	2 894.68	22.46
12-91	361.72	85.511 4	137.9	4.43	3 168.83	19.50
1-92	354.45	85.606 3	138.1	4.03	3 223.40	18.79
2-92	353.91	87.372 1	138.6	4.06	3 267.70	19.01
3-92	344.34	89.610 1	139.3	3.98	3 235.50	18.92
4-92	338.62	89.253 1	139.5	3.73	3 359.10	20.23
5-92	337.24	88.155 1	139.7	3.82	3 396.90	20.98
6-92	340.80	86.215 9	140.2	3.76	3 318.50	22.39
7-92	352.72	84.202 5	140.5	3.25	3 393.80	21.78
8-92	343.06	83.408 6	140.9	3.30	3 257.40	21.34
9-92	345.43	84.109 6	141.3	3.22	3 271.70	21.88
10-92	344.38	86.220 3	141.8	3.10	3 226.30	21.69
11-92	335.02	89.925 2	142.0	3.09	3 305.20	20.34
12-92	334.80	90.193 0	141.9	2.92	3 301.11	19.41
1-93	329.01	91.501 9	142.6	3.02	3 310.00	19.03
2-93	329.31	91.485 4	143.1	3.03	3 370.81	20.09
3-93	330.08	90.438 3	143.6	3.07	3 435.11	20.32
4-93	342.15	88.259 1	144.0	2.96	3 427.55	20.25
5-93	367.18	87.930 4	144.2	3.00	3 527.43	19.95
6-93	371.89	88.461 4	144.4	3.04	3 516.08	19.09
7-93	392.19	89.917 7	144.4	3.06	3 539.47	17.89
8-93	378.84	89.503 3	144.8	3.03	3 651.25	18.01
9-93	355.27	88.973 8	145.1	3.09	3 555.12	17.50
10-93	364.18	89.890 7	145.7	2.99	3 680.59	18.15
11-93	373.83	90.991 0	145.8	3.02	3 683.95	16.61
12-93	383.30	91.657 9	145.8	2.96	3 754.09	14.52
1-94	386.87	92.012 5	146.2	3.05	3 978.36	15.03
2-94	381.91	91.088 8	146.7	3.25	3 832.02	14.78

续表

Date	GP	USDX	CPI	IR	DJI	WTI
3-94	384.13	90.549 9	147.2	3.34	3 635.96	14.68
4-94	377.27	90.537 8	147.4	3.56	3 681.69	16.42
5-94	381.41	89.750 9	147.5	4.01	3 758.37	17.89
6-94	385.64	88.921 7	148.0	4.25	3 624.96	19.06
7-94	385.49	86.865 8	148.4	4.26	3 764.50	19.66
8-94	380.35	87.175 4	149.0	4.47	3 913.42	18.38
9-94	391.57	85.963 0	149.4	4.73	3 843.19	17.45
10-94	389.77	85.054 3	149.5	4.76	3 908.12	17.72
11-94	384.39	85.714 4	149.7	5.29	3 739.23	18.07
12-94	379.29	87.428 8	149.7	5.45	3 834.44	17.16
1-95	378.55	87.069 3	150.3	5.53	3 843.86	18.04
2-95	376.64	86.168 8	150.9	5.92	4 011.05	18.57
3-95	382.12	83.062 5	151.4	5.98	4 157.69	18.54
4-95	391.03	80.336 2	151.9	6.05	4 321.27	19.90
5-95	385.22	80.863 5	152.2	6.01	4 465.14	19.74
6-95	387.56	80.785 0	152.5	6.00	4 556.10	18.45
7-95	386.23	80.892 6	152.5	5.85	4 708.47	17.33
8-95	383.65	83.499 2	152.9	5.74	4 610.56	18.02
9-95	383.05	84.997 9	153.2	5.80	4 789.08	18.23
10-95	383.14	84.140 6	153.7	5.76	4 755.48	17.43
11-95	385.31	84.515 3	153.6	5.80	5 074.49	17.99
12-95	387.44	85.245 3	153.5	5.60	5 117.12	19.03
1-96	399.45	86.451 5	154.4	5.56	5 395.30	18.86
2-96	404.76	86.642 0	154.9	5.22	5 485.62	19.09
3-96	396.21	86.572 0	155.7	5.31	5 587.14	21.33
4-96	392.85	87.096 8	156.3	5.22	5 569.08	23.50
5-96	391.93	87.511 4	156.6	5.24	5 643.18	21.17
6-96	385.27	87.748 3	156.7	5.27	5 654.63	20.42
7-96	383.47	87.352 6	157.0	5.40	5 528.91	21.30
8-96	387.33	86.836 2	157.3	5.22	5 616.21	21.90
9-96	383.18	87.522 1	157.8	5.30	5 882.17	23.97
10-96	381.07	87.815 7	158.3	5.24	6 029.38	24.88
11-96	377.85	86.930 9	158.6	5.31	6 521.70	23.71
12-96	369.00	88.436 5	158.6	5.29	6 448.27	25.23
1-97	355.10	90.037 0	159.1	5.25	6 813.09	25.13
2-97	346.58	92.702 7	159.6	5.19	6 877.74	22.18
3-97	351.81	93.494 3	160.0	5.39	6 583.48	20.97

续表

Date	GP	USDX	CPI	IR	DJI	WTI
4-97	344.47	94.611 7	160.2	5.51	7 009.00	19.70
5-97	343.84	92.995 0	160.1	5.50	7 331.00	20.82
6-97	340.76	92.472 3	160.3	5.56	7 672.80	19.26
7-97	324.10	93.504 6	160.5	5.52	8 222.60	19.66
8-97	324.01	95.474 8	160.8	5.54	7 622.40	19.95
9-97	322.82	95.056 6	161.2	5.54	7 945.30	19.80
10-97	324.87	94.430 1	161.6	5.50	7 442.10	21.33
11-97	306.04	95.009 4	161.5	5.52	7 823.10	20.19
12-97	288.74	97.262 9	161.3	5.50	7 908.30	18.33
1-98	289.10	98.487 7	161.6	5.56	7 906.50	16.72
2-98	297.49	97.554 8	161.9	5.51	8 545.72	16.06
3-98	295.94	97.932 4	162.2	5.49	8 799.81	15.12
4-98	308.28	98.395 4	162.5	5.45	9 063.37	15.35
5-98	299.10	98.770 7	162.8	5.49	8 899.95	14.91
6-98	292.32	100.472 1	163.0	5.56	8 952.02	13.72
7-98	292.87	101.103 4	163.2	5.54	8 883.29	14.17
8-98	284.11	102.650 2	163.4	5.55	7 539.07	13.47
9-98	288.98	98.634 7	163.6	5.51	7 842.62	15.03
10-98	295.93	95.330 2	163.6	5.07	8 592.10	14.46
11-98	294.12	96.202 4	164.0	4.83	9 116.55	13.00
12-98	291.68	95.409 3	163.9	4.68	9 181.43	11.35
1-99	287.12	94.657 2	164.3	4.63	9 358.83	12.52
2-99	287.33	96.036 0	164.5	4.76	9 306.58	12.01
3-99	285.96	98.039 2	165.0	4.81	9 786.16	14.68
4-99	282.62	98.166 6	166.2	4.74	10 789.04	17.31
5-99	276.44	98.218 5	166.2	4.74	10 559.74	17.72
6-99	261.31	99.065 0	166.2	4.76	10 970.80	17.92
7-99	256.08	99.356 2	166.7	4.99	10 655.15	20.10
8-99	256.69	97.326 5	167.1	5.07	10 829.28	21.28
9-99	264.74	95.998 0	167.9	5.22	10 336.95	23.80
10-99	310.72	94.964 8	168.2	5.20	10 729.86	22.69
11-99	293.18	95.965 7	168.3	5.42	10 877.81	25.00
12-99	283.07	96.371 9	168.3	5.30	11 497.12	26.10
1-00	284.31	96.213 6	168.8	5.45	10 940.53	27.26
2-00	299.86	98.458 3	169.8	5.73	10 128.31	29.37
3-00	286.39	98.827 2	171.2	5.85	10 921.92	29.84
4-00	279.69	99.521 5	171.3	6.02	10 733.91	25.72

续表

Date	GP	USDX	CPI	IR	DJI	WTI
5-00	275.19	102.616 9	171.5	6.27	10 522.33	28.79
6-00	285.73	100.041 6	172.4	6.53	10 447.89	31.82
7-00	281.59	100.943 8	172.8	6.54	10 521.98	29.70
8-00	274.47	102.546 7	172.8	6.50	11 215.10	31.26
9-00	273.68	104.172 8	173.7	6.52	10 650.92	33.88
10-00	270.00	105.842 7	174.0	6.51	10 971.14	33.11
11-00	266.01	106.812 4	174.1	6.51	10 414.49	34.42
12-00	271.45	104.776 1	174.0	6.40	10 787.99	28.44
1-01	265.49	103.641 5	175.1	5.98	10 887.36	29.59
2-01	261.86	105.020 3	175.8	5.49	10 495.28	29.61
3-01	263.03	107.506 7	176.2	5.31	9 878.78	27.25
4-01	260.48	108.656 7	176.9	4.80	10 734.97	27.49
5-01	272.35	108.753 9	177.7	4.21	10 911.94	28.63
6-01	270.23	109.746 1	178.0	3.97	10 502.40	27.60
7-01	267.53	109.821 8	177.5	3.77	10 522.81	26.43
8-01	272.39	107.358 1	177.5	3.65	9 949.75	27.37
9-01	283.42	106.947 3	178.3	3.07	8 847.56	26.20
10-01	283.06	107.803 1	177.7	2.49	9 075.14	22.17
11-01	276.16	109.216 8	177.4	2.09	9 851.56	19.64
12-01	275.85	109.779 3	176.7	1.82	10 021.57	19.39
1-02	281.51	111.381 6	177.1	1.73	9 920.00	19.72
2-02	295.49	112.169 1	177.8	1.74	10 106.13	20.72
3-02	294.05	111.163 0	178.8	1.73	10 403.94	24.53
4-02	302.68	110.358 2	179.8	1.75	9 946.22	26.18
5-02	314.49	107.311 3	179.8	1.75	9 925.25	27.04
6-02	321.18	104.518 0	179.9	1.75	9 243.26	25.52
7-02	313.29	101.974 5	180.1	1.73	8 736.59	26.97
8-02	310.25	103.398 8	180.7	1.74	8 663.50	28.39
9-02	319.14	103.587 2	181.0	1.75	7 591.93	29.66
10-02	316.56	104.087 2	181.3	1.75	8 397.03	28.84
11-02	319.07	102.616 3	181.3	1.34	8 896.09	26.35
12-02	331.92	101.604 3	180.9	1.24	8 341.63	29.46
1-03	356.86	98.975 9	181.7	1.24	8 053.81	32.95
2-03	358.97	97.865 0	183.1	1.26	7 891.08	35.83
3-03	340.55	97.127 6	184.2	1.25	7 992.13	33.51
4-03	328.18	96.823 6	183.8	1.26	8 480.09	28.17
5-03	355.68	92.255 6	183.5	1.26	8 850.26	28.11

续表

Date	GP	USDX	CPI	IR	DJI	WTI
6-03	356.35	91.213 8	183.7	1.22	8 985.44	30.66
7-03	351.02	93.004 3	183.9	1.01	9 233.80	30.76
8-03	359.77	94.230 3	184.6	1.03	9 415.82	31.57
9-03	378.95	92.558 1	185.2	1.01	9 275.06	28.31
10-03	378.92	88.926 1	185.0	1.01	9 801.12	30.34
11-03	389.91	88.602 5	184.5	1.00	9 782.46	31.11
12-03	406.95	86.360 4	184.3	0.98	10 453.92	32.13
1-04	413.79	84.582 0	185.2	1.00	10 488.07	34.31
2-04	404.88	85.056 2	186.2	1.01	10 583.92	34.69
3-04	406.67	86.605 6	187.4	1.00	10 357.70	36.74
4-04	403.26	87.593 5	188.0	1.00	10 225.57	36.75
5-04	383.78	89.079 8	189.1	1.00	10 188.45	40.28
6-04	392.37	87.672 6	189.7	1.03	10 435.48	38.03
7-04	398.09	86.562 5	189.4	1.26	10 139.71	40.78
8-04	400.51	86.815 2	189.5	1.43	10 173.92	44.90
9-04	405.27	86.363 2	189.9	1.61	10 080.27	45.94
10-04	420.46	84.390 4	190.9	1.76	10 027.47	53.28
11-04	439.37	81.107 7	191.0	1.93	10 428.02	48.47
12-04	442.08	80.239 3	190.3	2.16	10 783.01	43.15
1-05	424.03	81.176 9	190.7	2.28	10 489.94	46.84
2-05	423.35	81.935 1	191.8	2.50	10 766.23	48.15
3-05	434.32	81.002 1	193.3	2.63	10 503.76	54.19
4-05	429.23	82.347 0	194.6	2.79	10 192.51	52.98
5-05	421.87	83.508 1	194.4	3.00	10 467.48	49.83
6-05	430.66	85.029 2	194.5	3.04	10 274.97	56.35
7-05	424.48	85.817 1	195.4	3.26	10 640.91	59.00
8-05	437.93	84.268 6	196.4	3.50	10 481.60	64.99
9-05	456.05	83.819 3	198.8	3.62	10 568.70	65.59
10-05	469.90	85.116 8	199.2	3.78	10 440.07	62.26
11-05	476.67	86.574 9	197.6	4.00	10 805.87	58.32
12-05	510.10	85.809 0	196.8	4.16	10 717.50	59.41
1-06	549.86	84.500 4	198.3	4.29	10 864.86	65.49
2-06	554.99	85.222 6	198.7	4.49	10 993.41	61.63
3-06	557.09	85.161 7	199.8	4.59	11 109.32	62.69
4-06	610.65	84.033 5	201.5	4.79	11 367.14	69.44
5-06	675.39	80.772 7	202.5	4.94	11 168.31	70.84
6-06	596.15	81.652 0	202.9	4.99	11 150.22	70.95

续表

Date	GP	USDX	CPI	IR	DJI	WTI
7-06	633.71	82.040 9	203.5	5.24	11 185.68	74.41
8-06	632.59	81.309 3	203.9	5.25	11 381.15	73.04
9-06	598.19	81.701 2	202.9	5.25	11 679.07	63.80
10-06	585.78	82.498 5	201.8	5.25	12 080.73	58.89
11-06	627.83	81.599 3	201.5	5.25	12 221.93	59.08
12-06	629.79	81.006 6	201.8	5.24	12 463.15	61.96
1-07	631.17	82.481 9	202.4	5.25	12 621.69	54.51
2-07	664.74	82.138 9	203.5	5.26	12 268.63	59.28
3-07	654.90	81.311 9	205.4	5.26	12 354.35	60.44
4-07	679.37	79.947 6	206.7	5.25	13 062.91	63.98
5-07	666.86	79.299 2	207.9	5.25	13 627.64	63.46
6-07	655.49	79.059 3	208.4	5.25	13 408.62	67.49
7-07	665.30	77.648 7	208.3	5.26	13 211.99	74.12
8-07	665.41	77.649 8	207.9	5.02	13 357.74	72.36
9-07	712.65	76.049 6	208.5	4.94	13 895.63	79.92
10-07	754.60	74.075 0	208.9	4.76	13 930.01	85.80
11-07	806.25	72.293 1	210.2	4.49	13 371.72	94.77
12-07	803.20	73.807 3	210.0	4.24	13 264.82	91.69
1-08	889.60	73.175 3	211.1	3.94	12 650.36	92.97
2-08	922.30	72.678 5	211.7	2.98	12 266.39	95.39
3-08	968.43	70.340 1	213.5	2.61	12 262.89	105.45
4-08	909.70	70.427 6	214.8	2.28	12 820.13	112.58
5-08	888.66	70.699 9	216.6	1.98	12 638.32	125.40
6-08	889.49	71.371 6	218.8	2.00	11 350.01	133.88
7-08	939.77	70.857 0	220.0	2.01	11 378.02	133.37
8-08	839.03	74.064 4	219.1	2.00	11 543.96	116.67
9-08	829.93	75.558 3	218.8	1.81	10 850.66	104.11
10-08	806.62	80.611 4	216.6	0.97	9 325.01	76.61
11-08	760.86	82.996 2	212.4	0.39	8 829.04	57.31
12-08	816.09	80.808 1	210.2	0.16	8 776.39	41.12
1-09	858.69	81.245 8	211.1	0.15	8 000.86	41.71
2-09	943.16	83.482 4	212.2	0.22	7 062.93	39.09
3-09	924.27	84.009 5	212.7	0.18	7 608.92	47.94
4-09	890.20	82.467 5	213.2	0.15	8 168.12	49.65
5-09	928.64	79.083 4	213.9	0.18	8 500.33	59.03
6-09	945.67	77.162 0	215.7	0.21	8 447.00	69.64
7-09	9 34.23	76.549 9	215.4	0.16	9 171.61	64.15

续表

Date	GP	USDX	CPI	IR	DJI	WTI
8-09	9 49.38	75.354 6	215.8	0.16	9 496.28	71.05
9-09	9 96.59	74.079 4	216.0	0.15	9 712.28	69.41
10-09	1 043.16	72.847 0	216.2	0.12	9 712.73	75.72
11-09	1 127.04	72.423 0	216.3	0.12	10 344.84	77.99
12-09	1 134.72	73.258 3	215.9	0.12	10 428.05	74.47
1-10	1 117.96	73.845 0	216.7	0.11	10 067.33	78.33
2-10	1 095.41	75.524 7	216.7	0.13	10 325.26	76.39
3-10	1 113.34	75.222 7	217.6	0.16	10 856.63	81.20
4-10	1 148.69	75.405 0	218.0	0.20	11 008.61	84.29
5-10	1 205.43	78.501 4	218.2	0.20	10 136.63	73.74
6-10	1 232.92	79.068 3	218.0	0.18	9 774.02	75.34
7-10	1 192.97	76.771 5	218.0	0.18	10 465.94	76.32
8-10	1 215.81	75.950 4	218.3	0.19	10 014.72	76.60
9-10	1 270.98	74.990 6	218.4	0.19	10 788.05	75.24
10-10	1 342.02	72.304 0	218.7	0.19	11 118.49	81.89
11-10	1 369.89	72.830 5	218.8	0.19	11 006.02	84.25
12-10	1 390.55	73.795 0	219.2	0.18	11 577.51	89.15
1-11	1 356.40	72.928 6	220.2	0.17	11 891.93	89.17
2-11	1 372.73	71.977 8	221.3	0.16	12 226.34	88.58
3-11	1 424.01	70.782 1	223.5	0.14	12 319.73	102.86
4-11	1 473.81	69.513 8	224.9	0.10	12 810.54	109.53
5-11	1 510.44	69.615 8	226.0	0.09	12 569.79	100.90
6-11	1 528.66	69.530 0	225.7	0.09	12 414.34	96.26
7-11	1 572.81	69.092 8	225.9	0.07	12 143.24	97.30
8-11	1 755.81	69.060 8	226.5	0.10	11 613.53	86.33
9-11	1 771.85	71.197 8	226.9	0.08	10 913.38	85.52
10-11	1 665.21	71.631 9	226.4	0.07	11 955.01	86.32
11-11	1 738.98	72.268 1	226.2	0.08	12 045.68	97.16
12-11	1 652.31	73.286 6	225.7	0.07	12 217.56	98.56
1-12	1 656.12	73.424 9	226.7	0.08	12 632.91	100.27
2-12	1 742.62	72.347 6	227.7	0.10	12 952.07	102.20
3-12	1 673.77	73.020 6	229.4	0.13	13 212.04	106.16
4-12	1 650.07	72.892 1	230.1	0.14	13 213.63	103.32
5-12	1 585.50	74.005 8	229.8	0.16	12 393.45	94.66
6-12	1 596.70	75.114 9	229.5	0.16	12 880.09	82.30
7-12	1 593.91	75.316 3	229.1	0.16	13 008.68	87.90
8-12	1 626.03	74.346 3	230.4	0.13	13 090.84	94.13

续表

Date	GP	USDX	CPI	IR	DJI	WTI
9-12	1 744.45	72.676 9	231.4	0.14	13 437.13	94.51
10-12	1 747.01	72.796 6	231.3	0.16	13 096.46	89.49
11-12	1 721.14	73.702 6	230.2	0.16	13 025.58	86.53
12-12	1 688.53	73.217 0	229.6	0.16	13 104.14	87.86
1-13	1 670.95	73.659 5	230.3	0.14	13 860.58	94.76
2-13	1 627.59	74.655 4	232.2	0.15	14 054.49	95.31
3-13	1 592.86	76.310 1	232.8	0.14	14 578.54	92.94
4-13	1 485.08	76.264 4	232.5	0.15	14 839.80	92.02
5-13	1 413.50	76.962 4	232.9	0.11	15 115.57	94.51
6-13	1 342.36	76.239 2	233.5	0.09	14 909.60	95.77
7-13	1 286.72	77.213 9	233.6	0.09	15 499.54	104.67
8-13	1 347.10	76.307 2	233.9	0.08	14 810.31	106.57
9-13	1 348.80	76.004 0	234.1	0.08	15 129.67	106.29
10-13	1 316.18	75.047 7	233.5	0.09	15 545.75	100.54
11-13	1 275.82	76.030 4	233.1	0.08	16 086.41	93.86
12-13	1 225.40	76.194 5	233.0	0.09	16 576.66	97.63
1-14	1 244.80	77.080 4	233.9	0.07	15 698.85	94.62
2-14	1 300.98	76.942 8	234.8	0.07	16 321.71	100.82
3-14	1 336.08	76.614 1	236.3	0.08	16 457.66	100.80
4-14	1 299.00	76.346 4	237.1	0.09	16 580.84	102.07
5-14	1 287.53	76.219 4	237.9	0.09	16 717.17	102.18
6-14	1 279.10	76.445 0	238.3	0.10	16 826.60	105.79
7-14	1 310.97	76.325 6	238.3	0.09	16 563.30	103.59
8-14	1 295.99	77.548 0	237.9	0.09	17 098.45	96.54
9-14	1 238.82	79.584 6	238.0	0.09	17 042.90	93.21
10-14	1 222.49	80.823 7	237.4	0.09	17 390.52	84.40
11-14	1 176.30	82.711 9	236.2	0.09	17 828.24	75.79
12-14	1 202.29	84.090 3	234.8	0.12	17 823.07	59.29
1-15	1 251.85	87.452 1	233.7	0.11	17 164.95	47.22
2-15	1 227.19	89.088 3	234.7	0.11	18 132.70	50.58
3-15	1 178.63	91.715 4	236.1	0.11	17 776.12	47.82
4-15	1 197.91	90.888 0	236.6	0.12	17 840.52	54.45
5-15	1 199.05	89.107 4	237.8	0.12	18 010.68	59.27
6-15	1 181.50	89.601 3	238.6	0.13	17 619.51	59.82
7-15	1 130.04	91.552 1	238.7	0.13	17 689.86	50.90
8-15	1 117.47	91.720 2	238.3	0.14	16 528.03	42.87
9-15	1 124.53	91.519 5	237.9	0.14	16 284.70	45.48

续表

Date	GP	USDX	CPI	IR	DJI	WTI
10-15	1 159.25	91.064 2	237.8	0.12	17 663.54	46.22
11-15	1 085.70	93.772 4	237.3	0.12	17 719.92	42.44
12-15	1 068.25	93.922 9	236.5	0.24	17 425.03	37.19
1-16	1 097.37	95.014 8	236.9	0.34	16 466.30	31.68
2-16	1 199.91	92.953 6	237.1	0.38	16 516.50	30.32
3-16	1 246.34	91.369 5	238.1	0.36	17 685.09	37.55
4-16	1 242.26	89.279 9	239.3	0.37	17 773.64	40.75
5-16	1 259.40	89.634 5	240.2	0.37	17 787.20	46.71
6-16	1 276.40	89.470 6	241.0	0.38	17 929.99	48.76
7-16	1 337.33	90.837 5	240.6	0.39	18 432.24	44.65
8-16	1 341.09	89.769 0	240.8	0.40	18 400.88	44.72
9-16	1 326.03	90.022 6	241.4	0.40	18 308.15	45.18
10-16	1 266.57	91.834 7	241.7	0.40	18 142.42	49.78
11-16	1 235.98	93.594 1	241.4	0.41	19 123.58	45.66
12-16	1 151.40	95.391 9	241.4	0.54	19 762.60	51.97
1-17	1 192.62	94.553 7	242.8	0.65	19 864.09	52.50
2-17	1 234.36	93.922 5	243.6	0.66	20 812.24	53.47
3-17	1 231.09	94.436 6	243.8	0.79	20 663.22	49.33
4-17	1 265.63	93.941 7	244.5	0.90	20 940.51	51.06
5-17	1 245.00	93.147 6	244.7	0.91	21 008.65	48.48
6-17	1 260.26	91.708 3	245.0	1.04	21 349.63	45.18
7-17	1 236.22	89.513 3	244.8	1.15	21 891.12	46.63
8-17	1 282.32	88.157 1	245.5	1.16	21 948.10	48.04
9-17	1 314.98	87.080 3	246.8	1.15	22 405.09	49.82
10-17	1 279.51	88.686 6	246.7	1.15	23 377.24	51.58
11-17	1 282.28	89.157 1	246.7	1.16	24 272.35	56.64
12-17	1 261.26	88.748 8	246.5	1.30	24 719.22	57.88
1-18	1 331.67	86.323 4	247.9	1.41	26 149.39	63.70
2-18	1 331.52	85.714 3	249.0	1.42	25 029.20	62.23
3-18	1 324.66	86.236 2	249.6	1.51	24 103.11	62.73
4-18	1 334.74	86.353 3	250.5	1.69	24 163.15	66.25
5-18	1 303.03	88.691 4	251.6	1.70	24 415.84	69.98
6-18	1 281.57	89.739 4	252.0	1.82	24 271.41	67.87
7-18	1 238.52	90.046 9	252.0	1.91	25 415.19	70.98
8-18	1 201.25	90.436 7	252.1	1.91	25 964.82	68.06
9-18	1 198.47	89.997 6	252.4	1.95	26 458.31	70.23
10-18	1 215.39	90.773 8	252.9	2.19	25 115.76	70.75

续表

Date	GP	USDX	CPI	IR	DJI	WTI
11-18	1 220.95	91.682 8	252.0	2.20	25 538.46	56.96
12-18	1 247.92	92.048 6	251.2	2.27	23 327.46	49.52
1-19	1 291.75	91.115 8	251.7	2.40	24 999.67	51.38
2-19	1 320.06	91.377 7	252.8	2.40	25 916.00	54.95
3-19	1 300.90	91.877 3	254.2	2.41	25 928.68	58.15
4-19	1 286.44	92.268 3	255.5	2.42	26 592.91	63.86
5-19	1 283.95	92.580 3	256.1	2.39	24 815.04	60.83
6-19	1 359.04	91.634 0	256.1	2.38	26 599.96	54.66

资料来源：Gold Price (GP) from the website http://www.gold.org；
Oil Prices (WTI) from the website http://www.eia.doe.gov；
Consumer Price Index (CPI) from the website https://www.bls.gov；
Dow Jones Industrial Average (DJI) from the website https://finance.yahoo.com；
Interest Rate (IR) from the website https://fred.stlouisfed.org/；
U.S. Dollar Index (USDX) from the website https://fred.stlouisfed.org/.

A.13 Data Set – Product Preference
A.13 数据集——购买产品时的选择偏好

Table A.18 Flavor Rating for Current and Spicy Flavors
表 A.18 对现有口味和辛辣口味的评分

No.	Participant	Spicy Score	Current Score
1	Arquette	14	12
2	Jones	8	16
3	Fish	6	2
4	Wagner	18	4
5	Badenhop	20	12
6	Hall	16	16
7	Fowler	14	5
8	Virost	6	16
9	Garcia	19	10
10	Sundar	18	10
11	Miller	16	13
12	Peterson	18	2
13	Boggart	4	13
14	Hein	7	14
15	Whitten	16	4

A.14　Data Set　– Forecasting Food and Beverage Sales

A.14　数据集——预测食品和饮料的销售额

Table A.19　Data for Vintage Food and Beverage Sales

表 A.19　Vintage 餐厅食品和饮料的销售额数据

Month	First Year	Second Year	Third Year
January	242	263	282
February	235	238	255
March	232	247	265
April	178	193	205
May	184	193	210
June	140	149	160
July	145	157	166
August	152	161	174
September	110	122	126
October	130	130	148
November	152	167	173
December	206	230	235

A.15　Standard Normal Distribution

A.15　标准正态分布表

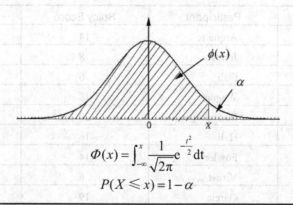

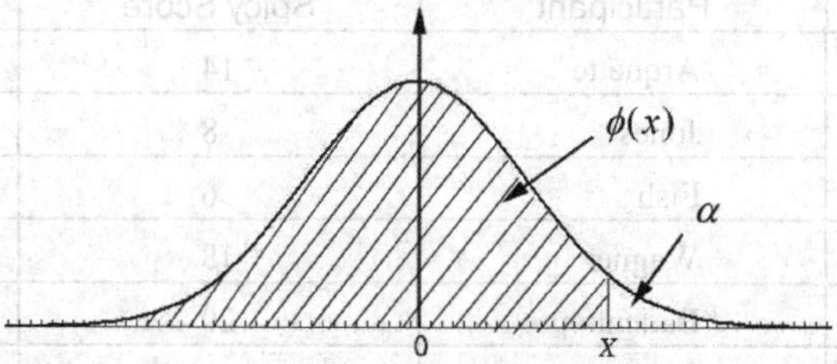

$$\Phi(x)=\int_{-\infty}^{x}\frac{1}{\sqrt{2\pi}}e^{-\frac{t^2}{2}}dt$$

$$P(X\leqslant x)=1-\alpha$$

x	0.00	0.01	0.02	0.03	0.04	0.05	0.06	0.07	0.08	0.09
0.0	0.500 0	0.504 0	0.508 0	0.512 0	0.516 0	0.519 9	0.523 9	0.527 9	0.531 9	0.535 9
0.1	0.539 8	0.543 8	0.547 8	0.551 7	0.555 7	0.559 6	0.563 6	0.567 5	0.571 4	0.575 3
0.2	0.579 3	0.583 2	0.587 1	0.591 0	0.594 8	0.598 7	0.602 6	0.606 4	0.610 3	0.614 1
0.3	0.617 9	0.621 7	0.625 5	0.629 3	0.633 1	0.636 8	0.640 4	0.644 3	0.648 0	0.651 7
0.4	0.655 4	0.659 1	0.662 8	0.666 4	0.670 0	0.673 6	0.677 2	0.680 8	0.684 4	0.687 9
0.5	0.691 5	0.695 0	0.698 5	0.701 9	0.705 4	0.708 8	0.712 3	0.715 7	0.719 0	0.722 4

续表

X	0.00	0.01	0.02	0.03	0.04	0.05	0.06	0.07	0.08	0.09
0.6	0.725 7	0.729 1	0.732 4	0.735 7	0.738 9	0.742 2	0.745 4	0.748 6	0.751 7	0.754 9
0.7	0.758 0	0.761 1	0.764 2	0.767 3	0.770 3	0.773 4	0.776 4	0.779 4	0.782 3	0.785 2
0.8	0.788 1	0.791 0	0.793 9	0.796 7	0.799 5	0.802 3	0.805 1	0.807 8	0.810 6	0.813 3
0.9	0.815 9	0.818 6	0.821 2	0.823 8	0.826 4	0.828 9	0.835 5	0.834 0	0.836 5	0.838 9
1.0	0.841 3	0.843 8	0.846 1	0.848 5	0.850 8	0.853 1	0.855 4	0.857 7	0.859 9	0.862 1
1.1	0.864 3	0.866 5	0.868 6	0.870 8	0.872 9	0.874 9	0.877 0	0.879 0	0.881 0	0.883 0
1.2	0.884 9	0.886 9	0.888	0.890 7	0.892 5	0.894 4	0.896 2	0.898 0	0.899 7	0.901 5
1.3	0.903 2	0.904 9	0.906 6	0.908 2	0.909 9	0.911 5	0.913 1	0.914 7	0.916 2	0.917 7
1.4	0.919 2	0.920 7	0.922 2	0.923 6	0.925 1	0.926 5	0.927 9	0.929 2	0.930 6	0.931 9
1.5	0.933 2	0.934 5	0.935 7	0.937 0	0.938 2	0.939 4	0.940 6	0.941 8	0.943 0	0.944 1
1.6	0.945 2	0.946 3	0.947 4	0.948 4	0.949 5	0.950 5	0.951 5	0.952 5	0.953 5	0.953 5
1.7	0.955 4	0.956 4	0.957 3	0.958 2	0.959 1	0.959 9	0.960 8	0.961 6	0.962 5	0.963 3
1.8	0.964 1	0.964 8	0.965 6	0.966 4	0.967 2	0.967 8	0.968 6	0.969 3	0.970 0	0.970 6
1.9	0.971 3	0.971 9	0.972 6	0.973 2	0.973 8	0.974 4	0.975 0	0.975 6	0.976 2	0.976 7
2.0	0.977 2	0.977 8	0.978 3	0.978 8	0.979 3	0.979 8	0.980 3	0.980 8	0.981 2	0.981 7
2.1	0.982 1	0.982 6	0.983 0	0.983 4	0.983 8	0.984 2	0.984 6	0.985 0	0.985 4	0.985 7
2.2	0.986 1	0.986 4	0.986 8	0.987 1	0.987 4	0.987 8	0.988 1	0.988 4	0.988 7	0.989 0
2.3	0.989 3	0.989 6	0.989 8	0.990 1	0.990 4	0.990 6	0.990 9	0.991 1	0.991 3	0.991 6
2.4	0.991 8	0.992 0	0.992 2	0.992 5	0.992 7	0.992 9	0.993 1	0.993 2	0.993 4	0.993 6
2.5	0.993 8	0.994 0	0.994 1	0.994 3	0.994 5	0.994 6	0.994 8	0.994 9	0.995 1	0.995 2
2.6	0.995 3	0.995 5	0.995 6	0.995 7	0.995 9	0.996 0	0.996 1	0.996 2	0.996 3	0.996 4
2.7	0.996 5	0.996 6	0.996 7	0.996 8	0.996 9	0.997 0	0.997 1	0.997 2	0.997 3	0.997 4
2.8	0.997 4	0.997 5	0.997 6	0.997 7	0.997 7	0.997 8	0.997 9	0.997 9	0.998 0	0.998 1
2.9	0.998 1	0.998 2	0.998 2	0.998 3	0.998 4	0.998 4	0.998 5	0.998 5	0.998 6	0.998 6
3.0	0.998 7	0.999 0	0.999 3	0.999 5	0.999 7	0.999 8	0.999 8	0.999 9	0.999 9	1.000 0

A.16 *T* Distribution Critical Value
A.16 *T* 分布临界值表

单侧（One-tailed）：

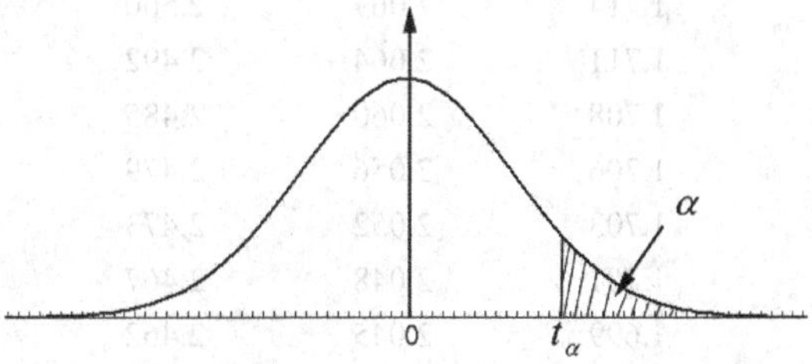

$$P\{t(n) > t_\alpha(n)\} = \alpha$$

双侧（Two-tailed）：

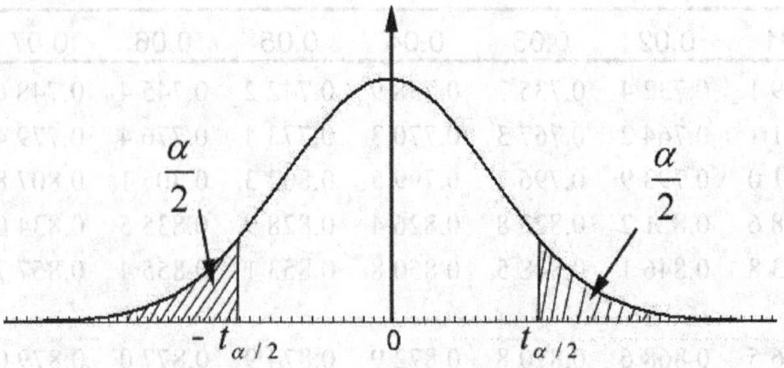

$$P\left\{t_{-\frac{\alpha}{2}}(n)\leqslant t(n)\leqslant t_{\frac{\alpha}{2}}(n)\right\}=1-\alpha$$

	单侧	0.1	0.05	0.025	0.01	0.005	0.001
Df	双侧	0.2	0.1	0.05	0.02	0.01	0.002
1		3.078	6.314	12.706	31.821	63.657	318.309
2		1.886	2.920	4.303	6.965	9.925	22.327
3		1.638	2.353	3.182	4.541	5.841	10.215
4		1.533	2.132	2.776	3.747	4.604	7.173
5		1.476	2.015	2.571	3.365	4.032	5.893
6		1.440	1.943	2.447	3.143	3.707	5.208
7		1.415	1.895	2.365	2.998	3.499	4.785
8		1.397	1.860	2.306	2.896	3.355	4.501
9		1.383	1.833	2.262	2.821	3.250	4.297
10		1.372	1.812	2.228	2.764	3.169	4.144
11		1.363	1.796	2.201	2.718	3.106	4.025
12		1.356	1.782	2.179	2.681	3.055	3.930
13		1.350	1.771	2.160	2.650	3.012	3.852
14		1.345	1.761	2.145	2.624	2.977	3.787
15		1.341	1.753	2.131	2.602	2.947	3.733
16		1.337	1.746	2.120	2.583	2.921	3.686
17		1.333	1.740	2.110	2.567	2.898	3.646
18		1.330	1.734	2.101	2.552	2.878	3.610
19		1.328	1.729	2.093	2.539	2.861	3.579
20		1.325	1.725	2.086	2.528	2.845	3.552
21		1.323	1.721	2.080	2.518	2.831	3.527
22		1.321	1.717	2.074	2.508	2.819	3.505
23		1.319	1.714	2.069	2.500	2.807	3.485
24		1.318	1.711	2.064	2.492	2.797	3.467
25		1.316	1.708	2.060	2.485	2.787	3.450
26		1.315	1.706	2.056	2.479	2.779	3.435
27		1.314	1.703	2.052	2.473	2.771	3.421
28		1.313	1.701	2.048	2.467	2.763	3.408
29		1.311	1.699	2.045	2.462	2.756	3.396
30		1.310	1.697	2.042	2.457	2.750	3.385

续表

单侧	0.1	0.05	0.025	0.01	0.005	0.001
Df 双侧	0.2	0.1	0.05	0.02	0.01	0.002
31	1.309	1.696	2.040	2.453	2.744	3.375
32	1.309	1.694	2.037	2.449	2.738	3.365
33	1.308	1.692	2.035	2.445	2.733	3.356
34	1.307	1.691	2.032	2.441	2.728	3.348
35	1.306	1.690	2.030	2.438	2.724	3.340
36	1.306	1.688	2.028	2.434	2.719	3.333
37	1.305	1.687	2.026	2.431	2.715	3.326
38	1.304	1.686	2.024	2.429	2.712	3.319
46	1.300	1.679	2.013	2.410	2.687	3.277
47	1.300	1.678	2.012	2.408	2.685	3.273
48	1.299	1.677	2.011	2.407	2.682	3.269
49	1.299	1.677	2.010	2.405	2.680	3.265
50	1.299	1.676	2.009	2.403	2.678	3.261
51	1.298	1.675	2.008	2.402	2.676	3.258
52	1.298	1.675	2.007	2.400	2.674	3.255
53	1.298	1.674	2.006	2.399	2.672	3.251
54	1.297	1.674	2.005	2.397	2.670	3.248
55	1.297	1.673	2.004	2.396	2.668	3.245
56	1.297	1.673	2.003	2.395	2.667	3.242
57	1.297	1.672	2.002	2.394	2.665	3.239
58	1.296	1.672	2.002	2.392	2.663	3.237
59	1.296	1.671	2.001	2.391	2.662	3.234
60	1.296	1.671	2.000	2.390	2.660	3.232
61	1.296	1.670	2.000	2.389	2.659	3.229
62	1.295	1.670	1.999	2.388	2.657	3.227
63	1.295	1.669	1.998	2.387	2.656	3.225
64	1.295	1.669	1.998	2.386	2.655	3.223
65	1.295	1.669	1.997	2.385	2.654	3.220
66	1.295	1.668	1.997	2.384	2.652	3.218
67	1.294	1.668	1.996	2.383	2.651	3.216
68	1.294	1.668	1.995	2.382	2.650	3.214
69	1.294	1.667	1.995	2.382	2.649	3.213
70	1.294	1.667	1.994	2.381	2.648	3.211
71	1.294	1.667	1.994	2.380	2.647	3.209
72	1.293	1.666	1.993	2.379	2.646	3.207
73	1.293	1.666	1.993	2.379	2.645	3.206
74	1.293	1.666	1.993	2.378	2.644	3.204
75	1.293	1.665	1.992	2.377	2.643	3.202
76	1.293	1.665	1.992	2.376	2.642	3.201
77	1.293	1.665	1.991	2.376	2.641	3.199
78	1.292	1.665	1.991	2.375	2.640	3.198

续表

Df	单侧 0.1 / 双侧 0.2	单侧 0.05 / 双侧 0.1	单侧 0.025 / 双侧 0.05	单侧 0.01 / 双侧 0.02	单侧 0.005 / 双侧 0.01	单侧 0.001 / 双侧 0.002
79	1.292	1.664	1.990	2.374	2.640	3.197
80	1.292	1.664	1.990	2.374	2.639	3.195
81	1.292	1.664	1.990	2.373	2.638	3.194
82	1.292	1.664	1.989	2.373	2.637	3.193
83	1.292	1.663	1.989	2.372	2.636	3.191
84	1.292	1.663	1.989	2.372	2.636	3.190
85	1.292	1.663	1.988	2.371	2.635	3.189
86	1.291	1.663	1.988	2.370	2.634	3.188
87	1.291	1.663	1.988	2.370	2.634	3.187
88	1.291	1.662	1.987	2.369	2.633	3.185
89	1.291	1.662	1.987	2.369	2.632	3.184
90	1.291	1.662	1.987	2.368	2.632	3.183
91	1.291	1.662	1.986	2.368	2.631	3.182
92	1.291	1.662	1.986	2.368	2.630	3.181
93	1.291	1.661	1.986	2.367	2.630	3.180
94	1.291	1.661	1.986	2.367	2.629	3.179
95	1.291	1.661	1.985	2.366	2.629	3.178
96	1.290	1.661	1.985	2.366	2.628	3.177
97	1.290	1.661	1.985	2.365	2.627	3.176
98	1.290	1.661	1.984	2.365	2.627	3.175
99	1.290	1.660	1.984	2.365	2.626	3.175
100	1.290	1.660	1.984	2.364	2.626	3.174
120	1.289	1.658	1.980	2.358	2.617	3.160
∞	1.282	1.645	1.960	2.326	2.576	3.090

A.17 *F* Distribution Critical Value

A.17 *F*分布临界值表

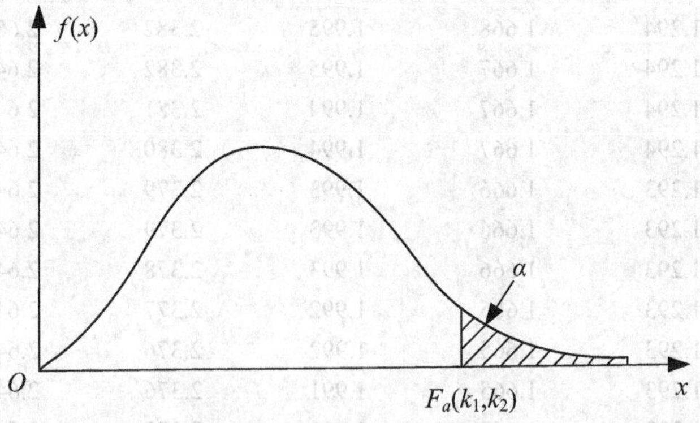

$$P\{F(k_1,k_2) > F_\alpha(k_1,k_2)\} = \alpha$$

$\alpha = 0.01$

k_2 \ k_1	1	2	3	4	5	6	8	12	24	∞
1	4 052	4 999	5 403	5 625	5 764	5 859	5 981	6 106	6 234	6 366
2	98.49	99.01	99.17	99.25	99.30	99.33	99.36	99.42	99.46	99.50
3	34.12	30.81	29.46	28.71	28.24	27.91	27.49	27.05	26.60	26.12
4	21.20	18.00	16.69	15.98	15.52	15.21	14.80	14.37	13.93	13.46
5	16.26	13.27	12.06	11.39	10.97	10.67	10.29	9.89	9.47	9.02
6	13.74	10.92	9.78	9.15	8.75	8.47	8.10	7.72	7.31	6.88
7	12.25	9.55	8.45	7.85	7.46	7.19	6.84	6.47	6.07	5.65
8	11.26	8.65	7.59	7.01	6.63	6.37	6.03	5.67	5.28	4.86
9	10.56	8.02	6.99	6.42	6.06	5.80	5.47	5.11	4.73	4.31
10	10.04	7.56	6.55	5.99	5.64	5.39	5.06	4.71	4.33	3.91
11	9.65	7.20	6.22	5.67	5.32	5.07	4.74	4.40	4.02	3.60
12	9.33	6.93	5.95	5.41	5.06	4.82	4.50	4.16	3.78	3.36
13	9.07	6.70	5.74	5.20	4.86	4.62	4.30	3.96	3.59	3.16
14	8.86	6.51	5.56	5.03	4.69	4.46	4.14	3.80	3.43	3.00
15	8.68	6.36	5.42	4.89	4.56	4.32	4.00	3.67	3.29	2.87
16	8.53	6.23	5.29	4.77	4.44	4.20	3.89	3.55	3.18	2.75
17	8.40	6.11	5.18	4.67	4.34	4.10	3.79	3.45	3.08	2.65
18	8.28	6.01	5.09	4.58	4.25	4.01	3.71	3.37	3.00	2.57
19	8.18	5.93	5.01	4.50	4.17	3.94	3.63	3.30	2.92	2.49
20	8.10	5.85	4.94	4.43	4.10	3.87	3.56	3.23	2.86	2.42
21	8.02	5.78	4.87	4.37	4.04	3.81	3.51	3.17	2.80	2.36
22	7.94	5.72	4.82	4.31	3.99	3.76	3.45	3.12	2.75	2.31
23	7.88	5.66	4.76	4.26	3.94	3.71	3.41	3.07	2.70	2.26
24	7.82	5.61	4.72	4.22	3.90	3.67	3.36	3.03	2.66	2.21
25	7.77	5.57	4.68	4.18	3.86	3.63	3.32	2.99	2.62	2.17
26	7.72	5.53	4.64	4.14	3.82	3.59	3.29	2.96	2.58	2.13
27	7.68	5.49	4.60	4.11	3.78	3.56	3.26	2.93	2.55	2.10
28	7.64	5.45	4.57	4.07	3.75	3.53	3.23	2.90	2.52	2.06
29	7.60	5.42	4.54	4.04	3.73	3.50	3.20	2.87	2.49	2.03
30	7.56	5.39	4.51	4.02	3.70	3.47	3.17	2.84	2.47	2.01
40	7.31	5.18	4.31	3.83	3.51	3.29	2.99	2.66	2.29	1.80
60	7.08	4.98	4.13	3.65	3.34	3.12	2.82	2.50	2.12	1.60
120	6.85	4.79	3.95	3.48	3.17	2.96	2.66	2.34	1.95	1.38
∞	6.64	4.60	3.78	3.32	3.02	2.80	2.51	2.18	1.79	1.00

$\alpha = 0.025$

F_α k_1 / k_2	1	2	3	4	5	6	8	12	24	∞
1	647.8	799.5	864.2	899.6	921.8	937.1	956.7	976.7	997.2	1 018
2	38.51	39.00	39.17	39.25	39.30	39.33	39.37	39.41	39.46	39.50
3	17.44	16.04	15.44	15.10	14.88	14.73	14.54	14.34	14.12	13.90
4	12.22	10.65	9.98	9.60	9.36	9.20	8.98	8.75	8.51	8.26
5	10.01	8.43	7.76	7.39	7.15	6.98	6.76	6.52	6.28	6.02
6	8.81	7.26	6.60	6.23	5.99	5.82	5.60	5.37	5.12	4.85
7	8.07	6.54	5.89	5.52	5.29	5.12	4.90	4.67	4.42	4.14
8	7.57	6.06	5.42	5.05	4.82	4.65	4.43	4.20	3.95	3.67
9	7.21	5.71	5.08	4.72	4.48	4.32	4.10	3.87	3.61	3.33
10	6.94	5.46	4.83	4.47	4.24	4.07	3.85	3.62	3.37	3.08
11	6.72	5.26	4.63	4.28	4.04	3.88	3.66	3.43	3.17	2.88
12	6.55	5.10	4.47	4.12	3.89	3.73	3.51	3.28	3.02	2.72
13	6.41	4.97	4.35	4.00	3.77	3.60	3.39	3.15	2.89	2.60
14	6.30	4.86	4.24	3.89	3.66	3.50	3.29	3.05	2.79	2.49
15	6.20	4.77	4.15	3.80	3.58	3.41	3.20	2.96	2.70	2.40
16	6.12	4.69	4.08	3.73	3.50	3.34	3.12	2.89	2.63	2.32
17	6.04	4.62	4.01	3.66	3.44	3.28	3.06	2.82	2.56	2.25
18	5.98	4.56	3.95	3.61	3.38	3.22	3.01	2.77	2.50	2.19
19	5.92	4.51	3.90	3.56	3.33	3.17	2.96	2.72	2.45	2.13
20	5.87	4.46	3.86	3.51	3.29	3.13	2.91	2.68	2.41	2.09
21	5.83	4.42	3.82	3.48	3.25	3.09	2.87	2.64	2.37	2.04
22	5.79	4.38	3.78	3.44	3.22	3.05	2.84	2.60	2.33	2.00
23	5.75	4.35	3.75	3.41	3.18	3.02	2.81	2.57	2.30	1.97
24	5.72	4.32	3.72	3.38	3.15	2.99	2.78	2.54	2.27	1.94
25	5.69	4.29	3.69	3.35	3.13	2.97	2.75	2.51	2.24	1.91
26	5.66	4.27	3.67	3.33	3.10	2.94	2.73	2.49	2.22	1.88
27	5.63	4.24	3.65	3.31	3.08	2.92	2.71	2.47	2.19	1.85
28	5.61	4.22	3.63	3.29	3.06	2.90	2.69	2.45	2.17	1.83
29	5.59	4.20	3.61	3.27	3.04	2.88	2.67	2.43	2.15	1.81
30	5.57	4.18	3.59	3.25	3.03	2.87	2.65	2.41	2.14	1.79
40	5.42	4.05	3.46	3.13	2.90	2.74	2.53	2.29	2.01	1.64
60	5.29	3.93	3.34	3.01	2.79	2.63	2.41	2.17	1.88	1.48
120	5.15	3.80	3.23	2.89	2.67	2.52	2.30	2.05	1.76	1.31
∞	5.02	3.69	3.12	2.79	2.57	2.41	2.19	1.94	1.64	1.00

$\alpha = 0.05$

F_α k_1 k_2	1	2	3	4	5	6	8	12	24	∞
1	161.4	199.5	215.7	224.6	230.2	234.0	238.9	243.9	249.0	254.3
2	18.51	19.00	19.16	19.25	19.30	19.33	19.37	19.41	19.45	19.50
3	10.13	9.55	9.28	9.12	9.01	8.94	8.84	8.74	8.64	8.53
4	7.71	6.94	6.59	6.39	6.26	6.16	6.04	5.91	5.77	5.63
5	6.61	5.79	5.41	5.19	5.05	4.95	4.82	4.68	4.53	4.36
6	5.99	5.14	4.76	4.53	4.39	4.28	4.15	4.00	3.84	3.67
7	5.59	4.74	4.35	4.12	3.97	3.87	3.73	3.57	3.41	3.23
8	5.32	4.46	4.07	3.84	3.69	3.58	3.44	3.28	3.12	2.93
9	5.12	4.26	3.86	3.63	3.48	3.37	3.23	3.07	2.90	2.71
10	4.96	4.10	3.71	3.48	3.33	3.22	3.07	2.91	2.74	2.54
11	4.84	3.98	3.59	3.36	3.20	3.09	2.95	2.79	2.61	2.40
12	4.75	3.88	3.49	3.26	3.11	3.00	2.85	2.69	2.50	2.30
13	4.67	3.80	3.41	3.18	3.02	2.92	2.77	2.60	2.42	2.21
14	4.60	3.74	3.34	3.11	2.96	2.85	2.70	2.53	2.35	2.13
15	4.54	3.68	3.29	3.06	2.90	2.79	2.64	2.48	2.29	2.07
16	4.49	3.63	3.24	3.01	2.85	2.74	2.59	2.42	2.24	2.01
17	4.45	3.59	3.20	2.96	2.81	2.70	2.55	2.38	2.19	1.96
18	4.41	3.55	3.16	2.93	2.77	2.66	2.51	2.34	2.15	1.92
19	4.38	3.52	3.13	2.90	2.74	2.63	2.48	2.31	2.11	1.88
20	4.35	3.49	3.10	2.87	2.71	2.60	2.45	2.28	2.08	1.84
21	4.32	3.47	3.07	2.84	2.68	2.57	2.42	2.25	2.05	1.81
22	4.30	3.44	3.05	2.82	2.66	2.55	2.40	2.23	2.03	1.78
23	4.28	3.42	3.03	2.80	2.64	2.53	2.38	2.20	2.00	1.76
24	4.26	3.40	3.01	2.78	2.62	2.51	2.36	2.18	1.98	1.73
25	4.24	3.38	2.99	2.76	2.60	2.49	2.34	2.16	1.96	1.71
26	4.22	3.37	2.98	2.74	2.59	2.47	2.32	2.15	1.95	1.69
27	4.21	3.35	2.96	2.73	2.57	2.46	2.30	2.13	1.93	1.67
28	4.20	3.34	2.95	2.71	2.56	2.44	2.29	2.12	1.91	1.65
29	4.18	3.33	2.93	2.70	2.54	2.43	2.28	2.10	1.90	1.64
30	4.17	3.32	2.92	2.69	2.53	2.42	2.27	2.09	1.89	1.62
40	4.08	3.23	2.84	2.61	2.45	2.34	2.18	2.00	1.79	1.51
60	4.00	3.15	2.76	2.52	2.37	2.25	2.10	1.92	1.70	1.39
120	3.92	3.07	2.68	2.45	2.29	2.17	2.02	1.83	1.61	1.25
∞	3.84	2.99	2.60	2.37	2.21	2.09	1.94	1.75	1.52	1.00

$\alpha = 0.10$

F_α k_1 / k_2	1	2	3	4	5	6	8	12	24	∞
1	39.86	49.50	53.59	55.83	57.24	58.20	59.44	60.71	62.00	63.33
2	8.53	9.00	9.16	9.24	9.29	9.33	9.37	9.41	9.45	9.49
3	5.54	5.46	5.36	5.32	5.31	5.28	5.25	5.22	5.18	5.13
4	4.54	4.32	4.19	4.11	4.05	4.01	3.95	3.90	3.83	3.76
5	4.06	3.78	3.62	3.52	3.45	3.40	3.34	3.27	3.19	3.10
6	3.78	3.46	3.29	3.18	3.11	3.05	2.98	2.90	2.82	2.72
7	3.59	3.26	3.07	2.96	2.88	2.83	2.75	2.67	2.58	2.47
8	3.46	3.11	2.92	2.81	2.73	2.67	2.59	2.50	2.40	2.29
9	3.36	3.01	2.81	2.69	2.61	2.55	2.47	2.38	2.28	2.16
10	3.29	2.92	2.73	2.61	2.52	2.46	2.38	2.28	2.18	2.06
11	3.23	2.86	2.66	2.54	2.45	2.39	2.30	2.21	2.10	1.97
12	3.18	2.81	2.61	2.48	2.39	2.33	2.24	2.15	2.04	1.90
13	3.14	2.76	2.56	2.43	2.35	2.28	2.20	2.10	1.98	1.85
14	3.10	2.73	2.52	2.39	2.31	2.24	2.15	2.05	1.94	1.80
15	3.07	2.70	2.49	2.36	2.27	2.21	2.12	2.02	1.90	1.76
16	3.05	2.67	2.46	2.33	2.24	2.18	2.09	1.99	1.87	1.72
17	3.03	2.64	2.44	2.31	2.22	2.15	2.06	1.96	1.84	1.69
18	3.01	2.62	2.42	2.29	2.20	2.13	2.04	1.93	1.81	1.66
19	2.99	2.61	2.40	2.27	2.18	2.11	2.02	1.91	1.79	1.63
20	2.97	2.59	2.38	2.25	2.16	2.09	2.00	1.89	1.77	1.61
21	2.96	2.57	2.36	2.23	2.14	2.08	1.98	1.87	1.75	1.59
22	2.95	2.56	2.35	2.22	2.13	2.06	1.97	1.86	1.73	1.57
23	2.94	2.55	2.34	2.21	2.11	2.05	1.95	1.84	1.72	1.55
24	2.93	2.54	2.33	2.19	2.10	2.04	1.94	1.83	1.70	1.53
25	2.92	2.53	2.32	2.18	2.09	2.02	1.93	1.82	1.69	1.52
26	2.91	2.52	2.31	2.17	2.08	2.01	1.92	1.81	1.68	1.50
27	2.90	2.51	2.30	2.17	2.07	2.00	1.91	1.80	1.67	1.49
28	2.89	2.50	2.29	2.16	2.06	2.00	1.90	1.79	1.66	1.48
29	2.89	2.50	2.28	2.15	2.06	1.99	1.89	1.78	1.65	1.47
30	2.88	2.49	2.28	2.14	2.05	1.98	1.88	1.77	1.64	1.46
40	2.84	2.44	2.23	2.09	2.00	1.93	1.83	1.71	1.57	1.38
60	2.79	2.39	2.18	2.04	1.95	1.87	1.77	1.66	1.51	1.29
120	2.75	2.35	2.13	1.99	1.90	1.82	1.72	1.60	1.45	1.19
∞	2.71	2.30	2.08	1.94	1.85	1.17	1.67	1.55	1.38	1.00

A.18 Wilcoxon Critical Value
A.18 Wilcoxon 临界值下界表

n	显著性水平	
	0.10（单尾 0.05）	0.05（单尾 0.025）
7	3	2
8	5	3
9	8	5
10	10	8
11	13	10
12	17	13
13	21	17
14	25	21
15	30	25
16	35	29
17	41	34
18	47	40
19	53	46
20	60	52
21	67	58
22	75	65
23	83	73
24	91	81